According to Luke

For
Bill and Glenda Cowell

According to Luke

A new exposition of the Third Gospel

David Gooding

Inter-Varsity Press
Leicester, England

William B. Eerdmans Publishing Company
Grand Rapids, Michigan

INTER-VARSITY PRESS
38 De Montfort Street, Leicester LE1 7GP, England

Wm. B. EERDMANS PUBLISHING COMPANY
255 Jefferson S.E., Grand Rapids, MI 49503

Published and sold only in the USA and Canada by Wm. B. Eerdmans Publishing Co.

First published 1987
Reprinted 1987

British Library Cataloguing in Publication Data

Gooding, D. W.
According to Luke: a new exposition of the Third Gospel
1. Bible N.T. Luke—Commentaries
1. Title
226'.406   BS2595.3

ISBN (IVP hardback edition) 0-85110-639-0
ISBN (IVP paperback edition) 0-85110-756-7
ISBN (Eerdmans edition) 0-8028-0316-4

Set in Bembo
Typeset in Great Britain by
Parker Typesetting Service, Leicester
Printed in Great Britain by
Richard Clay Ltd, Bungay, Suffolk

Contents

Preface

The seed from which this book has grown was planted in my mind some forty years ago by a remark made *en passant* by a preacher, Harry Lacey of Cardiff, that Luke would appear to set out the material in his Gospel in an almost geometrical order. Since then widely different authors, classical, rabbinic and Christian have contributed to the development of my thinking about the nature of Luke's writing, while more people than I can now remember have helped me by patient listening or active discussion to formulate my ideas. If I have unwittingly plagiarized anyone's material, I sincerely apologize.

Forty years ago study of the literary structure of biblical books (or rhetorical criticism as it is called in some circles) was but a trickle; in the last decade or so it has become a flood. Not until the flood subsides will it be possible to see clearly the final and permanent shape of the resultant landscape. Meanwhile a true sense of means and ends should remind us that a study of literary structure must always be kept subordinate to the primary ongoing endeavour to understand Luke's flow of thought and the message which he was inspired to convey. An introductory chapter offers an explanation of my approach to the study of Luke's work; but readers may well find it preferable to begin with the commentary proper (p.26) and to leave the introduction until they have completed the book.

Unless I have indicated otherwise, all quotations from the Bible are my own translation.

Various editors and advisers of the Press have made extensive and careful comments. I thank them all for their help, their enthusiastic encouragement, and not least for the tact with which they have coaxed and cajoled my English style to enter the last quarter of the twentieth century. For all remaining blemishes, linguistic, literary and theological, I, of course, and not they, am to blame.

The typing of part of the first draft was done by Mrs Sue Meara, of the rest of the first draft and of all subsequent drafts by Mrs Barbara Hamilton, and in both cases with impeccable expertise. I record my gratitude.

The book is dedicated to my life-long friends, Bill and Glenda Cowell. Bill was the one with whom I first explored the riches of Luke's Gospel; and all down the years Bill and Glenda's home has been to me and to countless others a shining example of that hospitality, which according to Luke, our Lord so much admired and so much commended. May he grant them his promised reward.

David Gooding

Luke's presentation of Christ

Luke's inspired presentation of Christ is arranged in two great movements: first the 'Coming' of the Lord from heaven to earth; and then his 'Going' from earth to heaven. The turning point between them stands at chapter 9 verse 51.

An unforgettable scene marks the beginning of the 'Coming': when Mary and Joseph arrive in Bethlehem to have their names registered in the census-lists of the then world-empire, there is no room in the inn for the world's Saviour to be born. Nonetheless the 'Coming' ends in glory: at the transfiguration Christ appears supreme and central in the coming universal kingdom of God.

An equally unforgettable scene marks the beginning of the 'Going' (see 9:51–56): certain Samaritans refuse to receive him into their village. Rebuking his disciples' revengeful anger, Christ later reminds them (see 10:20) that their names are already registered in the citizen-lists of a more glorious city. Appropriately, the climax of the 'Going' shows the man, Jesus, rejected and crucified on earth, but now risen and ascending, being received up into glory.

The 'Coming' and the 'Going': between them they sum up Luke's message of salvation. The pre-existent and eternal Son of God came to our world and became a man like us so that he might secure for us here in this world forgiveness, wholeness, peace with God and the certainty that God's will shall eventually be done on earth even as it is done in heaven.

But there is more. By his Going he has taken humanity to the pinnacle of the universe. Following the Captain of their salvation along that road, all who trust him will one day be brought to share his glory in that exalted realm, and to reign with him at his return.

And now for the first stage of the 'Coming'.

Aims, methods and explanations

(This parenthetical chapter is highly technical. Don't read it now, unless you wish to. Proceed straight to p.26 and come back to this chapter when you have finished the book.)

This study of Luke's Gospel sets out to discover, as far as may be possible, the point and purpose of each section of the narrative. So let us begin by explaining what we mean in this context by 'point and purpose'.

At one level there is no need to look far to discover Luke's purpose in writing: he has stated it himself in his prologue (see 1:1–4). He writes so that Theophilus may know the certainty of the things which he has been taught. This stated purpose implicitly claims that his record is reliable and authoritative; and naturally the claim has been endlessly debated. We do not intend to continue that discussion. This study accepts as a matter of faith the traditional view that Luke wrote under the inspiration of the Holy Spirit and that his account is reliable. This is not to say that scholarly investigation of the historicity of Luke's record is either improper or unprofitable: it is to say that the reader who wishes to follow the ongoing debate on this aspect of Luke's work is referred to the learned commentaries. Luke obviously expects us to believe him when he says that he has carefully consulted the contemporary sources, and he expects us to grant his claim to reliability. We grant it, and look to see what then he will tell us, and what he thinks its significance is, and why he thinks we ought to know about it, and what we are expected to make of it. His declared purpose is to convince us of the certainty of the Christian story: has he no intention of helping us to see its point?

Meanwhile, mention of learned commentaries makes it appropriate to remark that this present work is not written for professional New Testament scholars. It is written, with a great deal of fellow-feeling, for non-expert but serious readers of Luke's Gospel whose main difficulty lies not in understanding exactly what Luke is saying,[1] but in understanding why he says it. These readers, we imagine, may well find it comparatively easy to believe that any incident which Luke records did actually take place exactly as he says it did; but they will find it well nigh impossibl\` to believe that Luke saw no other reason for recording it beyond the sheer fact that it took place. They instinctively feel that Luke must have seen significance in the events which he selected for his record, and that he (or the Holy Spirit who inspired him) must have intended to convey that significance to his readers. And so when they have consulted the textual critics and translators, historians and exegetes, and have come to a clear and accurate understanding of what Luke says took place in some incident or other, they cannot always rest content. They feel that something still eludes them; and that something, of course, is *what the significance of the incident is meant to be*. They could write, if required, an exact précis of Luke's account; they could even, if driven to it, make up a sermon on the basis of Luke's record, for they are intelligent and creative thinkers. But they remain uncertain that the meaning their sermon gave to the incident would necessarily be the meaning which Luke intended it to have. How then are we to decide what Luke intended?

It is at this level that the present work offers its modest help by suggesting some ways and means by which we might come closer to perceiving the point and purpose of each section of Luke's narrative. In many places, of course, it will be obvious. When, for instance, Luke records long passages of our Lord's moral teaching, his primary purpose is doubtless, as the prologue says, to assure us that here is a reliable record of what Christ taught. But Christian instinct will tell us, even if strict exegesis cannot, that this will not have been his sole purpose: his object also will have been to lead us to accept this moral teaching and to put it into practice.

With other kinds of narrative, however, it is not always so immediately obvious what the point and purpose is. Take, for example, an incident from the birth narratives. Zechariah, we are told at some length (see 1:57–66), named his son John at the

---

[1]There is a wealth of learned exegetical commentaries available to help the non-expert discover exactly what Luke is saying in any given passage. Where Luke's meaning is obscure or disputed, the present work will refer the reader chiefly to I. Howard Marshall's *The Gospel of Luke, a Commentary on the Greek Text* (Exeter, Paternoster Press, 1978). Not only are its own judgments balanced and fairminded, but it carries an exhaustive range of references to other scholarly works of every shade of opinion. References in the form 'Marshall, p.—' are to this commentary.

insistence of the angel and in the face of stormy protests from his friends and relatives. Thereupon he was released from the dumbness imposed on him for his initial disbelief of the angel. 'What', we ask, 'are we supposed to make of that?' Doubtless it did Zechariah good to be made to do what the angel told him to do. But why do we have to be told about it? What, moreover, would it matter to us whether Zechariah called his son John, Timothy, Haggai, or Solomon?

Or take the incident which Luke chooses to record from Christ's boyhood days (see 2:41–51). It is the only story from the boyhood, and we are grateful for it and for Luke's assurance that it actually happened and is not a mere legend. But why tell us only this story from the whole of the boyhood and early manhood? It will obviously not do to say that Luke recorded this incident simply because it happened. Of course it happened. But so did many other things during that long period. And it is difficult to think that after all his research (see 1:1–3) this was the only story from the childhood days which Luke had heard. Why only one story, then? And why this one? Is it told us because it is typical of situations that constantly arose during those childhood days? Or for the very opposite reason that it was an untypical and special event? For whose benefit was the incident allowed to happen in the first place? The rabbis'? Or Mary's and Joseph's? Mary and Joseph hardly appear at their best in this story: they seem not a little flustered and anxious. Were we meant to conclude therefore that in spite of all that Mary had been told at the annunciation about the uniqueness of her child, she was not in fact expecting him to act in any unusual fashion? And if so, were we meant to find this astonishing, or understandable? Or is the story there so that preachers may use it as a warning to us not to do as Mary and Joseph did, and travel along carelessly imagining that Christ is with us when he isn't? Or is all this about Mary and Joseph and their anxiety merely circumstantial detail, the main purpose of the record being to supply the theologians with evidence for the self-consciousness of the child Jesus, which they can then use in the construction of their christologies?

Perhaps the proper response to all these questions is to observe that the story is not a myth, composed by its author to convey one particular message. It is a piece of history that like any other piece of history (only more so!) possesses multisignificance; and, therefore, we may – perhaps we are even expected to – deduce from it any and everything that may legitimately be deduced.[1] Even so, we might have expected Luke to give us some guidance as to how to interpret the stories he has recorded, and when he appears not to give us any, we can feel frustrated.

Our disappointment springs perhaps in part from the fact that as modern people we are used to the ways of modern historians. The modern historian is expected not merely to collect and record the facts of a case, but to point out the significance of the facts, to offer interpretations and to pass judgments. If he failed to do these things he would scarcely be regarded as an historian at all. Luke does not do these things. Indeed, like the other synoptic evangelists, he is notorious for the sparsity of his own interpretative comments.[2] But then he is not a modern, but an ancient historian. He writes in the tradition of the great biblical historians who also are renowned for relating the facts with a minimum of explicit comment.

Before, however, we hastily conclude that this means that Luke has done virtually nothing to guide our understanding and interpretation of the events he has recorded, we should observe that, thoroughly biblical historian though he is, Luke also has features in common with some of the classical historians and notably with that great pioneer of scientific history, Thucydides. Luke's use of speeches in his Acts of the Apostles has often been compared with Thucydides' use of speeches in his History.[3] Thucydides assures us that he has carefully investigated his sources, but he rarely cites them.[4] Luke likewise. And what is even more interesting, Thucydides has a way of juxtaposing two incidents or two speeches containing such clear similarities and/or contrasts that the reader is led to reflect on these similarities and contrasts. From there, without Thucydides' having to intrude any comment of his own, the reader is led to see for himself the irony, the tragedy, or whatever it is in human affairs that becomes apparent when one holds the two stories or the two speeches together in one's mind

---

[1]Notice the amount this leaves to the reader's own subjective interpretation – a point which it will be helpful to remember if later on anyone is inclined to complain that the present writer's methods of interpretation are inherently subjective.

[2]Of course he has some, like 18:1 and 19:11, for example.

[3]See, *e.g.* I. Howard Marshall, *The Acts of the Apostles: an Introduction and Commentary*, TNTC (IVP, 1980), p.42.

[4]See H. D. F. Kitto, *Poiesis, Structure and Thought* (University of California Press, 1966), pp.289, 349.

and thoughtfully compares and contrasts them.[1] Luke may have different lessons to teach, but he uses a similar method.

At 7:36–50, for example, he relates a story which no other evangelist records. A woman of the streets enters the house of Simon the Pharisee, where Christ is being entertained to dinner, and begins to pay Christ very close personal attention. 'And Simon said to himself, "This man, if he were a prophet, would have perceived who and what kind of a woman this is who touches him". . .' But Christ did not appear to perceive who touched him – or at least, so it seemed to Simon. And with that the story goes on to its conclusion.

In the next chapter he relates another story (8:43–48): 'A woman . . . came behind him and touched the border of his garment . . . and Jesus said, "Who touched me?" And when all denied, Peter said . . . "Master, the multitudes press you . . ." But Jesus said, "Someone did touch me, for I perceived that power had gone out from me." And when the woman saw that she was not hidden . . .' Had Luke been a modern historian he might well have introduced the second story with the remark: 'A moment ago we saw how Christ's prophetic ability to perceive the character of the woman who touched him was seriously called into question. Now we are to consider another incident which in part at least answers the doubts raised in the earlier story'. And then at the end of the second story he might well have added an interpretative comment as follows: 'These two incidents then have taken us to the heart of one aspect of Christ's ministry. Both incidents have concerned women, both have concerned sexual matters, both have concerned disorders: the first dealt with moral disorder, the second with physical. Both women would have known the hurt of being avoided by orthodox society, the first for fear of moral contamination, the second for fear of ceremonial defilement. Christ put an end to their isolation and proclaimed them fit to make contact again with decent and clean society, but in doing so he found his powers of moral and physical perception criticized as being superficial in the one case and exaggerated in the other. Notice, however, how precisely Christ's defence met the criticism on each occasion . . .' and so forth.

---

[1] The most famous example of this in Thucydides is the juxtaposition of the Melian Dialogue and the account of the Sicilian Expedition (end of Book V, beginning of Book VI). But there are others. See H. D. F. Kitto, *op. cit.*, pp.333–338 and the whole section, pp.279–354.

Luke has none of these preparatory observations or concluding interpretative comments; but we might be rash to deduce from their absence that when Luke, the only evangelist to use the story of the woman in Simon's house, selected it from the sources and placed it close to the story of the woman with bleeding, he did not himself notice the similarities and contrasts, or noticing them did not see any significance in them. Of course it is not possible to prove conclusively that Luke saw significance in these features of the two stories; but when we find this same phenomenon occurring in many pairs of stories throughout the Gospel, we may incline to think that the better explanation for Luke's lack of explicit comment is that he was an ancient historian in the tradition of the Old Testament historians and in the tradition of Thucydides. Like them he will have taken great pains in investigating his sources, in selecting his material, and in disposing that material so that its continuity of theme, its significant similarities and contrasts should be obvious to the thoughtful reader. But after that he will have been content to let the material speak for itself and to invite the reader's active co-operation in perceiving its significance without constantly intervening to explain and interpret. It is not, of course, a modern way of writing history; it is what H. D. F. Kitto[1] has labelled the 'dramatic' method.[2] The history it produces is none the worse for that. Thucydides combined this method with a passion for historical accuracy: there is no reason for thinking that Luke did less.

But this reference to Thucydidean studies may alert the reader that the present writer's approach will be that of a scholar who comes to Luke from the study of classical and hellenistic authors. Luke was doubtless as familiar with their methods as he was with those of Aramaic oral literature. Brought up on Aristotle the present writer supposes[3] that in whatever other directions one may look in order to detect the 'message' an author like Luke intended to convey, one must look first and foremost at three features of his work. Firstly, at his selection of material and the

[1]*Op. cit.* pp.282ff., 349–50.
[2]Not in the popular sense of vivid writing, but in the technical sense of allowing the narrative to speak for itself without explanatory and interpretative comments by the author.
[3]For discussion of the objection that it is false methodology to use Aristotle's canons of literary criticism, formulated in the fourth century BC on the basis of imaginative works like Greek tragedies, in order to interpret an altogether different kind of work, a factual history written in the first century AD, see Appendix I, p.357.

relative proportions he assigns to the various parts of that material. Secondly, at any themes or ideas that reoccur in the various and separate items which he has selected. It is in these repeated ideas, themes and emphases that the author's thought and his insights into the significance of his material are most likely to be detected. And thirdly one must look carefully at the author's disposition of his material, the *systasis tōn pragmatōn* as Aristotle would call it, the way he orders the individual parts of his material in relation to each other and to the whole, and the effect this has on the thought-flow of his narrative. What is the logic of his arrangement? Does he organize his material solely and strictly on chronological grounds, or does he group incidents together on grounds of similarity of topic? Does any one story continue the thought-flow of the previous story or break it? In any story or group of stories are there runs of thought with minor and major climaxes, suspensions, complications and dénouements? Has the author placed the climax in any given story where our understanding of the story would have placed it, or in some, at first sight, unexpected place?

First of all let us examine Luke's selection and proportioning of his material. He has obviously not told us everything Christ did and said. Consideration of what Luke has done, in cases where he and Mark seem to be dependent on the same source, shows that he has not even told us everything which he found in his sources. He has obviously selected what seemed to him important and given what space he pleased to the topics he selected. Take then the topic of Christ's conception, birth, infancy and boyhood. Mark tells us nothing. Matthew devotes four (or five or six, depending on how they are counted) stories to the topic: the genealogy, Joseph's reaction to the conception and birth, the visit of the wise men, the flight into Egypt to avoid Herod's massacre, and the return. And in all this, we should notice, there is not one word about the forerunner, John the Baptist, or his parents. Luke, by contrast, has selected no less than ten stories for his birth and infancy narrative, five of them dealing with events before the birth, and five with the birth and the events that followed. Luke, then, has more stories than Matthew. But not only more: his selection produces an altogether different emphasis. In every one of the first five stories, for instance, reference is made to John the Baptist (at 1:13–17; 1:36; 1:41–44; 1:57–63; 1:76–79). Almost as much space, if not more, is given to him as to the coming Christ. Obviously Luke was very interested in John the Baptist, and thought we ought to be too. Why?

To answer this question we could look in two directions. We could, if we wanted to, look outside Luke's Gospel; and we could conjecture that Luke must have had some external reason for putting all this emphasis on John the Baptist. Perhaps he had contact with, and was influenced by, groups of the Baptist's disciples who had maintained an independent existence even after Pentecost, like those he mentions in Acts 18:24 – 19:7. Perhaps he thought that John's ministry had not received the prominence it deserved, and he may have been wanting to restore the balance. The possibilities are many and some of our conjectures (who knows?) might even be right.

We should do better, however, in the first place at any rate, to look in another direction, namely to the internal evidence within the stories themselves to see what it was about John the Baptist that so interested Luke. And if we do that, we shall find our focus changing. Although, as we have said, John the Baptist is referred to in every one of the first five stories, the internal proportions of the stories[1] suggest that Luke is more interested in John's parents than in John.

And then if we look to see whether any notable theme or themes run through all of these five stories we shall find as follows:

In the first story (see 1:5–25) the angel comes and announces to Zechariah that he and his wife, though both elderly, are going to have a son; and the angel describes the exalted ministry that this son will eventually exercise. And there (see 1:17) Luke could have ended the story, had he chosen to; for at this point the story has told us all it is going to tell us about John the Baptist and his coming ministry as the forerunner. But Luke is not interested simply in John and his coming ministry: something else is pressing on his mind and he spends the next six verses telling us about it. Zechariah found the angel's announcement incredible, told him so and was struck dumb for his disbelief: 'You shall be silent and unable to speak until these things happen, because you did not believe my words, which shall in fact be fulfilled in due time' (1:20). And this, Luke explains, was all the more embarrassing because Zechariah

---

[1]For example, in the first story John gets five verses (1:13–17), his father and mother more than sixteen (1:5–13a, 18–25).

was in the middle of morning prayers in the temple at the time, and when he emerged to bless the people waiting outside he could not pronounce the blessing. After his tour of duty he went home and presently his wife conceived. At that the story breaks off and Luke turns to a different one. But notice what Luke has done: he has raised our interest in the question of the credibility of the angel's words, told us the penalty of unbelief, and then directed our minds forward: Zechariah will be dumb until . . . We shall not be satisfied now until we hear the end of this story. Luke has taken the first steps in building up a climax.

Story 2 (see 1:26–38) tells of the annunciation to Mary. Mary like Zechariah questioned the angel, but not like Zechariah out of unbelief. Her difficulty was a moral one: she could not see how an unmarried girl was going to become a mother. She was told how. And there again (see 1:35) the story might have ended, for at this point all that it has to tell us about the greatness of Mary's Son and the miraculous conception has now been told. But the story has something more to tell us, and when we hear it the theme will sound familiar. The angel evidently knew that Mary's faith would need to be supported and encouraged. So he assured her 'nothing shall prove impossible with God' (see 1:37) and for evidence to confirm her faith in that assurance he informed her of Elizabeth's miraculous conception (see 1:36).

Story 3 (see 1:39–56) tells us that Mary, naturally enough after what the angel had told her, went to see Elizabeth and while in her home gave voice to the *Magnificat*. The sentiments expressed in Mary's great outburst of praise are so sublime that one could not have been surprised if Luke had let it stand in solitary prominence introduced by the briefest of circumstantial detail. But not Luke. He first tells us what Elizabeth said to and about Mary: '. . . and blessed is she who believed, for the things which have been spoken to her from the Lord shall have fulfilment' (1:45). Stupendous things have been promised, and Luke is busy recording them; but at every turn he points out that believing such stupendous announcements was no automatic thing. Zechariah had found it impossible; if Mary believed, it was not to be passed by as a matter of course: it was a matter for holy congratulations.

After Mary went home Elizabeth gave birth to her son, who on the eighth day was duly circumcised and named John. Now when Luke comes to the naming of Mary's child, all he will say is: 'And when the eighth day came and it was time for him to be circumcised, his name was called Jesus, which was the name given him by the angel before he was conceived in the womb' (2:21). Had Luke wished, story 4 (see 1:57–66) could have given us an equally brief record of John the Baptist's birth, circumcision and naming, and he could have passed on without delay to story 5 (see 1:67–79) the prophecy which Zechariah pronounced over his infant son. Glorious as that prophecy is in itself as an expression of faith in the promises of the ancient prophets (see 1:70), in God's covenant (see 1:72) and in God's oath (see 1:73), we might well miss some of the significance Luke saw in it, if we lightly pass over the detail which Luke has deliberately put into story 4. Eight verses of vivid domestic detail (see 1:57–64) bring us to the climax: Zechariah recovers his speech. At which we remember, of course, that he had been struck dumb for his disbelief in the angel's words. Since then, we now perceive, he has recovered faith; he acts in obedience to the angel's command and against all protest names his son John. Luke devotes two further verses (see 1:65–66) to describing the impact made on all the people around by Zechariah's transition from the dumbness of unbelief to the eloquence of faith. We are at the climax Luke had in mind when he wrote story 1.

We pause to take our bearings. In our next chapter we shall have to look more closely at the significance of these first five stories. At the moment they are serving us as an example of how attention to Luke's selection of material, to his proportioning of it, and to the ideas which he repeats throughout a succession of stories can help us to perceive the way he is looking at the facts he records. In these five stories he relates the miraculous birth of John and the virginal conception of Christ. In one sense the importance of these two momentous events, taken by themselves, towers above all their circumstantial detail. But Luke has not chosen to record these two events simply as objective facts, leaving us to make of them what we will. He has invited us to look at them through the subjective experience of those to whom it was first announced that these events were about to happen, and he has repeatedly emphasized the demands it made upon their faith. In particular he has traced in detail one man's struggle with incredulity, from his initial defeat to his eventual triumph. This should not surprise us when we remember that Luke was writing so that Theophilus 'might know the certainty of the things in which he had been instructed' (1:4).

Perhaps Theophilus, called upon to believe such stupendous things as Luke is here recording, might at times have had a certain sympathy with Zechariah.

There remains the question of Luke's disposition of his material. In general he follows the chronological order, but not invariably or in every detail. To take one small example: in his account of John the Baptist's ministry (see 3:1–20) Luke follows the story right to its end when John is put in prison. Then *after* the imprisonment (see 3:20) he proceeds to tell of Christ's baptism (see 3:21–22) which, of course, happened *before* John's imprisonment, and was in fact performed by John though Luke does not say so. There is nothing strange in this. Luke is not falsifying history by departing from strict chronological order: he is simply finishing off one movement in his history before he begins another, regardless of the fact that chronologically the beginning of the second movement preceded the end of the first movement.

This is a perfectly valid thing to do and many historians and biographers do it. But even when Luke records two things in strict chronological order – and that is most of the time – it often becomes clear that the chronological sequence between the two things is not the most significant feature in their relationship. At 18:1, for instance, Luke tells us that our Lord spoke a parable. At 18:9 he tells us that he spoke another parable. Presumably the latter was spoken after the former, though how much later, and whether or not on the same occasion, we are not told. Perhaps there is significance in the chronological order in which they were spoken; but much more obviously significant is the fact that both parables deal with prayer and that (as we shall later see in detail, p.293) the first reminds us that our praying or our non-praying reveals what we think about the character of God, while the second reminds us that our prayers can show, at times all too revealingly, what we think of ourselves.

Or again, take the story of the blind beggar (see 18:35–43) and the story of Zacchaeus the tax-collector (see 19:1–10). Here for good measure Luke gives us both the chronological and the geographical relationship between the two incidents: the first happened 'as he drew near to Jericho', the second, 'as he entered and was passing through Jericho'. Is this then the only connection between the two stories? Hardly! The first incident is a salvation-story: 'your faith has saved you' (18:42). So is the second: 'today salvation has come to this house' (19:9). The first man was poor, the second rich. The first man made his living by begging; from which degrading occupation salvation delivered him. The second made his living by tax-gathering and in part, apparently (see 19:8), by extortion; from which despicable practice salvation delivered him also.

But that is not all. Eleven verses before the blind-beggar story Luke has placed the following sequence of thought: Christ: 'With what difficulty those who have riches enter the kingdom of God; for it is easier for a camel to enter through the eye of a needle than for a rich man to enter the kingdom of God'. Audience: 'Who then can be saved?' Christ: 'Things that are impossible with men are possible with God' (18:24–27). We cannot tell how long the interval of time was between this conversation and the incident of the blind beggar. From Luke's own narrative (see 18:21–34) we might deduce that a certain amount of time elapsed, and from Mark 10:23–45 we know that during the interval the incident of the request of the two sons of Zebedee took place. As far as chronology is concerned therefore the disciples may have had plenty of time to forget the conversation, by the time they witnessed the salvation first of the beggar and then of Zacchaeus. But – and here we come to the point – Luke has so arranged his material that in the narrative only seven verses (see 18:28–34) intervene between the end of the conversation and the beginning of the two salvation stories. Can we his readers possibly forget what he has told us about the wellnigh impossibility of a rich man being saved when seven verses later he tells us how a poor beggar was saved and then – wonder of wonders – how a filthily rich tax-collector was also saved? At least, if we have forgotten, it is scarcely Luke's fault.

Even so Luke has still not finished. Mark puts nothing between the story of the blind beggar (see Mark 10:46–52) and the ascent to Jerusalem (see 11:1). Luke interposes between these two points (see 18:43 and 19:29) not only the story of Zacchaeus (see 19:1–10) but also the parable of the pounds (see 19:11–28), which thus serves as the climax to his carefully arranged thought-flow: the difficulty of those who have possessions or riches in finding salvation; yet this is possible with God: witness the fact that Christ saved both poor and rich, and turned the crooked tax-collector into a philanthropist; and then taught his disciples to regard what resources they have as a sacred trust given them by Christ, for which they will be accountable when he returns.

If we are right, then, Luke has here taken items of conversation and teaching together with various incidents, which were all originally more or less independent in the sense that they took place at different times and in different places, and by careful selection and composition he has made them serve as a series of progressive lessons on a common theme. To do this he has not had to alter the meaning or significance of the original items: each still means, as it stands within the progression, what it first meant when it originally took place as an independent incident or conversation. Twenty separate and independent pearls, valuable and beautiful in their own right, do not lose any of their beauty or value if someone puts them on a common thread and turns them into a necklace. On the other hand a necklace is something more than a number of individual pearls. And so with this progression of items in Luke: each item by making its own contribution balances, complements and completes what the other items teach. If, therefore, one were looking in this part of Luke's Gospel for our Lord's teaching on riches it would be perfectly right to take his remarks on the almost impossibility of rich men being saved and to preach from them a warning to all rich people that their possession of riches is a very dangerous thing. Better be poor than miss salvation. Such a sermon would be perfectly true: but it would not be the whole truth. To present a balanced view of these matters the preacher ought perhaps to preach another sermon soon, this time on Zacchaeus. Despised and socially rejected by his fellow-townspeople because of his unacceptable ways of making money, he was nonetheless accepted and saved by Christ, much to the annoyance of the virtuous local people, many of whom unfortunately were never saved at all! Of course this second sermon would be careful to point out from Luke's story of Zacchaeus that Christ did not condone Zacchaeus' extortion but genuinely converted him to a better attitude towards possessions. To enforce this lesson and take it a stage further the next sermon would do well to use the parable of the pounds to point out that to avoid the danger of riches it is not enough simply to abstain from extortion, nor enough simply to be penniless and scrounge a living out of others as the blind man did before he was saved; nothing but a responsible use of our pounds, as stewards accountable to Christ, will be regarded as satisfactory when Christ comes again and calls us to account.

Now it does not follow that because Luke, by his selection and composition, has turned these items into a progressive series of complementary lessons on a common theme, that he has done this kind of thing everywhere else in his Gospel. It might well be that the meaning of some items in the Gospel is so to speak self-contained. Important in its own right, it has no direct bearing on its context within the Gospel. If on further study we find it so, we shall have no reason to complain. But the present work will start out with the assumption that it is worthwhile looking to see if there is a connection of thought between one part of the narrative and the next. Admittedly there is a danger that if one goes looking for connections of thought one will eventually see them where they do not exist; and it is not to be expected that the present work will everywhere succeed in avoiding this danger. In the borderlands between exposition and homiletics imaginative fairy-castles of subjective interpretation are liable to be constructed more frequently than in the sterner regions of exegesis which are unvisited by imagination. But the writer takes comfort from the critical good sense of his readers. He does not suppose that he will convince them that Luke intended all the meanings and all the connections of thought that the present writer will suggest. It will be enough if here and there the reader is helped by this book to see more clearly the significance of what Luke has written.

One more explanation and we shall be ready to begin our main work. At some levels of study it would be important to distinguish between the meaning which Luke saw in the words and deeds of Christ, and the additional meaning which we can see in them when we look back on them in the light of the Holy Spirit's further revelations in the Epistles. Since ultimately both the Epistles and the Gospel come from the same Holy Spirit, we have not thought it necessary in this work constantly to make this distinction.[1]

---

[1]Since this is a study book, it will yield its maximum profit to the reader who first reads what Luke says and then constantly refers to the biblical text in the course of following the commentary.

Part One
THE COMING

The arrival

Preliminary survey

The movements

1 The last hours before the dawn *(1:5–80)*
2 The rising of the sun *(2:1–52)*

Some further observations

Stage 1

The arrival

Preliminary survey

Without any doubt the prime purpose of the first two chapters of Luke's Gospel is to record the incarnation of the Son of God. No exposition of their contents can possibly be correct if it obscures the incomparable importance of that unique event. Nevertheless Luke has not been content simply to record the fact of the incarnation in a few majestic words in the manner of the fourth Gospel: 'And the Word became flesh and dwelt among us' (1:14). He has surrounded the story of the incarnation with a number of other stories. Their general function is obviously to tell of the preparations for the coming of Christ, of his conception and birth, of his infancy and

---

We suggest that stage 1 contains the following ten stories:

1	*1:5–25*	Zechariah in the temple.
2	*1:26–38*	The annunciation to Mary.
3	*1:39–56*	Mary's visit to Elizabeth; the *Magnificat*.
4	*1:57–66*	The birth and naming of John.
5	*1:67–80*	Zechariah's prophecy.
6	*2:1–7*	The birth of Jesus in Bethlehem.
7	*2:8–21*	An angel directs shepherds to the manger.
8	*2:22–35*	Simeon's prophecy.
9	*2:36–40*	Anna's prophecy.
10	*2:41–52*	The boy Jesus in the temple.

boyhood. What other functions they have will appear if we look carefully at their contents, proportions and arrangements.

Between story 10 and the next event recorded in the Gospel (3:1ff.) there is a chronological gap of about eighteen years. It is plain then that these ten stories form a closely knit group.

We already have had occasion to notice (pp.16–19) the internal proportions of this group; so now let us look at the way Luke has arranged the ten stories within the group, to see if that can tell us anything.

We find that though in one sense the ten stories present a continuous story-line, Luke does not allow the narrative to flow in one undivided stream from story 1 to story 10. Every now and then he brings the thought-flow to a temporary pause by inserting a general remark or summary, mostly with some indication of the time-lapse between one story or group of stories and the next. In tabular form the arrangement looks like this:

Story 1   1:5–23   Zechariah in the temple.

And after these days his wife Elizabeth conceived and hid herself for five months, saying, 'The Lord it is that has done this for me; he has graciously intervened to take away my reproach among the people' (1:24–25)

Story 2   1:26–38   The annunciation to Mary.
Story 3   1:39–55   Mary's visit to Elizabeth: the *Magnificat*.

And Mary stayed with her about three months and returned to her home (1:56)

Story 4   1:57–66   The birth and naming of John.
Story 5   1:67–79   Zechariah's prophecy.

And the child grew and became strong in spirit, and he was in the desert until the time came for him to appear publicly to Israel (1:80)

Story 6   2:1–7   The birth of Jesus in Bethlehem.
Story 7   2:8–21   An angel directs shepherds to the manger.

And when eight days later the time came for him to be circumcised, his name was called Jesus which was the name given him by the angel before he was conceived in the womb (2:21)

Story 8	2:22–35	Simeon's prophecy.
Story 9	2:36–39	Anna's prophecy.

And the child grew and became strong being filled with wisdom, and the grace of God was upon him (2:40)

Story 10	2:41–51	The boy Jesus in the temple.

And Jesus advanced in wisdom and in stature and in favour with God and men (2:52)

This arrangement produces a simple pattern in which a series of four pairs of stories is preceded by one single story standing by itself, and is followed by a single story standing by itself. But the arrangement is perfectly natural. Story 1 stands by itself not only because it relates a different incident from story 2, but because an interval of five months separates the two incidents (see 1:24).

Stories 2 and 3 stand together because their subject matter is interrelated and also because no time worth speaking of intervenes between them. In story 2 Mary is told about Elizabeth's miraculous pregnancy and therefore as soon as the angel departs she goes in story 3 to see Elizabeth 'in those days' (1:39). By contrast we are explicitly told that three months pass by between the end of the *Magnificat* in story 3 and the beginning of story 4.

Stories 4 and 5 form a natural pair. Their subject matter is closely related: in story 4 Zechariah recovers his speech, and in story 5 he forthwith uses it to pronounce his great prophecy. But then the interval-marker at the end of story 5 carries on the mind some many years to the beginning of John's public ministry; so that we have to retrace our steps a long way to begin story 6.

Stories 6 and 7 once more form a natural pair, for the birth of Christ in Bethlehem was followed that very same night by the visit of the shepherds to the manger. But at the end of story 7 there is mentioned first (see 2:21) an interval of seven days, and then (see 2:22) a further interval of thirty-two days (the time for purification being forty days after birth).

Again stories 8 and 9 have no interval-marker between them, for there was no interval: Anna came up 'at that very moment' (2:38) as

29

Simeon was concluding his prophecy. But naturally enough there is an interval-marker between stories 9 and 10: the interval covers some twelve years (see 2:42).

We are left with one story standing by itself. At its end one more general remark covers an interval of some eighteen years before the next event to be recorded.

From all this one thing immediately stands out: Luke's consistent concern to give us a precise and accurate timetable of events. He obviously considered that he was recording datable historical events, and not constructing myths, nor presenting general truths in mythical form. Now this observation is so important in itself, as we shall see later (p.39), that we might be inclined to think that Luke's arrangement of his material in this stage can be accounted for simply by his concern for precise timetabling and chronology. But at this point we remember the unanswered questions about story 10 left over from the Introduction (p.12). Why did Luke select only this story from the boyhood and place it all by itself at the end of this series of pairs of stories? And then we remember that he has placed one story all by itself at the beginning of the series as well. We had better look more closely at these two single stories. Chronology is important, but here it may not be Luke's sole concern.

Story 1 is about an old man in the temple, and practically the whole point of the story is based on the fact that he is an old man. Story 10 is about a young boy in the temple, and, once more, the whole force of the story rests on the fact that the one who is amazing the teachers of the law with his questions and answers is a young boy, only twelve years old. Interesting, but perhaps superficial? Let us look deeper. The question raised in story 1 is parenthood: can an elderly couple, all against nature, become parents? The question raised in story 10 is similar but significantly different. It is parentage. Mary says to the child 'Son why have you treated us like this? Look, your father and I have been very distressed searching for you'. And the child replies . . . 'Did you not realize that I must be in my Father's house?'[1] Your father and I . . . my Father . . . Without doubt the child is referring to supernatural parentage.

Miraculous parenthood, supernatural parentage. Quite clearly,

---

[1] Or, 'about my Father's business'. The difference in translation does not affect the point we are considering here.

there is something more here than superficial similarities and distinctions. These two stories are calling our attention to the two different kinds of miracle involved in the work of redemption. In other words the stories are not repetitiously recording the simple fact that miracles surrounded the coming of Christ into the world. The stories are complementary: they tell us that miracles of two essentially different orders were both necessarily involved in our redemption.

Zechariah and his wife were old. Nature in them was decrepit, the processes of generation already dead. For them to have a child would mean reversing the natural processes of ageing and decay (see 1:7,18), and restoring the malfunction of Elizabeth's barrenness which had been with her all her life. A miracle indeed; but if such a miracle is impossible, as Zechariah at first thought, all talk of redemption is idle talk, or at best a misnomer. A new body that had nothing at all to do with the old body, a new world that had nothing to do with the old world, this would certainly be a wonderful thing – but it would not be redemption. Redemption must mean turning back the decay of nature, renewing dying bodies, resurrecting dead ones, restoring fallen spirits.

But that is only half the story of redemption. The parentage of Jesus involved a miracle of a different kind: not restoring nature to her original unfallen state, but introducing into nature something that nature had never known before, the birth into the human race of one who was simultaneously God and man. Once more, if this miracle of Christ's divine parentage is not true, there is no redemption. No mere man, however holy, could offer himself as an adequate sacrifice to bear away the sin of the world, or impart resurrection life to the dead bodies of the myriads who have believed on him.

The conclusion seems inescapable therefore that Luke selected story 10 to complete his account of the incarnation because the special point of its subject-matter complemented the issues raised in story 1.

So much for Luke's selection and arrangement of the material in this first stage. We ought now to look to see if there is any common theme, or themes, running through the several stories. Our work is already half-done. Stories 1–5, so we noticed in the Introduction (p.17), all deal with the reaction of Zechariah, Elizabeth and Mary to the announcement of coming miraculous events. Mary at once believes, but is nonetheless given evidence to confirm and support her faith. Zechariah at first disbelieves; but his faith eventually recovers, and in stories 4 and 5 it comes to triumphant climax. In stories 6–10 a very similar, though significantly different, theme recurs: Mary's reactions to the things that begin to happen to, be said about, or be said by, her Son. As in stories 1–5 so here, we shall find no unbelief in Mary; but whereas in stories 1–5 the challenge to Mary as to Zechariah and Elizabeth was to believe that the miraculous was about to happen, in stories 6–10 the great miracle of the incarnation has happened, and the challenge is to face and try to understand the implications of that miracle as they begin to work themselves out. And here Mary who had no difficulty at all in believing that the miracle would happen, does have difficulties with understanding and accepting its implications.

In stories 6 and 7 Mary is obliged by Augustus' decree to give birth in Bethlehem and her child unexpectedly has to be laid, not in a cradle in the hotel, but in a manger. Yet a few hours later that very night shepherds arrive at the manger explaining by means of an extraordinary story how they knew exactly where to come to find the baby, and saying extraordinary things about him. All present are amazed; 'but Mary stored up all these things pondering them in her heart' (2:19).

In stories 8 and 9, Mary and Joseph are 'amazed at the things which were being said (by Simeon) about him (*i.e.* Jesus)', and then Simeon adds that one day, because of what shall happen in connection with her Son 'a sword shall pierce through your own (Mary's) soul' (2:33–35).

And finally, as we have already noticed, story 10 concentrates our attention on Mary and Joseph's anxiety at the temporary loss of Jesus, on their astonishment when they found him doing what he was doing, on Mary's worried remonstrance with him, and finally on their failure to understand his answer (see 2:48–50).

We notice the growing intensity: from one verse (see 2:19) mentioning Mary's continuing reflection on events, to three verses referring to Mary and Joseph's astonishment and Mary's coming sorrow (see 2:33–35), to virtually a whole story recording Mary and Joseph's distress, anxiety, amazement and failure to understand (see 2:43–51). And we notice the direction of this movement of thought. If in stories 1–5 Zechariah is moving from disbelief to triumphant faith, in stories 6–10 Mary is moving from surprise and interested reflection through foreboding of future sorrow to present anxious incomprehension.

But more of this presently. For the moment we may sum up the findings of our preliminary survey thus: in this stage Luke certainly puts before us the great objective facts of the conception and birth of the forerunner and the conception and birth of Christ with their precise timings. But he has done more than that. His selection, proportioning and arrangement of material has set the angle from which he means us to look at these things by concentrating our attention on the subjective reactions of Zechariah, Elizabeth, Mary and Joseph to these objective events. We are made to look at these events through their eyes, and as presently we analyse their reactions, we may well find that we are analysing our own. On the other hand their subjective reactions, being matters of history, are as much objective facts of history to us as the birth of John and the birth of Jesus. Our assessment of the evidence for these two miraculous births must necessarily include an assessment of the characters, motives, behaviour, credulity or incredulity of the people who were the leading human actors in these momentous events.

The movements

1. The last hours before the dawn (1:5–80)

Story 1.   Zechariah in the temple (1:5–25). If the birth of Christ, to borrow Zechariah's metaphor, was 'the Dawn from on high' (1:78), then chapter 1 of the Gospel covers the last few hours before sunrise. The night had been long and, for Israel, at times very dark. But through it all – through times of national success and disaster, through the conquest and the monarchy, through the exile and return – hope had persisted that the night would at last end and, as Malachi put it, 'the sun of righteousness would arise with healing in his wings' (4:2). Isaiah had prophesied (40:3–8) that before the 'glory of the Lord' should 'be revealed', a forerunner would be sent to prepare the way of the Lord. Malachi had added that before the day of the Lord came, the prophet Elijah would be sent to 'turn the hearts of the fathers to the children and the hearts of the children to their fathers, lest I come and smite the earth with a curse' (4:5–6). And now more than four hundred years after Malachi the seemingly interminable night was coming to its end: the dawn was about to break. Great preparations were afoot, and plans laid in the eternal past began to swing into action. The forerunner had to be born. A certain Zechariah and his wife Elizabeth, long since chosen to be his parents, had now to be advised of the coming birth and told how to bring up the child in the strict discipline appropriate to the unique Elijah-like ministry that he was destined to fulfil (see 1:13–17). And so in the last few months before sunrise the angel Gabriel was sent to tell Zechariah that he and his wife were soon to have a child. And Zechariah refused to believe the angel!

No doubt, Zechariah's disbelief, coming at this critical point in history makes a very dramatic story; but we may be sure that it was more than a fine sense of the dramatic that made Luke tell the story. Nor was it merely Luke's concern to tie John the Baptist's life and ministry to its historical context that made him tell the story in such great detail. The requirements of historical dating and identification would have been satisfied without any record at all of Zechariah's temporary lapse into unbelief; and if honesty demanded that some mention be made of it, mercy might have kept it brief. Instead, Luke has told the story in great detail. Why? Presumably, because he thought that Zechariah's lapse into disbelief raised important issues which ought to be considered.

Take first the grounds of his disbelief, as Luke gives them to us. Zechariah's difficulty was not that he was taken aback by the suddenness of the angel's message, and genuine humility made it difficult for him to believe that he and his humble wife had been singled out for such high honour as to be the parents of Messiah's forerunner. Had that been the case he would have replied to the angel as Gideon did on another occasion: 'But my family is the poorest . . . and I am the least in my father's house . . .' (Jdg. 6:15), or words to that effect. What he actually said was 'On what evidence can I be sure of this? For I am an old man and my wife is well on in years' (1:18). This was his real difficulty: for him and his wife to have a child would mean a miracle of divine intervention; and Zechariah considered such a miracle to be so extremely unlikely that even if it was an angel of God who announced it – and Zechariah did not dispute that – he was not prepared to believe it, not at least unless he were given some stronger grounds for belief than the bare word of an angel.

Now Zechariah had no time to think through his response before he blurted it out, and that is why perhaps it revealed an attitude grievously inconsistent and bordering on the irrational.

After all, Zechariah was no atheist nor deist. He was not even a layman, but a priest, who at the time the angel appeared to him was publicly officiating at morning prayers in the temple. Moreover, as we learn from the angel, Zechariah in his private devotions had been praying to God for a child; and there is no point in praying to God for something which nature is refusing to do by herself, and at the same time believing that God is never likely to intervene in nature anyway.

Of course, to be fair to Zechariah it may be that he and his wife had gone on praying only so long as they were still of normal child-bearing age, when all that they were asking the Creator to do was to give nature a little push forward to get on with the job which the Creator had designed her to do. They were long past that age now. For them to have a child now would require the Creator's intervention to put the processes of ageing and decay into reverse. Perhaps, then, they had ceased praying for a child after middle life, in the belief that these processes of ageing and decay were also designed by the Creator and that he would not intervene to reverse processes which he himself had created.

Be that as it may, for a private person to refuse to believe the word of an angel over some personal matter is serious enough; but, as we have already noticed, at the time of the angel's visit Zechariah was not a private person: he was the official public, priestly representative of the people of God. Moreover the good news which the angel was bringing to Zechariah was not simply a private or personal gospel message: it was, as the angel had carefully explained (see 1:15–17), a preliminary and integral part of *the* gospel itself. Yet here was Zechariah refusing to believe this particular gospel message on grounds that would deny the very basis of the gospel in its entirety. If God could not restore the processes of nature in Elizabeth's body, what hope was there that creation itself should ever be delivered from its bondage to corruption? If God could not revivify Elizabeth's ageing and dying body, how should he ever raise from the tomb the body of Jesus already three days dead? And if that resurrection were impossible, no resurrection would ever be possible. The grounds which Zechariah gave for his disbelief were, without his knowing it, utterly subversive of the entire gospel.

We are told that the angel struck him dumb. The action was neither vindictive nor arbitrary. In a few minutes Zechariah was expected to go outside and, as priest on duty for the day, in God's name pronounce God's blessing on the waiting people. But a priest who cannot believe the authoritative word of an angel of God, because he cannot accept the possibility of divine intervention to reverse the decay of nature, has lost faith in the basic principle of redemption. Without redemption, he has no gospel. Without a gospel, any blessing he pronounced upon the people would be the emptiest of professional formalities. If Zechariah could not believe the angel's gospel, it were better that he did not pretend to bless the people. Fittingly the angel struck him dumb.

At this point we should notice how fair Luke is to Zechariah. He exposes the whole story of his disbelief; but that does not mean that he impugns either his loyalty to ecclesiastical order or his moral integrity. Luke points out that Zechariah as a priest had married within the priestly family of Aaron (see 1:5), and as far as morality and personal holiness went 'they were both righteous in the sight of God, blamelessly observing all the Lord's commandments and requirements' (1:6). But Israel's religion was concerned with far more than correct morality and ceremonial. Israel's prophets and priesthood, indeed Israel's very existence were meant to stand as a testimony to God's redemptive interventions in nature and in world-affairs. In fact, though Israel doubtless had priests of some kind before the Exodus, her special role among the nations as a kingdom of priests (see Ex. 19:4–6) was a direct historical outcome of God's miraculous intervention in nature in the plagues of Egypt and at the Red Sea, and of his redemptive intervention in the Passover. The Levites, too, who were assistants to the priests, likewise owed their existence as an institution to God's intervention at the Passover in Egypt (see Ex. 13:11–16 with Nu. 3:1–13). Moreover these great historical interventions of God on Israel's behalf were not regarded as mere past events: for Israel they were pledges and patterns of God's future intervention for the purpose of the restoration of all things. Every Passover at which Zechariah assisted was a memorial of past, and a prophecy of future, divine redemptive intervention.

When therefore the angel came and announced to the priest Zechariah that God had heard prayer and was about to fulfil his prophetic promises, that Messiah was coming to effect the restoration of all things, and that Zechariah had been chosen to be the father of the forerunner, Zechariah as a priest ought not to have been unduly surprised. That he should disbelieve the angel on the grounds that miraculous divine intervention was incredible, made a nonsense of the very faith which as a priest he was appointed – and paid – to represent and maintain.

But we have no basis for thinking that Zechariah's disbelief at the angel was the expression of some well-thought-out position whose implications he had worked out to their logical conclusions. It was more likely instinctive, an instance of that disbelief of God and of his Word which ever since the Fall has been endemic in the human race, and which, however deeply suppressed by religious discipline, is liable in unguarded moments to reassert itself. It reminds us that much of our modern disbelief springs from the same source. We flatter ourselves if we think that it necessarily arises from our scientific outlook. Happily for Zechariah his lapse was only temporary, and in any case it did not nullify God's purpose. Not long after he got home from his tour of duty as a priest, Elizabeth conceived.

Stories 2 and 3.   The annunciation and the Magnificat *(1:26–56).* We must now leave Zechariah and his initial disbelief in the possibility of divine intervention, though we shall have to return to him and his problems later. For the moment Luke moves our attention to Mary and her story. Her story, as given here, is in fact two stories: the annunciation and the *Magnificat*. The one is Mary's explanation of how she became pregnant before marriage; the other is her reaction to that pregnancy. At least, that is what these two stories are, if Luke is writing history.

But is he? The traditional answer to this question has always been and still is, yes. But in more recent decades expressions of the contrary opinion have grown louder and more frequent. Many hold that Luke's and Matthew's accounts of the incarnation are of very doubtful historical worth; but they are inclined to add that this does not matter because these accounts are imaginative statements of theological truths about Jesus; not history but religious myth. One can therefore deny the incarnation as a historical fact, but still believe the truth expressed by the incarnation-myth.

It would be both out of place and impossible here to discuss, or even report, what exactly the truth is which it is claimed that the incarnation-myth expresses; the scholars who maintain that the story is a myth are not all agreed – and not altogether certain themselves – as to what that truth is. But some of their reasons for not accepting the incarnation as a historical fact are clearly relevant to our present study. The basic contention is that divine intervention is impossible, and that therefore the incarnation cannot have taken place. If that is so it raises some very grave questions about the nature of Luke's and Matthew's narratives. These questions have recently been stated very succinctly and forcibly by Mr Clifford Longley:[1]

> If . . . nothing miraculous occurred at the event of Jesus's conception, the implications are enormous . . . It means Jesus had a natural father. This was either Joseph or someone else. If it was Joseph, those New Testament references to his thinking his betrothed wife was made pregnant by another man are not just "religious myth" – they are deliberate lies, either by Joseph himself, or someone else who made them up. If it (*scil.* the natural father – addition mine) was not Joseph but indeed another man, then Mary's story was a lie, Joseph was deceived (or an accomplice in the lie), and the Gospel writers were "taken in".
>
> The question . . . is . . . how do they (*scil.* modern liberal theologians) avoid casting aspersions at the integrity (and chastity) of Joseph and Mary?

The only way of rebutting these charges would be to say that the New Testament references to Joseph never had any basis in anything that Joseph or Mary ever said or did; that as to the historical fact Jesus was probably born to Joseph and Mary in the normal way after their marriage; and that Matthew's story about Joseph finding Mary pregnant by someone else before they were married is simply part of the myth; that Matthew and Luke (or some other person) who fabricated this myth would have been the first to admit that if taken as history it would be preposterously untrue; but that they cannot be charged with lying since they never attempted to give the impression that they were writing history. According to this theory they must have thought that everyone (except the most stupid) would see that their story was a myth designed to convey a

[1] 'A Conservative case for Christ' *The Times* (London, June 4, 1984, p. 18).

38

religious truth (and presumably that everyone would see what that truth was); that neither Mary nor Joseph, had they lived to read the story, would have been offended or mystified by their distortion of the historical facts in the interests of religious myth; and that none of their contemporaries, not even Jewish ones, would have sought to deny this religious truth simply on the grounds that the details of the myth were not historically true. And finally this theory would have to admit that though the early Christians were sophisticated people and recognized the myth for what it was, after a few decades Christians became less sophisticated, mistook the myth for literal history and continued to do so for centuries.

The whole idea is, of course, preposterous; but close examination of the way Luke writes wrecks the theory completely. It shows unmistakably that he regarded the incarnation as literal, factual history, and that he intended his readers to do so too. First, in his prologue he assures his reader that he has carefully consulted the oral and written sources, and that his account is reliable. Then as we have already noticed (p.30), he organizes his material relating to the incarnation according to the precise timings of its main events. Then again, his record of the two miraculous pregnancies becomes even more precise in its timings. He tells us that after conception Elizabeth hid herself five months (see 1:24), that the angel visited Mary in the sixth month of Elizabeth's pregnancy (see 1:26), that the angel informed Mary that Elizabeth was already six months pregnant (see 1:36) and that after the visitation Mary visited Elizabeth, stayed with her about three months, and then returned home before Elizabeth's child was born (see 1:56). Finally when Mary's child is born, he dates the birth by reference to contemporary secular history (see 2:1–2). So Luke has not simply related these stories and left us to make of them myth or history as we will. He has indicated beyond all doubt that he intends us to take them as history. It is illegitmate, therefore, to take what Luke intended as factual history, deny its historicity and then interpret it as though he meant it to be a religious myth. Certainly Luke intended to convey a religious truth, namely that Jesus is the Son of God; but in his account the religious truth is explicitly based on the historical fact: 'the Holy Spirit shall come upon you and the power of the Highest shall overshadow you; *for this reason moreover* the holy one to be born shall be called Son of God' (1:35).

There is only one escape open to the myth-theory. It is this. Luke in consulting his sources came across the myth already fabricated (it must then have been fabricated very early). Unquestioningly, and very unintelligently, he mistook it for history. Physician though he may well have been, and travel companion of Paul though he was, he was not sufficiently disturbed by the story of a miraculous, virginal conception as to consult his educated and sophisticated Christian friends who would at once have told him that it was myth; but innocently proceeded to assure his reading public that it was history. This explanation is so utterly improbable that to borrow some more words from Mr Longley[1] 'it may be easier to believe in miracles . . . or in atheism'.

According to Luke, then, the incarnation was an historical event and that means that the story of the annunciation originates with Mary and the report of the *Magnificat* originates with Mary and/or Zechariah and Elizabeth. In telling these stories Luke has called our attention to two things: first, as we have just seen, to a number of precise timings related to the onset and development of the two miraculous pregnancies, and secondly to the question of Mary's reaction to the great announcement.

The precise timings (see above p.39) allow us, whether Luke intended it or not, to work out when Mary first told her story. She must have gone and told Elizabeth almost immediately after the annunciation. And that means that she did not wait until undisguish-able evidence forced her to offer some explanation of her state. Who would have believed her then? She went at once, while there was still no physical evidence, perhaps none that even she could observe herself, to tell Elizabeth that an angel had visited her and had announced that she was going to have a child without being married.

What possible reason could she have had at that stage for invent-ing the story and telling it to others if it were not true? It may be said that like any Jewish girl she was full of dreams of becoming the mother of Messiah. That in itself is very doubtful. But even if it were true, she had no dreams of its coming about that way, as is shown by her immediate retort to the angel, 'But I'm not married!' (1:34). And to think the unthinkable for a moment, what girl in her position would try to explain a pregnancy (for which there was as yet no evidence) resulting from some casual affair, by claiming that

[1] *Art. cit.*

an angel had told her that she was going to become pregnant by a
divinely induced conception, and that her child would prove to be
the Messiah? Who would she expect to believe the story? She was
not a Greek teenager, with her head turned by reading too many
ancient Greek myths about gods coming in to human women. And
her relatives were certainly not Greeks either. The only story in
their Old Testament about supernatural beings coming in to
human women was a story of illicit demonic unions (see Gn. 6:4).
As a Jewess living among humble, conservative, believing Jews,
she would have known instinctively that her story, had it been
invented, would not have had the slightest hope of being believed.
We know what Joseph thought when he first heard the story (see
Mt. 1:19); and we know what action he initially proposed to take.
He, and all his social class, would have regarded Mary as guilty of a
criminal breach of the law of betrothal, for which Scripture
(though it was no longer normally carried out) prescribed the death
penalty (see Dt. 22:23–24). We also know what some people who
knew that Jesus was conceived before Mary was married, continued to think of the matter long into the life of our Lord, in spite
of Mary's story (see Jn. 8:41). All this, with a woman's instinct,
Mary would have instantaneously foreseen the moment the angel
made the announcement. It magnifies the faith and devotion which
made her submit herself to the will and word of God (see 1:38); but
it also makes it utterly incredible that she invented the story.

The second matter Luke calls our attention to in great detail is
Mary's reaction to the annunciation. First her faith and then her
joy.

Towards the end of the annunciation the angel virtually suggested to Mary that she should go and visit Elizabeth to obtain
confirmation of her faith. It takes little imagination to see why her
faith would need strengthening. She had been chosen for a gigantic,
unprecedented, unrepeatable task: how should her mortal flesh
stand the psychological and spiritual strain in the long nine months
of waiting? We have earlier thought of modern man's difficulty in
believing Mary's story. That is not the question that concerns Luke
here. He is concerned rather with how Mary herself, being an
ordinary human girl of flesh and blood, believed it, and went on
believing it, and bore the incalculable honour and the immeasurable
burden without losing faith and nerve and proper humility and
sanity itself.

When the angel departed the first temptation would have been to think that she had imagined the whole thing. But when she arrived at Elizabeth's, she found not only that Elizabeth was, as the angel had said, miraculously pregnant, but that Elizabeth knew by prophetic inspiration without Mary's having to tell her that Mary was going to be the mother of the Lord. And Elizabeth confirmed Mary in her faith.

So now Mary knows for sure that she is to be the mother of the Son of God. How will she react? We cannot but scrutinize her reaction very carefully since it is part of the evidence presented to us for the truth of her story. If she does not show herself emotionally aware of the immeasurable greatness of the honour she claims, we shall feel uneasy: does she even understand the claim she is making? If on the other hand she shows the slightest trace of pride or self-centredness, we shall feel uneasy again: how could a woman who claimed to be about to become the mother of the Son of God be proud and arrogant on that account without totally undermining her claim? As therefore Mary breaks out into praise and prophecy we must try to listen critically.

Her phraseology, we notice, is formal, archaic and poetic, drawn in great part from the Old Testament. This is not grotesque, as some have suggested, a sign that Luke is here concocting an artificial story. Anyone who has attended meetings where non-literary people of moderate education engage in extemporary prayer, will know that such people generally use language laced with archaic expressions taken from some old translation of the Bible which they have heard read ever since they were children, and mixed with words of hymns written a century or more ago. And so with Mary now. This is for her an exalted and intensely spiritual moment. Probably the only exalted language she knows is biblical language. We are not surprised by its style, though presently we may be by its contents.

She begins by praising God (see 1:46) – a normal opening to any prayer. Then at once (see 1:47) she confesses to great joy (the Greek word Luke uses to translate her original Aramaic indicates exultant, overwhelming, religious joy). She is, then, emotionally aware of the stupendous wonder of the thing that is happening to her. Aware also of the immeasurable contrast between her present obscure, humble state, and the immense publicity and honour which inevitably shall be hers throughout all succeeding generations (see 1:48).

What effect, we wonder, will all this have on her personality, on her concept of herself and of her status, on the relationship, as she now feels it, between herself and all other people, between herself and God?

Here a very striking thing meets us: never once in all the *Magnificat* does she mention the fact that she is going to be the mother of the Son of God. Of course that is the reality which underlies her joy and praise; but the way she refers to this great fact shows us what, as she sees them, are the implications of it for her.

Her joy arises, she explains, because in acting as he is towards her, God is acting as her Saviour (see 1:47). We note with more than interest that she still regards herself as someone who needs to be saved like the rest of mankind.

'All generations shall call me blessed' – but she does not add 'because I am to be the mother of the Son of God' but 'because the Mighty One has done great things for me' (1:49). In other words, what God has done, rather than what she is, is the aspect of the matter that is filling her mind.

But what, in the light of these great things which God has done for her, is her relationship with God as she now sees it? The Old Testament had always insisted on the impassable gulf that separates the name of God from any other name: God's name alone is holy. Have the great things elevated her to a position where for all practical purposes the distance and distinction between her and the Divine Persons reduce to vanishing point? Not in Mary's estimation. Even in these moments of intense spiritual exultation, she has no illusions, no incipiently blasphemous thoughts. All generations of creatures shall call her blessed; but she immediately takes her stand as a creature with all those other creatures: for Mary still 'Holy is his name' (1:49).

She has now spoken three couplets. In all three she has said something about herself, though without either self-importance or self-centredness. And this is the last we shall hear from Mary about herself. There are twice as many couplets still to come, but Mary will not speak of herself personally and explicitly again.

This may strike us as remarkable humility, but actually it arises naturally from the way she looks at the event itself. Utterly unique though it is in one sense, in another it appeals to Mary as nothing unusual. It is an act of God's mercy. But then, 'God's mercy comes to generations after generations for those who reverence him' (1:50). Anyone of the millions in these innumerable generations could tell a tale of God's mercy just as she could. She does not feel the specialness of her case, because her eye is not on herself but on the constancy of God. In the infinite class of God's merciful acts her case, however large, is but a single member.

But surely humility can sometimes arise out of ignorance, and if so, it is not the genuine article. Could it be that Mary in first claiming to be the mother of the Messiah and Son of God, and then in regarding the whole affair as simply one more example of God's common mercy to all generations is giving the game away? Never having known anything outside her own humble artisan class could it be that she has no concept of what is involved in being, say, the high priest of her nation, or the Caesar Augustus of the Roman world, let alone Messiah of the royal house of David and Son of God; and therefore sees nothing incongruous in the notion that God should by-pass the rich, noble, educated and powerful families and choose a little artisan-class girl from some obscure family to be the mother of the King of kings and Lord of lords?

It is almost stupid to have asked the question; but it is important to see why the answer is no. Mary is aware of the great differences in ability, resources and power which separate the philosophers, the rich and the aristocrats from the uneducated, the poor and the weak, and she herself observes that for the purposes of the incarnation God has deliberately by-passed the former class and chosen someone from the latter. But to explain it she launches into a string of verbs in the aorist tense (see 1:51–53), which have the exegetes undecided whether she is describing God's action in the past, God's action in the future viewed prophetically as though already accomplished, or God's habitual action. We need not decide the exegetes' question. Mary means all three. She sees God's choice of her as merely one example of what God always does, has done, and will do. And the reason for this is that, as she has told us in her very first couplet, what is happening to her is an activity of God as Saviour. In salvation he always scatters the proud, puts down princes, sends the rich away empty, but exalts the lowly and feeds the hungry. That is why she uses the poetic language of the centuries to describe her own experience, for this has always been the experience of any who have at any time experienced any aspect of God's salvation. Hannah (see 1 Sa. 2) found it so in her domestic situation, very different though it was from Mary's. Paul was to observe that this is the principle, in the highest sense of the term, on which God's salvation works (1 Cor. 1:18–31).

And finally Mary puts what has happened to her in another larger context. 'He has helped Israel, his servant, remembering to put into action his mercy (as he promised to our fathers) to Abraham and to his seed for ever' (1:54–55). Hundreds of times since her childhood, in the home, in the synagogue, at the religious festivals, Mary had heard of God's calling out of Abraham, of the formation of her nation from him, of God's great covenants to him and to his seed: of the way God had honoured those covenants in the past, and how he would do so again. When, therefore, the mighty event happened to her, she had its proper context already imprinted on her mind. What was happening to her, was happening to her as part of her nation, not because she personally and individually was special but because of God's faithfulness to Abraham and to his seed. This context would not detract from the uniqueness of what was being done in and through her; but it would help her to see herself in true perspective as part of God's ways with her nation, its election, history and destiny. That awareness of context doubtless both sustained her faith and at the same time kept her, in her exalted office, from any exaggerated sense of self-importance. And, by pointing it out, Mary helps our faith too. Seen as part of that unique nation's unique history, the unique event of the virgin birth and the incarnation looks almost natural.

Stories 4 and 5. The birth and naming of John and Zechariah's prophecy (1:57–80). The next two stories revert to Zechariah. The first (see 1:57–66) relates the birth, circumcision and naming of his son; the second (see 1:67–79) records the prophecy he pronounced over that son.

In the course of the first story Zechariah will recover his power of speech. So let us briefly recall how and why he lost it. The angel said to Zechariah: 'You shall be silent and not able to speak until the day these things happen, because you did not believe my words which shall be fulfilled when their time comes' (1:20). Zechariah's disbelief did not last long. Perhaps it scarcely survived his being struck dumb; for when he completed his tour of duty and went home Luke briefly notes: 'And after this Elizabeth his wife conceived' (1:23–24). Here was the angel's word being fulfilled in front of his eyes: he could not but believe it. But he remained dumb. The beginning of our present story (see 1:57) relates the child's birth.

This surely destroyed any lingering doubt in Zechariah's mind: but still he remained dumb. Obviously, therefore, the story could not stop here: it must go on to tell us what had to happen before Zechariah was allowed to recover his speech, Even so, Luke, had he chosen, could have informed us briefly in so many words that it was when Zechariah did as the angel had told him to, and named his son John, that he was released from his dumbness. And if Luke had done so, we might reasonably have concluded that what the angel wanted was not only belief but also obedience on Zechariah's part, and that with obedience achieved, the story had reached its proper climax.

In actual fact Luke has given the story a different focus and a different climax from what we have just suggested. It is not, of course, that Zechariah's faith and obedience are merely secondary matters in this story: they are crucial. Nor are we denying that Zechariah's faith will be the climax of the Zechariah-story taken as a whole. But that climax will come in 1:67–79 when, with his speech recovered, Zechariah will fill the stage and the one-time disbeliever will deliver a prophecy triumphant in its faith from beginning to end. Here in 1:57–66, however, the focus of the story is not Zechariah nor Elizabeth, but their neighbours and relatives. When Elizabeth's child is born, it is the reaction of these neighbours and relatives to which Luke devotes a whole verse (see 1:58). When the naming day comes, it is the neighbours and relatives who take the initiative: it is they who are for calling the child Zechariah; and when Elizabeth objects they appeal over her head to Zechariah; and when he takes his tablet and writes 'John is his name', Luke pauses to record their astonishment (see 1:63b) before he adds that at this juncture Zechariah recovered his speech. Quite clearly Luke is focusing on the neighbours and relatives. And when Zechariah's silence is broken, Luke does not forthwith end the story: he spends no less than two whole verses more depicting the effect it had on them and on people throughout the whole of Judaea (see 1:65–66). Here then is the climax and we must notice precisely what the stated effect was: 'All who heard them stored these things in their memories, saying, "What then shall this child be?"' So we ask next what it was about the happening recorded in Luke's story that led to their being so impressed about the child and his future.

We notice that it was not simply the birth that impressed them. They realized that the birth of a child to such elderly parents was a remarkable thing, and they were prepared to attribute it to God's extraordinary goodness: 'they heard that the Lord had magnified his mercy to Elizabeth, and they rejoiced with her'. But when they saw what happened at the naming ceremony, they did not rejoice so much as they were astonished and overawed. Even before Zechariah recovered his speech they may have heard Zechariah's story of the angel in the temple via Zechariah's writing tablet and Elizabeth; if not, they certainly heard about it afterwards. It had two parts. First the angel had predicted the miraculous birth. Whatever anybody might think of Zechariah's story, there was the baby as large as life. But according to Zechariah the angel had also announced that his child was destined to be the Messiah's forerunner. This was a story of an altogether different order, earthshaking in its implications. If it was true, they were standing on the verge of the messianic age. But was it true? After all, most parents think their first child is somehow special and dream up a marvellous future for it. Elderly parents are especially prone to such doting. Could it not be that Zechariah carried away by paternal pride was exaggerating or even fantasizing? It would be only natural.

Time would tell, of course, but meanwhile the child, whatever his future, must be named. Naturally the relatives were especially interested in this. In their society it was considered a disaster if a man died without a son to carry on the family name.[1] The relatives therefore would have been tremendously relieved that Zechariah's branch of the family now had a son to keep the family name going, and they were already calling him Zechariah after his father when Elizabeth said, 'No: he had to be called John'. The relatives were shocked and tried to get her to see that this would break the family tradition completely (see 1:61). But Elizabeth insisted. They appealed over her head to Zechariah; and to their astonishment and dismay he agreed with his wife. It was all so contrary to natural feeling, family interests and accepted practice. Why must they deliberately break the connection between the child and his family tradition especially if, as they claimed, he was destined to be the illustrious forerunner of Messiah?

And then dumb Zechariah spoke, and explained (or explained again) that this break with family tradition was not his idea: the

---

[1] This is the crucial point on which the whole of the Old Testament book of Ruth turns.

angel had told him that he must call the child John. The neighbours and relatives were overawed, as were people in general as the news spread through Judaea; for here, they needed no telling, was something that was so contrary to nature that it was obviously not a story invented by Zechariah, and they fell to considering its implications: 'What then shall this child be?'

John eventually grew up, claimed to be the forerunner and announced Jesus as the Messiah. John was murdered, Jesus was crucified. We today still have to ask the question, Was John really the forerunner? And that means asking, among other things, what motives Zechariah had in naming his son John.

So much then for story 4; but we have not finished yet with what happened at the naming ceremony. With his infant son lying before him in his cradle, Zechariah was moved to prophesy, by the Holy Spirit, so we are told (see 1:67); and 1:68–79 (story 5) records what he said. We listen critically. Will it in fact bear the hallmark of the Holy Spirit's prompting, or will it turn out to be little more than the expression of paternal pride, a glorification of his son, disguised in the phraseology of religion?

Note first his sense of proportion. Of the twelve verses of his prophecy the first eight go by without his mentioning his son at all (see 1:68–75). Then come two verses (see 1:76–77) in which he refers to John and his destined ministry; and after that the last two verses (see 1:78–79) revert once more to something else. The proportion is healthy, but it implies no belittling of John or false humility on Zechariah's part. On the contrary it arises out of Zechariah's conviction that John is to be the forerunner. Zechariah sees that if John is indeed the forerunner, something is happening that is infinitely more important than the birth of one prophet, however exalted he proves to be: here is an intervention of God in history that vindicates every prophetic promise truly made in God's name ever since history began (see 1:68–70). Again, since John is to be the forerunner, Zechariah realizes that there is soon to appear someone infinitely more important than John. In Zechariah's mind John is already outshone by the rising sun (see 1:78). God has intervened. The long night for Israel and the world is over. The sunrise from above is about to dawn (1:78). It will mean redemption (see 1:68); and salvation (see 1:69); and deliverance from servitude and freedom to serve God (see 1:74–75): forgiveness of sins and therefore freedom from the fear of death, and peace (see

1:77–79). God has intervened. He has raised up a horn of salvation, that is a mighty Saviour, in the house of David (see 1:69). And that horn, of course, is not John, but Jesus.

And now we become aware of a remarkable thing. Zechariah throughout his prophecy has been using the past tense. 'God has visited . . . has raised up a horn of salvation.' In one sense quite correctly: the Saviour had already come. But at the moment he was an unborn infant, not yet viable. As far as the world was concerned, the sun had not yet risen. It was still dark. Yet Zechariah's faith was already sensing vindication and victory. It was long ago now since the prophets first preached the promise of God (see 1:70), and God himself swore a covenant on oath to Abraham (see 1:73). Since then faith had often been tempted to say that those old prophecies were only myths, an expression of man's belief in hope itself as a principle of life (for life without hope is unbearable); that they were never meant to be taken literally, that there never would be any real dawn in this world; that the only way for faith to survive was to reinterpret the dawn as a way of expressing a belief that the never-ending night had a pleasant side to it, if you only learned to adopt the right attitude to it. And faith had had to fight back and say that God cannot lie; that he must have meant what he said; that the prophets were not all self-deceived fools, unable to distinguish their own thoughts from the voice of God; that it was God who spoke to that long succession of unique prophets; that he must one day honour his oath, and honour the faith of generations of men.

And now it had happened. Faith had been vindicated. But faith was also sober. It could afford to be. Zechariah looks back at his own baby. Yes, you my child, will have your necessary preliminary work to do. Messiah will save us from all our enemies (see 1:74), the great imperialist Gentile powers included. But first, Israel must repent. There can be no salvation in other senses until Israel has learned the way to salvation in the sense of forgiveness of sins and reconciliation with God. That alone is the way out of the darkness of death's shadow and into peace. It will be Messiah's task, my son, to give his people not only forgiveness of their sins, but the knowledge that they have been forgiven. But you must go in front and prepare his road (see 1:76–79).

Zechariah knew the people. He was not a priest for nothing. They would be more interested in political deliverance than in repentance and forgiveness of sins and in getting right with God. It would be difficult for John building a road down which Messiah could travel to get at their hearts. But nothing could alter the fact, or spoil the triumph for Zechariah's faith. The Messiah had come.

Luke is half-way through his first stage, his account of the last few hours before the dawn. At the beginning Zechariah's faith was decidedly shaky. It is delightful here to see that before Messiah actually came physically and publicly into the world, Zechariah's faith recovered and triumphed. So may ours before Messiah comes again.

2. The rising of the sun (2:1–52)

Stories 6 and 7.   The birth of Jesus in Bethlehem and the visit of the shepherds (2:1–21). Stories 4 and 5 told of the birth, circumcision and naming of the forerunner; stories 6 and 7 tell of the birth, circumcision and naming of the Messiah. At once a vivid contrast appears between the two sets of stories: in the naming of John great stress was laid on the break with family tradition; at the birth of Jesus we shall find great stress laid on the maintenance of family tradition. This contrast is no mere superficiality. As the forerunner of Christ John was to be 'the voice of one crying in the wilderness' (3:4), a voice, that is all. It was irrelevant to his ministry who he was and of what family he came. On the other hand, as forerunner John led a movement that at the beginning was independent of Jesus, and in a sense continued to be independent even after Jesus began his own public ministry. John himself never became one of Christ's apostolic band; his converts were regarded as his disciples (see 5:33); and though John's disciples frequently left John and attached themselves to Jesus (see Jn. 1:35–37; 3:25–26), John still went on making disciples (see Jn. 4:1). Moreover John made such a great impact on the nation that many people wondered whether he was in fact the Messiah. He carefully and clearly denied it, and publicly declared Jesus to be the Messiah (see 3:15–17; Jn. 1:19–34); but in case any doubt should arise then or later, the angel in naming him saw to it that family tradition, which was essential to Messiah, should be declared to be irrelevant to John's ministry. It did not matter who his father or family was.

For Jesus, by contrast, the maintenance of family tradition was, as we have said, all important, and that for obvious reasons. To claim to be the Messiah was to claim to be the Son of David and heir to the covenant and the promises made by God with David. So in the annunciation Gabriel describes the destined role of Mary's child as follows: '. . . and the Lord God shall give to him the throne of his father David and he shall reign over the house of Jacob for ever, and of his kingdom there shall be no end' (1:32–33). Likewise Zechariah in his prophecy speaks of Jesus as a horn of salvation raised up by God in the house of David (see 1:69). Nor is this a little local colouring which came from Christ's Palestinian Jewish origin, but which disappeared when the Christian gospel moved out into the Gentile world: it remained an essential part of the gospel. Paul the apostle to the Gentiles describes the gospel as '. . . the gospel of God . . . concerning his Son who was born of the seed of David according to the flesh . . .' (Rom. 1:1–3). And years later writing from a Roman prison Paul bids Timothy 'remember Jesus Christ, risen from the dead, of the seed of David according to my gospel' (2 Tim. 2:8). This emphasis on the Davidic tradition springs from the very nature of the gospel. The gospel is not a set of timeless universal truths expressed in the language of myth. The gospel is that centuries ago God started a great movement in history with Abraham and his seed and then with David, a movement which was every bit as literal and historical as the rise of the Roman Empire; and that Jesus the Messiah and Saviour is the culmination of that historical movement, come to fulfil all the promises made to and through David.

It was therefore indispensably necessary for this royal family tradition to be maintained at the birth of Jesus, and one feature of it in particular. The prophet Micah had predicted that the Messiah would be born in Bethlehem (see 5:2); in Bethlehem, therefore, Jesus must be born. Notice at once how our two stories together emphasize the place where Jesus was in fact born: in the city of David, in Bethlehem, in a manger (see 2:4, 7, 11–12, 15–16); but notice next that the chief concern of 2:1–7 (story 6) is to explain how he came to be born there.

It was not Joseph or Mary who arranged it in order to lend credibility, when the day should come, to Jesus' claim to be David's Son. Divine providence so ordered things that it was the supreme organizing genius of the ancient world who arranged for Jesus to be born in Bethlehem. Caesar Augustus ordered a census. The organizing principle of the census was that every man must return to the city from which his family sprang in order to be registered. Joseph belonged to the house and line of David and he therefore had to go to David's city. He could not avoid maintaining the family tradition: the census compelled him.[1] Of course Augustus knew nothing about this effect of the census, and the last thing he or his vassal Herod would have done would be to strengthen the credentials of a messianic claimant to the throne of Israel. For Augustus the taking of censuses was one of the ways he employed to get control over the various parts of his empire. But – and here is the irony of the thing – in the process, as he thought, of tightening his grip on his huge empire, he so organized things that Jesus, Son of Mary, Son of David, Son of God, destined to sit on the throne of Israel and of the world, was born in the city of David, his royal ancestor. Fulfilling, all unknowingly, the prophecy of Micah, he established this particular detail in the claim of Jesus to be the Messiah.[2]

It is a most interesting example of God's providential government of the world of men. When John the Baptist was conceived, God turned back the processes of nature. When our Lord was conceived there was introduced into nature something which nature had never known before and which nature by herself could never have produced. But when God's Son and destined ruler of the kings of the earth entered the world of men, there was apparently no interference with men's will or freedom of action whatsoever. Augustus had his own completely adequate reasons for his action and he did exactly what he wanted to do. Yet he did what, had he known, he would not have wished to do: he established the claim of the royal Son of David. He did in fact what had been predetermined by the counsel and foreknowledge of God.

So much then for story 6; what about story 7 (see 2:8–20)? The story of the angelic hosts and the visit of the shepherds to the manger is perhaps the best known of all the nativity stories. The marvellously rich imagery of the story appeals to some of the profoundest feelings in the human heart: shepherds caring for their sheep, the mother for her baby, and the angel choir breaking into

---

[1]The historians cannot tell us for certain exactly why Joseph's being of the house and family line of David should have obliged him under the terms of the census to return to Bethlehem. Two or three reasons are possible, none is certain. Red tape in the different provinces and vassal kingdoms of the Roman Empire was almost as complicated as ours is today. For discussion see Marshall, p.100–102.

[2]For another instance in Luke's writings of an imperial decree unintentionally helping forward the gospel at a crucial stage, see Acts 18:1ff.

the darkness of earth's night to herald the long-awaited sunrise, assuring the humble poor that whatever the mighty governments of the world might be doing, God cares for his people, and with a shepherd's heart has chosen that his Son should be born not in a palace but in a manger. Nor do we need to deny the symbolism of the story in order to maintain its historicity. History is solid, but without poetry it is dull and in danger of being meaningless; poetry is glorious, but without history, insubstantial. In the gospel of Christ both meet. Only the dullest of pedestrian minds would insist that an event must be either symbolic or historical and cannot be both.

Our chief concern with story 7, however, is to discover, if we can, how it fits into its context in Luke's narrative. And there are clues. We have already noticed how both stories 6 and 7 emphasize the place where Jesus was born: in the city of David, in Bethlehem, in a manger (see 2:4, 7, 11–12, 15–16). But there is this difference: story 6 explains how Jesus came to be born in this place; story 7 explains how a few hours after he was born, certain shepherds knew exactly the place to come to in order to find him: an angel, they said, had told them. Next we notice the effect of this whole incident as Luke himself has related it. The shepherds were the only ones, as far as we are told, to hear or see the angels. After they had visited the manger and told their story, they went off singing praise to God, and are never heard of again. The people standing around who heard what the shepherds said to Mary and the people who subsequently heard their story, 'marvelled' (2:18); but we hear nothing more of them either. And then we are told of Mary's reaction, as we shall be also in the next pair of stories (see 2:33–35), and even more so in the final story (see 2:43–51; see pp.61–62): 'Mary was storing up all these things pondering them in her heart' (2:19).

And no wonder. They would have been an incalculable comfort to her. Preparing for the arrival of an ordinary baby, especially if it is her first, is responsibility enough for most mothers. Mary had been told that her miraculously conceived child was the Son of God. But since the annunciation no further angel had appeared to instruct her from time to time as to what preparations and arrangements would be appropriate for the Son of God. Imagine her concern! How would she know if she was doing everything right, as it ought to be done?

At home in Nazareth she would have been making the best

preparations she could for the birth, when the census demands had put all her plans awry. To have to take a journey, and stay in a public hotel at such a time was bad enough. Imagine her distress when she got there and found all the rooms were taken. Their house in Nazareth was not a palace; but Joseph was a master builder and doubtless they had reasonable comfort. Now she would have to give birth in some make-shift quarters, half in public. And where could she put the child when it was born? Her first baby! And God's Son! How could she put God's Son in a rough manger?

And then the shepherds arrived enquiring where the baby was. When asked how they knew where to come they replied that an angel of the Lord had told them that the Saviour, Christ the Lord, had been born this very night in the city of David.

With this, if not before, things must have begun to make sense to Mary. Gabriel had told her that her child should have the throne of his father David; and here was an angel sending these shepherds to David's city. She and Joseph had not intended to come to Bethlehem, but Augustus, or so it had seemed at the time, had compelled them to come to David's city. Now she saw what plan it was that lay behind Augustus and his administration, and had shepherded her and Joseph to Bethlehem. But there was another question. Perhaps, with the sudden increase in the population caused by the census, there might have been more than one baby born in David's city that night. How did the shepherds know that Mary's baby was the right one? The answer was simple: the angel had given them a sign: they would find the right baby lying in, of all places, a manger.

Ordinary women in Bethlehem did not put their firstborn infants in mangers, we may be sure, at least not if they could help it. For Mary it must have been unspeakably distressing to have to do so. Yet here were these shepherds, and according to them angels knew that the Son of God was lying in a manger, and were glad of the fact: they could use it as a sign to guide humble shepherds to where they might find the Saviour. Since then, of course, uncounted millions have been grateful for this sign, for at the higher level of meaning the birth in a manger has guided them more surely to the recognition of Jesus as God's Son and as Saviour of the world than birth in a palace would have done. Mary, of course, could not have foreseen that; but this much surely she saw: if angels were glad to use the manger as a sign for shepherds, another Shepherd must have guided her and Joseph and the child to the manger in the first place. All, then, was well and would be well: the responsibility for shepherding the infant Son of God was in higher hands than hers.

Stories 8 and 9.   The prophecies of Simeon and Anna (2:22–40). We may have forgotten it by now, but in stories 2 and 3 we listened to Mary expressing her intense joy: 'My soul magnifies the Lord and my spirit has rejoiced in God my Saviour' (1:46–47). In stories 8 and 9 (see 2:22–39) we are to hear of Mary's anguish: '. . . and your own soul shall be pierced through with a sword' (2:35). It goes without saying that this contrast is not an artificial literary creation of Luke's; still less is it the product of the present writer's subjective imagination. The contrast is inherent in two essential elements in God's programme of redemption: the incarnation with its joy and the cross with its inevitable anguish. The chief concern of our two stories will be to tell us how, when, and in what circumstances the warning of coming anguish was conveyed to Mary. Earlier (p.41) we found ourselves wondering how Mary, being an ordinary mortal of flesh and blood, would bear the enormous strain of the prospect of becoming the mother of the Son of God. We can now also perceive that when she saw the one she believed to be the Son of God rejected by his nation and crucified, her faith would have been overwhelmed with indescribable dismay and bewilderment, if it had not been adequately prepared. Stories 8 and 9, then, will describe that preparation. For the incarnation Mary was first prepared by Gabriel and then her faith was further strengthened by Elizabeth; for the cross Mary will first be prepared by Simeon, and then consoled and encouraged by Anna. Let us begin by studying these two people.

Both Simeon and Anna had a vigorous and active faith in what they believed to be the divinely inspired prophetic programme for the restoration of Israel. Simeon is described as 'looking for the consolation of Israel' (2:25). The delightful term 'consolation of Israel' suggests that his expectation was based on the programme enunciated in such passages as Isaiah 40ff. He was looking for the day when Israel's warfare and chastisement would be over, and God would 'comfort his people'. Nor was Simeon narrow-mindedly concerned simply for the future of Israel. Basing himself again on Isaiah's predictions (*e.g.* 42:6; 49:6 *etc.*) he foresaw the time when the light of God's salvation would spread to the very ends of the earth (see 2:31–32).

Anna, for her part, is described as speaking of Jesus 'to all those who were looking for the redemption of Jerusalem' (2:38). That expectation, again, was not mere wishful thinking or narrow-minded jingoism. It was solidly based on the repeated promises of the prophets. Jeremiah (see ch.33), for instance, had spoken of the matter. Daniel (see ch.9) had been given a timetable for Jerusalem's partial restoration, its consequent renewed desolations, and its ultimate complete restoration. After the return from the exile in Babylon, the prophet Zechariah had repeatedly (see 1:12 – 2:13; 8:1–23; 9:9; 12:1 – 13:1; 14:1–21) affirmed that Jerusalem would one day be finally and permanently redeemed, and his language had made it clear that he was thinking of a restoration far more glorious than what was achieved when Nehemiah rebuilt the city's walls. Since that time Jerusalem had been desecrated by Antiochus Epiphanes, and now downtrodden by the Romans. But Anna, and those like her, were undaunted in their faith: Daniel had said that after the partial restoration following the exile, desolations would supervene until the final restoration. In Anna's mind things were going according to plan. Jerusalem's 'widowhood' (see La. 1:1) had lasted a long while; but Anna, too, in the literal sense had been a widow for a very long time, and in a way her personal experience mirrored that of her city. Constant in her prayers and supplications, she was undaunted in her faith that the city's sorrows and desolations would one day be a thing of the past, and Jerusalem would be redeemed (see 2:37–38). If Mary should need to be consoled and fortified to face the prospect of Messiah's 'being cut off', as Daniel had phrased it (see 9:26), there was none more suited to the task than Anna.

We return to Simeon. Not only had he a firm faith in the prophetic programme in general, but he had been given a personal revelation relating to the timetable for the fulfilment of some of the details of that programme: 'it had been revealed to him by the Holy Spirit that he should not see death before he had seen the Lord's Christ' (2:26). From that revelation one might have jumped to the conclusion that Simeon would live to see the messianic kingdom established and the consolation of Israel, for which he looked, fully realized. But Simeon did not take it so. He recognized in Jesus

God's salvation (see 2:30). He did not mean, of course, 'salvation accomplished': the Saviour was still only a baby; he meant 'the means, or instrument of salvation'.[1] Obviously the baby would have to grow up before he could accomplish salvation. Even so, having seen God's instrument of salvation actually born into this world, Simeon did not make it the basis of a prayer to be allowed to live on to see salvation accomplished; instead he took it as an indication that he was now going to be allowed to depart in peace. He could go in peace, in the certain knowledge that if the Saviour had actually come, salvation would eventually be accomplished, however long it took. But he was happy to go because he knew also – and this he began to tell Mary – that even after he had grown up, the Saviour would not immediately be welcomed by the nation, drive out the enemy, liberate Jerusalem city, 'console' Israel and put the world right. On the contrary, the Saviour would meet bitter opposition and rejection, and Mary would find the anguish of witnessing it like having a great military sword thrust through her soul.

Nor did Simeon get all these foresights simply from his private revelation. 'This child' he said 'is set for the falling and rising up of many in Israel, and for a sign that is spoken against . . . so that the thoughts of many hearts may be revealed' (2:34–35). Both the language and the ideas were taken from the Old Testament. Isaiah had early prophesied that the Lord would be 'a stone of stumbling and a rock of offence to both the houses of Israel . . . many shall stumble over it and be broken . . .' (8:14). Similarly the phrase 'a sign that is spoken against' carried overtones from the Old Testament. The noun-form (*antilogia*) of the participle which Luke uses for 'spoken against' (*antilegomenon*) is the word which was used in the Greek translation of the Old Testament to record Israel's rebellion against God in the wilderness (see Nu. 20:13).[2] And when Simeon explains that the purpose behind Christ's being a 'sign that is spoken against' is 'that the thoughts of many hearts might be revealed', his words take us back to the explanation God gave to Israel as to why he had allowed them to undergo such traumatic

---

[1] The Greek word *sōtērion* can mean, like its cognate *sōtēria*, 'salvation accomplished'. But its primary meaning is 'means or instrument of salvation', and that is the sense in which it would appear to be used here.

[2] *Cf.* its use in Heb. 12:2–3: '. . . him who endured such contradiction (*antilogia*) by sinners against himself '.

experiences in the wilderness: '. . . that he might humble you, to prove you, to know what was in your heart, whether you would keep his commandments or not' (Dt. 8:2).

Israel had never been a nation marked by unqualified obedience, any more than other nations had. When they came out of Egypt singing their songs of redemption, no-one had dreamed that hidden in the hearts of many of them lay as yet unformed thoughts of sheer rebellion against God their Redeemer. But the wilderness, by God's deliberate intention, exposed them. And Simeon knew what Isaiah knew, that human nature is the same in all ages. Much therefore as he looked for the consolation of Israel, he knew that beneath the outward forms of religion there lurked still in many hearts that same spirit of rebellion, and that the first effect of the coming of Christ would be to provoke their hidden rebellion into open antagonism. In a sense Christ had to do that, for there could be no consolation of Israel until the latent rebellion against God had been brought out into the open, had been recognized for what it was, repented of and forgiven.

Simeon was no pessimist: he believed that Christ would be not only the cause of many in Israel falling but also the means of their rising again (see 2:34). Exposure, confession and repentance would lead to forgiveness, reconciliation; even the Gentile nations would be embraced in the scope of that reconciliation. But Simeon was a realist. To him was given the delicate task of gently warning Mary that before the final consolation of Israel there must come bitter anguish for Israel, for her Son and for herself.

Mary may well not have understood at the time all that Simeon told her; but later when the opposition against Jesus mounted, hardened and became official, and Mary was tempted to think that God's programme and timetable of redemption had gone wildly astray, she would look back to this meeting with Simeon and Anna in the temple and take comfort. Perhaps she would reflect on the providentially precise timing that brought Simeon into the temple at exactly the right moment on the right day to meet her and the child. And then she might even reflect on how she and the child came to be in the temple on that day to hear what Simeon had to say about the programme of redemption – at least, if she did not, Luke has done his best to make sure we do. Five times over (see 2:22, 23, 24, 27, 39) Luke has told us that the reasons for, and the timing of, her visit to the temple were controlled by the law of the

Lord. That law required from her two things: the sacrifice connected with the purification of a woman after childbirth and the presentation of her firstborn son to the Lord. Since her child was a male, forty days had to elapse before she was allowed to come to the temple to offer her sacrifice (see Lv. 12:1–8); and so it was 'When their days of purification were complete' (2:22) that Mary brought Jesus to the temple to present him to the Lord. The timing of her visit was not a matter of chance: in this particular she was controlled by the timetabling of God's law.

Nor was the presentation of her firstborn Son to the Lord an empty formality or a mere superstition. The law (see 2:23) went back to the time of Israel's redemption from Egypt, when under God's judgment Egypt's firstborn were slain, but Israel's firstborn were saved by the blood of the Passover sacrifice (see Ex. 12; 13:11–16). Ever after this, Israel's firstborn males, in recognition that their predecessors in Egypt owed their lives to God's redeeming mercy, had to be consecrated to the service of God. Since such consecration meant a life of religious service to God, like for instance that of Samuel (see 1 Sa. chs. 1 and 2) or that of the whole tribe of Levi, parents were normally allowed to redeem their firstborn from that life of service by a payment of five shekels (Nu. 18:15–16).[1] But every firstborn male still had to be formally presented to the Lord; and the constantly recurring presentations had reminded Israel, as they were intended to do, that redemption was the basis of God's deliverance of his people. At the same time they had indelibly impressed on the nation's consciousness the basic principle and programme of redemption: the price of redemption is the sacrifice of the substitute.

It was on the very day when Mary came to present her firstborn to the Lord and stood there with her own sacrifice in her hand, that Simeon had approached her and had gently indicated that for Israel's redemption her firstborn must suffer. The message was at the time veiled in a certain obscurity, and that was kind: but when eventually Mary came to understand its full import, she would see that God had controlled both the time and the occasion of the

---

[1] Luke makes no explicit mention of the payment of five shekels to redeem Jesus, and the commentators disagree over whether Mary and Joseph did, or did not, decide that the child must be left consecrated utterly to God's service and not redeemed (though unlike Samuel, he seems to have worked later at a secular trade as a carpenter: Mk. 6:3). We need not try to decide the matter here.

message's delivery. And she would perceive that her Son's suffering and death were not untimely, some tragic accident: they were a necessary part of an eternal purpose.

One more small detail of timing might well have occurred to her as she reflected on that day in the temple. Anna had spoken of Jesus to those who were looking for the redemption of Jerusalem. Now had Anna appeared first, delivered her message and then left Simeon to finish the story, Mary might have concluded that Simeon's announcement annulled Anna's enthusiastic message; that Israel's rejection of God's Son, although it meant that salvation would go to the Gentiles, made it doubtful that Jerusalem city would ever be restored. But Anna had come up after Simeon; and in spite of all that Simeon had said, she had still assured her listeners that Jerusalem city would be redeemed. Remembering this, Mary would be prepared to hear the worst without losing heart.

She would one day hear that her Son had stood and wept over Jerusalem 'O Jerusalem, how many times would I . . . and you would not. Behold your house is left to you desolate' (13:34–35). She would one day hear, until her blood ran cold, how he had warned that Jerusalem would be surrounded by armies, its inhabitants butchered, or taken captive, and the city itself trodden down until the times of the Gentiles were fulfilled (see 21:20–24). But she would lose neither heart nor faith; for she would also hear that he said, a few sentences later, '. . . they shall see the Son of Man coming in a cloud with power and great glory. But when these things begin to come to pass, look up, and lift up your heads; because your redemption draws near' (21:27–38). Hearing that, she would remember Simeon and then Anna.

Story 10. The boy Jesus in the temple (2:41–52). We have already considered this final story in different connections (pp.12 and 32) and there is no need to repeat here what we discovered there. It will be enough perhaps, if we observe here how natural and true to life Luke's narrative is and yet how skilfully he has caught the dramatic climax of the incident.

As pilgrims Mary and Joseph were travelling in a large caravan which included a number of friends and relatives (see 2:44). It was not careless of them but very natural therefore, that during the first day of the return journey they did not know exactly where the boy Jesus was. He could have been with any one of the members of their extended family, or even with friends; and anyway he was a boy of twelve and well able to look after himself during the day.

It was also very natural, and typical of thousands of parents who have temporarily lost a child, that when at last they found him, Mary's sudden relief should allow her pent-up anxiety to express itself, even in front of such a distinguished company, in a clear, if restrained, reprimand of her child.

But now notice how Luke times the climax. At 2:46a he has the parents finding Jesus; but he does not immediately give us Mary's reprimand. At this point he first switches our attention to Jesus sitting among the teachers of the law, astonishing everybody by the depth of his understanding and the quality of his answers. In a situation where an unaccompanied child is found in a public building, the most natural questions for the authorities to ask are 'Hello son, are you all alone? Where's your father? Who *is* your father?' On this occasion the remarkable ability of the child must have given these questions an even greater interest in the minds of the theologians. When therefore Jesus' parents came in and identified themselves as the child's parents by Mary's reprimand: 'Son, why have you treated us like this? Your father and I . . .', the theologians must have watched and listened with intense interest: 'so this is his father, then; I wonder exactly who he is.'

At that dramatic moment the child spoke: 'Why were you searching for me? Did you not realize I had to be in my Father's house?' (2:49).

My Father's house? The learned doctors knew their Old Testament inside out. In all the long biblical record, not even Moses who had built the tabernacle, not David who had longed to build the temple, nor Solomon who had actually built it, no prophet, no king or commoner, not the most exalted of them, had ever referred to the tabernacle or temple as 'my Father's house'. The child was conscious of a relationship with God that none had conceived of, let alone expressed, before. And with that relationship, a compelling devotion: 'I had to be in my Father's house.'

'Did you not realize it?' he asked Mary and Joseph. The question was asked with all the delightful simplicity of a child. Mary, at least, ought to have realized it, and ought to have worked out some of the implications of what Gabriel had told her; but in her defence it can be said that she was not the last one to believe Jesus to be the Son of God, and then with unfortunate inconsistency to express ideas and views implying that in some things Jesus was in error. She had had, moreover, such little time to think through those implications; even we who know the subsequent story of the life, ministry, death, resurrection and ascension, and believe most firmly in the incarnation, even we have not managed to think through fully all its implications.

But now both Mary and Joseph were flustered, and they did not understand what he said (see 2:50). Did it mean that from now on he was constantly going to assert independence of them? That would make it very difficult to bring him up; and after all, he was a child still. He had still to grow in wisdom and stature (see 2:52). No, he would not be asserting premature independence. Mary and Joseph still had their task to fulfil as parents, and he would be subject to them (see 2:51). He was a real child.

But they had been given an early warning; and Mary kept all these sayings in her heart (2:51). The time would come when she must let him go. Her unique task would be over. She would then have to let him go at the level of the mere human relationship of child, that she might receive him as Saviour, Lord and God. As she thought over this incident, it would prepare her, so that when the break came it might not be so much a break as the eclipsing of one unique joy and responsibility, by an infinitely greater wonder, worship and obedience.

Luke in all his Gospel will mention Mary only once more (see 8:19–21), and then not by her personal name. By that time the human, physical relationships of mother and brothers of the Messiah will already be starting to give way to the higher spiritual relationship to Christ of those who hear the word of God and do it.

Some further observations

We set out in our study of this first major section of the Gospel to examine Luke's selection of material, sense of proportion, repetition of ideas and themes, thought-flow, composition and structure. We early noticed that he had chosen five stories to cover happenings before the birth of Christ and five to cover the birth and what followed. That in itself suggested that Luke had a carefully balanced sense of proportion. Then we noticed (p.30) that story 10 contained striking similarities and contrasts with story 1; and we concluded that story 10 was selected by Luke because its theme complemented the theme of story 1. Since then we have noticed that a leading theme in stories 6 and 7 contrasts vividly with a leading theme in stories 4 and 5; and similarly stories 8 and 9 show a marked contrast with stories 2 and 3.

This suggests not only that Luke has arranged his selected material in a carefully composed structure, but also that the structure is in fact symmetrical. The matter can best be represented in tabular form:

i	*Story 1*	An old man in the temple. Question: miraculous parenthood? Zechariah's disbelief.
ii	*Stories 2 and 3*	Mary's joy at the incarnation: the words of Gabriel and Elizabeth: the timing of Mary's visit to Elizabeth.
iii	*Stories 4 and 5*	Family tradition deliberately broken at the birth, naming and circumcision of John.
iv	*Stories 6 and 7*	Family tradition carefully maintained at the birth, naming and circumcision of Jesus.
v	*Stories 8 and 9*	Mary's anguish at the cross: the words of Simeon and Anna: the timing of Mary's visit to the temple.
vi	*Story 10*	A young boy in the temple. Question: supernatural parentage? Mary and Joseph's failure to understand.

This observation calls for comment, if for no other reason than that many people have an instinctive aversion to such structural symmetries. In a purely literary work they would regard symmetry as a cheap device, tending to triviality, and a sign of poor taste. They cannot think that a writer of holy Scripture would so far demean himself as to employ it. In a serious historical work they would regard symmetrical structure as being quite impossible. History by its very nature, they argue, is not symmetrical, and therefore no account of it can be given in symmetrical form without serious distortion of the historical facts. Moreover in recent years many scholars have claimed to detect symmetrical structures in Luke's writings; but their schemes are often mutually exclusive.

This proves, their critics argue, that these symmetries are not objectively present in Luke's work: they are creations of the subjective imagination of the commentators.

The question of literary taste is not so serious as it first appears. Granted that symmetrical structures in literature do not please modern taste, there is abundant evidence that they were to the taste of ancient writers of the highest excellence. C. H. Talbert refers in this connection to Homer, Aeschylus, Euripides, Herodotus, Thucydides, Pindar, Catullus, Horace, Virgil, Propertius and Plutarch.[1] Luke's taste is more likely to have been that of the ancient world than that of ours.

More serious is the charge that the use of symmetrical structures is incompatible with a concern for historical accuracy. We have already hinted (p.15) that this charge is mistaken; we will discuss it more fully in Appendix 2, p.358.

The third objection rests on an all too true observation, but on a false deduction. Granted that the differences between the symmetries which scholars of a literary bent have claimed to detect in Luke – Acts are so great that they cannot all be right, but could all be wrong. The same could be said often enough about the learned views of the exegetes and historians; and we do not on that account rule out in advance all attempts at exegesis or historical criticism. We patiently seek for sound criteria for judging between the conflicting views put forward. This likewise we shall discuss later in Appendix 3, p.360.

For the moment, however, certain practical considerations call for our attention. In the rest of his Gospel Luke will constantly do the kind of thing we have found him doing in this first section. He will group passages by common theme, and he will frequently tell a story which expresses one aspect of a matter and then shortly afterwards balance it with another story which expresses a complementary or opposite aspect of the same matter. He will do it because he wishes to present a balanced account of our Lord's life, work and teaching. The result, intended or otherwise, will be that his work will often give the impression of being symmetrically structured. In some places the impression will be striking, in others not so clear; it is perhaps to be expected that if he has used sym-

---

[1] *Literary Patterns, Theological Themes and the Genre of Luke – Acts*, (Scholars Press, 1974), p.67. The present writer would not necessarily agree with all the structures proposed by Dr Talbert.

metry at all, he is more likely to have used it in the arrangement of incidents and parables than in the record of long stretches of detailed teaching. But – and here is our first practical point – the question whether and to what extent Luke may have intended to construct symmetrical structures will not be our main concern. Our prime concern will be to perceive the flow and balance of Luke's thought. Symmetries if they exist, certainly do not exist for their own sake: they are the result of the balance of Luke's thought. It is possible to follow the flow and balance of his thought without deciding whether the structure of his narrative is intended to be a perfect symmetry or not.

Our second practical point is that to avoid excessive tedium in what follows we shall not necessarily refer explicitly to the considerations of selection, proportion, repetition of ideas, thought-flow, composition and structure which have guided our exposition in those cases where it is self-evident what they are.

And one final practical point, concerning a labour-saving device. Towards the beginning of each stage we shall place a kind of table of contents, drawn up for the purpose of suggesting what the main ideas and themes of the stage are and how they relate to one another. Some of them will show clear, detailed and complete symmetry; some will show little or none. Let each reader see in them as much or as little symmetry as he pleases.[1] But even those who cannot accept any, may still find it useful to turn to the tables from time to time and to use them as maps to help them maintain a bird's-eye view of the terrain as a whole while the commentary is moving inch by inch through that terrain in its necessarily more pedestrian fashion.

---

[1] See C. H. Talbert's remarks on the dislike of perfect, unbroken symmetry among the ancients of both the classical and Near Eastern worlds, *op. cit*, pp.78–9. His remarks are valid enough, even if in practical literary criticism it is all too easy to appeal to this principle in order to claim partial symmetry in passages where it is very doubtful.

The introduction of the Son of God

Preliminary survey

The movements

1 John in the desert and at the Jordan *(3:1–20)*
2 Christ at the Jordan and in the desert *(3:21–4:13)*
3 Christ at Nazareth *(4:16–30)*
4 Christ at Capernaum *(4:31–43)*

Stage 2

The introduction of the Son of God

Preliminary survey

If the main topic of chapters 1 and 2 was the arrival of the Son of God in our world, it is easy to see that the next main topic is going to be his official introduction to the world of men and the beginning of his public ministry. The question arises, however, whether Luke intends us to read all the following chapters in one unbroken stream, or whether here, too, as in stage 1, he has grouped his narratives so that we might the better see their significance. Let us begin, therefore, by mapping out the successive movements of thought which we now encounter.

Chapter 3 opens by dating the beginning of John's ministry, then identifies his role and gives examples of his preaching until at 3:20 Herod puts an end to it by imprisoning him. John is not heard of again until 7:18ff. So let us call 3:1–20 movement 1.

Next Luke records not the beginning of Christ's public ministry – that does not come until 4:14 – but three other matters linked together by a very pronounced, common theme. First the baptism (3:21–22) at which the Voice from heaven proclaims: 'You are my beloved Son'. Then the genealogy (3:23–38) which demonstrates Jesus to be '. . . son of Adam, son of God'. Then the temptation (4:1–13) in which the devil twice questions 'if you are the Son of God'. And when the temptations are over Luke brings the section to a clear-cut end by the formal remark: 'And when the devil had completed every temptation, he departed from him until the next suitable occasion' (4:13). Let us label 3:21 – 4:13, then, movement 2.

At this point Luke calls our attention to geography. All the events of movements 1 and 2 have taken place in the south of the country: at 3:2–3 John came out of the wilderness to the Jordan; at 4:1 Jesus returned from his baptism in the Jordan to the wilderness, and then at 4:9 to Jerusalem. But now to begin his public ministry Jesus goes north to Galilee and Luke begins his account of that ministry with a lengthy general statement: 'And Jesus returned in the power of the Spirit into Galilee and reports of him spread throughout the country. And he was teaching in their synagogues and being praised by everybody' (4:14–15). After that general description Luke gives a particular instance: his teaching in the synagogue at Nazareth (see 4:16–30). It comes to a very decided end: the people are enraged and try to destroy him; but 'he passed right through them and went on his way' (4:30). Let us call this incident movement 3.

Another geographical note separates movement 3 from what follows: 'and he came down to Capernaum, a city of Galilee' (4:31). Here the reception is very different: far from attempting to get rid of him, they try to persuade him to remain with them; but he insists on leaving in order to preach elsewhere (see 4:42–43). We may call the Capernaum incident (4:31–43) movement 4.

Now notice what Luke does at this point. Instead of passing on to the next incident he calls a temporary halt by inserting (4:44) a general summary remark: 'And he was preaching in the synagogues of Judaea'.[1] This summary virtually repeats the summary at 4:15, and the effect is that these two summaries, standing one at the beginning of movement 3 and the other at the end of movement 4, bracket the two movements together. The two movements, after all, are giving two specific instances of the general activity described by the summaries: Christ's teaching and preaching in the synagogues. Moreover, when we look beyond the summary at 4:44 into chapter 5 we find that synagogues are no longer mentioned: we shall not find Christ in another synagogue until 6:6.

Let us therefore take the hint, pause at 4:44, and look at the four movements we have so far encountered. Much of the material in these movements is shared by Luke with the other evangelists. He includes it doubtless because he wants to say for his own reasons what they say for theirs. But there are certain features which are

---

[1]This (and not '. . . of Galilee') seems to be the correct reading. 'Judaea' presumably means, as in 1:4, 'the whole country of Palestine', see Marshall, p.199.

peculiar to Luke, and these may help us more quickly to perceive the direction of his own thought. Let us look at some of them.

Apart from a few phrases and ideas the Nazareth incident at 4:16–30 (movement 3) is peculiar to Luke. Its first main message is obvious and explicit: Christ identifies himself and his ministry by reading a passage from Isaiah 61 and claiming to be its fulfilment. This at once recalls 3:2–6 (movement 1) where the Baptist was introduced and his ministry identified by a similarly lengthy quotation from Isaiah (see 40:3–5). The parallel is hardly accidental; it is certainly not insignificant.

Movement 1 also has its own peculiarity. Like Matthew, Luke has the Baptist calling on the people to give practical evidence that their repentance is genuine, and not to parry the thrust of his preaching by a false defence: 'Do not begin to say within yourselves, "We have Abraham as our father"' (3:7–8; Mt. 3:7–10). Unlike Matthew, however, Luke chooses to emphasize the need for this practical evidence: he alone records that three lots of people came to ask John what works they had to do to prove their claim to have repented (see 3:10–14). But at this point we look again at the Nazareth incident. There, at 4:23, things go into reverse, so to speak, for the people demand that Christ produce more works to justify his claim: 'Doubtless you will quote this proverb at me: "Physician heal yourself; whatever we have heard you have done in Capernaum, do here also in your own native city."' Of course, Christ regards this demand for further evidence as nothing but the people's false defence of their unwillingness to believe, and he spends the rest of his time in the synagogue proving it to be so. But our interest at the moment lies in simply observing that leading ideas in movement 3 balance and complement ideas in movement 1. What the point is of their doing so we must consider later; but the fact that they do so we presumably owe to Luke's deliberate selection and arrangement of his material.

Or take yet another of Luke's peculiar features. At 3:23–38 he records Christ's genealogy. Now Matthew also has a genealogy of Christ, but he puts it at the beginning of the birth narratives (1:1–17), not between the baptism and the temptation as Luke does; and Matthew's genealogy works forwards from Abraham to Christ, not backwards from Christ to 'Adam, son of God' (3:38). Luke's deeper reasons behind this arrangement will be considered later on; but its superficial effect we have already noticed (p.67): it gives to Luke's movement 2 (3:21–4:13) as compared with Matthew's comparable passage, a further instance of the term 'Son of God' and an additional sense in which it is used (additional that is, to the sense in which it is used at the baptism and in the temptations). But with this compare one of Luke's peculiarities at 4:41 (movement 4). Matthew (8:16), talking of what happened in Capernaum at even when the sun was set, says simply: '. . . and he cast out the spirits with a word . . .'. Mark (1:34) says more: 'and he cast out many demons and he did not allow the demons to speak, because they knew him'. Luke (4:41) says more still: 'And demons also came out from many, crying out and saying, "You are the Son of God." And he rebuked them and did not allow them to speak, because they knew that he was the Christ.' The term 'Son of God' will not be found again in Luke until 8:28 and only rarely thereafter. Our exposition will have to ask why he lays so much emphasis on it in both movements 2 and 4.

For the moment the similarities we have noticed between movements 1 and 3 and then again between movements 2 and 4 strongly suggest that these four movements were meant to stand together as a closely-knit group. We shall refer to them as stage 2 of the Gospel. We shall, of course, wish to penetrate beneath their superficial similarities to discern, if we can, what Luke was intending to show us by this selection and arrangement of material. To help us do that let us construct a table of contents which will present at a glance the major features of the four movements (see opposite page).

The movements

1. John in the desert and at the Jordan (3:1–20)

Stage 1 recorded the arrival in our world of the Son of God as a human baby and his growth as a child. Though prepared for and announced by an angelic visitor and celebrated by the choirs of heaven, on earth the birth passed by almost completely unnoticed. It was a deliberately private affair. As to the baby's identity, few people beyond the families of Mary and Elizabeth knew who the child was, or knew more than that he was somehow special. The shepherds in the fields of Bethlehem and their restricted circle of friends and acquaintances knew something. Simeon and Anna knew more. The learned doctors in the temple had their curiosity

Stage 2 of the Coming 3:1 – 4:44

Preparation for the public ministry 3:1 – 4:13.

1 John in the desert and at the Jordan 3:1–20.

1 *John's identity and function* 3:4–6: the fulfilment of Isaiah 40:3–5.

2 *The demand for evidence from the people:* 'bring forth fruits worthy of repentance and do not begin to say . . . "We have Abraham for our father . . ." (3:8).

3 *The people's reaction:* . . . the people were full of expectation and were all wondering . . . whether John might not possibly be the Messiah . . . (3:15).

4 Herod imprisons John (3:20–21).

2 Christ at the Jordan and in the desert 3:21–4:13.

1 *Christ's identity:* 'My beloved Son' (3:22); son of Adam son of God (3:38); 'If you are the Son of God' . . . (4:3, 9).

2 *The demand for evidence from Christ:* 'If you are the Son of God, command this stone to become bread . . . throw yourself down from here' (4:3, 9).

3 *A question of authority:* The devil said . . . 'To you will I give all this authority, . . . if you will worship before me, yours it will be, all of it . . . .' (4:6–7).

The beginning of the public ministry 4:14–44.

3 Christ at Nazareth 4:16–30.

1 *Christ's identity and mission* 4:17–19: the fulfiller of Isaiah 61:1–2.

2 *The demand for evidence from Christ:* 'Doubtless you will say to me . . . "Physician heal yourself: whatever we have heard done at Capernaum do here also in your native city"' (4:23).

3 *The people's reaction:* All admitted that they were amazed at the gracious words that came from his lips, and they said, 'Is not this Joseph's son,' (4:22).

4 The people try to destroy Jesus (4:28–30).

4 Christ at Capernaum 4:31–43.

1 *Christ's identity:* 'the Holy One of God' (4:34): 'the Son of God' (4:41); 'the Christ' (4:41).

2 *The refusal of evidence from demons:* Jesus rebuked him saying, 'be quiet' . . . And rebuking them he did not allow them to speak, because they knew that he was the Christ (4:35, 41).

3 *A question of authority:* . . . and they spoke . . . saying 'What is this word? For with authority and power he commands the unclean spirits and they come out' (4:36).

aroused and provocatively answered. Beyond that the matter was almost completely private, as any healthy normal childhood needs to be.

All this changes with stage 2. The privacy is gone for ever. The time has come for the Son of God to be openly and publicly introduced to the world. Two major questions will therefore now be answered: exactly who is Jesus Christ, and exactly what has he come to do? The people of his own day would have needed to have these things explained and demonstrated very carefully, for their expectations of who or what the Messiah would be when he came, and what he would do, were often uncertain, frequently confused and conflicting. And things are not much better today: christendom itself is marked by uncertainty and confusion on these questions. Luke therefore will not leave us to deduce, as best we may, from a mass of individual incidents and sayings, who Jesus was and what he came to do. He will record what was said at the official introductions by the divinely appointed forerunner, by God the Father, by Christ himself, and even by the demonic world. Moreover, the very formality of the structure in which Luke presents these introductions will carry its own message. Here is no haphazard collection of items, whose unstructured lack of proportion gives more prominence to some features than they deserve and less to others. Luke has aimed to give us a complete and rounded picture, the essential elements of which are presented in careful balance, due proportion and proper emphasis.

Movement 1 (3:1–20) describes the ministry of the forerunner. Notice the impressive list of names with which it begins: the Emperor Tiberius Caesar, the military governor of Judaea, Pontius Pilate, the tetrarch Herod, Philip and Lysanias, and the chief priests Annas and Caiaphas This list serves to date the beginning of John's ministry; but it does more: it helps us to perceive John's stature. If these men possessed the highest authority in the land, John came with a higher authority. They were the establishment of organized society; John came out of the desert. But in that desert the word of God had come to John son of Zechariah (note the formal patronymic) and it had constituted him a prophet of the order of men like Isaiah, Jeremiah and Ezekiel, who under direct inspiration of God had counselled, and sometimes rebuked and denounced, emperors, kings and priests as well as the nations at large.

He came, says Luke, preaching baptism as an expression of

repentance which should in turn lead to forgiveness (3:3). In one sense, of course, a call to repentance was the stock-in-trade of any prophet or preacher; but John's call to repentance was different from all others: how different, Luke now shows us by citing a prophecy from Isaiah (40:3–5). The heart of that prophecy was a metaphor drawn from the ancient custom that when an emperor or some other eminent personage was about to visit a city, the citizens could be required to prepare a well-constructed approach-road along which he could advance with due pomp and dignity on his way into the city. Using that metaphor Isaiah predicted that one day Israel would be called upon to prepare an approach-road for such a visitor. What visitor? Isaiah left his hearers in no doubt: 'Prepare . . . the way of Yahweh . . . a highway for our God . . . say to the cities of Judah, Behold, your God! Behold, Adonay Yahweh will come as a mighty one . . . his reward is with him and his recompense before him' (40:3, 9–10).

So said Isaiah, and Luke now uses Isaiah's words in order to describe John's ministry and to identify the person whom John announced. It is of the utmost importance therefore to notice that Luke is not simply borrowing a felicitous phrase or two from Isaiah to describe John's ministry on the grounds that John's ministry bore a certain resemblance here and there to what Isaiah was talking about. Luke is stating that John's ministry was the fulfilment of Isaiah's prophecy. John's was the voice that according to Isaiah was destined to call upon the people to prepare the approach-road; and it follows that the visitor whom John announced was the visitor announced by Isaiah: Yahweh himself.

Luke, of course, cites Isaiah's prophecy in a Greek translation. For Isaiah's 'Prepare . . . the way of Yahweh', he puts 'Prepare the way of the Lord (Greek: *kyriou*); but he means exactly the same as Isaiah: the Greek word *kyrios* is the standard translation of Yahweh in the Greek Old Testament. For Isaiah's 'make straight . . . a highway *for our God*', Luke puts 'make straight *his* paths'; but that does not mean that Luke is scaling down Isaiah's prophecy to make it apply to some lesser figure: grammar shows that the pronoun 'his' refers to 'the Lord' – 'Yahweh' of the previous line; and consideration of poetic parallelism will deliver the same verdict. For Luke, then, the visitor announced by John is none other than the visitor predicted by Isaiah: it is the Lord God, Yahweh himself, coming to his people, incarnate in the person of Jesus Christ. One could scarcely overestimate the importance of John's ministry in preparing the way for the coming of such a visitor.

But Luke is not finished with Isaiah's metaphor yet. The ancient Hebrew ran: 'and the glory of the Lord shall be revealed and all flesh shall see it together' (Is. 40:5). The Septuagint Version had used an interpretative rendering: 'and the glory of the Lord shall be seen and all flesh shall see the salvation of God'; and from this Luke is content to cite the second of the two clauses. For him doubtless salvation was the form in which the glory of God was especially revealed through the coming of Jesus; and we can see the flow of his thought: 'John came preaching the baptism of repentance unto the forgiveness of sins, as it is written ... "All flesh shall see the salvation of God"' (3:3,5). It will be a marked theme of Luke's Gospel that our Lord possessed the glorious, divine prerogative of granting absolute forgiveness of sins and used it to confer salvation on people (see 5:20–24; 7:48–50). But Isaiah had said that to see the glory of the Lord, the people would have to construct a road for him to approach them; and John, and Luke his historian, lay down the same condition: if the people would see the salvation of God in the form of forgiveness of sins, they too must build God his approach-road: its name would be repentance. Seeing and enjoying God's glory, salvation and forgiveness would not follow automatically upon the physical arrival and presence of God incarnate; only those would see and enjoy these divine gifts, into whose hearts repentance had made a way of access.

Luke therefore now spends no less than eight verses (see 3:7–14) describing the difficulty and the thoroughness with which John attempted to prevail upon the people to build the road. He pointed out that the Old Testament had spoken not only of the coming Messiah, but also of the coming wrath (3:7; see e.g. Mal. 4:1). Forgiveness was an urgent necessity. But as now, so then, people would readily stop short of thorough-going repentance. They behaved, he said, like vipers in front of a bush fire: trying to escape the flames but without any intention of having their evil natures changed. They behaved as though to escape the coming wrath all they needed to do was to submit to the mere outward rite of baptism without giving any practical evidence of genuine repentance. John protested that he had not taught them any such escape-route, whoever else might have done (3:7). Or, rather than repent they would try to hide behind the fact that they were physically descended from Abraham, and John had to warn them that physical descent from Abraham was no substitute for repentance, no defence against the coming wrath (see 3:8). As a tree is not assessed by its botanical label but by whether its fruit is good or bad, so would they be one day soon. If their lives were found to have produced bad fruit, they would be cut down and consigned to the fire (see 3:9), no matter whose children they were – unless they repented, and produced practical evidence to show that their repentance was genuine.

Perturbed by this preaching various kinds of people came asking John what repentance would mean in their case (see 3:10–14). Private citizens were told that for them a work of repentance would be their willingness to share life's necessities of food and clothing with those in need; tax-collectors, that for them it would be their ceasing to demand more than the appointed amount of tax; and soldiers, that for them it would be refraining from extorting money or goods by force or by falsely accusing people; they must be content with their army wages and provisions.

So far, then, Luke has first identified the visitor for whom the road had to be made, and then shown us what making the road involved. Now in his next three verses (see 3:15–17) he reverts to the theme of the immeasurable greatness of the coming visitor. John's prophetic authority and unique ministry naturally created a tremendous sense of expectancy among the people, so much so that some began to wonder if John were himself the Christ. John denied it, of course, but took the occasion to prepare the people for the fact that when the Christ came he would be infinitely greater than John, as would be shown by his immeasurably superior ministry. He would be more powerful than John, but not simply in the sense that he would have more of the same power as John had: there would be a whole category of difference between John's power and the Christ's. John baptized in water; the Christ would baptize in the Holy Spirit and in fire (see 3:16). The Christ would thereby do two things which neither John nor any other mere man, however exalted, had either the power or the authority to do: he would impart spiritual life to those who repented and believed, and he would execute the wrath of God upon the unbelieving and unrepentant. We do not know how much John would have under-stood of what would eventually prove to be involved in the bap-tism in the Holy Spirit; but he certainly knew enough to know that the Holy Spirit is no impersonal power, but the very life of God. John could put repentant people in water; in a sense, anybody could. Only One who was God could put people in the Holy Spirit, or the Holy Spirit in people.

John could also – and he often did – rebuke unrepentant sinners and warn them of the wrath to come (see 3:7). But it was not given to John, and he knew it, to exercise the final judgment, to make the ultimate discrimination between men, to convey the wheat to the heavenly garners, and to execute the wrath of God upon the chaff (see 3:17). But an office which it would have been both lunacy and blasphemy for John to claim for himself or for any other mere man, that office he asserted the coming visitor would have.

From what Luke says, the way John's ministry ended was highly significant, perhaps symbolic. He had announced the coming visitor and called on people to prepare to receive him. Herod not only refused to repent: he decided to silence John. So he shut him up in prison. That was tantamount to closing the door on the visitor even before he arrived. One day, so Luke will eventually tell us (see 23:8–9), Herod got the chance, so he thought, to satisfy his curiosity and ask the visitor many questions. But the visitor stayed silent.

2. Christ at the Jordan and in the desert (3:21 – 4:13)

And now the visitor arrives. John had announced him as none other than Yahweh, the bestower of forgiveness, the baptizer in the Holy Spirit, the final judge of men, the executor of the coming wrath. All that was true, of course, but it was not the whole story. To complete the account of who he is we shall need to listen to movement 2. At the baptism it will tell us that he is, in a sense unique to him, the Son of God. Through the genealogy it will tell us that he is, in a sense common to all men, son of Adam, son of God. And then in the temptations it will show him demonstrating himself to be the true Son of God by his undeviating loyalty to the essential principles of sonship.

Luke spends only two verses (see 3:21–22) on the baptism: deliberately he eliminates or reduces to a minimum everything except those features on which he wishes us to concentrate. They, of course, are unspeakably sublime. The baptizer is not mentioned: Luke has chosen to follow John's public ministry right to its end, before he then reverts to Christ's baptism. He does not intend to deny or hide the fact that it was John who did the baptizing: but the person who did the baptizing and even the process of the baptism itself lie outside the centre of his interest. The circumstantial detail is brief: all the people were being baptized, Jesus had been baptized and was praying. Up to that point he could have been simply one more person among the thousands of others. And then the sublime happening took place that declared and demonstrated Jesus to be utterly unique: 'the heaven was opened, and the Holy Spirit descended in bodily form as a dove upon him, and a voice came out of heaven, "You are my beloved Son, in you I have found delight"'. Three facts are thus told us, and for a while three Persons only, in their solitary divine splendour, are allowed to fill our vision.

Two things are said to come out of the opened heaven, the Holy Spirit and the voice. Both are directed to Christ. The Holy Spirit comes down upon him in bodily form as a dove. Why a dove? Perhaps it was meant to recall Noah's dove which 'found no rest for the sole of her foot' on the flood-waters, and to emphasize by contrast that the Son of God, having come through Jordan's baptismal waters, was a fit resting-place for the Spirit of God. Perhaps there is no need to summon up echoes from the past. At the coming of the Holy Spirit at Pentecost (see Acts 2) the tongues of fire are self-evidently emblematic of the divinely empowered utterance which the Holy Spirit at that moment is said to give to the disciples. So here the descent of the Holy Spirit as a dove could conceivably be an emblematic expression of the Father's complacent and satisfied delight in the Son which the voice from heaven simultaneously announces. Whatever the truth of the matter, the main thing we must grasp is Luke's insistence that the Holy Spirit came down in bodily form, that is, visibly. We are not dealing here with some private experience within Christ's inner consciousness, invisible to others, and only known about because Christ later on told his disciples about it. The express point of Luke's narrative is that the procession of the Holy Spirit from the Father to the Son was on this occasion deliberately made visible (in Jn. 1:32–34, John the Baptist is on record as claiming to have seen it). And with the Holy Spirit's presence made visible the Father's presence is made audible as he declares 'You are my beloved Son: in you I have found delight'. The words were addressed to the Son: 'You are . . .'. According to Matthew (3:17) other people heard them and rightly interpreted the voice as giving them to understand '*This is* my beloved Son'. But for his part Luke is content to concentrate our attention solely on the three Persons so that we might see Jesus as the Son of God in his unique relation with the Father and with the Holy Spirit. Here is no doctrine of the Trinity in complicated philosophical-theological terminology, appropriate and necessary as that would later become. Here is a revelation from an open heaven and a demonstration, divine in its sublime simplicity, of the delightful relationships of the three Persons of the Trinity. It points to the unique sense in which Jesus is the Son of God.

There is, of course, another sense in which he was son of God; and Luke, careful as always to maintain the balance of truth, now inserts Christ's genealogy to show that he was '. . . son of Adam, son of God', that is, that he was son of God in the sense that Adam was son of God. Jesus was truly human.[1] God and man: not one without the other, but both. Truly man, but not merely man.

With this Luke passes to the temptation. The flow of the narrative – the son of Adam, son of God, being tempted by the devil in respect of, among other things, eating – takes us back in thought to the story of Adam's disobedient eating of the tree; and that in turn throws further light on our two basic questions: who is Jesus and what has he come to do? He is the second man come to triumph where the first man failed, destined in resurrection to be the beginning and head of a new humanity as Adam was the beginning and head of the old. Yet the first temptation shows the difference between him and the first man. 'If you are the Son of God', said the devil, 'command this stone to become bread' (4:3). Such a suggestion, needless to say, would never have been a temptation to Adam, any more than it would be to any of us. Adam did not have the power to turn stones into bread, nor has any mere man since. For Christ, by contrast, the whole force of the temptation lay in the fact that he, as Son of God, had the power to turn stones into bread if he pleased. He did not reply to the devil – let it be said reverently – 'Don't be foolish: I have not the power to turn stones into bread', but 'Man shall not live by bread alone'. The Greek word for man which Luke uses (*anthrōpos*) is the one which means man in the sense of human being. Christ's reply, therefore, indicates that while

---

[1]For the difficulties connected with the details of the genealogy see Marshall, pp.157–65. Whatever is the true solution of these difficulties, it goes without saying that in recording that Jesus was the son, as was supposed of Joseph, Luke is not forgetting or contradicting his account of the virgin conception.

he is indeed the Son of God, he is also human and proposes to live on the terms that are right and appropriate for a man, a son of Adam.

And so the first victory was won. It was not, however, a victory for mere asceticism. Human life, if it is going to be truly life, and not a form of living death, needs more than bread for its maintenance: it depends on God's Word and on fellowship with him in loving obedience to that Word. Adam in the garden, surrounded by every conceivable kind of food, was tempted to disobey God's word, disobeyed it and found that disobedience led to death. Israel in the desert was allowed to hunger (see Dt. 8:3) and then fed with manna so as to be taught that man does not live by bread alone but by every word that proceeds out of the mouth of God. Now hungry after his forty days of fasting in the desert, Christ willingly submits to the written Word – 'It stands written' – and refuses to eat independently of God's Word spoken to his heart.

The second temptation did not rely for its force on the question of who Jesus was so much as on the authority which the devil himself claimed to have: 'all this authority . . . has been given to me and I give it to whomsoever I will'. We need not try to decide to what extent the claim was true. Some of it certainly was. Compare Revelation 13:2 where Scripture says of the beast 'the dragon gave him his power and his throne and great authority'. Admittedly, the very phrase 'all this authority . . . has been given to me' shows the devil's ineradicable sense that he is a creature and derives his power ultimately from the Creator. But in this very fact lies the force of the temptation: why does God allow the devil such long-lasting and apparently successful power? If the first temptation tested faith in God as the provider of life's necessities, the second is going to test faith in God as the moral governor of the universe, and in his promises that 'the Son of Man and the saints' (see Dn. 7) should be given universal dominion.

The worship demanded by Satan did not presumably include that element of admiration and praise which worship of God normally includes. What Satan was demanding was that Christ should recognize him as an ultimate fact and authority which cannot be overcome but has to be reckoned with and compromised with. On those terms the devil was prepared to let Christ gain worldwide success. Many movements, before and since, both political and religious have bought success and power on those terms, justifying their attitude on grounds of expediency or realism or necessity. The result has been to leave mankind in spite of much apparent progress a prisoner to demonic forces of evil both in their personal lives and in their social and political institutions. Christ citing Scripture once more as the authoritative expression of God's absolute authority (see 4:8), refused to bow down to any but God. In the mystery of God's purposes and government of the universe this refusal would cost Christ the cross; but it would win for mankind that possibility of freedom of which we shall soon hear him speak when he begins his public ministry (see 4:18).

The third temptation relied for its power once more on the fact that Jesus was the Son of God, but also on his demonstrated determination to trust Holy Scripture and to obey God. The devil therefore quoted a Scripture which promised Messiah angelic protection, and challenged Christ not just to trust it, but to give evidence of his trust by acting upon it. The temptation was exceedingly subtle. We recall how John the Baptist had rightly urged it on the people that it was useless simply claiming to be children of Abraham: they must act, they must produce practical evidence of the validity of their claim. Moreover to the godly mind the challenge to trust God's word and 'step out in faith' has a powerful attraction, and refusal or even hesitancy to act can appear as lack of faith. But Christ saw through the deception: it was in fact a challenge not to trust God but to tempt him, not to prove his Sonship, but to abuse it. No word had come from God bidding Christ jump off the temple; no necessity of God's work or human need required it. The only motive for doing it would either be vainglory or the desire to test God to see whether he would keep his promise; and Scripture forbids man's testing of God in that way. God is not on probation; there is no doubt about his faithfulness that has to be cleared up by putting him through an examination. To jump off the temple would have been to take the initiative and force God into a situation where he would have no choice but to back up the action in order to avert disaster, or else to be accused of unfaithfulness if he did not. That would have been to reverse the role of man and God, and of Son and Father. Satan's demand for action as evidence of Christ's Sonship was false, and Christ refused to act. All the devil had succeeded in doing was to demonstrate that Jesus was indeed the true Son of God.

3. Christ at Nazareth (4:16–30)

It is at first sight remarkable that for his first major example of Christ's public ministry, Luke should have chosen an incident in which the people's reaction was so hostile and their verdict on his claims so decidedly negative. Admittedly, Luke carefully indicates that before Christ met with this negative response at Nazareth he had been very well received throughout the whole of Galilee (see 4:14–15); and he immediately balances the rejection at Nazareth with the good reception at Capernaum (see 4:31–43). Even so, why give such prominence to the Nazareth incident?

One reason could be that the sermon at Nazareth was programmatic. It therefore makes a fitting introduction to Christ's public ministry. To identify himself and his mission Christ cited Isaiah 61:1–2 and 58:6, and it recalls the way Luke identified John and his mission at 3:4–6 by a similar quotation from Isaiah. It is an essential part of the gospel that neither John nor Jesus came in order to start some new religion or movement never heard of before. Both claimed to be the fulfilment of Scripture's prophetic programme. Naturally, of course, no responsible person was going to accept Christ's claim without examining the evidence for it. The people of Nazareth, however, decided that the evidence was inadequate and the claim spurious. In recording their decision Luke is obviously not intending to admit that it was a fair decision; but having advertised it so boldly, Luke will presumably take great pains to show us why it was false.

Before, however, we consider why the people of Nazareth decided against the claim, we had better consider exactly what the claim was. First Christ claimed to be the anointed Servant of the Lord: 'The Spirit of the Lord is upon me because he has anointed me . . .' (4:18). Secondly he described his mission as a preaching mission: 'to preach good news to the poor'. Poor in what sense? There is no reason why the term should not mean among other things the financially poor; but it will certainly include poverty of other kinds. Before Christ's sermon is over he will have cited two people who in times past had received God's grace: one was a poor widow (see 4:26), but the other was an exceedingly rich nobleman, commander of the Syrian armies, whose poverty lay not in lack of money but in his utter resourcelessness against leprosy (see 4:27). And to go no further than the next chapter, 5:27–30, some of the first to benefit from the gospel were the financially rich tax-collectors. Their poverty was moral and spiritual. This in fact is the pattern throughout the Gospel: the term 'poor' covers poverty of every kind, but denotes above all else the spiritual poverty from which all alike suffer.

In what then did the good news for the poor consist? Presumably the next clauses and phrases of the quotation tell us. One element, 'release', receives a double emphasis: 'release to the captives . . . to send forth the crushed in freedom (literally, in release)'. The Greek word for 'release' on both occasions is *aphesis*. Its associated verb carries a wide range of meaning: 'to send away, discharge, let go, release, allow' and then the specialized sense 'to forgive', since to forgive is to release someone from his debts, guilt, obligations and deserved penalties. The noun *aphesis* can mean 'release', 'discharge', 'setting free' in a general sense or else 'forgiveness'. Its meaning in this passage will depend on the sense in which the terms 'captives' and 'crushed' are intended. Let us notice then that the word for 'captive' in Greek (*aichmalōtos*) means, at the literal level, a war-captive. It is not the word one would use for someone imprisoned for a crime or for a political offence (which in New Testament language would be *desmios*). It follows therefore that our Lord could not have been using the word in its literal sense in the synagogue at Nazareth. He claimed that the promise of Isaiah was being fulfilled that very day in the ears of the congregation: captives were having release offered to them. Obviously he was not talking of literal captives of war. In the metaphorical sense, on the other hand, there are plenty of examples in the Gospel of Christ's giving freedom to people who were captives to guilt (see 7:41–50), to the crushing and bruising power of Satan (see 8:26–39), to the love of money (*e.g.* 19:1–10) and so forth. One must conclude, therefore, that this was the sense in which he spoke of captives.

The other element in the gospel to the poor was the offer of recovery of sight to the blind. This obviously included the offer of literal sight to the physically blind, since various cases of healing of blind people are recorded in the Gospel (see 7:21, 18:35–43). But once more it is impossible to think that the offer was restricted to the blind in this literal sense. What kind of a programme would it have been that announced that it had two major concerns: freedom for literal prisoners-of-war and physical sight for the blind? Under-stood in a spiritual sense, however, the twin offer was an apt summary of the gospel, as is seen from the fact that the same two elements, expressed in other words, reappear in other summaries of the gospel by later preachers. Here for instance is Paul, as recorded by Luke, explaining his mission before Agrippa: 'to open their eyes that they may turn from darkness to light (*i.e.* the recovery of sight to the blind) and from the power of Satan unto God, that they may receive forgiveness (*aphesis*) of sins (*i.e.* the release for captives) and an inheritance among those who are sanctified . . .' (Acts 26:18). Understood in this spiritual sense, moreover, the offer was immediately relevant to the congregation in the synagogue at Nazareth – disturbingly so, as we shall see in a moment.

The final element in the programme had to do with timetable. Isaiah's prophecy had predicted that the anointed Servant of the Lord would 'proclaim the Lord's favourable year and the day of vengeance of our God' (61:2); and Luke is obviously concerned to make sure that we understand exactly how much of this programme Christ claimed was being fulfilled that day in Nazareth. He paints the scene in graphic detail. Christ stands up to read; the attendant hands him the scroll; he finds the passage in Isaiah and reads it through until he comes to this twin phrase; he reads the first part up to 'the Lord's favourable year', stops in the middle of the sentence, and with the eyes of everyone in the synagogue rivetted on him, deliberately rolls up the scroll, gives it back to the attendant, sits down, and begins to say 'Today this Scripture has been fulfilled in your hearing'.

It is almost impossible to exaggerate the importance of the point which Christ was so dramatically making: he was the Messiah, his coming had instituted the Lord's favourable year; but it had not begun the day of vengeance: he had no intention of executing the wrath of God upon evil men or evil societies and institutions at this stage in history.

For many people, particularly those who believed in him, this was a shock and a disappointment, especially when they found out what it would mean. John the Baptist, we recall, had announced that the Christ would do two things: he would not only impart God's Holy Spirit to those who believed; but he would also burn up the chaff with unquenchable fire (see 3:16–17). The expectation was true: Christ will one day execute the wrath of God (see 2 Thes. 1:7–10). John's disappointment seems to have arisen, however, from the mistaken idea that Christ would immediately proceed to put down evil and destroy unrepentant men. In the name of the coming Christ John had denounced Herod's sins, and Herod, unrepentant, had John imprisoned. John therefore apparently expected Christ to come, chastise Herod and release him; and when Christ made no attempt to do so, John was disappointed (see 7:18–23), and had to be reassured that the fulfilment of the prophetic programme had not failed, ceased or gone astray. It was not that evil was so powerfully entrenched and Christ and his followers so few and weak that it was not prudent just yet to attack Herod and try to break his power. Christ had no intention of overthrowing Herod's political power in order to open John's prison door, or of executing judgment on Herod or on any other evil men. He had come to institute the Lord's favourable year, the purpose of which was the proclamation of the gospel and the provision of a way of escape from the wrath to come. Not until that year was over – and God's merciful longsuffering would see to it that it was a very long year – would the comparatively short, sharp day of vengeance come.

That then was the claim and that was the programme. The congregation had to admit the astonishing grace of his words; but on the other hand, to them his relatives, friends and neighbours, he was after all only Joseph's son (see 4:22). And where was there any evidence enough to prove the stupendous claim that he had just made?

Christ read their thoughts. 'I am sure,' he said, 'you will quote this proverb at me, "Physician heal yourself."' It is perfectly clear what they meant by their unspoken proverb: it was their defence against the charge of unbelief. They did not believe him, that they admitted. But the fault was not theirs, but his, for not supplying adequate evidence. The cure was in his own hands. It was no good finding fault with them for not believing; they were prepared to believe if he provided them with sufficient evidence. It was up to him to provide it. They had heard that he had done many marvellous things in Capernaum. But that wasn't enough; if he wanted them to believe his claim, he would have to prove it true by doing many more works like that in his own home town.

Put like that (and notice it was Christ who put it like that, see 4:23) the people's case seemed eminently reasonable. Had not John argued in the very same way with the people that it was no use merely saying they were Abraham's true children and had repented: they must produce practical evidence that their claim was true? It would be very strange therefore if, as some commentators seem to think, Christ not only refused to give them the evidence they so reasonably asked for, but instead said many things which were not strictly relevant and served only to anger them beyond endurance. In fact, what Christ said was neither irrelevant nor rude. It was an attempt to get them to see first that the kind of evidence that they were asking for was not the kind of evidence that could ever give them proof of his claims; secondly, that the evidence which could give them perfect assurance that his claim was true was readily available to them; and thirdly, that whether they took advantage of this available evidence was not up to him, but up to them. To borrow their metaphor: as a physician he could heal them, and their resultant good health would be incontrovertible evidence that his claim was true; but whether they would admit they were sick and in need of healing, and whether they would allow him to heal them and so supply them with the desired evidence was not up to him, but up to them.

First, then, Christ reminded them of the reports of his miracles at Capernaum. They had already provided them with objective *prima-facie* evidence that his claim was not nonsense, but had genuine substance. To have gone on simply repeating that kind of objective evidence at Nazareth, however, would not have advanced the case any further.

Secondly, he pointed out that their difficulty in accepting his claim did not arise solely from the lack of objective evidence. There was another factor involved, a subjective psychological difficulty so well and universally recognized that it had been expressed in the common saying: no prophet is acceptable in his hometown (see 4:24). The difficulty was nothing to do with the adequacy of the evidence. It had nothing to do with logic. It was an irrational – or at least non-rational-instinctive, emotional bias. It would be difficult for them to overcome this emotional bias; but the difficulty was on their side not on his. They would have to recognize its existence, and overcome it, if ever they were going to be fair to the evidence. If they did not recognize it in themselves, their complaint that the evidence was inadequate could be a mere rationalization of their bias.

Thirdly, Christ cited a couple of Old Testament case histories – but at this point we must proceed very carefully, since many commentators have found it difficult to see the relevance of the two stories to the question of the congregation's demand for evidence which Christ was supposed to be discussing. Some indeed have claimed that the stories have no relevance to the preceding discussion: Luke has simply done a rather poor scissors-and-paste job with his sources and stuck a couple of stories in here which originally had nothing to do with the Nazareth incident. Others, observing that Christ emphasizes the fact that in both stories God's prophet was sent to bring blessing to Gentiles and not to Israelites, have thought that Christ was criticizing the narrow-mindedness of his Jewish congregation. This explanation is certainly better than the first, in that it suggests a reasonable flow of thought; Jesus is defending himself against the Jews' refusal to believe him by using these two Old Testament stories as a kind of a prophecy to predict that though rejected by his fellow-nationals he will one day be believed in by millions of Gentiles. But this explanation still does not get to the heart of the matter. The congregation was complaining that the evidence for his claim was inadequate. It was hardly enough to reply 'never mind; millions of Gentiles will believe it, just like Gentiles in the past have believed God's prophets when Israel did not'. The real question was on what grounds did the Gentiles in the past believe and on what grounds would the millions of Gentiles in the future believe? If the Jews of Nazareth found the evidence inadequate for their faith, how could it rightly be adequate for the Gentiles' faith? Were Gentiles simply credulous simpletons? Obviously we ought to take Christ's reference to these two Old Testament stories seriously and look at them in more detail.

When the widow of Zarephath met Elijah she had never set eyes on him before as far as we know (see 1 Ki. 17:8–16); and the demand he made on her was, in a sense, outrageous. She had only one handful of meal left, yet he insisted that she first make him a cake. He added, of course, that if she first did that and gave him the cake, then after that her supply of meal would be miraculously maintained. But she had to use up her handful of meal in making him a cake first. Why then did she trust him? He claimed to be a prophet, but what evidence could she have that his claim was true? Had she been like the people of Nazareth, she would have demanded that Elijah must first do a miracle – filling her barrel miraculously would have been an appropriate one – and then she would believe him and make him a cake. But Elijah insisted that it must be the other way round. Without any evidence except Elijah's solemn promise in God's name, she had to use her last lot of meal to make him a cake first, and then, so he said, the miracle would happen.

Fortunately she did trust him, made the cake, and the miracle happened: she and her son were supplied with food for the rest of the famine. She had proved by experience that Elijah was true. She now had incontrovertible evidence. But what made her trust him in the first place? The answer is simple: it was the realization of her extreme poverty and fatal lack of resources. If she refused to trust him, she would keep her last handful of meal for herself and her son; they would eat it, and within a few days be dead. If she gave her last handful to Elijah and he turned out to be a fraud, what would it matter? She would die a few hours sooner, that's all. If she trusted him and he turned out to be true, she and her son were saved. Actually her extreme poverty made it easy for her to see the reality of the situation. Had she still had half a barrelful when she met Elijah, she might have been tempted to refuse to risk trusting him, in the vain hope that her half barrelful might somehow see her through to the end of the famine.

The relevance of the story to the congregation at Nazareth is not difficult to see. They wanted evidence that Christ's claim was true. Christ was saying that conclusive evidence was readily and immediately available. What after all was the claim? It was that he had come, as God's anointed Servant, to give salvation, forgiveness, release from guilt and from spiritual bondage to people who were spiritually captives, poor and resourceless. If they were poor and resourceless, they had only to call on him and he would demonstrate to them in their own personal subjective experience that his claim was true. Let them apply to him. If he turned out to be a fraud, they would have lost nothing.

But there, of course, lay the trouble; they were not poor, at least, in their own estimation they were not. They were respectable, spiritually resourceful people, kind parents, loyal citizens, honest traders, regular attenders of the synagogue. His claim to be the Messiah come to put the world right was fantastic enough for a young man whom they had known from infancy; but they were prepared to consider the objective evidence of further miracles if he could repeat what he was reported to have done in Capernaum. But they were not in any urgent personal need. To suggest that there was any parallel or relevance to them in the story of this Gentile widow was an insult. Did he think that they, his aunts and uncles, sisters, brothers, cousins, friends and neighbours were going to admit to him that they were morally and spiritually poor, inadequate and resourceless, and call on him as their only hope? It was humiliating and offensive in the extreme.

But that is why the story of Naaman was so apt; for when Naaman heard what Elisha said he must do to get rid of his leprosy, he felt so humiliated that at first he went away in a rage (see 2 Ki. 5:9–14). What made him change his mind and submit? The simple but hard fact that he was a leper. His servants pointed out that if it was humiliating to be asked to do such a mean thing as to dip himself in the Jordan, it was better to do that and be cured than to let the leprosy go unchecked and eventually to suffer the humiliations which the advancing disease would inflict.

But the congregation at Nazareth had had enough. To be told that they were spiritually blind, resourceless and poverty-stricken was bad enough; now to be told that they were less wise than this Gentile leper was intolerable. They tried to destroy Christ.

Now we can see perhaps why Luke has given the Nazareth incident such prominence. It was, in the first place, an important statement of Christ's claim. But Luke was aware that it was not enough simply to make the claim: there had to be evidence to support it. Doubtless it was sad to have to report that Christ's own relatives and townspeople rejected the claim; but it was also important that he should be able to show Theophilus and us on what grounds they rejected it. It may be that the people of Nazareth would have continued to argue that it was because the evidence for the claim was inadequate; we can now see that it had little to do with inadequacy of evidence, but everything to do with their refusal to face their true spiritual condition, their refusal, in other words, to repent. They could not see that Joseph's son was the Messiah. But then Isaiah had said, and John the Baptist had repeated it, that if the people would see the glory of the Lord when he came, and the glory of his salvation, they would have to build him an approach-road.

4. Christ at Capernaum (4:31–43)

For the final movement in his 'Introduction of the Son of God'

Luke has chosen virtually the same material as Mark has put in his first chapter, 1:21–39. The fact that he shares this material with Mark does not mean, of course, that Luke is not to be credited with having intended to say everything he says in this movement to the same extent as he is in movements like movement 3 that are peculiar to him. When Luke takes over material from some source or other, by the very decision to take it over he makes it his own. If he says the same as Mark it is because he wants to say the same as Mark. When he wants to emphasize certain features in the material more than Mark, he certainly feels free to do so as we have already seen (p.70). Our task now is to see if we can, why Luke has chosen this material to complete his introductory account of who Jesus was and what he came to do.

Movement 4, then, tells us that when Christ went to Capernaum he taught in the synagogue (see 4:31) as he had done in Nazareth. But on this occasion we are not told the contents of his sermon. Instead Luke concentrates on the authority of his preaching and its effects; and of the varied effects of his ministry Luke concentrates again on one thing more than others: his power over evil spirits. In the synagogue he cast out an unclean spirit from a man, and it forms for Luke the chief topic of interest (see 4:33–36). Leaving the synagogue he went to Peter's home and there healed his mother-in-law (see 4:38–39), and later that evening he healed a large number of people of various (unspecified) illnesses (see 4:40). But with that Luke reverts once more to Christ's power over demons and spends another whole verse describing it (see 4:41). It is evident that for Luke the opposition of demons and Christ's triumph over it were not incidental to his ministry: they lay at the very heart of it. The emphasis within movement 4 is enough by itself to show it; but when we recall what we have so recently been told in movement 2 about Satan's attack on Christ in the temptations it puts the matter beyond doubt. We shall find in fact that as we consider this question of Christ's power over demons, it will bring together the major themes that have dominated this stage 2: the nature and purpose of Christ's mission, the authority of the Word, the identity of Jesus and the evidence for his claims.

First, then, the nature and purpose of his mission. At the temptation Satan's attempt to pervert the Son of God had failed; now in movement 4 we see the Son of God turning to the offensive.

Luke reports how the demon-possessed man in the synagogue at

Capernaum cried out at the top of his voice 'Ha! what do you want with us, Jesus of Nazareth? Have you come to destroy us? I know who you are, the Holy One of God' (4:34–35). It was a rhetorical question; but if we must answer it, we might well borrow the words of John: 'For this purpose was the Son of God manifested that he might destroy the works of the devil' (1 Jn. 3:8). It is at this level of spiritual warfare that the battle for man's salvation must ultimately be fought out.

It would, of course, be untrue, foolish and dangerous to suggest that every man is possessed by some demon or other. Demon-possession, according to the New Testament, is an extreme form of spiritual bondage. On the other hand the writers of the New Testament are serious in their assertion that every unregenerate man is in a very real sense under the power of Satan (see *e.g.* Acts 26:18; 2 Cor. 4:3–4; Eph. 2:2; Col. 1:13; 1 Pet. 2:9), and needs to have his eyes opened to the fact, and allow Christ to bring him out of his spiritual darkness and bondage into the freedom of God's light. And that is, of course, what Christ was talking about when at Nazareth he asserted that he had come to bring release to the captives and recovery of sight to the blind. The congregation not only could not see he was the Messiah, but actually became enraged, and in a frenzy tried to destroy him. It was all too clear evidence that they were in captivity to Satan, blind to their own condition and to where their salvation lay. If ever such people were going to be liberated, Christ would have to break the power of Satan over them.

In this great spiritual warfare two matters are of supreme importance: the authority of the Word of God, both written and proclaimed, and the identity of Jesus. The first three movements have relentlessly emphasized the authority of the Word, the necessity of obeying it, the strategic importance of proclaiming it (3:2, 3–4; 4:4, 8, 12, 15, 16–21). Now movement 4 takes up the story. It shows us Christ going forth to war against spiritual forces. How will he proceed? What weapons, what methods will he use? It was, says Luke, while 'he was teaching . . . on the Sabbath day and they were astonished at his teaching, for his word was with authority' (4:32) that the man with an evil spirit cried out in recognition of the superior power of Christ. Nor is Luke content to record the fact that Christ cast out the demon: Luke must give us the effect on the congregation: 'And amazement came on everybody and they talked together among themselves, saying, "What is this word? For with authority and power he commands the unclean spirits and they come out"' (4:36). The emphasis is inescapable. In the temptation Christ had rejected the false authority the devil had offered him and had staked everything on the authority of the written Word of God. Now triumphant he exercises the very authority of God through his own spoken word. Nor only against demons; for when Luke comes to record how Christ delivered Peter's mother-in-law from her fever, he simply repeats the phrase he uses of Christ's methods with the demons: 'he *rebuked* the fever' (4:39, and *cf.* 4:35 and 41).

The message of movement 4 is clear. We know of course that for mankind's deliverance and redemption Christ would later have to fight another battle of a different kind at Calvary. But that does nothing to diminish the importance of the point that movement 4 is making: in the fight for man's deliverance from the power of Satan, the first and foremost tactic is the proclamation of the supremely and absolutely authoritative Word of God. And it follows that to neglect the preaching of that Word, or in any way to cast doubt in people's minds as to its authority and trustworthiness is to play directly into Satan's hands and to help maintain his bondage over them. It was a sense of the supreme importance of preaching the Word to as many as possible, says Luke (see 4:42–44), that made Christ leave Capernaum, in spite of his popularity there, in order to preach elsewhere.

The second matter of supreme importance in the war against spiritual wickedness is the identity of Jesus. Twice over we are told (see 4:34 and 41) that demons as they left their victims cried out in recognition that Jesus was the Christ, the Son of God. On each occasion Christ silenced them. At first sight that is perhaps surprising. Throughout this stage the question of the necessity of evidence to prove who Jesus is has been very much to the fore. We might have expected Jesus therefore to call the attention of the people to the testimony of these defeated demonic forces. But of course he did not. In the course of the great war, Satan and his demons may for tactical reasons sometimes say what is true – in the third temptation Satan even quoted Scripture – or they may be forced against their will to say what is true: they never say it out of loyalty to the truth or with any intention of leading people to believe the truth. Truth is ultimately a Person; in the great warfare of the ages his identity is all-important. Only those are to be trusted, in the ultimate sense, who speak in loyalty to that Person. Those of course who deny that Jesus is the Christ, the Son of God, thereby declare plainly that they fight on the other side.

Christ's way with sin and sinners

Preliminary survey

The movements

1 Christ and the authorities *(5:1–26)*
2 Christ's principles of spiritual discipline *(5:27–39)*
3 Christ and the authorities *(6:1–19)*
4 Christ's principles of morality *(6:20–49)*

Stage 3

Christ's way with sin and sinners

Preliminary survey

In the chapters which now follow, one topic is prominent above all others: Christ's moral teaching. Chapter 6, for example, contains Luke's counterpart (6:20–49) to Matthew's Sermon on the Mount. We need not decide the question whether the matter which Luke records here was spoken on the same occasion as the matter which Matthew records in the Sermon, or whether Christ, like many other preachers, gave many similar, but not identical, sermons on different occasions. Nor for the moment need we stay to consider the difference in proportions: the Sermon in Matthew fills no less than three whole chapters (5–7), while Luke's counterpart occupies merely thirty verses (6:20–49). The general similarity between Luke's material here and the Sermon on the Mount is enough to alert us to the fact that a sizeable part of the next two chapters is going to be taken up with Christ's moral teaching.

Equally obvious is the repetition throughout these two chapters of the words sin, sinners and sinful. The first story in chapter 5 is peculiar to Luke, and we may presume that he chose it to stand in this prime position because he judged its message especially suitable for the beginning of this new section of his Gospel. Here is the climax of the story in Luke's own words: 'But Simon, when he saw it, fell down at Jesus's knees, saying, "Depart from me, for I am a sinful man, Lord"' (5:8).

In the third story (see 5:17–26) a man, brought to Christ to be healed of paralysis, is unexpectedly given something else first: 'Man, your sins are forgiven you' (5:20). And when the scribes object: 'Who can forgive sins but God alone?' (5:21), Christ replies: 'Which is easier, to say, "Your sins are forgiven you," or to say, "Arise and walk"? But that you may know that the Son of Man has authority on earth to forgive sins . . .' (5:22–24).

Again, in 5:30–32 we find the following sequence: 'And the Pharisees . . . complained . . . saying, "Why do you eat and drink with the tax-gatherers and sinners?" And Jesus . . . said . . . "I have not come to call the righteous but sinners to repentance."'

Again in 6:32–34 we find Christ reminding his disciples that 'If you love those who love you, what credit is that to you? Even sinners do the same. And if you lend to those from whom you expect repayment, what credit is that to you? Even sinners lend to sinners . . .'

But if the words 'sin' and 'sinners' are prominent in these chapters, so are other words of similar meaning. In 6:2 the Pharisees accuse Christ's disciples of doing 'what it is not lawful to do on the sabbath'. Christ counters their accusation by pointing out that David and his men on one occasion ate 'what it is not lawful for anyone to eat except the priests' (6:4).

Similarly the whole crux of the story of the man with the withered hand (6:6–11) is 'Is it lawful on the sabbath to do good or to do evil?' (6:9).

In addition there are other places in these chapters where without actually using the words wrong, or unlawful, or sinful, the Pharisees by their questioning imply that Christ is doing wrong. In 5:30 their question 'Why do you eat and drink with tax-gatherers?' implies that it is wrong to eat with them. In 5:33 their statement, 'The disciples of John fast often . . . but yours eat and drink', implies that Christ is wrong in not making his disciples fast.

Clearly, then, these chapters are going to be concerned with Christ's teaching on right and wrong, on what is lawful and unlawful, on doing good and doing evil, on sin and sinners and on how to treat them, on justice and forgiveness, uncleanness and cleansing, in other words, on morality.

Our first task is to discover, if we can, how far through the coming chapters this topic is meant to extend before Luke allows another topic to dominate his narrative. Our task is easy: at the end of the long sermon on morality Luke, in his typical way, has placed a concluding remark which formally brings stage 3 to its end and separates it from stage 4: 'When he had completed all his words in the hearing of the people, he entered Capernaum' (7:1).

Next we ought to look at the selection and ordering of his material. Much of the material which Luke has put into this stage is common to him and Matthew and/or Mark; but certain notable features are peculiar to Luke. As we have already noticed, the very first story in this stage is altogether peculiar to Luke (see 5:1–11). Again, Mark has no equivalent of Matthew's Sermon on the Mount; Luke has, but he puts it in a very different position from Matthew: Matthew puts the Sermon *before* the cleansing of the leper (8:1–4), the healing of the paralytic (9:2–8), the call of Levi and the criticisms made by the disciples of John (9:14–17), the choosing of the apostles (10:1–4), the incident in the cornfield (12:1–8) and the man with a withered hand (12:9–14); Luke puts his equivalent *after* all these things, and some even of these things he puts in a different order from Matthew. Luke's basic selection and order are nearer to Mark's; but his inclusion of the miraculous catch of fish (5:1–11) and an equivalent of the Sermon on the Mount, inevitably means that his flow of thought is different from Mark's. We must look, therefore, to see whether Luke's arrangement of his material will give us any help in perceiving the particular way he is looking at things.

He starts off in chapter 5 with three stories each introduced by a formal 'And it came to pass',[1] and each recording a miracle. In the first (see 5:1–11) Peter is brought to realize and confess his sin, and is made 'a fisher of men'. In the second (see 5:12–16) a man is cleansed of leprosy and sent as a testimony to the priests. In the third (see 5:17–26) a man is forgiven his sin, cured of paralysis and made an object-lesson to the teachers of the law. Since, even superficially read, they seem to have certain features in common, let us label these three incidents movement 1.

'After these things he went out', says Luke (5:27), and there follows a discussion, provoked by the conversion of Levi, on the spiritual discipline which Christ imposed on his 'converted sinners' and on himself in his contacts with them (see 5:27–35). Christ concludes the discussion with a parable which turns out to be threefold: old and new garments, old and new wineskins, old and new wine (see 5:36–39). Let us call this discussion, movement 2.

---

[1]This phrase is omitted for the sake of idiomatic English in many modern versions. It is common enough in Luke's Gospel, but it is not invariably used to introduce every incident.

Chapter 6 starts off with three stories, each introduced by a formal 'And it came to pass'. In the first (see 6:1–5) the Pharisees criticize him and his disciples for plucking and rubbing ears of corn and eating them on the sabbath. Christ refutes the criticism. In the second (see 6:6–11) Christ defies the scribes and Pharisees and heals a man with a withered hand in the synagogue on the sabbath. The Pharisees are furious and begin to plot revenge. In the third (see 6:12–19) Christ carefully chooses twelve special disciples, calls them apostles, publicly associates them with himself as he continues his work of healing before vast multitudes from all over the country. A discernible current of thought runs through all three stories. Let us call them movement 3.

'And he lifted up his eyes on his disciples' says Luke (6:20), and there follows a long statement of Christ's moral teaching (see 6:20–38). Christ concludes the statement with a parable which turns out to be three-fold: it is based on eyesight (see 6:39–42), fruit-trees and fruit (see 6:43–45),[1] and building (see 6:46–49). Let us call this statement of Christ's moral teaching, movement 4.

Judged merely from the point of view of its superficial, formal arrangement, the material in this stage has certainly been organized in a very neat and orderly fashion. Our exposition will have to keep an eye on this arrangement, just in case Luke is using it to help us to see the significance of the facts he records. There follows a map to enable us to see the contents of this stage at a glance (see over).

The movements

The central feature of Christ's moral teaching, when we first become aware of it, is undeniably astonishing: according to Christ, he himself is the criterion and touchstone of what is right and wrong.

At the beginning of the stage (see 5:5), it is Christ's word, and no other consideration, which Peter at his daily work of fishing must obey in order to achieve success. At the end of the stage (see 6:46–49) it is the hypocrisy of calling Jesus Lord and then failing to do the things which *he* says, that leads to ultimate disaster. In

---

[1]The mention of treasure in 6:45 does not introduce another parable based on treasure-hoarding; it is simply a metaphorical phrase used *en passant* to help the application of the fruit-tree parable: a good tree brings forth good fruit: a good man out of the good treasure of his heart brings forth good fruit.

The new way 5:1-39

1 Christ and the authorities 5:1-26

1 In the fishing-boat 5:1-11: Christ the Lord of daily work. Peter, the expert fisherman, is convicted of sin, but is made into a fisher of men.

2 The untouchable leper 5:12-16: Christ 'stretched out his hand and touched him'. The cleansed leper is sent as a testimony to the priests.

3 The healing of the paralytic 5:17-26: Present were Christ and Pharisees and teachers of the law from all over Galilee, Judaea and Jerusalem. 'And the power of the Lord was there for him to heal' (5:17). The paralytic is made a testimony to the theologians.

2 Christ's principles of spiritual discipline 5:27-39

1 Attitude to the sinfully rich and socially ostracised tax-collectors 5:27-28: Christ converts the tax-collector, Levi, who abandons his unacceptable way of making money and follows Christ.

2 Attitude to mixing socially with sinners 5:29-32: Pharisees criticize Christ for attending a dinner-party with rich tax-collectors and sinners. Christ gives his reasons: the sick need a doctor.

3 Attitude to fasting and spiritual exercises 5:33-35: Behaviour of the 'sons of the bride-chamber' is regulated according to the presence or absence of the bridegroom.

4 A threefold parable 5:36-39: (*a*) old and new garments, (*b*) old and new wineskins, (*c*) old and new wine.

The only way 6:1–49

3 Christ and the authorities 6:1–19

1 **In the cornfield** 6:1–5: Christ the Lord of the sabbath. The disciples are accused of sin, but Christ defends and justifies them.

2 **The man with a withered hand** 6:6–11: Christ says 'Stretch out your hand'. The man's healing is made a lesson to the scribes and Pharisees.

3 **The healing of the multitudes** 6:12–19: Present were Christ and his newly appointed apostles. A great crowd assembles from Judaea, Jerusalem, Tyre and Sidon. 'Power came out from him and healed them all' (6:19).

4 Christ's principles of morality 6:20–49

1 **Attitude to poverty, hunger, sorrow and social ostracism** 6:20–23: 'Blessed are you poor . . . blessed are you when men shall . . . ostracise you . . . for the Son of Man's sake'.

2 **Attitude to riches, society, laughter and social acceptance** 6:24–26: 'Woe to you who are rich now . . . who are full . . . when all men speak well of you . . .' for 'you have received all the comfort you are going to get'.

3 **Attitude to enemies and would-be borrowers** 6:27–38: Behaviour of 'sons of the Most High' should conform to that of their Father.

4 **A threefold parable** 6:39–49: (a) good and bad eyesight, (b) good and bad fruit-trees, (c) good and bad building.

5:21–25 it is because Jesus is the Son of man that he has the authority, which God alone has (see 5:21), to forgive sins in the ultimate sense. In 6:5 it is because he is the Son of man that makes it lawful for his disciples to work for him on the sabbath. And in 6:22 it is because he is the Son of man that persecution for his sake is a supreme blessing.

This central feature of his moral teaching is all the more astonishing when we remember that he was not addressing himself to a morally and religiously backward people: he was living and teaching in a nation whose moral and religious sense was developed beyond that of any other nation in the world. Its Old Testament was unmatched in the ancient world not only for its lofty monotheism and morality, but also for its insistence that religion and morality were, and must be, the two inseparable sides of one and the same coin. By the time our Lord came Judaism's meticulous priests, careful exegetes and sophisticated theologians had given, and were still giving, endless thought to the question of deducing from the Old Testament what was right and what was wrong in any given situation. Judaism had no lack of experts. Most of them accepted the Old Testament as the Word of God and therefore as the basic authority on all moral and religious matters. Many of them held that the traditions of the elders were equally binding on the people as God's Word. Others disagreed and this naturally led to much disputing among the different schools of thought. But as they watched Christ act and heard him teach, most experts were agreed that he was blasphemous (see 5:21), lax and careless (see 5:30, 33), and positively lawless (see 6:2); and they sought grounds for accusing him (see 6:7), deliberated how to stop him (see 6:11) and ostracized his disciples as evil men (see 6:22). Christ, of course, defended himself and his disciples and on occasions went over to the attack and criticized the experts for what he maintained were perverse distortions both of religion and morality. Not surprisingly this stage is full of disputing (see 5:21–24, 30–32, 33–35; 6:2–5, 7–11, 22–23); and Luke is not afraid to tell us about it. Better a vigorous moral awareness, even if it leads to much controversy, than peace that arises out of moral indifference.

Luke, then, will show us Christ in contrast with Judaism and its experts at two different levels. In chapter 5, speaking generally, Luke shows us Judaism as a system which in its day was good, indeed God-given; no criticism is levelled against it except that it is now old and beginning to be obsolete. Against this background Luke represents Christ as bringing something that was completely new, higher and better. In chapter 6, on the other hand, again speaking generally, Luke presents Judaism as a system which has been distorted by the perverse interpretations of the religious and theological authorities. These perversions Christ exposes for what they are, and in their place he presents himself, his example and his Word as the only true and final authority.

But it is time we began to look at the detail of Luke's narrative.

1. Christ and the authorities (5:1–26)

From many points of view the first three stories of stage 3 hang together as a group. In each we find Christ in relation to an expert authority in some field or other. In story 1 (see 5:1–11), the field is that of fishing, and the expert authority is Peter, a master fisherman. In story 2 (see 5:12–16) the field is that of ceremonial cleanness and uncleanness, and the expert authorities are the priests. And in story 3 (see 5:17–26) the field is that of biblical interpretation and the expert authorities are the doctors of the law (see 5:17).

In each field Christ, to everyone's amazement (see 5:9–10, 15, 26), does better than the experts can do, indeed better than they can imagine is possible. When, having protested that there are no fish about (see 5:5), the master fisherman lets down his nets at Christ's word, he takes an enormous catch (see 5:6). The priest was expert at diagnosing leprosy (see Lv. chs. 13 & 14) and had the authority to pronounce a leper clean, if he ever recovered; but the priest could not cure a leper. Christ could and did. The doctors of the law were expert theologians. They could have discoursed at length and with great profit on the Old Testament doctrine of divine forgiveness. But they could not, of course, exercise that divine forgiveness and release a sinner from the guilt of his sins. Nothing less than that was what Christ claimed to have the authority to do; and he backed up his claim by the performance of a miracle (see 5:20–26).

Each of these stories in fact relates a miracle, and, as we have already observed, the people whom Christ thus miraculously treats are made a testimony to others. Peter is given a ministry to all men in general: 'from henceforth you will catch men' (5:10). The leper is deliberately sent to the priest 'for a testimony to them' (5:14). The paralytic and his forgiveness and healing are made a testimony both to the theologians (see 5:17) and to the lay-public (see 5:26). But the miracles carry no implied criticism of Judaism's experts, and it is important to notice it here, because in chapter 6 Christ will criticize some of those experts very severely. The miraculous catch of fish is not meant to imply that if Jewish fishermen were only more efficient they too would always secure bumper catches; the miraculous cleansing of the leper is not meant to suggest that if Judaism's priests were only more holy they too would be able to heal lepers; and the miraculous healing of the paralytic is not meant to demonstrate that if Judaism's teachers of the law were only more knowledgeable or more exact in their exegesis, they too would be able to exercise the divine prerogative of forgiving people's sins. Of course not. The miracles are frankly miracles. They reveal the uniqueness of Jesus: he is the Son of man; and they demonstrate that with the arrival of the Son of man a new age has dawned and a new way of dealing with the age-old problem of sin and sinners. The demonstration will cover three fields: daily work and its motivation; religious discipline and its relation to personal purity; biblical interpretation and its relation to practical living.

Let us look at the stories individually.

i. In the fishing-boat (5:1–11). It makes excellent sense in a series of stories and sermons dealing with the topic of sin that the first story should deal with Christ's ability to awaken a man to his sinfulness. How will a man correct sinful attitudes if he is not aware of them? It also makes sense that the first story should deal with sinfulness in the widest possible area, daily work.

One day, so we are told (see 5:3), Christ used Peter's boat as a pulpit from which to preach a sermon. Peter sat by Christ's side right through the sermon, but as far as we are told, the sermon did not convict him of sin. After the sermon was over, Christ told Peter to put out into deep water and let down the nets for a catch. Now sermons may not have been much in Peter's line, but fishing certainly was. On that he was an authority, and from his expert knowledge and recent experience, he knew it was no good letting down the nets for a catch: there were no fish about. A long night's fruitless fishing had shown that, and he told Christ so (see 5:4–5). But then he made a decision which was to revolutionize his whole attitude to daily work: 'Nevertheless', he said, 'if you say so, I will' (5:5). Before this Peter's motive for letting down his nets had always been the obvious and natural one, the hope of catching fish and making a profit. Why not? But this day, with no hope of fish or profit, he let down his nets for another reason and motive entirely: simply because Christ told him to, in obedience to Christ, in order to please Christ. The result was an enormous catch of fish, bigger than his tackle could cope with.

The effect upon Peter was understandable. The miracle was not teaching better techniques which, if followed, would improve Peter's profits: it was calling his attention to the Person of Jesus. However dimly Peter perceived who Jesus was at this stage, he had in fact discovered the Holy One of God. Here was the Lord of fish and fishermen, the Lord of nature, the Lord of men and of their daily work. And here was that Lord not simply in a pulpit preaching sermons, but beside Peter in his boat at his daily job, seeking to be not only the director of his work but the one whose pleasure Peter is to seek in doing that work. And to think that a few minutes ago Peter, relying on his expert knowledge, had presumed to tell him that his command to let down the nets was misguided. It made Peter so aware of his sinfulness that he felt unfit to be in the same boat and engaged on the same work as Christ. 'Depart from me', he said, 'for I am a sinful man, Lord' (5:8).

Christ did not depart, of course, nor even criticize Peter. It was not Peter's fault that up till this point he had gone to work simply to make a living and for what enjoyment there was to be had in the process. He had not realized before who Jesus was, and Jesus had never before indicated that he wanted to be the director of Peter's work. When he had been asked, Peter had readily agreed to loan his business plant for the good of Christ's religious cause; but even so he had not realized that it was open to him to work for Christ in everything that he did. As soon as he realized it, he at least showed himself ready to respond to the challenge.

We who have long known who Jesus is, however, and what he requires of us in the sphere of our daily work, might well have cause to feel more sinful than Peter. Our sinfulness as Christians is perhaps seen most not in the occasional, glaring misdemeanour of which we may be guilty, but in the chronic sub-standard quality of the motivation of our daily work. How long is it since we went about a day's work, not primarily for its necessary material profit, or for the enjoyment to be got out of doing it, but primarily in order to please the Lord and obey him? And if it is a sin for the Christian to have any prime motive for doing his daily work other than to please the Lord (see Mt. 6:31–32; Col. 3:23), how many days have we spent totally in sin!

Peter's confession of sinfulness, however, was not answered by some such word as 'Do not be afraid, your many sins have all been forgiven'. Peter was not thinking of specific and particular sins which he had committed, but of his general sinfulness and unworthiness as a person: 'I am a sinful man'. Christ's reply was, in effect, 'Don't worry; in spite of that I can make something of you and use you: from now on you will catch men.' The phrase 'catch men' is instructive. At his daily work he caught fish and a skilful job it was. Now those skills were not to be abandoned, but applied at a higher level. Peter's daily work was to be elevated to the higher spiritual level for which the lower material level is but the necessary, practical foundation. To live we must eat, and fish will do for that as well as anything. But there is more to life than eating: and therefore even catching fish, done for the right motives, has ultimate purposes far beyond merely keeping people alive. Therefore the Lord of daily work having taught Peter to go about that work with the right motive ('Nevertheless at your word I will'), now calls Peter to serve at the level of the ultimate purpose of life's work. 'From now on', he says, 'you will catch men', catch them, of course, for God and for his kingdom. With that Peter left his secular employment to devote himself to spiritual work (see 5:11). But it is to be remembered that the experience which launched him on his great spiritual labours was an experience which he had of Christ in his secular work. For the believer secular and spiritual work are simply different ends of an undivided spectrum, and the secular work can and must have the same ultimate objectives in view as the spiritual. Since Messiah has come, we, in our daily work may no longer be content to aim at less than serving him and his cause.

ii. *The untouchable leper (5:12–16).* After Peter's sinfulness had been exposed there came to Christ a man 'full of leprosy' (5:12). His uncleanness needed no exposure: he had long since been diagnosed by a priest and was obliged to cry, 'Unclean! Unclean!' (Lv. 13:45–46). His leprosy was obvious to everybody anyway: he was full of it.

We do not know exactly what disease, or cluster of diseases, was referred to in biblical times by the term 'leprosy'. Whatever it was, the disease, like any other disease, was sometimes regarded as having been imposed on some people as a divine chastisement for their sins (*cf.* the case of King Uzziah, 2 Ch. 26:16–21); but it was not always thought to be so.[1] Nonetheless in Old Testament days leprosy, in common with many other physical functions and mal-functions (see Lv. 15), was thought of as rendering a person not only physically unclean, but ceremonially unclean as well; and the ceremonial as well as the physical uncleanness was regarded as contagious. The disease, therefore, had to be diagnosed by a priest, and upon such diagnosis the sufferer had to be officially pro-nounced unclean, and segregated from the presence of God in the temple and from social contact. When, if ever, the leper was cleansed in the sense of being physically healed, he then had to visit the priest again to have his physical healing certified, and in addi-tion he had to offer certain sacrifices and perform certain ablutions before he could be finally and officially pronounced ceremonially clean (see Lv. 14). The regulations were severe on the sufferer: they were necessary for the protection and health of the nation.

This elaborate ceremonial treatment of leprosy and its cleansing have naturally led Christians all down the centuries to regard leprosy as a kind of picture of the uncleanness of sin, and Christ's cleansing of the leper as a parable of his ability to purify a man's life. It is true that in more recent times some sensitive people have objected to this idea on the grounds that it casts a terrible stigma on people suffering from physical leprosy. The objection is under-standable, but, if one may say so respectfully, illogical. Paralysis (see Heb. 12:12), blindness (see Jn. 9:1–3, 40–41) and gangrene (see 2 Tim. 2:17) are all used in the New Testament as metaphors of spiritual malaise. Leprosy is but one among many physical illnesses that can helpfully be used as a metaphor or parable of moral and spiritual disease; and we are all morally and spiritually unclean in God's sight. The greater saint a man is, the more readily he will acknowledge it (see Is. 6:5). But sheer common experience will tell us that moral and spiritual uncleanness is not imaginary, nor is the danger of contagion. These things trouble our modern world still, and we therefore look with interest to see what Christ's attitude was both to the unclean man and to Judaism's laws on uncleanness.

---

[1]The New Testament also teaches that while sickness can be a divine discipline upon a believer for his sin (1 Cor. 11:29–32), sickness is not by any means always the result of personal sin (Jn. 9:1–3).

Christ's cleansing of the leper demonstrated two things simultaneously: his divine compassion and his miraculous power. He might have cured the man simply by speaking the command, 'Be clean'; but in his compassion he stretched out his hand and touched him (see 5:13). It requires little effort to imagine what the touch of that hand meant to a man who had been segregated from society as an untouchable. But we must not misinterpret Christ's compassion: it carried no criticism of the Jewish priests. He was not suggesting that if they had only been more compassionate they would not have segregated the man. Christ's touch had the miraculous ability to banish leprosy. The priests had no such power. For them to have touched the leper would have been to spread the uncleanness by contagion; and that would have been pseudo-compassion. Their God-given duty was to maintain standards of cleanliness, to diagnose leprosy, pronounce lepers unclean, and, painful and drastic though it was, to segregate them. In touching the leper Christ was doing nothing to undermine the priests' stand against uncleanness; on the contrary, he upheld their authority: for when he had cleansed the man he sent him to the priests for their inspection, and told him to offer the sacrifices required by the law of Moses (see 5:14).

The analogy will hold for moral and spiritual uncleanness too. Many people nowadays seem to imagine that Christ's compassion for unclean people justifies permissiveness. But that is mistaken and dangerous. The law of God condemns uncleanness, and warns that if persisted in it will lead to eternal segregation (see Rev. 21:27). Christ certainly can do what the law cannot do: he can cleanse a man (see Jn. 13:10; Eph. 5:26). But that does not mean that he disagrees with the law. Cleansing a man is not the same thing as saying that on grounds of compassion dirt should no longer be so strictly regarded as dirty. Cleansing presumes that dirt is dirty, ugly, dangerous and unacceptable. Indeed Christ is on record (see 16:14–18) as having explicitly denied that he had come to encourage a more permissive attitude towards the law's moral demands; and his apostles later on solemnly warn us that various forms of moral uncleanness are contagious (see 1 Cor. 5:6; Heb. 12:14–15).

On the other hand, in carefully sending the cleansed leper to the priests 'for a testimony to them', Christ was making a second, supremely important point. He was inviting them to observe that someone had arrived with a power infinitely greater than they or their rituals possessed. They could not heal a leper: he could.

Once again the analogy holds at the moral and spiritual level, and here is the glory of Christ's power. It is not simply that Judaism's concepts of ceremonial defilement and its rituals, sacrifices and ablutions were eventually to pass away as being elementary, external symbols inappropriate in a world come of age. It is that the law entrusted to Israel, divine in its origin though it was, could not, even at its deepest and most spiritual level, produce in a man's heart and life the cleanness that it rightly demanded. But what the law could not, and cannot, do that Christ can. This is the constantly repeated theme of the New Testament (see *e.g.* Acts 15:8–9; Rom. 7:7 – 8:11; Tit. 3:3–7; Heb. 9:9–14).

iii. The healing of the paralytic (5:17–26). Both Matthew (see 9:1–8) and Mark (see 2:1–12) record the healing of the paralytic which Luke now presents (see 5:17–26); but only Luke tells us in the opening verses that there were . . . 'doctors of the law sitting by, who had come out of every village of Galilee and Judaea and Jerusalem' (5:17). Indeed, the term 'doctor of the law' (*nomodidaskalos*) occurs only twice elsewhere in the New Testament; which seems to show that Luke is wishing to emphasize here that on this occasion a number of Judaism's official teachers of the Old Testament were present. These men were different from the priests of whom we have just been thinking: the priests were experts in the practice of Judaism's rituals, the doctors of the law in Judaism's theology.

Now the lesson which Christ taught them was not that God being a forgiving God delights to forgive the repentant sinner. That the Jewish theologians (one suspects, even the Jewish schoolchildren) knew already from the Old Testament. What Christ taught them was something startlingly new: he personally released a man from the guilt of his sins (see 5:20). The theologians immediately picked up the implications of this claim. The Old Testament gave no one, not priest, nor prophet, nor theologian any such authority. They could pronounce in God's name that God had forgiven, or would forgive, such and such a sin; but none had authority to pronounce forgiveness in his own name, as Christ had just done. They accused him of blasphemously arrogating to himself a divine prerogative (see 5:21). And Christ's reply was not to explain that they had misunderstood him. Far from it. He proceeded to demonstrate by a miracle that he personally as Son of man had authority here on earth, without waiting for some final judgment, to pronounce absolute and final forgiveness in his own name (see 5:22–25).

Astonishing as this was to the theologians, an even fuller statement of the wonderfully new element which Christ has introduced into the concept and enjoyment of forgiveness, came with Christ's death, resurrection and ascension. Judaism, it goes without saying, had all the way along, known and enjoyed divine forgiveness. But it was forgiveness of a kind that left even the saintliest of them with a conscience 'not yet made perfect' (Heb. 10:1–23), with no sense at all that sin had been finally and fully put away, and therefore with the need constantly to bring further sacrifices to put away further sin. With them, therefore, the question of forgiveness was always at any given time incomplete. They had no freedom to enter the most holy place of God's presence, and the question of ultimate acceptance with God was left uncertain. By contrast the forgiveness which Christ gives makes the conscience 'perfect', in the sense that the one forgiven is assured that God will never again 'remember his sins against him', will never raise again in the court of divine judgment the question of his guilt and its legal penalty. It therefore frees the one forgiven from the need to offer any more sacrifices for his sins and gives him complete freedom of access into, and welcome in, the presence of God both here and now, and in the hereafter.

We should notice at once, however, that when the theologians objected that Jesus' claim was blasphemous they were not (at this stage, at least) being perverse. If he had not been the divine Son of man, his claim would have been blasphemous; and as yet they had little evidence (many of them had come up from the south, see 5:17) to prove that this particular claim was true. To set their minds at rest, therefore, Christ proceeded to do a miracle. Not just any miracle, of course, but a miracle designed to show that the forgiveness he had just pronounced was not bogus, or rank antinomianism, but real and genuinely divine. Having forgiven the paralytic he proceeded to release him from his paralysis and to give him the strength to walk to the glory of God. The man himself, says Luke, went off to his home glorifying God; and everybody who saw it was amazed, and they too glorified God at the sight of the one-time paralytic walking (see 5:25–26).

Now it so happens that in Hebrew 'walking' is a standard meta-phor for a man's way of life and behaviour (*e.g.* Eph. 4:17). Christ's demonstration, therefore, easily becomes for us a parable of what his apostles mean when they talk of the provision Christ makes for those whom he forgives to enable them 'to walk in newness of life' (Rom. 6:4).

2. Christ's principles of spiritual discipline (5:27–39)

Having recorded three examples, drawn from different but repre-sentative areas, of Christ's new and better way with sin and sinners, Luke now turns to deal with the spiritual discipline which Christ expected from his converts and which he imposed on himself and his disciples in his dealings with them. To illustrate the question clearly Luke cites some extreme cases.

i. Christ's attitude to the sinfully rich and socially ostracized tax-collectors (5:27–28). All men are sinners, but in the estimate of Jews tax-collectors were triply bad. Firstly, they worked for the hated imperialists, and that in the eyes of many made them traitors. Secondly, as a class they were extortionate and fraudulent: the rabbis classed them as robbers. Thirdly, since their occupation necessarily involved them in constant contact with Gentiles, they were regarded by Jews of the stricter kind as permanently ritually unclean. Added together this meant that tax-collectors were regarded as the lowest of the depraved to be classed along with 'sinners', that is, prostitutes, and socially ostracized.

Levi was a tax-collector: what would Christ require conversion to involve for him?

We may recall that John the Baptist had taught that there was nothing morally wrong in tax-collecting for the imperial power; the wrong was in the fraud and extortion that tax-collectors generally practised. True repentance, therefore, according to John did not necessarily mean giving up tax-collecting, but it did mean giving up all fraud and extortion (see 3:12–13). Christ seems to have taken the same basic view. His convert Zacchaeus, for instance, renounced fraud and extortion, promised reparations, but did not promise to give up his tax-collecting; nor apparently did Christ require him to (see 19:1–10).

But with Levi there was no question of simply satisfying the minimum necessary requirements of morality. Christ called him to follow 'and he left everything and rose up and followed him'. Christ did nothing less than break his love of money and turn him into an altruistic follower of Christ. It was something that years of the synagogue's discipline and of social ostracism had been unable to achieve.

ii. *Christ's attitude to mixing with sinners (5:29–32)*. Conversion to Christ immediately gave Levi a love and concern for his former fellow sinners such as he had never had before for them or for anybody else: it was, of course, a desire to see them also converted. Has a man been genuinely converted by the grace of Christ, if he does not in consequence have a desire that others be converted too? Levi's desire led to action: he threw a large dinner-party at which his former colleagues could meet Christ and hear him preach.

The Pharisees and their biblical experts, however, criticized Christ and his disciples for attending the dinner. To their way of thinking mixing socially with such grievously antisocial sinners merely condoned their sin, and that in turn discredited Christ's evangelism. Perhaps those Pharisees' attendance at such dinner parties might have condoned sin. They had no gospel, they had not Christ's power to convert sinners, they were not as he was the Great Physician. They might even have been in danger of succumbing to moral contagion themselves. Christ did not tell them they ought to attend such parties. After all, one does not send just anybody to attend to a patient suffering from smallpox. On the other hand, if no doctor or nurse visits and tends such a patient, the patient will die without any chance of recovery. Someone, therefore, must go where the sick patient is. 'The healthy do not need a doctor,' said Christ, 'but the sick do. I have not come to call the righteous but sinners to repentance' (5:31–32).

It would certainly be a strange doctor who considered that he was doing all he could and should against disease by lecturing the healthy on the dangers of disease, and never going anywhere near the sick. And then, again, 'righteous' and 'sinners' – were they not in this context relative terms? Were the Pharisees altogether so righteous that they did not need the Doctor at all?

iii. *Christ's attitude to fasting and spiritual exercises (5:33–35)*. But Christ's critics had another criticism, and this time it concerned not what he was prepared to do in order to make converts, but what he did with them when he had made them. Said his critics: 'John's disciples frequently fast and engage in solemn prayers, and so do the Pharisees' disciples; but yours eat and drink' (5:33). They found such laxity disturbing: it seemed to take the seriousness out of true religion.

Christ replied with an analogy: 'Can you make the sons of the bridechamber, that is, a bridegroom's guests, fast while the bridegroom is with them?' (5:34). No, of course not. To try to enforce fasting on such an occasion would be absurdly inappropriate.

'On the other hand', said Christ, 'the days will come when the bridegroom shall be taken away from them, and they will fast then' (5:35). But by now the analogy had begun to merge into a metaphor. Christ was the Bridegroom. For his disciples his presence, his forgiveness, their release from spiritual bondage, and the new vistas he opened up before them, made their joy like that of a wedding banquet. To have imposed fasting on them at that stage in their spiritual experience would have been highly incongruous and artificial. There is no point in fasting just for the sake of fasting. To be of any use it must be related to the spiritual realities of any given situation.

That did not mean that they would never fast. They would when the Bridegroom was taken away. Historically that happened at the crucifixion, though their sorrow was soon overtaken by the joy of the resurrection, the ascension, and the coming of the Holy Spirit (see Jn. 16:19–22). Spiritually, it can happen that a believer may lose, not the Lord's presence with him, but a sense of the unclouded joy of that presence. Or he may find himself in the thick of some spiritual battle. Fasting may well be appropriate then.

Two things must strike us about Christ's answer to this criticism. The first is its plain common sense: there was obviously no trace of religiosity about him. The second is a matter of much greater importance. Once again, as so often in this stage, Christ puts himself forward as the key, the controlling factor, the regulator of true spirituality. His disciples' lives are ordered not so much by rule and regulation as by the practical realities of a living relationship with a living Lord. For them forgiveness, salvation, morality, ethics, religious discipline, all hinge upon a personal relationship with Christ.

This was a new thing in Judaism. And Christ will now tell us about the relation of the new to the old.

iv. A threefold parable (5:36–39). It has become more and more evident as we have progressed through this first part of stage 3, that in his way with sin and sinners Christ has not been calling the people back to a more rigorous and devoted obedience to the Judaism they already knew. Rather his coming has introduced something altogether new and better. In him, as another was yet to put it, (Heb. 11:40) 'God has provided some better thing'.

To explain the relationship between this new thing and the old Christ now tells a parable (see 5:36–39). It is one single parable, but it has three parts; and all three parts have in common that the 'old thing' represents Judaism and the 'new thing' Christ and Christianity.

The old and new garments. Judaism's rituals and disciplines, the 'righteousness which is of the law' (Rom. 10:5), however good originally, are now a worn out garment. It is impossible to maintain their usefulness by attempting to patch them up with a few new elements taken from the gospel of Christ. The old garment must be discarded and the new assumed in its place.

This proved a difficult lesson for some Jewish Christians to learn. People like Paul and Barnabas accepted it at once (see Acts 15; Gal. 5:3–4; Phil. 3:2–14). Others like Peter accepted it (see Acts 15:7–11), but sometimes were tempted to compromise (see Gal. 2:11–21). Christendom has not always resisted the temptation of imagining that the Christian gospel can be expressed in rituals, ceremonies, sacrifices and priestly orders taken over from Judaism. But Christ's warning stands: try to patch an old garment with a piece of cloth taken from a new, and both garments will be spoiled and the attempted repair will not work.

The old and new wineskins. Christ produces a new ferment of joy in the hearts of his disciples. The old traditional Jewish forms for the expression of religious life have now grown hard and unpliable. The new wine of new life in Christ could not possibly submit to their unyielding restrictions. Not that Christian joy and fervour intend to dispense with discipline and restraint altogether; but new forms will have to be devised, more pliant and yet, in consequence, stronger.

The old and new wine. The wine of Judaism has become mellow and settled by centuries of experience and increasing tradition. The gospel of Christ and the salvation it provides are new wine. A man who has cultivated a taste for the traditional, settled dignity of

Judaism, will not at once relish Christianity; he might even resent its novelty. Many did. Some still do.

It will be noticed, however, that while comparison is made throughout between Judaism and the gospel of Christ altogether to the advantage of the gospel, nothing disrespectful is said of Judaism. The garment of Judaism is now old; but there is no denying that it was a good, God-given garment in its day. The wineskins of Judaism have grown old and too tight for the new wine; but they served a good purpose for the old wine. Indeed, it is finally admitted that in some respects to some people Judaism will at first taste better than Christianity. In a word, the Christian gospel is being compared with good, healthy Judaism, which God had himself instituted to serve a very real need until Christ should come.

3. Christ and the authorities (6:1–19)

We have reached the half-way point in this stage and things now begin to take on a more serious tone. Christ's gospel is no longer being compared with features of Judaism which were good in their time but which are now becoming old and obsolete. Rather it is being compelled to stand against inadequate interpretations, and then positive perversions, of Judaism. In the first story of this movement the Pharisees accuse Christ and his disciples of breaking God's law, and Christ has to point out that their accusation is based on an inadequate interpretation of holy Scripture. In the second story Christ has to defy the Pharisees' interpretation of the law of sabbath as being not only inadequate but positively immoral. In the third story, Jesus as Israel's Messiah bypasses all the traditional religious authorities in Judaism and appoints twelve apostles to be his own authoritative representatives to the nation. He thus takes an early step on the path that should eventually lead to the complete divergence of Christianity from Judaism. Let us look at these stories in detail.

i. In the cornfield (6:1–5). The Old Testament law of sabbath (see Ex. 20:8–11) forbade work on the sabbath day. About that there was no doubt. When, therefore, our Lord's disciples plucked ears of corn on a sabbath, rubbing them in their hands and eating the kernels, some of the Pharisees accused them of breaking the sabbath (see 6:1–2). If the accusation had been valid, it would have convicted the disciples of sin, and by implication Christ as well.

This incident is recorded also by Matthew (see 12:1–8) and Mark (see 2:23–28). Both of them inform us that our Lord in reply gave a number of different reasons in justification of his disciples' behaviour. Luke chooses to dwell on only one of them, and we therefore are here concerned only with that one reason. Our Lord did not choose, as he might have done, to point out that their definition of what constituted work on the sabbath was quite arbitrary and had no authority within Scripture. What he did point out was that their application of the general law of sabbath was wrong in this particular case: it overlooked the fact that Scripture itself allowed exceptions to religious regulations under certain circumstances, witness the precedent established by David's eating of the shewbread (see 6:3–4; 1 Sa. 21).

The law governing shewbread was not a moral law but only a religious regulation. The strict consecration of the shewbread to God and to his priests was designed to teach Israel the holiness of the Lord, the sacredness of his service and the sanctity of those whom he chose to minister to him in the special ministry of the priesthood. Normally, therefore, the symbols of that service were forbidden to non-priests. But the occasion recorded in 1 Samuel 21 was no normal occasion. In the first place David himself was no ordinary citizen. He was the Lord's anointed (1 Sa. 16). He was God's viceroy in Israel. Moreover at this time he was fleeing for his life from evil Saul, and desperately hungry. It was of paramount importance to the Lord that the Lord's anointed should be fed; and it was perfectly proper, therefore, that a symbol whose strict consecration was designed to teach Israel to revere the service of the Lord, should be used to serve the needs of the Lord's anointed. And if serving his needs meant serving the needs of his servants, there was nothing improper about it.

Now comes the analogy between the law of the shewbread and the law of sabbath, between David as the Lord's anointed and Jesus as the Son of man. The sabbath was instituted for this primary reason among others, to teach men to cease one day a week from serving themselves and to devote the day to the service of God. But Jesus was no ordinary man. He was the Christ, the Son of David (see 1:32), the Lord's Anointed (see 4:18), the Son of man in the fullest possible sense and as the Son of man he declared himself to be Lord of the sabbath. He had a right to his disciples' incessant service. If plucking the corn was done in his service, then it was perfectly proper to do it even on the sabbath.

If a tourist is looking round a stately home and comes across a door marked private, he must respect the owner's prohibition. But if the owner's son comes out and invites him to dinner, the tourist is not disregarding the owner's prohibition by following the owner's son through the door marked private. Let us admit that the Pharisees did not realize that Jesus was the unique and more than human Son of man (see Dn. 7:13–14); it was nonetheless a mis-application of the law of sabbath, though made in ignorance, to accuse the disciples of sin for working for God's Son on God's sabbath.

Before we leave this incident, we should perhaps reflect how it raises, not lowers, the standards which God expected of Israel. They were taught to do their own work six days a week, and then to reserve one day in seven holy to the Lord. It is perilously easy in our secular world for the Christian to fall into the mistake of imagining that Christian liberty allows him to lower that standard, until no day is holy to the Lord; whereas in fact our Lord's teaching is that for the Christian every day should be consecrated to his service. We may recall that at 5:1–11 Christ taught Peter that he was Lord of the believer's daily work; here he teaches his disciples that he is Lord of their sabbaths as well.

ii. The man with a withered hand (6:6–11). There follows now another confrontation between Christ and the Pharisaic interpreters of Scripture. It happened in a synagogue on another sabbath day. Present in the synagogue was a man with a withered hand and the Pharisees were watching to see if Christ would heal him; they were ready to accuse him of sin if he did, since according to them the healing of a man's hand was work and was therefore forbidden on the sabbath.

And Christ who at 5:14 had been so careful to uphold the authority of the priests, now defied these would-be authorities. Reading their unspoken thoughts he told the man to step forward where everybody could see him. That certainly concentrated everybody's attention on the man's poor, shrivelled, useless hand. How could anyone think that sabbath-keeping was meant to pro-long that state of affairs? God in his great compassion had instituted the sabbath so that men's hands might rest and regain strength for further work, not so that it might prolong their disability to do any work at all. Christ who in his compassion had stretched out his own hand and touched the leper (see 5:13), now bade this man stretch out his hand, and healed him.

But it was not merely compassion that moved Christ; nor did he appeal this time to his special status and rights as the Son of man and Lord of the sabbath, nor even to the authority of some particular Scripture. He appealed instead to the authority of morality, and argued that an interpretation of the sabbath law that conflicted with basic morality must be wrong, for it would involve slander on the very character of God who ordained the sabbath. To forbid the healing of a man's hand would be to do him an injury. 'I ask you', said Christ, 'is it lawful on the sabbath day to do someone good, or to do him an injury, to save life, or to destroy it?' (see 6:9).

Yet when Christ defied the scribes and the Pharisees and healed the man, 'they were filled with madness, and discussed among themselves what they might do to Jesus' (6:11). The religious mind is a curious thing. It is not necessarily interested in common morality; still less in relieving human misery and affliction. It is interested in keeping rules; particularly the rules which spring from its own cherished interpretations of Scripture or tradition; and to these interpretations it will attribute the inflexible authority of God himself. Let God incarnate, contrary to its interpretations, interpose with a miracle of divine goodness to relieve human misery, then instead of revising its interpretations it will plan to stop such miracles happening again. Luke rightly describes this attitude as mindless folly (see 6:11). It goes without saying that this was never true Judaism, but a perversion of it. It also goes without saying that Christianity has not always escaped similar misinterpretations.

iii. The healing of the multitudes (6:12–19). The anger of the scribes and Pharisees at Christ's public defiance of their authority and his exposure in front of the people of the folly of their cherished interpretations of Scripture was more serious than might at first appear. It would lead eventually to his death. 'In these days', therefore says Luke (6:12) our Lord spent a night in prayer on a mountainside, and after that did two things.

First, he carefully chose twelve men from among his disciples and appointed them as his apostles. What these men were to be and do we learn later from Luke and from the rest of the New Testament. They were presently to be sent out as Messiah's official emissaries to the nation, their very number, twelve, being matched to the number of the tribes of Israel. To them he would delegate his power and authority (see 9:1). After Pentecost they would be his official witnesses (see Acts 1:8,22) and leaders of the new community, the Christian church. From their number some would be chosen to become the inspired writers of the New Testament, the official channels of the revelation given to the church from the risen Lord by the Holy Spirit (see Jn. 14:26; 15:27; 16:13–15).

Secondly, after choosing them he came down with them from the mountain, where he had been at prayer, and stood on the plain, before a tremendous gathering of disciples and of the general public from all over the country, north and south (see 6:17). This was the first time that these men had stood with him publicly in their official capacity before such a representative crowd from all over the nation. They would never forget that occasion nor the demonstration he gave them that day of what he and his teaching stood for. The people came, Luke tells us, 'to hear him and to be healed of their diseases and . . . power came out from him and healed them all' (6:17–19). We recall that other gathering of which Luke has recently told us (see 5:17) when there was assembled a representative collection of teachers of the law from every village of Galilee and Judaea and Jerusalem. On that occasion he had given those teachers a demonstration of the distinctive quality of his teaching. The power of the Lord was with him to heal, and the healing character of his teaching was manifested as he first forgave a paralytic's sins and then released him from his paralysis and gave him the power to walk to the glory of God. And so now, as his newly appointed apostles stood with him on the plain, power came out from him and he healed the crowds; and in that context of healing he 'lifted up his eyes on his disciples' (6:20) and taught them what the pastoral epistles would later describe as 'healthy, wholesome words, even the words of our Lord Jesus Christ' (1 Tim. 6:3).

4. Christ's principles of morality (6:20–49)

We come now to Luke's equivalent of the Sermon on the Mount. We have no need to decide the question of whether or not the material recorded by Luke was spoken by Christ on the same occasion as the material recorded in the Sermon by Matthew. Many preachers preach similar, but slightly varied, material on different occasions; and Christ may well have done so too. For our purposes the differences between the material presented by Luke and Matthew will be especially helpful. We cannot hope to do justice to the whole of our Lord's moral teaching summarized here by Luke; that would need a close exegesis of every detail and wide-ranging discussion of its practical applications. Such a study would lead us far beyond the proportions of this present work. We must be content to observe the general flow of Luke's thought, and for that purpose those features which distinguish Luke's presentation from Matthew's Sermon will prove a useful guide.

i. *The right attitude to poverty, hunger, sorrow and social ostracism (6:20–23).* First we notice that whereas Matthew's Sermon has nine beatitudes, Luke's has only four (see 6:20–23). Here no blessing is pronounced on the positive states of being meek, merciful, pure in heart or peacemaker; only the negative states of poverty, hunger and weeping are mentioned, and those who suffer them are pronounced happy because of the compensations which they do, and shall, enjoy. Then one final blessing is given more prominence than the other three combined. It pronounces blessed those who are hated, separated from men's company, reproached, and whose name is cast out as evil for the Son of man's sake: in a word, those who are socially ostracized not just for any cause whatever, good or bad, but for Christ's sake.

ii. *The right attitude to riches, society, laughter and social acceptance (6:24–26).* The 'woes' which Christ pronounces in these verses have no counterpart in Matthew's Sermon: they are peculiar to Luke. They express a mixture of indignation and sorrow, and more of sorrow than of indignation. They largely repeat in reverse terms, and thus underline, what the 'blessings' say. Now the biggest emphasis among the 'blessings', as we have just noticed, falls on those who are hated, ostracized and denigrated for the Son of man's sake: they suffer, Christ explains, the same as the prophets did (see 6:23). So here the corresponding 'woe' observes (6:26) that those who are spoken well of by all men, are being treated as the false prophets were. Luke leaves us in no doubt, therefore, as to what Christ had in mind. He was thinking of the bitter criticisms of his teaching, examples of which we have had throughout this stage, and even more of the hostility which his exposure of the Pharisees'

118

false teaching was beginning to stir up. We have already had one unpleasant instance of it at 6:11; eventually, as we know, it would lead to his murder, and as Luke records in Acts to outbursts of persecution against the church.

Then one further, small but significant Lucan peculiarity is worth noticing. In Matthew, Christ phrases himself thus: 'Blessed are the poor in spirit, for *theirs* is the kingdom of heaven' (5:3), in Luke he 'lifted up his eyes on his disciples and said, Blessed are *you* poor, for *yours* is the kingdom of God' (5:20). And this use of the second person plural instead of the third continues throughout the 'blesseds' and the 'woes'.

The effect is that Christ divides the great company of people listening to him into two groups: you who are poor, are hungry and weep, and you who are rich, are full and laugh; you who are to be congratulated, and you who are to be sorrowed over. The final contrast is particularly significant. It is not between those who are reproached and those who are spoken well of by all. It is between those who are reproached *for the Son of man's sake*, and those who are spoken well of by all. And the same applies to the other contrasts. In other words, the two groups are not those who are for any reason poor, hungry and sorrowful, and those who likewise for any reason are rich, full and laugh. The basic criterion that divides the great throng into two groups is whether they are Christ's genuine disciples or not.

The case of Levi, the tax-collector (see 5:27–32) will illustrate the point. Before his conversion, he was like all his fellow tax-collectors, hated by the people, socially ostracized, and spoken very badly of. That did not mean, of course, that he enjoyed the blessedness of which Christ speaks. He did not incur this treatment for Christ's sake. He was in fact among the rich, the full, those who laugh – an apt description of the guests at his pre-conversion banquets. But then Christ changed him: he stopped all his extortion, abandoned his lucrative occupation and shared a meagre common purse with Christ and his travelling band of evangelists in order to take the gospel to the nation. Curiously enough, his conversion did not alter things much in one respect: he was still spoken ill of. The Pharisees, much as they disapproved of tax-collecting, were not pleased with his conversion to Christ nor with his attempts to get other tax-collectors converted (see 5:29–30). And as for the poor, while they were doubtless glad to have a few less tax-collectors around, when they discovered that Jesus was not prepared to lead a revolution against the imperialists, they eventually joined with the Pharisees and Sadducees, rejected Christ and his apostles, Levi included, and chose by preference a revolutionary activist (see 23:18–25). But now Levi did qualify for the blessedness of which Christ spoke: the poverty, suffering, criticism and ostracism which he now endured were being endured for the sake of loyalty to Christ and to his gospel.

One further element in this section of Christ's teaching may detain us for a moment: his remarkable compassion for the unscrupulously rich. At 5:27–31, in spite of heavy criticism by the Pharisees he had gone among them with the compassion which a true physician has for the desperately sick. Now here at 6:25–26 he tells us what moves him to pronounce his 'woe' of sorrow upon them: it is the thought that the comfort which they enjoy in this life is all the comfort which they are ever going to get. When we come to the story of the rich man and Lazarus (see 16:19–31) we shall see more fully what he means by saying that such people have received all the comfort they are ever going to get (see 16:25); and we shall the more readily understand his compassion. It will be interesting to see also that by that stage (see 15:13–15) the Pharisees have somewhat changed their tune regarding the seriousness of serving mammon.

iii. The right attitude to enemies and would-be borrowers (6:27–38).

There follows now a number of detailed moral exhortations. Important in their own right, they also balance what has just been said. A man who rejoiced when he was cast out of men's company, reproached and rejected as evil, and who considered it a woe to be spoken well of by all, might be in danger of becoming a very unpleasant character, a veritable Ishmael, his hand against every man, and every man's hand against him. Christ obviates this danger by telling his disciples what their attitude must be to the very enemies who have cast them out and spoken evil of them. 'Love your enemies, do good to those who hate you, bless those who curse you, pray for those who ill-treat you . . . lend . . . be merciful . . . do not judge . . . do not condemn . . . release . . . give'.

Running through these exhortations are two basic principles. The first is that followers of Christ are called upon to behave in ways far superior to those of sinners (see 6:32–34). It is the fact that many of the kind and generous attitudes and acts on which we all congratulate ourselves, are the attitudes and acts which all members of all groups show towards members of their own groups. We all love our fellow-socialists, or fellow-capitalists, or fellow-nationals, or fellow-religionists. But there is nothing very special about that. Even sinners do the same. Christ calls his followers to love their enemies, their oppressors, their robbers and those that show them violence, and to do them good (see 6:27–29).

The second is that followers of Christ must show the same character as their Father (see 6:35–36). He is just, but he is more than just: he is merciful. So must his sons be. It is not so much a question of following rules, or even of clamouring for justice. It is a question of inheriting by the new birth the Father's nature and exhibiting that nature by behaving as his mature sons. Sonship, one might almost say, is the key to Christ's moral teaching. We recall how at 5:34–35 he explained that the behaviour of 'sons of the bride-chamber' (which is what the Greek calls the bridegroom's guests) will be regulated by the presence or absence of the bridegroom. And the analogy turned into a metaphor: he is the Bridegroom and his disciples are his 'sons of the bride-chamber'. Now here his disciples are sons of the Father. And once more we conclude that for them true moral behaviour is not so much a matter of keeping rules but a matter of developing a Godlike character as a result of enjoying the life of God in fellowship with Christ.

iv. A threefold parable (6:39–49). The second half of stage 3 ends, as does the first half, with a parable in three parts. But there is an important difference in the message of the two parables. The first tripartite parable (see 5:36–37) was concerned to contrast the new and the better with what was good in its day, but is now old and inadequate. The second tripartite parable is concerned to contrast the true, good and correct with what is downright false and unrelievedly bad.

The first part of the second parable (see 6:39–42) is based on an analogy with eyesight, and applies to those who would teach others. It castigates two faults. First there is the fault of the man who has no sight at all, and yet professes to lead others (see 6:39–40), with the inevitable result that he himself falls into the ditch and his disciples, who by definition can get no further than the teacher they are depending on, fall into the ditch as well. It is a pathetic thing to listen to a man who has no personal experience of Christ's salvation trying to instruct others like himself in the gospel of Christ.

Secondly there is the fault of the man who has sight, but whose visual judgment is grievously impaired: he has a baulk of timber, says our Lord, with delightful hyperbole, in his eye and he can't really see straight. In prosaic language, he has some glaringly wrong habit or attitude in his life which everybody else can see; but strangely enough, not only can he apparently not see it himself, but he is the very one who is constantly pointing out other people's minor faults and failings, and offering to correct their vision by casting out these motes from their eyes. Actually, he could see the beam in his own eye if he wanted to: his finding fault with others is but compensation for allowing his own major fault to continue unjudged. Our Lord calls him a hypocrite (see 6:41–42).

The second part of the parable (6:43–45) is based on an analogy with fruit-trees and their fruit. The fruit of a tree is an unfailing indication of the nature of the tree. So a man's actions, words and attitudes are an unfailing indication of the state of his heart. But there is an ever present temptation to avoid drawing the painful conclusions that result from applying this principle to myself, by regarding my few good actions and words, as 'typically me', and my many bad actions and words as 'not being me at all, really'. But we deceive ourselves thus. True, a Christian, if he knows what he is talking about, can say with Paul 'But if what I would not do, that I do, it is no more I that do it, but sin which dwells in me' (Rom. 7:20). But Paul is explaining why believers sin, not giving them an excuse for continuing to sin and not troubling themselves too much about it. A man whose conversation (6:45) is constantly full of evil things, great or small, has an evil heart; for a man's talk is the overflow of his heart. The saintliest man may be appalled by the occasional overspill whose sudden eruption escapes the filter of his moral judgment and reveals what pollutants still remain in the depths. But if the general tenor of a man's conversation is evil, the source must be evil too. No excuse can break the connection between a tree's fruit and the nature of the tree.

And finally, the third part of the parable is based on an analogy with building (see 6:46–49). There is only one way to build a house secure against a storm and that is to dig down deep and lay its foundations on the rock. But digging deep can be troublesome. It is all too easy to be content with a superficial knowledge of Christianity and a superficial, nominal profession of faith without real obedience to Christ (6:46). But just as there is only one foundation, so only those who are by personal contact with him built directly and squarely on the foundation of his Word, believed, applied and performed, will survive the storms here and hereafter.

Christ's way of salvation

Preliminary survey

The movements

1 Salvation from death: a gift to faith *(7:2–17)*
2 False expectations of salvation, and rejection of the Saviour
     (7:18–35)
3 Salvation and the love and service of the forgiven *(7:36 – 8:3)*
4 The mysteries of the kingdom relating to salvation
     (8:4–21)
5 Salvation from the physical elements *(8:22–25)*
6 Salvation from spirit powers, and rejection of the Saviour
     (8:26–39)
7 Salvation from the waste of life's vital forces *(8:40–48)*
8 Salvation and a 'secret' raising of the dead *(8:49–56)*

Stage 4

Christ's way of salvation

Preliminary survey

Chapters 7 and 8 of the Gospel contain for the most part individual stories of healings and miracles performed by Christ himself. Then at 9:1 Luke turns from Christ's own ministry to report the mission of the twelve apostles. It looks then as if chapters 7 and 8 might well be intended to stand together as stage 4 of the Gospel.

One theme receives special emphasis in these two chapters; the topic of salvation. That we can see in the first place from the repetition of the Greek verb for 'save', *sōzō*. This verb and its compound *diasōzō* (to rescue, bring safely through, save) can carry a wide range of meaning. In the New Testament *sōzō* is used of saving people in a physical sense from danger or disaster, for example from drowning (see Mt. 8:25). It can also denote 'saving' in the sense of 'healing' as in Mt. 9:22. It can and frequently does have the deeper sense of 'forgiveness' and 'salvation from a life of sin' (see Lk. 7:50; Tit. 3:5). The related nouns *sōtēria* (salvation) and *sōtēr* (Saviour) are used in connection with the consummation of salvation at the second coming of Christ (see Rom. 13:11; Phil. 3:20–21). In a sense, therefore, one could claim that virtually the whole of the New Testament is taken up with the theme of salvation. Nonetheless it remains true that in Luke's two chapters 7 and 8 there is a higher than average concentration of the term 'save'. The verb *diasōzō* occurs at 7:3 and nowhere else in the whole of the Gospel. Before chapter 7 the verb *sōzō* occurs only once (see 6:9); but in chapters 7 and 8 it occurs five times (see 7:50; 8:12, 36, 48, 50). Let us consider these occurrences.

The story of the woman in Simon's house (see 7:36–50) is peculiar to Luke. It is in fact a moving story of salvation: 'your faith has
saved you: go in peace' says Christ to the once fallen and now
forgiven woman (7:50).

The remaining stories Luke shares with the other evangelists but
he uses the word 'save' more than they do.

In describing the healing of the centurion's slave Matthew uses
two verbs: *therapeuō* (8:7), which means 'to treat' or 'to heal', and
iaomai (8:8, 13) which means 'to heal'. Luke uses three verbs: *iaomai*
(7:7) and *hugiainō*, which means 'to be well', but in the introduction
to the story (7:3) *diasōzō* meaning 'to save' in the sense of saving the
slave from dying.

At 8:4–15 Luke records the parable of the sower, as do also
Matthew (see 13:3–23) and Mark (see 4:3–20). All three evangelists,
of course, explain who are the people represented by the seed
which fell by the wayside: they are those who hear the word, and
immediately the devil comes and snatches away what has been
sown in their hearts. Only Luke adds why the devil does it: 'so that
they may not believe and be saved' (8:12).

Matthew (8:28–34), Mark (5:1–20) and Luke (8:26–39) all tell the
story of the demoniac, and all three record how the bystanders told
the crowds who came out from the nearby city what had happened.
Luke, and only Luke, phrases their explanation like this: 'those who
saw it told them *how the demon-possessed man was saved*' (8:35).

All three synoptic evangelists tell the interconnected stories of
the woman subject to bleeding and Jairus' daughter. All three relate
that the woman 'was saved' (*i.e.* healed, Mt. 9:22; Mk. 5:34; Lk.
8:48). But when it comes to Jairus' daughter Matthew does not use
the term 'saved' at all. Mark uses it in the request for help which
Jairus made to Christ while the girl was still alive (see 5:23). Luke,
by contrast, uses the term, but not at that point in the story. He
waits until the girl is dead and everyone has given up hope, and
then records Christ's words to Jairus: 'Only believe and she shall be
saved' (8:50). That certainly gives the word 'save' a remarkable
connotation.

Luke, then, in these two chapters has collected a number of
stories which he presents to us as instances of salvation. The merest
glance will show that they are not all instances of the same aspect of
salvation. Moreover, along with these instances he presents other
incidents which without actually using the term 'save' are clearly

intended as further instances of salvation. Together they form an impressive array. The centurion's slave is saved from dying (see 7:2–3); the widow of Nain's son, already dead and on his way to be buried, is raised from the dead (see 7:12–15). The woman in Simon's house is saved from her guilty past by the gift of forgiveness (see 7:47–50). The disciples on the lake are saved from drowning in the storm (see 8:23–24). The demoniac is saved from the power of demons (see 8:27–36). The woman subject to bleeding is saved from a debilitating physical weakness (see 8:43–48), while Jairus' daughter is saved from the sleep of death (see 8:50–55).

Presumably Luke means these incidents to be in some sense representative examples of Christ's power to save. But in addition to these incidents, chapters 7 and 8 contain two lengthy passages of comment and teaching: the first deals with matters that arose over John the Baptist (see 7:18–35) and the second contains a selection of parables, that of the sower being the most prominent (see 8:4–21). The question naturally arises whether or not the topics discussed in these two passages have anything to do with the topic of salvation, and if so, what. We have already noticed that Luke has explicitly connected the parable of the sower with the question of salvation (see 8:12); but the passage dealing with John the Baptist does not explicitly use the term. Mark has no counterpart to this passage; Matthew (see 11:2–19) has, but he puts it in an altogether different context from Luke, after the mission of the twelve apostles, and not like Luke, before that mission. To discover, if we can, why Luke has put it in the position he has and what if anything it has got to do with its context, we could look at the way Luke has arranged his material in this stage as a whole. Very early on in our study (p.14) we noticed that the story of the woman in Simon's house, which is peculiar to Luke, has striking similarities with the story of the woman subject to bleeding, which he shares with other evangelists. Perhaps he has included the passage about John the Baptist in this context because it also raises questions that in his mind are related to matters raised elsewhere in this stage of the Gospel. We can but look and see. Let us begin by making a list of contents.

The first story (see 7:2–10) records the salvation of the centurion's servant from dying. Luke joins it by means of the words 'and it came to pass soon afterwards' (7:11) to the story of the widow of Nain's son (see 7:11–17) whom Christ raised from the dead. Since Luke seems to link these incidents together and they both deal with salvation from death let us call 7:2–17 movement 1.

Next (see 7:18–23) Luke tells how John the Baptist sent two of his disciples to Christ with a question, and what answer Christ gave to that question. This is followed, after the departure of John's disciples, by a long rebuke of the crowd for their perverse attitude towards both John and Christ (see 7:24–35). Since both these passages involve John, let us call them movement 2.

There follows the story of the woman in Simon's house, who attended Christ with tears, kisses and ointment. Luke then links this story by means of the words 'and it came to pass soon afterwards' to his record of a group of women who followed Christ and his disciples and 'supported them out of their private means' (8:1–3). Let us call these two stories about women devoted to Christ movement 3.

From 8:4 onwards Christ begins to teach in parables. There is the parable of the sower (8:4–15), the parable of the lamp (8:16–18), and then at the end when his mother and brothers come looking for him he announces in metaphorical language 'my mother and brothers are those who hear the Word of God and do it' (8:19–21). Let us call this parable section (8:4–21) movement 4.

At this point the narrative turns to relate a voyage which Christ and his disciples made across the lake and back again. The story contains four distinct episodes. One, the storm, occurred as they were crossing the lake (see 8:22–25). We may call it movement 5. The next, the saving of the demoniac, occurred when they landed on the other side (see 8:26–39). We may call it movement 6. The other two episodes took place when they arrived back. The first was the saving of the woman subject to bleeding (see 8:40–48), and we may call it movement 7; and the second was the saving of Jairus' daughter (8:49–56): we may call that movement 8.

Now in the same way as the story of the woman in Simon's house and the story of the woman subject to bleeding show certain similarities and contrasts in the detail of their subject-matter so do some of the other stories, as will appear if we now map out the main details of the eight movements. (See pp.130–131.) It will be one of the chief tasks of our exposition to try to see the point of these similarities and contrasts.

The movements

1. Salvation from death: a gift to faith (7:2–17)

There is no doubt what aspect of salvation is presented by the stories of the centurion's slave and the widow of Nain's son: it is salvation from death. The stories are very dramatic: one man was on the point of death, the other was already dead and in process of being buried; and both were saved and given life.

These are the basic facts of the stories; but we are not left to make of them what we will. It is the explicit concern of the stories themselves to tell us on what conditions these men were saved from death and given new life.

Take first the centurion. He was a Gentile, and in his humility (see 7:7) he sent some Jewish elders to ask Christ to come and save his slave. They, however, made the common mistake of pleading for this salvation on the basis of the centurion's meritorious works. Now certainly the centurion had a remarkable record of good works. He loved the Jewish nation and had built the local Jews a synagogue (see 7:5). When we take into consideration the cost of such a building, and the fact that normally Romans, like the later satirist Juvenal, despised the Jews, their faith and their prayer-houses, we can understand perhaps why the Jews pleaded that 'this man is worthy to have you do this for him'. Christ listened to their plea and began to go with them to the centurion's house. In the centurion's works Christ doubtless saw evidence of an honest heart genuinely seeking to please God the best he knew how.

But the centurion knew better than to rest his plea for the salvation of his slave on his personal merit. When he realized that the Lord was approaching his house, he sent friends to tell him, 'Lord, don't trouble yourself; I am not good enough for you to come under my roof. That is why I did not even consider myself worthy to come to you' (7:6–7). Had it been only the emperor, Tiberius Caesar, from whom he had wished to receive some favour, much as he wanted it, he would not have considered himself sufficiently worthy or important to ask the emperor to come to his house personally to bestow the favour. He knew then enough etiquette, let alone spiritual sense, to realize that it was utterly out of place and irrelevant to prate about his own merits in the presence of Christ, or to suggest that upon consideration of his

Stage 4 of the Coming 7:2–8:56

1 Salvation from death: a gift to faith: the centurion's slave and the widow of Nain's son 7:2–17

1 The centurion to Christ: 'Speak the word and my slave will be healed. For I also am a man set under authority . . . and I say . . . Go, and he goes . . . and I say . . . Come, and he comes' . . . And . . . Jesus was amazed . . . and said . . . 'I have not found so great faith, no not in Israel.'

2 The widow of Nain's son was about to be buried when Christ said, 'Young man . . . get up' (Gk. *egerthēti*). And the dead man sat up and began to speak . . . And fear seized all of them.

2 False expectations of salvation and rejection of the Saviour: John and the 'men of this generation' 7:18–35

1 John wonders if Jesus is 'the Coming One' or if they should be looking for someone else. Jesus does many miracles in the presence of John's messengers and bids them 'Go and report to John what you have seen and heard . . .'

2 'What did you go to see? . . . a man clothed in soft raiment? . . .' Those who are splendidly dressed and live in luxury are in kings' palaces. But what did you go out to see? A prophet? Yes . . . and more than a prophet.

3 'All the people . . . justified God, being baptized by John's baptism. But the Pharisees . . . rejected the counsel of God, not being baptized by him.' They said John had a demon!

5 Salvation from the physical elements: the disciples and the storm on the lake 8:22–25

1 And he (Jesus) rebuked the wind and the raging water, and they ceased . . . And he said, 'Where is your faith?' And . . . they were amazed saying . . . 'Who then is this that he commands even the winds and the water, and they obey him?'

2 Christ fell asleep and the boat was filling with water and they were in danger of going down. 'And they . . . roused him (Gk. *diegeiran*) . . . and he got up (Gk. *diegertheis*) and rebuked the wind . . . And they were afraid . . .

6 Salvation from spirit powers, and rejection of the Saviour: the demoniac and the men of the country 8:26–39

1 The saved demoniac asks to accompany Christ, but Christ sends him away saying, 'Go back home and recount what great things God has done for you . . .' And he went away, and told all over the town what great things Jesus had done for him.

2 And they went out to see what had happened . . . and they found the man (who for a long time had worn no clothes) . . . sitting, clothed and in his right mind at the feet of Jesus.

3 And they . . . told them *how* the demon-possessed man was saved (*i.e.* they told them about the demons entering the pigs and the pigs being drowned in the lake); and all the people . . . asked Jesus to depart.

3 Salvation and the love and service of the forgiven: the woman in Simon's house and the women who served 7:36 – 8:3

1 'a . . . woman . . . standing behind at his feet . . . began to wet his feet with her tears . . .'.

2 '. . . the Pharisee . . . said . . . If this man were a prophet, he would have perceived who and what kind of woman this is that is touching him . . .'

3 'And he said to the woman, Your faith has saved you; go in peace.'

4 'Certain women who had been healed . . . served and supported them out of their own private means.'

4 The mysteries of the kingdom relating to salvation: the parables of the sower, the lamp and the family 8:4–21

1 'To you is given to know the mysteries (i.e. the revealed secrets) of the kingdom of God, but to the rest in parables, that seeing they may not see and hearing they may not understand.'

2 '. . . the devil . . . takes away the word from their hearts so that they might not believe and be saved.'

3 The true family circle: Christ's mother and brothers are those who hear the word of God and do it.

7 Salvation from the waste of life's vital forces: the woman subject to bleeding 8:40–48

1 . . . a woman . . . came behind him and touched the border of his garment . . .

2 . . . Jesus said, 'Who is it that touched me?' And when all denied . . . Jesus said, 'Someone did touch me, for I perceived that power had gone out from me.'

3 And he said, 'Daughter, Your faith has saved you; go in peace.'

4 A woman . . . who had spent all her living on doctors and could not be healed . . .

8 Salvation and a 'secret' raising of the dead: the awakening of Jairus' daughter from the sleep of death. 8:49–56

1 He allowed no-one to enter with him except Peter, John, James and the girl's parents. And . . . he said . . . 'She is not dead, but asleep.' But they (the crowd) laughed at him knowing that she was dead. . . . And he ordered the parents to tell no-one what had happened.

2 One said, 'Your daughter is dead, don't trouble the teacher any more.' But Jesus . . . replied, 'Only believe and she will be saved.'

3 The restored family circle: Christ, his apostles, the father and mother and the child raised from the dead.

merits Christ ought to take the trouble to come to his house to effect the salvation he deserved. The very first thing he did was to disclaim all merit.

And then the centurion had perceived that such was the authority of Christ that he did not need to come to his house anyway. Christ need only speak a word of command, and the slave would be healed instantaneously (see 7:7–8). As an officer in the army the centurion had only to issue an order and soldiers sprang to carry it out, because behind him and his order lay the authority of the supreme commander of the Roman forces, his imperial majesty. What authority Christ commanded the centurion did not fully know; but his very request presumed Christ had authority over the forces of life and death. Recognizing that all the merit, power and authority lay in Christ and Christ's word, he humbly made his appeal: 'Say the word, and let my servant be healed'. Christ's amazed comment was (and notice that it is Christ's comment and not our own idea injected into the story): 'I tell you, not even in Israel have I found such great faith' (7:9).

This first instance of salvation, then, has itself explicitly laid down the fundamental principles on which salvation was given and received on that occasion, and presumably on all other occasions: salvation is not granted on the basis of a man's good works, worth or merit. It is given on the grounds of faith. And faith according to this story, is not confidence that we have done the best we could, that God will assess our merits generously; faith is abandoning trust in our works and merit and any thought of deserving salvation, and relying totally and without reserve on the Person of Christ and the authority of his word.

But this lesson is so important and so difficult to grasp – notice again Christ's astonishment that a Gentile got it right when many Jews did not – that Luke has reinforced it by adding here a story which no other evangelist records, the story of the widow of Nain (see 7:11–17). What a contrast she makes with the centurion: he a strong, commanding type of man with ample resources and many noble works to his credit; she a weak desolate widow. Now she was following her only son to the grave when Jesus moved with compassion stopped the sad procession of death, raised the young man to life, and gave him to his mother (see 7:15). Notice the verb: he *gave* him to her. In that wonderful moment, no conditions were laid down, no promises extracted. The awesome gift of new, unexpected life was apparently an unconditional gift, an action of the unqualified grace of God.

Put both stories together, and they lay down positively and negatively what the conditions of salvation are. If you have many good works to your credit and good resources like the centurion, or nothing at all like the widow, it makes no difference: for salvation is not of works, whether many or few, whether good or bad; it is by grace through faith, it is the gift of God.

The last two clauses, as the reader will have realized, are borrowed from Paul (see Eph. 2:1–10). Not altogether arbitrarily: in the context in which he employs them, he is talking of salvation from spiritual death by the gift of new life in Christ. But obviously, whether it is salvation from physical death, as with the centurion's slave and the widow's son, or whether it is salvation from spiritual death, the basic principles of salvation are the same.

But to return to the centurion for a moment. In praising his faith Christ confessed that he had not found so great faith, no not in Israel (see 7:9). Why not, we wonder? If salvation from death was a gift, why were people not clamouring for it?

One answer is that salvation was not simply by faith: it was by faith in Christ; and that meant, as many of the stories in this stage will make clear, recognizing, however dimly, who Jesus was, as the centurion or as the crowd at Nain did (see 7:16). And this is where for many people the doubts and difficulties began, as we are now about to see.

2. False expectations of salvation, and rejection of the Saviour (7:18–35)

If salvation depends on faith in Jesus as the Christ, the Son of God, it is at once evident why many of his contemporaries did not even apply to him for salvation: they did not believe that he was the Christ. The evidence for his claim, they would have said, was not only inadequate, it was negative. Luke candidly tells Theophilus – and us – about it. He records what Christ's contemporaries said and did and the reasons they gave for their rejection of both John the Baptist and Jesus. He records also what Jesus said and did in reply. And then he allows his readers to make up their own minds.

Of all that the present passage tells us perhaps the most disturbing thing is that John the Baptist himself at one stage suffered certain doubts and perplexities about Jesus. In his public ministry he had announced Jesus as the 'Coming One', that is the One whose coming had long been promised by the prophets. He had declared that the Coming One would exercise a twofold ministry: he would baptize in the Holy Spirit all those who repented and believed; but he would also 'burn up the chaff with unquenchable fire' and 'cut down every tree that did not bear good fruit and cast it into the fire' (3:9, 16–17). It would seem from his phrase 'even now is the axe laid at the root of the trees' (3:9) that he believed the judgment was imminent, and that the execution of God's wrath would follow shortly.

But at the time of which our passage speaks John was now in prison (see 3:20; and compare 7:18–19 with Mt. 11:2–3). There it was reported to him by his disciples that Jesus was doing marvellous, miraculous things (see 7:18); and that, of course, fitted in exactly with half of John's expectations of what the Coming One would do. But Jesus was apparently making no attempt whatever to fulfil the other half of his expectations. He had not even made the slightest move to get John out of prison, or to execute God's judgment on the evil Herod who had put him there. Why not? How could he be the Messiah if he didn't? It was all right his going about healing an odd slave here and raising a widow's son from the dead there – John had nothing against that. But what about the big issues? When was Jesus going to start putting oppressive governments right? Abolishing evil rulers like Herod? Putting down the Roman tyranny and giving Israel her political independence under a just government once more? How could Jesus convincingly claim to be the answer to the world's problems if he failed to do these things, and merely contented himself with saving individuals? The matter perplexed John very deeply and he sent two disciples to Christ with the question: 'Are you the One who was destined to come, or should we be expecting someone else?'

John is not the only one to have felt the problem. To this very day there are many who feel that they cannot believe in Jesus if he is interested merely in the saving of individuals and not in putting right the great political, economic and social evils of the world.

The Lord's reply (see 7:21–23) was not to deny that he would ever execute God's judgment on evil men and governments. His reply was to do a number of miracles, such as Isaiah had prophesied Messiah would do (see Is. 35:3–5; 61:1–3), and to send John the story of them, that he might see beyond doubt that Jesus was fulfilling part of the programme that the prophets had laid down: and that if he was fulfilling one part already, he would fulfil the other part later on.

Messiah's programme, it is evident, had certain inbuilt priorities. In the fulfilling of Old Testament prophecy, Christ insisted that the preaching of the gospel to the individual (see 7:22) must take precedence over the executing of God's judgment on the wicked in general and on unjust governments in particular. It would be a sorry thing for us all if that were not so. The day of the Lord will certainly come in spite of all complaints and criticisms that it is too long delayed (see 2 Pet. 3:3–10); and it will come too soon for many people. The reason it waits is that 'God is longsuffering . . . not wishing that any should perish, but that all should come to repentance'. We may feel, like John, that the injustices we suffer cry out to be avenged. We may feel, again like John, that by delaying to right the world's wrongs, Jesus is putting his own reputation as Messiah at risk. But we serve a Messiah who in his compassion for men puts the salvation of the individual before his own reputation.

But for most of Christ's contemporaries, the difficulty they found in admitting that Jesus was the Messiah was altogether different from John's difficulty. So when John's messengers left, our Lord began to speak to the crowds about John, and in so doing to probe their consciences. The fact is that when John first began to preach in the wilderness, these people had gone out to him in their thousands (see 3:7). Since then, however, many of them had tried to forget it. But our Lord would not allow them to. With powerful and deeply probing irony he reminded them not only that they had gone out into the desert to John the Baptist, but why it was they had gone out (see 7:24–28). They had not gone out into the desert to see a reed shaken by the wind, or a man dressed in fine clothes. Obviously not. They had gone out to John the Baptist because they had believed that he was the forerunner of Messiah prophesied of by Isaiah (see ch. 40). But if John was Messiah's forerunner, then Jesus was the Messiah, and the people, one and all, ought to have put their trust in him and to have received him as Saviour and sovereign Lord. Many had in fact done so; but many had not, and were busy trying to forget that they had ever thought there was anything in John the Baptist at all. They now maintained that John had a demon, that is, he was mad, and that Jesus was morally lax, irresponsible and dissolute (see 7:33–34).

It is a common thing for people to get caught up in some religious experience or other and afterwards to change their mind about it and to be embarrassed by their former excitement. The thing that must interest us, at our distance in history, is what it was that made them change their minds. From what Luke tells us it was John's preaching, and in particular the significance he gave to his baptism (see 7:29–30). John preached that the people's sins were intolerably obnoxious to God. They stood exposed to the wrath of God. 'You offspring of vipers' he thundered at them, 'who has warned you to flee from the wrath to come' (3:7). Many of the crowd including, and perhaps especially, the tax-gatherers, recognized that John's preaching was true (see 7:29). They knew they were sinners. John's condemnation of their sin, his warnings of God's wrath, they accepted as God's just verdict on their lives; and they had themselves baptized in humble confession of their sin and of their need of salvation. Not so the Pharisees and the experts in the law. These were men who prided themselves on their meritorious keeping of the law of God and they were quite happy to rest their hope of salvation on their merits. Not that they would have claimed that they had kept God's law perfectly. But they felt sure that God Almighty, when it came to the final examination, would behave like a kindly schoolmaster or indulgent don, overlook their shortcomings and grant them an honourable pass. John's insistence that God's holiness could not countenance any shortcomings, they regarded as extreme. When he added that they had in principle (if not in extent – though there was real doubt about that too) broken the law just like the tax-collectors and the ignorant masses, and stood equally exposed to the wrath of God and in equal need of salvation, they decided that John's preaching was simply grotesque, and that John himself had a demon and was emotionally unbalanced. 'Just look at his ascetic diet', they said, as if the moral truth of a sermon could be settled by an appeal to the preacher's personality and habits. It was, Christ pointed out, God's law that John was expounding: in rejecting John's preaching on the holiness and wrath of God they were rejecting the very counsel of God (see 7:30).

But then Christ went on to point out that to be consistent with their reasons for rejecting John they ought to have received Jesus. Though he, too, at times preached the wrath of God, more solemnly perhaps than any other had done (see Mt. 5:21–22; 10:15;

Mk. 9:45–48; Lk. 16:22–31), yet he brought a message of forgiveness and salvation and of the love of God delightful and joyful beyond all expectation. He had authority, he claimed, to grant men here on earth forgiveness in the full and absolute and final sense (see 5:24). This surely would have pleased the Pharisees. They had not liked John's preaching of the wrath of God, understandably. But this preaching of the love of God, of a forgiveness so generous, so certain, that one could know oneself accepted with God here on earth without waiting for the final judgment – this they surely would have welcomed. The repentant tax-collectors and sinners welcomed it of course. But not the Pharisees! They pointed to Christ's lack of ascetic diet, and to his social mixing with tax-collectors and sinners (for the purpose of converting them), and denounced him as a religiously undisciplined man whose teachings positively encouraged people to neglect the law and live sinfully.

Christ's comment was that they were like children in the market-place content with neither dancing nor weeping (see 7:31–32). They would neither have the holiness and wrath of God, nor the love and forgiveness of God. All they wanted was a God small enough to compromise and to pretend that their imperfect keeping of the law was adequate, a salvation small enough for their merits to earn it, and a doctrine of salvation that left the verdict of the final judgment decently uncertain.

If these then were the historical reasons why many of Christ's contemporaries rejected both John the Baptist and Jesus, we shall at least have no difficulty in understanding them: we hear them voiced frequently enough in our own day. But the charge that Christ's doctrine of salvation is a form of antinomianism is a serious one, if for no other reason than that a superficial and unbalanced statement of the doctrine can in fact make it sound very antinomian. At this point, however, Luke adds two stories, peculiar to himself, which have the effect of demonstrating the charge to be false. The effect is scarcely unintended.

3. Salvation and the love and service of the forgiven (7:36 – 8:3)

The two stories of movement 1 demonstrated that salvation is not of works, but by grace through faith. Movement 3 will now present two stories to show that while salvation is not of works, once it is received it leads to good works. In so doing movement 3

137

will answer the criticisms launched by the Pharisees and lawyers against Christ in the passage we have just considered.

One of the Pharisees invited Christ to a meal (see 7:36). Perhaps he was in two minds about Jesus, impressed by his moral teaching to the point of thinking he might be a prophet, but distressed by the type of people he mixed with and claimed as his converts. At any rate, when a woman of the streets suddenly entered the dining room, and began to pay Christ personal attention, and Christ made no attempt to stop her, Simon decided that this finally proved that Jesus was no prophet: 'This man, if he were a prophet, would have perceived who and what kind of a woman this is that touches him, that she is a sinner' (7:37–39). Prophets above all people should have a true discernment of moral character.

Now it is true that this woman had been immoral; but apparently she had since been saved by faith in Christ (see 7:50) and her sins had been forgiven. [It is important to notice that the tense of the verb in 7:48 is perfect. Not, 'your sins are now (at this moment) forgiven you'; but 'yours sins have been (at some time in the past, however recently) forgiven'. And so also in v. 47.] The difficulty, however, would lie in convincing Simon of that. Any believer in Christ would have accepted Christ's word for it. But Simon was not a believer in Christ. He would need some very convincing evidence before he believed it. So Christ began by telling him a parable about two debtors, the nub of which was that a debtor who has been forgiven a debt by his creditor will love his creditor for it; and the bigger the debt forgiven, the greater will be the love. As a story the parable was true to life: there was nothing forced or strained about it. Indeed, Simon himself was happy to state the universally recognized principle of behaviour which the story illustrated; which made the application of the parable, when it came, unanswerable. If we may paraphrase that application it ran like this.

'Simon, I'm telling you', said Christ, 'that this woman's many sins have been forgiven. If you ask on what grounds I am claiming that, look at the evidence. This weeping over my feet, this wiping of them with her hair, this kissing and anointing of my feet – what does it all spring from, Simon? Did you not yourself say just now that where a debtor has been freely forgiven a large debt, he will feel immense gratitude and love towards the creditors who forgave him? This woman had certainly piled up an enormous debt. But look at her extreme gratitude and love towards me. Is that not, on your own admission, evidence that she has been forgiven that enormous debt?' Certainly it would be, if Christ were the Great Creditor who had authority to forgive human sin. A gasp of astonishment went round the room as the other guests suddenly saw the implication of what Christ was saying and tried to comprehend it: 'Who is this that even forgives sins?' (7:49).

Meanwhile, Simon had his own problem to wrestle with. His own treatment of Christ, as Christ had reminded him (see 7:44), had scarcely risen to the normal courtesies of a host towards a guest. If gratitude and affection to Christ were the evidence that one's sins had been forgiven, what did Simon's ingratitude reveal about Simon?

But to recur to the woman. Luke could scarcely have chosen a more appropriate example to place at this point in his narrative. Forgiveness is that aspect of salvation that most of all raises the question of its validity. Is it more than a condoning of sin? And of all the types of sinner who call for forgiveness, is not a woman of this kind one whose repentance people are most likely to doubt, whose return to her former ways people most readily expect, and whose conversion they are most likely to regard as bogus? Her kissing and anointing of our Lord's feet, her wiping of his feet with her hair, could it not be merely fleeting emotionalism? Or worse?

But let Luke tell his full story. 'And it came to pass soon afterwards', he says (8:1), that as Christ went on his preaching tours through villages and towns up and down the country, there followed him certain women who spent their time, money and energy looking after Christ and his band of apostles (8:1–3). Socially they were a very mixed group, and one of them, at least, came from the privileged classes. But what they all had in common was gratitude to Christ for having saved them from evil spirits and diseases. Not content to let their gratitude spend itself in mere emotionalism, they had voluntarily undertaken this tiresome, unromantic work at their own expense.

Together then the two stories of movement 3 have made their common point: though salvation is, and must be, not by works, but by grace through faith, none the less where it is genuinely experienced, it will lead to love and gratitude to the Saviour, and love and gratitude will in turn lead to devotion and practical good works. Not that all professions of salvation are genuine, of course – but it is the function of the next movement to tell us about that.

4. The mysteries of the kingdom relating to salvation (8:4–21)

In movement 3 we were offered evidence that the salvation preached by Christ is genuine and effective. To many people, however, the whole question of salvation, its reception and out-working is a baffling mystery. They understand the importance of morality, and exhortations to lead a better life make good sense to them. It also seems reasonable to them to hope that if we do our best, in spite of our weaknesses and temptations, God will in the end be merciful in his verdict on us. But the idea that a person can in this present life hear the Word of God, believe and be saved (see 8:12) makes little sense to them. A mystery in itself, it is also the one idea above all others that Satan will do his utmost to prevent from taking root in their hearts (see 8:12). And when the matter is further complicated by the self-evident fact that many professions of salvation are very dubious or even false, they are inclined to dismiss the whole thing as incomprehensible if not a delusion.

According to Christ in the passage now before us (see 8:10) this difficulty in understanding salvation is to be expected. God's way of salvation, that is, his way of establishing his kingdom, is admittedly a mystery; though the word 'mystery' has a somewhat different meaning on the lips of Christ from what it has in our normal modern parlance. He means that God's way of salvation is a plan devised by God which no-one would ever have known anything about if God had not revealed it. He has of course revealed it through his Word and finally and fully through Christ and his apostles (see Eph. 3:1–13). It is therefore an open secret. And yet for all that it is an open secret, people will never understand it unless Christ reveals it to them through speaking the living word of God into their hearts.

That does not mean that certain people are automatically and forever excluded from the possibility of understanding salvation, witness what happened when Christ spoke the parable of the sower. This parable was explaining the processes and reactions which are set in motion when the word of God is preached with all its living power to produce faith and with faith salvation and the understanding of salvation. The disciples no more understood the meaning of the parable when they first heard it, than the rest of the people. But they had the sense to come and ask Christ for further

140

illumination (see 8:9), and he, of course, gave them their request. And so it is with all matters relating to salvation. If the offer of salvation itself seems at first to the hearer to be wrapped up in obscure language, difficult to make sense of, the hearer can always apply in prayer to Christ for the necessary illumination. And it will be granted.

But now to the parables that were spoken on this occasion, that of the sower, the lamp and the family.

The parable of the sower (see 8:4–15) declares that there are four different responses among people to the offer of salvation presented by the preaching of the Word of God. One is the immediate thwarting of any effect at all by Satan himself (see 8:12). The second is that while the word is superficially received, it is never allowed to take root; and when temptation comes, it exposes the reception as having been shallow and rootless. The third is that the word is listened to with some seriousness; but before the resolve to receive it and obey it can be acted upon, it is choked by the cares or the riches and pleasures of this life, and comes to nothing.

None of these reactions is any good. The only response that is of any use is when people in an honest and good heart, having heard the word, hold it fast and bring forth fruit with endurance (see 8:15). The Word of God is a living thing like seed. Where it is given the opportunity, it will show its living power by producing fruit. If no permanent fruit is produced, then one may question whether the word of God was truly received, just as Simon's complete lack of love and gratitude towards Christ showed that he had never received forgiveness and salvation. Nor is a temporary outburst of joy and enthusiasm valid evidence that the word has been received. There must be a patient continuing, a bringing of fruit to full growth (see 8:13–14).

Similarly, the parable of the lamp (see 8:16–18) is directed to warning us to 'take heed how we hear' (8:18), that is to be careful what we do with what we hear. There are people who if they could be brought to confess where they stand, would profess to have received the gospel. And yet they never speak to anybody about it, not even to their friends or children. But that is very strange behaviour. The gospel by its very nature is light. No-one would ever light a lamp and then put it under a pot or under a bed; he would put it where it could give its light and be seen. It is impossible anyway permanently to hide where one stands in relation to the gospel. What is hidden will come out sooner or later – that is, it will if it is really there. The danger is, as 8:18 points out, that the man who thinks he has received the gospel, and keeps it hidden and never lets the fact be known, may find one of these days, when he comes to look for the reality of the gospel within him, that it is not in fact there – and never was.

Finally, the parable of the family (8:19–21) presses home the same point: if we claim to have a living relationship with Jesus Christ, then the evidence that we do in fact have that relationship will be found not simply in our claiming to have it, but in our hearing, obeying and doing of the word of God. If the hearing, obeying and doing are lacking, the existence of the relationship is brought seriously into question.

5. Salvation from the physical elements (8:22–25)

The table of contents for this stage (pp.130–131) suggests that we shall be doing what Luke intended us to do, if as we think over the contents of movements 5–8 we hold in our minds the events and lessons of movements 1–4.

At 7:11–17 we were told of the widow of Nain's son who was on the very point of being buried when Christ intervened, and bade him get up. So the young man was saved just, as we might think, in the nick of time. At 8:22–25 the position seems to go into reverse. Christ was asleep in a boat when there came a violent storm. The boat was filling with water and in imminent danger of going down to the bottom with all its passengers, but Christ slept on, apparently unaware of the danger. The disciples in alarm roused him: 'Master, Master, we are perishing.' At that he got up and rebuked the wind and waves and there was a great calm. Then he rebuked his disciples: 'Where is your faith?', he asked.

At first sight the rebuke might seem harsh. Their fear was so natural, and it did look as if they were going down any minute, and that Christ was unaware of it. Had Christ been awake and clearly conscious of what was going on, and still had done nothing about it, that might have been different.

But though their fear was natural, the more we think about it, the less excuse there is for their lack of faith. The Gentile centurion (see 7:2–17) had perceived that Jesus had powers of command over the forces of life and death. The disciples had been present when Jesus had rescued the widow's son from the very jaws of the grave;

and the people of Nain had had enough perception to see that this was a divine intervention (see 7:16) and that Jesus was, to go no further, a great prophet raised up by God. Had the disciples not listened to the conversation between Jesus and John's messengers, and heard his renewed affirmation, on the strength of his many miracles, that he was the 'One that should come', the Messiah come at last after centuries of prophecy and preparation to accomplish the purposes of God for the deliverance and redemption of Israel and of the Gentiles?

Granted then that the disciples' fear was natural and instinctive; but where was their logic? If Jesus was what even at this early stage in their experience they believed him to be, logic should have told them that the divine plan for the redemption of mankind was not about to founder because a sudden storm had caught the long-promised Messiah asleep and he had inadvertently perished. But fear is a powerful demolisher of logic, and in any case they were still learners: they believed John and they believed Jesus and accepted his miraculous demonstrations of his Messiah-hood; yet it still surprised them to find he was Lord of the physical elements (see 8:25).

There is less excuse for our lapses of faith and logic, if at one extreme we confess Jesus as God incarnate and then dismiss this present story contemptuously as a mere 'nature-miracle', or if at the other extreme, we confess Jesus as Lord of the universe and then fear that he has forgotten about us and our circumstances.

We live in a universe that is lethally hostile to human life: only the miracle of creation and divine maintenance preserves our planet and its wonderful adaptations and provisions for the propagation of human life. Within our earth itself wind, wave, lightning, storm, flood, drought, avalanche, earthquake, fire, heat, cold, germ, virus, epidemic, all from time to time threaten and destroy life. Sooner or later one of them may destroy us. The story of the stilling of the storm is not, of course, meant to tell us that Christ will never allow any believer to perish by drowning, or by any other natural disaster. Many believers have so perished. It does demonstrate that he is Lord of the physical forces in the universe, that for him nothing happens by accident, and that no force in all creation can destroy his plan for our eternal salvation or separate us from the love of God which is in Christ Jesus our Lord (see Rom. 8:38–39).

6. Salvation from spirit powers, and rejection of the Saviour (8:26–39)

Movement 5 depicted salvation from the physical forces of nature. But physical forces are not the only powers in the universe that are potentially hostile to man. There are spirit powers that seek man's destruction: seducing spirits as Scripture calls them (see 1 Tim. 4:1–2) and Satan himself (see Acts 26:18). The demoniac is an extreme example of what satanic forces can do with a human personality that has come under their complete domination. Unlike the Holy Spirit, who always sets a man free, develops his personality and increases his self-control and dignity, satanic forces seem to strive to overpower a man's personality, and ultimately to break down his self-control, and to rob him, as they did the demoniac, of self-respect. These spirit forces gave the man great power: he had often broken the chains and fetters with which well-meaning friends had bound him (see 8:29). Unfortunately some people are fascinated by spirit-power. Any experience that gives them what appears to be more than human power will automatically commend itself to them as valid and good. And therein lies the deception. Spirit beings can indeed give people amazing power; but in the end those powers will prove destructive of human personality and self-control. So it was with the demoniac. When asked what his name was, he did not reply, John or Thomas, or whatever name it was his parents had given him (see 8:30). Long since he had given up the struggle to be himself, to control his own life. A legion of evil powers controlled him. Morbid and shameless he dwelt among the tombs (see 8:27). Of course the man was an extreme case, but a warning nonetheless of what it will mean for human beings to perish, as they will unless they are set free from the power of sin and Satan by Christ (see Eph. 2:2; Col. 1:13).

Movement 6, then, is the story of how Christ delivered the man's personality from the domination of evil spirits, and restored his freedom and self-control. But it is more. Had it been only that, the story could have concluded at 8:33, but Luke spends another four verses (see 8:34–39) describing the response of the local townspeople to Christ's deliverance of the demoniac. A solemn story it is too. When Christ first approached the demoniac, the man had pleaded to be left alone. Christ overruled him. The man was not a free agent; acting under *force majeure* he was but voicing the will of his demonic masters. Christ disregarded the request for he was concerned to give the man his freedom, and to bring him to the point where any request he would make would be the expression of his own free will. But when the townspeople asked Christ to depart, he granted their request at once and departed (see 8:37). Their request was the expression of their own free choice made with their eyes open and in full view of all the evidence; and Christ respected their choice. He will never remove a man's free will, not even in order to save him.

Even so Luke has not finished with his story, but spends another two verses (see 8:38–39) telling us that as Christ was leaving, the demoniac, now set free, asked Jesus to be allowed to accompany him. His request was refused; for what reasons we shall see presently.

Now if we think back to 7:18–35 we shall recall that that passage described the rejection of Christ by a group of people, as does the present passage. The 'men of this generation' (7:31) had gone out into the desert to see this startling phenomenon that was John the Baptist, originally under the impression that he was the forerunner of the Messiah. Eventually they repudiated him and his preaching, claiming that his ascetic habits showed that he had a demon. It was a highly doubtful accusation; but it is understandable that no one would want a man with a demon about the place.

Against that, put the case of the demoniac of our passage. There was no doubt about his demon-possession. Some of the local townspeople had at times tried to bind him with chains and to restrain his self-destructive and anti-social behaviour. Yet when Christ not simply restrained the man, but expelled the demons and saved him completely, they did not like it. They who had helped the man before, now asked his Saviour to depart.

Why? They were afraid, says Luke. Twice over he tells us so (see 8:35, 37). Strange. Luke does not say that they were afraid of the man when he roamed the cemetery naked. Perhaps they were, perhaps they weren't. But whether they were or not, was it not strange that they should be afraid now that they saw the man sitting clothed and in his right mind? What had they to be afraid of? One can only conclude that they were afraid of Christ, afraid of his supernatural, and to them mysterious, power to cast out demons. They could not understand the change that had come over the man.

To them the power that had brought it about was frightening. But what a sad comment on man's fallen and unregenerate state it is, that man should feel more at home with demons, than with the Christ who has power to cast out demons.

Yet it is often so. Men who would try to help a criminal or a drunkard, or, if they should prove incorrigible, would want the one imprisoned and the other put into hospital, find it embarrassing and somewhat frightening if the criminal or drunkard is saved by Christ and turned into a sane, wholesome, regenerate, disciple. They do not understand how the change has been effected. They may be pleased for the man's sake that his condition has improved; but they want nothing to do with the One who has made the improvement: they do not intend themselves to become his disciples.

There was also another reason, of course, for the people's fear. Luke stresses the fact that the herdsmen who had witnessed what had happened to the herd of pigs told the people of the district 'how the demoniac was saved' (8:31–36). The story of the pigs is a strange one in our ears. The demons asked that if they must be expelled from the man, they might be permitted to enter the swine; but when the swine ran into the lake and were drowned, the demons presumably lost their temporary embodiment once more. Christ had surely anticipated what would happen, and had deliberately allowed it. The destruction of the pigs would vividly demonstrate what must have been the even greater eventual destruction of the man, had the demons been left in control. In a sense the pigs had acted as the man's substitute. Had the man himself been drowned in the lake, that also would have got rid of the demons from him; but it would have got rid of the man himself as well. So the pigs died and were buried in the sea; the man himself walked free. But that faced the people of the district with a big and a frightening choice: they were gripped with a tremendous fear, says Luke (see 8:37). Some of them, as we have noticed, had been willing to help the man when it was a matter of chaining him up; but if a man's deliverance from demons was going to cost a whole herd of pigs, that was a different matter altogether. A herd of pigs represented an enormous amount of food and money! They decided they must ask Christ to depart before, perhaps, he started saving any further demoniacs.

Christ granted their request; but when the saved demoniac asked to be allowed to accompany Christ, Christ refused him. Freedom for this man would not mean pleasing himself, even though his pleasure was to be with Christ, where doubtless he felt safest. Freedom was in freely obeying the commands of the One sitting at whose feet he had found peace and sanity. So the man was sent back to his home and town as a witness, and a very enthusiastic witness he proved to be (see 8:39). If ever 'wisdom was justified by her children' (7:35), it was in the case of this man whom incarnate wisdom had restored to soundness of mind. Perhaps in the months that followed, as the people of the countryside observed him and heard his story of what Christ had done, they lost their fear of Christ, as John the Baptist lost his doubts when his disciples reported to him the wonderful things that Christ had performed (see 7:21–23).

7. Salvation from the waste of life's vital forces (8:40–48)

'When Jesus returned the crowd welcomed him, for they were all expecting him' says Luke (8:40), using a word for expecting (*prosdokaō*) which he had earlier used in John the Baptist's question 'or do we *look for* another' (7:20). What expectations filled the minds of the crowd! A certain Jairus, in particular, was eagerly awaiting the Lord's return. His only daughter lay dying, and it was doubtless with some impatience that he was waiting for Christ to come back so that he could ask him to come to his house to save his daughter (see 8:41). As soon then as Christ arrived he came and put his request, and Christ began to go with him to his house. But as he went, Luke explains, the crowds thronged him (see 8:42) and Christ was held up and could make no progress. Then a woman came for healing (see 8:43) and that detained Christ still further. It must have been torture for Jairus.

At this point, if we are used to reading the Gospel stories each one separately as virtually independent units, we shall see no problem in what we are now being told. If, on the other hand, we have managed to remember what Luke so very deliberately told us in the story of the centurion, a question may well arise and it will run like this: What did it matter if the Lord was held up and could not make his way to Jairus' house? Was it not the central point of the centurion's story that Christ had the ability to save at a distance, and did in fact save the centurion's slave from dying without having to go to the centurion's house? Why then did Christ not put Jairus out of his agony of waiting by simply speaking the word and saving Jairus' daughter from dying without waiting to get to Jairus' house? Has Luke himself so far forgotten what he took such pains to tell us about the centurion that he does not realize that this present story must raise a question in the mind of anyone who has taken the earlier story seriously? Luke, of course, does not answer the question here; and when he finally gets round to finishing Jairus' story, some of the further details he gives will but only add to the mystery.

Meanwhile he follows the interruption in the proceedings brought about by a woman who tried to obtain healing simply by touching the border of Christ's garment. Luke presents her case as another example of 'salvation' (8:48) and since his examples so far have illustrated different aspects of salvation, we might well begin by asking what aspect of salvation is presented here. Like the demoniac's this woman's case was chronic (see 8:27–29 and 43); but her case quite clearly had nothing to do with demons. It was a physical weakness, probably a uterine haemorrhage. It was sapping her vital physical forces, and also apparently draining away her monetary resources (see 8:43): she had spent all her living in a vain attempt to find a cure.[1] It is part of the weakness and brokenness which we humans inherit as a result of the Fall that in addition to straightforwardly physical mechanisms, various psychosomatic processes can also sometimes go wrong, with similar results. Fear is a notable example. Designed to promote or protect life, it can run out of control, and waste the body's energies all to no purpose.

Be that as it may, the chief interest in the story lies once more in how the sufferer was healed: over and over again we are told about her touching Christ. Four out of the story's six verses are spent on telling us how the woman tried to gain healing by touching the edge of Christ's garment without being observed; but this proved impossible because Christ perceived that someone had touched him, and insisted on knowing who it was that had touched him; at which point the disciples protested that with the crush of people round him, it was silly to ask who had touched him; but Christ insisted that someone had touched him and would not be content

---

[1]The phrase at 8:43 'having spent all her living on doctors' is absent from many manuscripts (though a similar phrase is present in Mk. 5:26) and for that reason it is omitted from some translations. According to Marshall, p.344, no clear-cut decision is possible either for or against omission.

until the woman came forward and in front of all the people confessed why she had touched him. If after all this we have not realized that Luke wants us to take seriously Christ's ability to perceive someone's touch we have just not been paying attention to what Luke is saying. Moreover we cannot help recalling that the story of the woman in Simon's house (see 7:36–50) was very concerned about a woman's touching Christ. The crucial question for Simon was whether or not Christ could perceive the character of the woman who was touching him. Simon initially decided that Christ could not, for if he had been able, he would not, in Simon's judgment, have allowed the woman to touch him at all. We must, therefore, examine these twin matters of touching and our Lord's powers of perception in these two stories.

We notice to start with that the trouble with both women was related to their sex: with the first it was a moral weakness, with the second it was physical. In Jewish thinking the touch of both women would have brought defilement: this was what Simon felt about the woman in his house, and what Leviticus 15:19–27 declared about the woman with bleeding. She herself was unclean (see Lv. 15:25) and therefore whoever touched her became unclean. It meant that both women would have known the hurt and alien- ation of being regarded unfit to have contact with clean and decent people. For both women salvation removed the alienation by removing its cause and reintroduced them into healthy society. Perhaps one reason why the woman with bleeding tried to be healed without anyone knowing was not only natural modesty, but also fear of the people: religious people in the crowd could have been angry with her for mingling with them and thus infecting them with her uncleanness. If so, not the least benefit of her healing was that from then on she could mix freely with people without the hidden fear of her weakness being detected. At the moral level forgiveness did the same for the woman in Simon's house: Christ's public validation of the genuineness of her salvation made it pos- sible for her to feel accepted in decent society without the fear of her past being constantly brought up against her. Salvation meant reintegration.

In the second place we notice that though both stories raise the question of Christ's powers of perception, the point at issue is different on each occasion. In the first story the question is whether Christ can perceive the character of the woman who is touching him; in the second whether he can perceive the fact that someone has touched him. Strict moralist that Simon was, he would have been aware of people's tendency to put on false fronts and poses to hide their real characters; and although his attitude was one which could easily degenerate into hard, unloving, suspicion and lack of trust, his concern to protect decent people from the deceptions of undesirable characters was surely in itself sound and realistic. According to him a prophet should be more than naturally shrewd at penetrating disguises and seeing through people (see 1 Ki. 14:2–6); and he concluded that Christ could not read the woman's true character and therefore was no true prophet and was being taken in. The event as we know proved Simon wrong. Simon had kept his thoughts to himself (see 7:39), but Christ read his thoughts without being told them (see 7:40). Moreover he showed himself fully aware of the kind of person the woman had been. He interpreted her 'touching' of him very differently from Simon; but he also provided Simon with an undeniable argument that his interpretation was correct.

The need for correctly interpreting the evidence in such cases remains a constant practical problem. People like this woman, and criminals of various kinds, are notorious for making false professions of salvation and trading on the gullibility of the Christian community. Where that community is taken in, moreover, a scandal can arise against the gospel and against the whole concept of conversion and salvation. On the other hand, when people of this kind are genuinely converted, it can gravely damage their spiritual progress if the Christian community is unduly suspicious and refuses to trust and accept them. It certainly requires more than human wisdom to interpret correctly the evidence presented by such professed converts.

In the case of the second woman the crucial question was Christ's ability to perceive not merely something about the woman but also something about himself. He knew, so he said, that someone had touched him in a more than casual or superficial way, because he perceived that power had gone out from him (see 8:46). This tells us the supremely important fact that the power that saves us is not an impersonal power. True, the power of Christ was transmitted to the woman when she touched not him but merely the border of his garment. She was healed because hers was genuine faith and not mere superstition (see 8:48); but she found out what genuine faith must mean: we cannot be saved by the power of Christ without having to do with Christ as a person. It is impossible, for the simple reason that we cannot exercise faith in Christ and draw on his power without his knowing; but the impossibility saves us from at least two dangers. It saves faith from degenerating into superstition and regarding Christ (or his garments) like a relic possessed of some magical impersonal power. It also saves faith from being merely a form of selfishness and salvation from being regarded as merely self-improvement. Many a man has first come to Christ simply to get power to overcome some weakness or other like, say, obsessive gambling or alcoholism that is ruining his body and wasting his resources. Christ stands ready to answer every such call for help. But in his mercy he will not have such a person treat his salvation as a cure; he will insist that such a man come to know him as a person, and, like the woman, to confess him publicly as Saviour.

8. Salvation and a 'secret' raising of the dead (8:49–56)

Luke now resumes the story of Jairus and his daughter, and we remember our question: why did not Christ relieve Jairus of his agony of suspense by using his well-advertised power of saving at a distance and by delivering his daughter from dying without waiting to come to his house?

We may surmise that one reason might have been to test and so to strengthen Jairus' faith. When the centurion said to Christ 'Lord don't trouble yourself' (Gk. *mē skullou*) it was an expression of faith (7:6). When someone from Jairus' house told him not to trouble the Teacher any more (Gk. *mēketi skulle*), it was a temptation to give up faith in Christ on the grounds that it was now too late, the situation had gone beyond Christ's ability to do anything about it. Christ countered that temptation and saved Jairus from hoepless sorrow by challenging him to persistence in faith: 'only believe and she shall be saved' (8:50).

Then, of course, there is the simple and obvious fact that if Christ had saved the girl at a distance, the last example of salvation in this series of examples would have been a case of salvation from dying; as it is, it is appropriately enough a case of salvation from death itself. Now the widow of Nain's son was saved from death; but his story, we found, was part of a lesson on the conditions upon which salvation is granted. The lesson of the story of Jairus' daughter is different: the centre-point is that while all the people knew that the girl was dead – and she was really dead – Christ insisted that death for her was only sleep (see 8:52). Taught by Christ believers ever since have regarded the death of the body as a sleep, and through the apostle Paul they have been further taught to believe that the final phase of their salvation will occur when the Lord comes and awakens their dead bodies from the sleep of death (1 Thes. 4:14–17).

In light of this, one would have to be impervious to every drop of imagination not to treat the story of the raising of Jairus' daughter as the Fourth Gospel treats the raising of Lazarus (see ch. 11). In that case also Christ refused to heal Lazarus at a distance or to go to Bethany in time to save Lazarus from dying. He first stayed away until Lazarus 'fell asleep' (11:11), then came to Bethany to wake him out of sleep (11:11), and finally made his raising from the dead a foreshadowing of the great resurrection of the dead at the second coming (11:24–27).

If there is any truth in the suggestion that the raising of Jairus' daughter was intended as a prefiguration of the resurrection at the Lord's coming, it might also help to explain the other problem that besets this story: Christ's insistence on secrecy. No-one was allowed into the house except three disciples and the parents (see 8:51); and after the girl was brought back from the dead, the parents were commanded not to tell anyone what had happened (see 8:56). How, we wonder, could the matter possibly be kept secret? All the people outside knew she was dead. The professional mourners had been hired for the funeral and were already busy weeping and wailing. Were they not to be told that their services were no longer required, and why? And even if they were not told, they would soon see the girl alive once more, and the news would spread like wildfire. If it was to be a secret, it would be an open secret.

But then that is what a 'mystery' in the New Testament sense of the word is. And a mystery is what certain details of the resurrection at the coming of Christ are said to be (see 1 Cor. 15:51). If in movement 4 Christ explains one mystery of the kingdom which he had communicated by means of a parable (see 8:10–15), it is not perhaps altogether unthinkable that in movement 8 he is illustrating another great mystery by means of a miracle.

Christ and the goal of redemption

Preliminary survey

The movements

1 The setting up of the kingdom viewed from our world
   (9:1–27)
2 The setting up of the kingdom viewed from the other world
   (9:28–50)

Stage 5

Christ and the goal of redemption

Preliminary survey

We now enter stage 5 and our first task is to decide its extent. The task is easy, since 9:51 is the pivotal verse in the thought-flow of the whole Gospel. Though little more than a third of the way through the book, it announces that the time for Christ to be taken up into heaven is now approaching, and Christ accordingly sets himself resolutely to go to Jerusalem. From this point onwards the narrative will become a record of our Lord's journey from earth to heaven, which is why we have labelled all that follows 9:50 'The Going'. But if 'The Going' starts at 9:51, we are left with a mere fifty verses (9:1–50) to form the last stage of 'The Coming'.

At first sight this is a little surprising. We might reasonably have expected that as the last stage of 'The Coming' stage 5 would have functioned as an obvious and powerful climax to all that has gone before. Perhaps it does, for importance and power do not necessarily depend on length. Even so, with only fifty verses stage 5 is the briefest stage of 'The Coming'. Why so brief?

Whatever the reason, the brevity is at least deliberate. Comparison of this part of the Gospel with its counterparts in Matthew and Mark reveals that while Luke has chosen to put very little in this stage which Matthew and Mark do not have, he has chosen to leave out large amounts of what they do have. After his brief mention of Herod at 9:7–9 he has no account of the birthday dance that led to John the Baptist's execution as Matthew (see 14:1–12) and Mark (see 6:14–29) have. All three have the feeding of the five thousand and the confession of Jesus as God's Messiah. Between these two stories, however, Matthew (see 14:22 – 16:12) records the walking on the sea, the return to Gennesaret, the controversy over washing of hands, the Syrophoenician woman, healings and the feeding of the four thousand, the demand for a sign, and the warning against the leaven of the Pharisees. Mark in this position (see 6:45 – 8:26) has this same long list of stories and a few more of his own. Luke has none of them: in his narrative the feeding of the five thousand (see 9:10–17) is followed immediately by the confession of Jesus as God's Messiah (see 9:18–27).

Luke's brevity, therefore, was not it seems forced upon him by any lack of source material. We can say, if we wish, that it came about because he wanted to include in the second part of his Gospel a large amount of interesting material which Matthew and Mark do not record (which is perfectly true); but that he was hard up for space because of the limit imposed on book length by ancient methods of book production (a very doubtful argument, since he could have written a many-volumned work like Thucydides if he had so wished); and that therefore the mechanical necessity of creating room later on for his special material compelled him to omit from chapter 9 most of the stories which Matthew and Mark have included. Whether we find such an explanation sufficient will depend, in part at least, on whether we think that practical necessity is enough by itself to account for the choices and decisions of a writer of Luke's ability – let alone for the mind of the Holy Spirit who inspired him. After all, another – or an additional – reason is possible. It could be that Luke wrote these fifty verses, these and no more, because this particular selection of material said all that he wanted to say at this point in his Gospel, and that he would not have said more even if he had had all the space in the world to say it in.

Whatever the truth of the matter, when we look at the way he has put his selected material together, the marks of very deliberate composition are at once apparent. See the table of contents for stage 5 (p.156).

We notice that the effect of Luke's selection and arrangement of material is that the leading themes of verses 1–27 recur in a kind of mirror-image in verses 28–50. Since the effect is presumably deliberate on Luke's part, our exposition will have to try to see the point and purpose of this arrangement.

Meanwhile one thing is obvious: the most important part of the

Stage 5 of the Coming 9:1–50

1 The setting up of the kingdom viewed from our world 9:1–27

A *The briefing and sending out of the twelve* 9:1–9

a Power and authority over demons given to the twelve 9:1–2.

b Instructions on how to react to being received or not received 9:3–6.

c Herod is perplexed by reports that Jesus is John the Baptist, whom he beheaded, risen from the dead, and wonders who Jesus really is 9:7–9.

B *The feeding of the five thousand* 9:10–17

The disciples are told to feed the multitudes: they protest that they cannot: then Christ feeds them miraculously.

C *The confession of Jesus as God's Messiah* 9:18–27

a Jesus was praying alone 9:18.

b People wrongly identify Jesus as John and Elijah; Peter confesses him as God's Messiah 9:18–20.

c Announcement of Christ's rejection, death and resurrection: exhortation to disciples to take up the cross in light of the coming in glory: promise of a view of the kingdom 9:21–27.

2 The setting up of the kingdom viewed from the other world 9:28–50

C' *The transfiguration of Jesus* 9:28–36

c' View of Christ, Moses and Elijah in glory: discussion of Christ's death, resurrection and ascension to be accomplished at Jerusalem 9:28–32.

b' Peter implies that Moses and Elijah are in the same class as Christ; but the Voice proclaims Jesus as 'My Son, My Chosen' 9:33–35.

a' Jesus is found alone 9:36.

B' *The healing of a father's only son* 9:37–43

The father begs the disciples to cast out the demon, but they cannot: Christ heals the boy miraculously.

A' *Further instruction of the twelve* 9:43–50

c' Disciples are perplexed by Christ's statement that he must be delivered into the hands of men 9:43–45.

b' 'Whoever receives this little child in my name receives me, and whoever receives me receives him who sent me' 9:46–48.

a' John objects to Christ's power over demons being exercised by any but the twelve: he is corrected by Christ 9:49–50.

material lies in the two central paragraphs, 9:18–27 and 9:28–36. These two paragraphs make, each in its own way, three major statements. The first concerns the identity of Jesus. At 9:20 Peter on behalf of all the apostles formally states the conviction to which they have come, that Jesus is God's Messiah. Then at 9:35 the voice from the cloud declares Jesus to be 'My Son, My Chosen One'. The second concerns Christ's imminent rejection, death, and resurrection. 9:22 announces these events in plain straightforward language; 9:31 refers to the same events but in the richly evocative phrase 'his exodus which he must accomplish at Jerusalem'. The third concerns Christ's second coming. At 9:26 Christ openly speaks of the time when the Son of man shall come in his own glory and that of the Father and of the holy angels; while the transfiguration (see 9:28–36) according to one of the participants in that glorious event, was a foreview of the second coming. 'We were not following cunningly devised stories', says Peter, 'when we made known to you the power and *parousia* of our Lord Jesus Christ, but we were eye-witnesses of his majesty . . . when we were with him on the holy mountain' (2 Pet. 1:16–18). The term *parousia* when used in connection with our Lord in the New Testament refers without exception to his second coming.

With this we can already see that stage 5 is in fact going to function as a climax to the first half of the Gospel. There can be no greater climax to anything than the second coming of the Lord; and stage 5 not only presents the first explicit statement in the Gospel that there is going to be a second coming, but it gives us a magnificent foreview of that coming glory.

The movements

1. The setting up of the Kingdom viewed from our world (9:1–27)

Stage 4, we may remember, presented us with many different instances and aspects of salvation. Wonderful as they were, they were all of them instances of the salvation of the individual, and for that very reason stage 4 could not stand as the climax of the first half of the Gospel. The salvation of the individual is infinitely important; but it is not everything. True, the last incident in stage 4 proved to be, for those with eyes to see it, a prototype of the resurrection of those who sleep in Jesus at his coming. But there is a whole disordered world to think of; and nothing less than the universal establishment of the kingdom of God in every corner of the earth could satisfy the hunger of our hopes. Stage 5 is going to talk about that kingdom: how Christ had it proclaimed to all Israel (see 9:2) by his apostles; how he spoke about it himself to the crowds that sought him (see 9:11); and how to a favoured few he gave a foreview of it (see 9:27). Stage 5 will, as we have said, mention nation-wide preaching and explanations and exhortations given to the crowds. But for the most part the lessons of this stage will be given to the close circle of the twelve – on one occasion to only three of them – and sometimes it will be indicated that they were for their ears only (see 9:21, 36, 43–44). Until Christ was actually crucified, God's strategies for the setting up of his kingdom were part of that hidden wisdom (see 9:45 and 1 Cor. 2:7–8), which none of the rulers of this world knew, for if they had known it they would not have crucified the Lord of glory. Movement 1 will relate the processes by which the apostles were prepared to be told explicitly what those strategies must be.

The briefing and sending out of the twelve (9:1–9). The contents and proportions of the narratives of the mission of the twelve are at first sight a little strange. One verse (see 9:1) describes the delegation of the necessary power to the apostles. Four verses (see 9:2–5) describe their briefing. Five verses in all of preparation – and then the whole mission itself is dismissed in one solitary verse: 'And they departed and went through the villages preaching the gospel and healing everywhere' (9:6). No sample sermons are given; no exorcisms or cases of healing are described; no detailed report is made on how well or otherwise they were received in this or that town or village. Obviously Luke has not told us much of what we would like to hear; but he has presumably told us what he thinks we need to hear, and we ought therefore to stay a little while on the detail of it.

We are told that the first part of the apostles' mission was to preach. The content of their preaching was to be the kingdom of God (see 9:2), and their message is further described as gospel, as good news (see 9:6). What they were to announce doubtless included a call to repentance such as John the Baptist had issued; it may also have included some indication of the ethical standards which would be required of members of the kingdom, such as

Christ had spoken of in his sermon on the plain (6:20–49). But primarily their preaching was to announce the good news that the long expected kingdom of God was really coming. For any Jew who knew the glorious descriptions of the age to come given in the Old Testament, the announcement that the kingdom of God was 'at hand', was self-evidently good news. But the reality and nature of that kingdom were further to be demonstrated by the second part of the apostles' mission: they were given supernatural power and authority to set people free from the domination of evil spirit powers, and to heal them physically. Here was not merely exhortation to do better and to fight one's weaknesses: here were what a later writer (Heb. 6:5) was to describe as 'the powers of the age to come' breaking in on the world to heal and to save.

Next (9:3–4) the apostles were told to expect the nation to defray the expenses of their food, lodging, clothes and travel. The nation's King – though as yet they did not recognize him as such – was 'coming to his own' (Jn. 1:11) and he had a right to call on the nation to maintain his messengers. 'His own', as we know, did not receive him; and when that happened and he was officially declared to be an outlaw, he explicitly countermanded the instructions given here (see 22:35–38). But at this stage the apostles were to expect reception and maintenance. Indeed, they were to understand that refusal to receive them was an exceedingly grave matter: wherever it happened, they were, on leaving, to shake off the dust from their feet as a testimony against those who had rejected them. They were given no powers, such as Elijah had once possessed (see 9:54; 2 Ki. 1:9–14), to execute summary judgment upon their rejectors. On the other hand, they were to make it clear to everyone that the kingdom of God whose coming they heralded, was not simply a set of suggestions for an alternative life-style, nor one among several options for the future; it was the kingdom of God: to reject it was to be guilty of rejecting God himself, to stand in danger of eternal perdition.

So the apostles went off on their mission, and while, as we remarked above, we are not given a detailed account of it, we are given a description of its general impact on the nation. It is given, however, in an indirect fashion (see 9:7–9): the impact made on the nation is presented through the eyes of Herod. The impression on the people at large was that they were witnessing a visitation by someone from the world beyond. They speculated that it might be

John the Baptist risen from the dead, or Elijah returned from heaven to inaugurate the age to come (see Mal. 4:5), or one of the ancient prophets resurrected. That in itself is interesting. They no longer felt simply, as they had earlier done, that a great prophet had arisen among them (see 7:16); they now felt that in the person of Jesus this world had been invaded from the world beyond. Their speculations as to the identity of Jesus were admittedly inadequate; but their basic idea was absolutely right. Isaiah, Jeremiah and Ezekiel, for instance, were great prophets; but their births were those of ordinary men, the kingdom of God did not come through them, they were not, so to speak, an invasion from the world beyond. Jesus was.

But, as we have said, Luke asks us to look at the impact on the people not directly but through the eyes of Herod. And that is even more interesting, for the apostles had been heralding the approach of the kingdom, that is, the rule of God, and Herod was one of the rulers of this world – a rather small ruler no doubt, but a ruler nonetheless. What is more, when John the Baptist had called on the people to prepare for the coming of the Messiah, Herod had resented John's moral demands and had silenced him, pretty con-clusively he had thought, first by imprisonment and then by death. If, then, there was any foundation to what the people were saying, Herod was in grave trouble. Prophets of morality could be awk-ward, particularly if they were popular with the masses; but they could all in the end be silenced – if death was the end of everything as far as this world is concerned. If, however, death and the grave were not adequate barriers against John's re-entry, or Elijah's, then Herod and his throne were desperately insecure. Doubtless Herod told himself that the masses were victims of gross superstition; but he was left uneasy, not so much now about particular questions of morality – that was a second-order matter – but about the person of Jesus. Who exactly was he? Was he just one more prophet or holy man? Or was he really some kind of invasion from the world beyond? And he sought to see Jesus (see 9:9). If that, then, was the impact of the apostles' preaching and ministry in the days before the resurrection of Christ, it goes without saying that it should be the effect of our preaching also since Pentecost. We are failing in our main task if we give people the impression that the kingdom of God is solely concerned with the regulation of morality in this present age, and do not bring them to see that the crucial question is who Jesus is, and whether he is one day to invade our world again when he comes in his glory and in that of the Father and of the holy angels (see 9:26).

The feeding of the five thousand (9:10–17). There follows now the story of the feeding of the five thousand, and to understand the point of it, we must pay attention to its context and to its position in the thought-flow of the whole stage. The miracle was doubtless a lesson to the people; but it was even more so to the apostles. We see this first from the internal proportions of the story, and then also from the fact that the apostles' inadequacy which is exposed and corrected in this story is re-echoed and emphasized in the story of that other miracle (see 9:37–42) which stands opposite this one in Luke's carefully arranged scheme (see the table of contents p.156).

It happened, says Luke, when the apostles returned from their mission and reported what they had accomplished (see 9:10). Christ withdrew with them to Bethsaida; but the crowds, finding out where they had gone, followed them. Understandably: the preaching and ministry of the apostles all round the nation would have raised in them expectations and wistful hopes that the ancient prophecies of a coming age of universal peace and sorrowless paradise might after all be true and on the point of fulfilment. And Christ who knew the hunger of the human heart for release from the frustrations and disappointments and pain of life in this present age, did not rebuke the crowd for intruding on his privacy; he welcomed them and spoke to them of the kingdom of God and healed those who had need of healing (see 9:11). That would have fed their hopes still further.

But presently the apostles intervened to point out to Christ (as if he had not realized it) that the hour was getting late, that there were no shops or lodging houses in the remote area where they were, and that he had better send the crowd away to find food and lodging in the nearest villages. Perhaps this unintended impertinence in taking the initiative and telling Christ what to do was the result of a sense of power and authority induced in them by the success of their recent mission. But what happened next shows how inadequate their ideas were even yet about the Person and powers of Christ, and the nature of the coming kingdom which they had been heralding round the country. Christ had no intention of sending the people away. He was going to give them a foreshadowing of what the kingdom of God, fully come, would mean. Isaiah in his poetic way had promised (see 25:6–9) that one day God would spread a banquet for all the nations of the world, a feast of rich food, vintage wines, succulent satisfying dishes and the finest of beverages. One element in that divinely satisfying banquet would be the banishing of death for ever and the wiping away of every tear. The time for the spreading of that actual banquet had, of course, not yet come; but Christ was going to give the crowds and the apostles a vivid foretaste of it and a demonstration of the powers that would eventually bring it about. It would involve a miracle of course, and a miracle on a grand scale: nothing less than a miracle of that order could prefigure the great banquet-to-be. But first Christ did an interesting thing: he told his apostles to feed the crowds themselves. Now the apostles had never seen a miracle on this scale before. They had witnessed the healing of individuals; indeed, they had themselves been allowed in their recent mission to use supernatural power to expel demons and to heal. But to feed this tremendous mass of people, numbering some five thousand males let alone women and children, was altogether a different proposition. Even so their response was not all that intelligent. Christ was not in the habit of talking practical nonsense, nor was he mocking their feeble powers. If he told them to feed the crowd, it ought at least to have startled them into thinking that there might be more to the kingdom of God and the powers of Jesus than they had yet realized. Instead of that, the highest their thoughts could rise to was the possibility of going to the nearest merchants (wholesalers, of course) and of buying the necessary quantity of food; otherwise, they remarked, they had only five loaves and two fish.

But the pitiful inadequacy of their resources and the utter impossibility of the situation as long as their ideas were limited to the ordinary natural processes of life in this world provided the contrasting background against which Christ could vividly demonstrate what will be involved in the coming of the kingdom. Looking up into heaven (see 9:16) he brought the powers of heaven irrupting once more into this world and transformed its meagre resources into more than enough to feed the multitudes. The lesson is still needed. We rightly stress the moral laws of the kingdom of God, and strive to see them applied even now to the world's social and economic problems. But we should beware of allowing that present concern to limit our ideas of what the kingdom of God will one day involve. The kingdom of God, fully come, will not mean simply the carrying on of present activities in a more caring, more just, more efficient way. It will be nothing less than the invasion of our world by the powers of the world beyond, releasing nature from her groanings and frustrations, and transforming creation from a system of inevitable decay into a world of freedom, satisfaction and perfect fulfilment, with death destroyed and sorrow gone.

The confession of Jesus as God's Messiah (9:18–27). We have reached the climax of the first movement. As we have noticed, Luke does not tell us that between the feeding of the five thousand and the confession of Jesus as God's Messiah a considerable time and a number of events intervened. He does not deny it, of course. But when in Luke's narrative we hear the Lord ask the apostles: 'Who do the crowds say I am?' and the apostles reply 'John the Baptist, or Elijah, or one of the old prophets risen again', it is impossible for us to forget that we have heard all these suggestions before, a mere ten verses earlier. Why the repetition? Why, having left out so much material, could Luke not have omitted Christ's first question as well, and have proceeded to the second which after all is the heart of the matter: 'Who do you say that I am?'

We can judge only by the effects of the repetition. Whatever else it does, it emphasizes the simple but important fact that when the apostles confessed Jesus as God's Messiah, they did so in full knowledge of all the other suggestions and conjectures that were being made. When they confessed him as Messiah, therefore, it was not because they had been impressed by the supernatural element in his ministry, and could not think of any other, and less extreme, way of accounting for it. The people's suggestions all implied something supernatural about Jesus and his ministry; and Jesus took the trouble to get his apostles to review all these suggestions before they finally and formally expressed their own conviction. Their confession thus stands in deliberate contrast to, and contradiction of, all the other suggestions. It says that those other suggestions, however exalted, are inadequate to express who Jesus is: he is nothing less than the incomparable and unique Messiah of God. With this formal, considered, collective, explicit confession on the part of the apostles we have reached not only a climax in stage 5 of Luke's Gospel, but also a turning point in the history of the world.

But the apostles had no sooner been brought to realize fully that Jesus was the Messiah, than Jesus proceeded to announce the sequence of events that should lead to the setting up of the kingdom. We cannot know exactly what ideas the apostles themselves may already have had on this matter; but we learn from their later remarks and behaviour that the last thing they would have been expecting was that the Messiah would be rejected by the nation and crucified. They were therefore told at once. To have allowed them to go on for some months under the impression that he was expecting the present interest and enthusiasm of the crowds to grow into a national acceptance of him as the Messiah, only to discover later that the nation would do the very opposite, would have given them grounds for supposing that he had misread the situation and that his hopes and plans for setting up the kingdom were liable to be proved wrong. Now, therefore, when his popularity with the masses was at its height, and the apostles' faith and insight into his true identity had reached their acme, he at once gave them to understand clearly that he knew he was going to be rejected.

Next we should notice exactly by whom he said he was going to be rejected. It is not strictly true to say as we did a moment ago that he predicted that the nation would reject him. It was the religious leaders, he said, that would repudiate his claims and have him crucified. With the people he was very popular as we have just seen, and he remained so according to Luke (see 19:47–48; 20:1, 45; 21:37–38; 22:2–6) right up until the final week. Only at the last minute were the religious leaders able to bring the crowds over to their side to shout for his crucifixion. One might have thought, therefore, that the obvious thing to do at this stage was to get his apostles to mount a nation-wide campaign to inform the people that Jesus was the Messiah and then to use massive popular support to overwhelm the opposition of the religious leaders. Our Lord did the very opposite: he forbade his apostles to tell anyone that he was the Messiah (see 9:21).[1] One reason for this prohibition was doubtless what many have suggested: the people's ideas of what the

---

[1]This prohibition seems not to have been either absolute or permanently in force even before the resurrection. When the blind man (18:38) called on him as the Son of David, Jesus did not tell him never to say it again. When at the triumphal entry (19:38–40) the crowds hailed him as 'the King that comes in the name of the Lord', he refused the Pharisees' demand to have them silenced. And he himself from time to time continued to refer to himself publicly in terms that to the perceptive at least implied that he was the Messiah, *e.g.* 'a greater than Solomon' (11:31).

Messiah would be and do were so inadequate, not to say perverted, and mixed up with contemporary politics, that to have announced nation-wide that Jesus was the Messiah could well have started a highly undesirable political movement and have created masses of enthusiastic but unregenerate followers, quite unprepared to take up their cross daily in order to follow Christ, more likely in fact to take up the sword to fight for what they imagined to be his rights. The explanation which Christ gave for the prohibition, however, was that he must be rejected and killed: not simply would be, but must be. The 'must be' was doubtless dictated by the divine strategy for the setting up of the kingdom. It meant that any attempt at avoiding or opposing this rejection and death would be not only useless, but contrary to the divine will. In announcing the necessity, however, Christ did not stay to explain the reasons behind it; he simply stated it and moved on to the remaining steps in the process of setting up the kingdom. His death would be followed by his resurrection. That would certainly vindicate his claim; but he indicated (see 9:23–26) that his resurrection would not forthwith put an end to all opposition and there and then establish the kingdom of God. Far from it. Anyone who was thinking of following him was warned that it would mean, even after the resurrection, denying himself and taking up his cross daily, bearing the same hostility from the world that Christ bore, and sharing the shame and reproach of being a follower of a Christ who had been crucified. Indeed a would-be disciple, far from reigning with a triumphant Christ over a subdued world (see 1 Cor. 4:18), would have to be prepared to lose his very life for Christ's sake.

Nor did Christ hold out any hope that if his disciples were prepared to endure such suffering for a while, the opposition would eventually be won over and the world gradually converted, so that little by little the kingdom of God would be established on earth. The kingdom of God, in the sense in which he was talking of it, would be established only by Christ's personal coming again in his own glory and in the glory of the Father and of the holy angels (see 9:23–26). Then, and only then, would the time come for the reward of those who had suffered for his sake; and then those who had denied him in his absence would discover the eternal loss incurred by that denial.

If the apostles' confession of Jesus as God's Messiah was a high-point and climax in their experience of Jesus, this announcement must have seemed a fearful anti-climax and must have filled them with dismay. If the kingdom was not to be established on earth until the second coming, then before them lay a bleak prospect of cross-bearing and suffering without much likelihood that they would ever see the kingdom. They might well be dead before it arrived. How then would they find the faith to go on believing in and hoping for the coming of a kingdom that they were never likely to see?

Christ saw the problem and the need to strengthen the faith of his apostles, and through them the faith of subsequent generations of believers (see 2 Pet. 1:12–21), both in the reality of that kingdom and in the certainty of its coming. 'But I tell you' he added (9:27) 'there are some among those standing here, who will certainly not experience death before they see the kingdom of God'. He was, of course, referring to what three of the disciples were to see, a few days later, the transfiguration on the mountain.[1]

2. The setting up of the kingdom viewed from the other world (9:28–50)

It is no accident that the material in the second half of this stage presents a kind of mirror image of the material in the first half. Take, for instance, the paragraph we have just considered (see 9:18–27) and the paragraph which now follows (see 9:28–36). In one sense both of them, as we have already noticed (p.157), deal with exactly the same things: the identity of Jesus compared with Moses and Elijah, his death, resurrection and second coming. The difference is that these two paragraphs look at these things from two completely different points of view: the first from the point of view of men in this world, the second from the viewpoint of persons in the other world. In 9:18–27 the identity of Jesus is

---

[1] Some find it difficult, if not impossible, to think that this promise referred to the transfiguration. In particular they feel that the expression 'they will certainly not experience death before they see . . .' would be very odd if it referred to seeing something within the next few days. This difficulty is real enough, if one thinks of the kingdom of God only as something that is destined to come on earth in the future. But, as we are about to suggest, the kindgom of God will not begin to exist only when it comes on earth. It already exists in the other world. Indeed, Moses and Elijah were already 'seeing the kingdom of God' as Christ stood talking to his disciples before ascending the mountain. But, of course, before that kingdom comes in open manifestation on earth, the normal way for a human being to see it would be to die, like Moses, or to be translated, like Elijah. To be allowed to see it without and before dying was something extraordinary. At the same time to see the kingdom as it was already in the eternal world would be to see what that kingdom would be like when eventually it came and was established on earth.

something which men are gradually brought to realize fully by experience; in 9:28–36 it is something which has always been known. In 9:18–27 the death of Christ is something which the apostles are told will take place as the result of his rejection by the religious leaders at Jerusalem. It sounds like (at least temporary) defeat. In 9:28–36 the death of Christ is something long since planned and now about to be triumphantly fulfilled. Moreover in 9:18–27 the confession of Jesus as God's Messiah and the announcement of his death, resurrection and coming in glory are the climax to which everything in movement 1 has led; whereas in 9:28–36 the glory of the kingdom, the long-planned 'exodus' at Jerusalem, the certainty of the eventual establishment of the kingdom on earth at the second coming, these things are the starting point in the light of which the rest of movement 2 proceeds.

The transfiguration of Jesus (9:28–36). The first effect of the transfiguration on the apostles was doubtless to convince them beyond any shadow of doubt of the real existence of the other world, the eternal kingdom. Our world is not the only one: there is another. Next they were given to see that that other world is not just future to our world, but concurrent with it, though also before it and beyond it. They further saw that though that world is normally invisible to ours, Christ had contact with both worlds simultaneously; and what is more, though he was still on earth, his person and clothes could and did take on a radiance suited to the glory of the other world (see 9:29). Moreover 'there talked with him two men, Moses and Elijah who appeared in glory' (9:30–31). That is very interesting, because in our world these two men were separated by time, since they lived in two completely different centuries; in that world they were together. Clearly time and change do not affect that world as they do ours. And yet it would be false to jump to the conclusion that in that world there is no past or future, but only one eternal present, for we are told that Moses and Elijah were talking with Christ about an event that apparently was future to all three of them: Christ's death and resurrection (literally, his 'exodus') which he was about to accomplish at Jerusalem (see 9:31). He had not yet died: he knew it, of course; but they also knew it.

Their conversation was about Christ's exodus. In this world Moses had superintended the offering of the Passover sacrifice to save Israel from the wrath of God as the first step towards their liberation from bondage and their exodus from Egypt. In that world, if not before, he would long since have discovered that his Passover sacrifice and exodus had another dimension: they were a prototype and prophecy of the sacrifice of Messiah, a pledge which one day would have to be 'fulfilled in the kingdom of God' (22:16). And he would further have learned that his own Passover in Egypt was not simply a useful analogy that fortunately happened to lie to hand when God decided that Messiah must die: the sacrifice of Messiah to save Israel and all who will from the wrath of God and the domination of Satan had been decided upon ages before Moses' Passover.

Elijah, too, when in this world, had offered a sacrifice (see 1 Ki. 18). Its purpose had been to win back Israel from her vain idolatries to serve the true and living God. Its method was simple: the God who could show, by fire from heaven, his acceptance of the sacrifice offered on Israel's behalf, was to be acknowledged as the true God. In that world Elijah too would have learned that his sacrifice was also a prototype of the way by which God had already purposed to bring back Israel and all mankind from their false gods: the sacrifice of Messiah offered on behalf of all men and its acceptance demonstrated by the resurrection of Christ and the coming of the Holy Spirit from heaven.

A few days before, news of the coming death of Christ had appeared to the apostles as a sudden unexpected shock, an obstacle in the way of their hopes put there by the perversity of the religious leaders of their nation. Now on the mount of transfiguration they were beginning to discover that the death of Christ was a sacrifice, foreknown before the foundation of the world, spoken of and foretold by both the law and the prophets, and now about to be as deliberately fulfilled as it had been deliberately planned.

Moreover, what the apostles saw on the mount of transfiguration was not merely a sight of the past and of the near future as it appeared to persons in glory: it was also evidence of the utter certainty of Christ's second coming. This is not something which we are left to deduce from the narrative: Peter himself, as we have earlier observed, tells us (see 2 Pet. 1:12–18) that this among other things is what the transfiguration convinced them of. The evidence which he cites is the evidence both of sight and of hearing: they were, he says, eyewitnesses of Christ's majesty, and they heard the voice from the majestic glory (so NIV). Let us notice, therefore, what exactly it was among all that happened on the holy mount, which led Peter on subsequent reflection to be so certain that the crucified Jesus would one day come again in glory. 'We were not following cunningly devised stories' he says 'when we made known to you the power and coming of our Lord Jesus Christ, but we were eye-witnesses of his majesty, for he received from God the Father honour and glory when there was borne to him from the Majestic Glory a voice to this effect: "This is my Beloved Son in whom I have found delight".' That is, Peter is not referring simply to the fact that on the holy mount Christ's face was transfigured and his clothes transformed. He is observing that at a certain point in the proceedings, Jesus received from God the Father a tremendous accolade of honour and glory. With Peter as our guide we had better look back at Luke's narrative to see exactly at what point this accolade of glory was given him.

The conversation between Christ, Moses and Elijah, as we have noticed, was about Christ's exodus at Jerusalem, about the fact that he must leave the glory of the transfiguration mount, go down into the squalid sinful world below, on to Jerusalem and death: the Son of man had to go even as it had been ordained (see 22:22). Moses and Elijah therefore were now already beginning to depart (see 9:33) when Peter suggested that it would be good if they did not go, but all stayed where they were on the mountain. He proposed in fact to make three tents, one each for Christ, Moses and Elijah, to facilitate their stay. He like the other two apostles had been asleep, Luke says – obviously he had not followed the conversation too closely – and he did not realize what he was saying. It was nonetheless a most unfortunate suggestion. Not only did it imply putting Moses and Elijah on a level with Christ, but it would have impeded and delayed the very going which had been planned from eternity and for which the time had now come. It was at that point in the proceedings, when having discussed his exodus Moses and Elijah were departing and Christ was turning to go down the mountain and on to his exodus, that the cloud came and Jesus received from the 'Majestic Glory' himself the tremendous accolade of honour and glory: 'This is My Son, My Chosen One; hear him'. Not only had the exodus been planned by the Father: Christ's willingness to fulfil it filled the Father's heart with delight and moved him thus to honour the Son.

As Peter reflected on this glorious event in later life, it convinced him of two things. First, the death of Christ was no tragic accident: it was foreknown, that is foreordained, before the foundation of the world (see 1 Pet. 1:20). Secondly, the shame and death of the cross were no obstacle in the way of Christ's setting up of the kingdom. His willingness to suffer was the reason for the Father's delight, the grounds for his bestowing on Jesus the supreme glory. Not only had he already raised him from the dead and given him glory (see 1 Pet. 1:21): one day he would do before the whole universe what he had done on the mount of transfiguration. He would glorify and vindicate his Son: Christ would come again (see 2 Pet. 1:16) not only in his personal glory but in the glory of the Father himself and of the holy angels (see 9:26). No glory would be too great for the Father to bestow upon the One crucified.

With the coming of the voice, says Luke, Jesus was found alone. The lawgiver and the prophet had gone. For all their eminence they were but men. Their role in history had been preparatory to the incarnation, death and resurrection of Christ. Now that he had come, they retired. The actual redemption of the world would depend on Christ and on Christ alone.

The healing of a father's only son (9:37–43). The next day they came down from the mountain, says Luke (9:37); and if our imaginations have caught any glimpse at all of the glory of the transfiguration, we shall not miss the poignancy of these words, particularly when we see the spiritual squalor and distress with which they were immediately surrounded in the world below.

Two things will help us to see the significance of the next incident as Luke wants us to see it. First we may compare his account with those of Matthew and Mark. Like Matthew (see 17:14–20), Luke does not include the four verses of conversation between Christ and the father of the demon-possessed boy on the question of the length of the boy's disorder and of the necessity and possibilities of faith, which Mark records at 9:21–24. Unlike both Matthew (see 17:19–20) and Mark (see 9:28–29), Luke does not record the subsequent conversation between the apostles and Christ on why they could not cast out the demon. On the other hand Luke has some small but telling features which the others do not have. Only Luke records that the boy was his father's only son and that the father based his appeal to Christ in part upon this fact (see 9:38); and only Luke tells us that when the boy was cured Christ 'gave him back to his father' (see 9:42). A whole world of meaning is captured in these small phrases: the unique relationship and the special affection of a father for an only son; the tragic effect of the physical distortions and personality changes induced by demon-possession which had in a very real sense taken the boy away from his father and ruined the enjoyment of the relationship; and the delightful outcome of the healing, that the boy was 'given back' to his father and the enjoyment of the relationship restored.

And then only Luke records the impact this made upon the crowds: 'they were all amazed at the majesty of God' (9:43). The word Luke uses for 'majesty' (Greek: *megaleiotēs*) is interesting. It occurs elsewhere in the New Testament only twice, once at Acts 19:27 and once at 2 Peter 1:16; and on the latter occasion it is used by Peter to describe the majesty of Christ which Peter had seen on the mount of transfiguration. Luke's brief description of the impact made on the crowds, then, gives us to see what Christ did by the miracle he performed: in coming down from the mount of trans-figuration where the majesty of God as it appears in the eternal kingdom had been on display, he brought some of that glory with him down into the spiritual squalor and distress of our world and gave men to catch a glimpse of the majesty of God.

There is, moreover, another thing we can do to help ourselves perceive what Luke wants us to see in this story: we can compare and contrast it with the story at 9:10–17 which we have already studied. That also was a story of a miracle involving the crowds, and just as there the disciples were asked to provide the necessary relief and were unable to (see 9:13), so here (see 9:40). But there are differences as well as similarities: at 9:13 it was Christ who told the disciples to feed the crowds and they were unable to, whereas here in 9:40 it was the father who pleaded with the disciples to heal his boy and they could not. Again, the miracle of the feeding of the five thousand was also, we discovered, an enacted parable. It is likely that the miracle of the healing of the father's son will turn out to be an enacted parable as well. But the need which Christ met on the first occasion was hunger; the need which Christ meets in our present story is something altogether different, though no less illustrative of the general human condition.

Now, as we have already noticed, Luke in his version of the story does not record the subsequent discussion between the disciples and Christ on why it was they were unable to cast out the demon. Luke concentrates our attention solely on Christ's rebuke (if that is what it was) of the crowd: 'O faithless and perverse generation, how long shall I be with you and bear with you? Bring your son here' (9:41). What, we ask, was the reason for that somewhat severe remark? Was not the situation distressing enough, particularly to the father, without adding to his distress by this rebuke? And was it not doubly distressing when he had pleaded with Christ's own apostles to cast out the demon and they could not? Why seem to be impatient with the man and the crowd?

Let us recall the situation. Here was a father and his only son. Imagination will tell us the love, affection and hopes which he had for that only child. And now the father was being cruelly robbed of his enjoyment of his son by demon-possession which convulsed the boy, twisting his limbs and distorting his features till he foamed at the mouth, and quite possibly perverting his personality as well. And adding to the anguish of it was the inability of even the disciples to do anything about it. Certainly it was distressing to the father; but it was equally, perhaps more, distressing to Christ to see the people of God, reduced to such helpless anguish, as a result ultimately of the nation's departure from, and lack of faith in, God. In his distress Christ described the situation by using a phrase which we first find in Deuteronomy 32:5ff. It is worth quoting the phrase in its context. Moses is rebuking Israel for forsaking God and going after idols. 'They are a perverse and crooked generation. Is this how you repay the Lord, you foolish and unwise people? Is he not your Father who created you, who made you and formed you? (32:6) . . . But . . . they sacrificed to demons which were not God, gods they had not known (32:17) . . . and the Lord saw it and rejected them, because he was provoked by his sons and daughters (32:19) . . . and he said, I will see what their end shall be, for they are a very perverse generation, children who are unfaithful' (32:20).

This is a very moving passage and its relevance to the situation in our story is at once evident. The boy's twisted limbs, convulsed features and disturbed personality, and the distress of the father at seeing his only son in that condition were an all too eloquent picture of the distress of the Father at seeing his sons and daughters in Israel gone from him, attracted by false religion and demonic powers, and become perverse, crooked and twisted at the deeper level of their spiritual relationships. And all this as a result of loss of faith in, and love of, and obedience to, the Father. For *the* Son of the Father it was an almost intolerable distress to have to remain among such faithless and perverted sons: 'how long shall I be with you, and bear with you?' he said.

How then should the trouble be put right and Israel's sons and daughters be won back to the Father? If the trouble began with ingratitude and then unbelief, deepening into disobedience, and alienation and faithlessness until any old religion, demonic power or superstition was more attractive and fascinating than the Father himself, it is obvious that mere moral sermons and exhortations would be inadequate to bring them back. They would need a new revelation of the Father, a vision of his majesty and glory, to break the fascination of sin and the attractiveness of idolatry, and to reawaken a sense of the incomparable wonder of God and evoke faith and worship and obedience.

And that is what Christ did for the people in our story. The disciples had been unable to do it. They were, of course, the ones who had been left behind when Christ and the three had gone up the mountain, and they had not even seen the glory and the cloud or heard the Father's voice. It took the Son of the Father to do it. From the splendour of the transfiguration where the voice from the 'Majestic Glory' had proclaimed him 'My Beloved Son', he had come come down the mountain to the spiritual squalor of the plain in order to make known what the Father was really like and to reveal his glory to some of his long-lost sons. And the effect on the people, says Luke, was this: they were all amazed at the majesty of God.[1]

Luke's story is, of course, history. It all actually happened. But it takes little imagination to see that it is a parable as well, of how the Son of the Father came down not simply from the mount of transfiguration but from heaven itself by way of the incarnation to tell out the Father (see Jn. 1:18; 14:9), and went at last to Calvary that we poor deluded and perverse men and women, far gone from God, might see 'the light of the knowledge of the glory of God in the face of Jesus Christ' (2 Cor. 4:6); and seeing it be redeemed and restored to the Father.

---

[1] Cf. what is said of the present role of the believer in the world in Phil. 2:15 which also uses the language of Dt. 32:5: 'children of God without fault in a crooked and perverse generation among whom you shine as lights in the world' (or, 'as luminaries in the universe'. The Greek word translated 'shine' is used for the rising and appearing of the heavenly bodies).

Further instruction of the twelve (9:43–50). If that then was why
Christ came down from the glory, it follows that until he comes
again his apostles and servants must offer themselves to be used for
that same purpose. To that end the final paragraph of stage 5 is
devoted to further instruction of the twelve on how they were to
go about their mission in the world. In particular they would need
to know what attitude to take towards the power and authority
entrusted to them for their work of representing their Lord. History has surely shown the importance of the lesson: the church's
attempts to exercise power and authority in the world in the name
of Christ have sometimes forfeited the respect of the world as being
self-evidently inconsistent with what Christ stood for.

While, then, everyone was still amazed at the tremendous acts of
power which Christ was performing (see 9:43), Christ impressed
on his apostles that he who was doing these powerful deeds would
eventually be 'delivered up into the hands of men'. The apostles did
not understand what he said. In the first place they did not
apparently understand to what 'being delivered up into the hands of
men' referred, and they were afraid to ask (was it because they were
subconsciously afraid of what the answer would be?) And then the
phrase itself seemed to imply weakness and helplessness; and it
probably did not make sense to them that someone who could
wield the supernatural power that Christ was wielding, would be
delivered into the hands of men as though completely unable to
save himself. Luke explains that it was not altogether their fault that
they could not understand the lesson: 'it was concealed from them
so that they should not perceive it' (9:45). When Christ was
arrested, condemned and crucified they saw all too clearly what it
meant, and saw it with shock and consternation. In a world that
worshipped power, to be crucified was the extreme of disgrace and
shameful weakness, and a crucified Messiah seemed an absurd
contradiction in terms. Later they came to see and admire the
divine wisdom of the strategy of the cross. They saw that mere
power is inadequate to change a man's heart, to reconcile a man to
God, to change his rebellion into faith and love and obedience; and
inadequate therefore to solve the human problem and bring in the
kingdom of God. And then they saw that the cross with all its
apparent weakness and shame was able to do what power by itself
could not do: 'the weakness of God was stronger than men' (1 Cor.
1:25). They saw too that Christ's suffering of the cross was not an

unfortunate obstacle on Christ's path to glory: he had come down from glory deliberately in order to suffer the cross. The cross was an expression of the wisdom of the 'Majestic Glory'. And then they woke up to the fact that the message of the cross is the only message of any use in the evangelization of the world, and the principle of the cross the only safe principle to follow in the organization and running of the churches (see 1 Cor. 1:18 – 4:13).

Then there was another lesson which Christ had to teach them (see 9:46–48). When Christ had sent them out on their mission, he had given them power and authority (see 9:1) and had impressed on them that it was very important how people received them (see 9:3–5): to reject them was to stand in danger of the judgment of God. Perhaps it was this, coupled with the different degrees of success achieved by the different apostles in their mission, or perhaps the fact that only three of them had been allowed to accompany Christ on the mount of transfiguration, or perhaps it was all these things and more besides – whatever it was, it led them to think that they themselves were important, and then to argue among themselves which of them was the most important. Christ cured their mistake by pointing out that if he sent a mere child as his representative on some mission or other, it would be equally important whether people received the child or not as it would be whether they received an official apostle or not. The importance did not reside in the child itself or in the apostles themselves, but in the fact that they represented Christ and Christ represented God. In this sense there were no degrees of importance: even the least among them, if he represented Christ and the Father, was great, nor could anyone ever attain to a more magnificent greatness than to represent, never mind in what lowly mission, the 'Majestic Glory'.

Finally there was a third lesson (see 9:49–50). When the apostles had been sent on their mission (see 9:11), they had been given power and authority over all demons. That was wonderful. To their amazement, however, they came across someone else casting out demons in the name of Christ. That, they could see at once, was highly improper. We forbade him, says John.

Perhaps we should not condemn John too hastily. The reason he gives – 'because he does not follow with us' – is perhaps ambiguous. Was he including Christ in the 'us', or was he thinking only of the twelve? If he meant simply the twelve, then they were surely guilty of narrow-minded self-importance. On this showing, it would not have troubled them that by forbidding this man to cast out demons in the name of Christ they were condemning many people to remain in spiritual bondage. And what is even worse, we have just been told (see 9:40) that on one occasion, at least, nine apostles had been unable to cast out a demon themselves. Not to be able to do it themselves and yet to forbid somebody else to do it, was hardly the best way of furthering the work of the Lord.

On the other hand, John's 'us' may have been intended to include Christ. In that case his concern would have been that the man who was casting out demons in the name of Christ, was attempting to do Christian work, without being willing to take his stand unreservedly with Christ, and to follow along with Christ and his apostles in the path of discipleship to which Christ had called them. The modern equivalent would be people who engage in all kinds of relief work in the name of Christ, but are not prepared to obey and follow all the commandments and disciplines laid down by Christ for his church. It is not a matter of indifference whether professing Christians do, or do not, observe all things that Christ has commanded the apostles (see Mt. 28:20). Failure to can sometimes be symptomatic of a very serious spiritual condition (see Mt. 7:22–23; 1 Jn. 2:19).

Whichever of the two attitudes John and his fellow apostles were taking, Christ's reply calmed their spirits. Notice he did not say on this occasion, 'He who is not against me is for me', but 'He who is not against you is for you'. Christ was thinking of the practical difficulties that would arise in the path of the apostles as they went about their work for the Lord. It would make life easier for the apostles if all who attempted to use the name of Christ followed all the commandments of Christ. On the other hand, in a world where obedience is rarely perfect, the apostles were to comfort their hearts with the reflection that he that was not positively against them, was for them. Besides, Christ had already pointed out to them that when the Son of man comes in his glory, all questions of loyalty and disloyalty, obedience and disobedience, will be fully assessed and suitably rewarded (see 9:23–26).

Part Two
THE GOING

The nature of the journey

We have reached the turning point in the Gospel. Up till now Luke has been describing the Coming of our Lord Jesus Christ into our world. But at this point there comes a very significant change: our Lord begins to go, and the whole of the remainder of the Gospel is devoted to an account of that Going. First the turning point is very clearly marked: 'When the days drew near for him to be received up, he resolutely set his face to go to Jerusalem' (see 9:51); and then throughout the rest of the Gospel Luke will from time to time remind us that Christ is on a journey (see 9:52,57; 10:1,38; 13:22,33; 17:11; 18:35; 19:1,11,28–29,37,41,45; 24:50–51).

We should at once notice carefully what the goal of the journey is said to be. It is sometimes stated on the basis of 9:51 that our Lord's goal on this journey was Jerusalem. But that is not so. Our Lord's journey certainly lay *via* Jerusalem; but the goal of the journey was what Luke here describes as 'being received up'. The phrase has the same sense as that given it by the early Christian hymn quoted by Paul (1 Tim. 3:16) which says that Christ 'was believed on in the world, *received up in glory*'. In other words by 'being received up' Luke is referring to Christ's ascension into heaven. That and no less was the goal of the journey.

This observation is important. A journey from Galilee to Jerusalem need be nothing more than a literal, geographical journey; but a journey from Galilee to heaven cannot be simply a literal geographical one. Moreover, when we take into account what the goal of the journey was, it becomes obvious that the reason why the journey had to go via Jerusalem was not geographical either. Jerusalem is not geographically nearer heaven than anywhere else on earth. The reason for going via Jerusalem was in the first place historical. Jerusalem was the capital city of the Jewish nation to whom God had promised the Messiah. It was the capital city of the kings of Judah, who were the ancestors and prototypes of the Messiah. In that city God had deigned to localize his presence in the temple in a way in which he had not done in any other temple on earth. To that city God had sent a succession of inspired prophets, predicting with ever more detail the Coming of Messiah. Jerusalem, then, was Messiah's city, where he had a right to be received and acclaimed and enthroned. To present himself as Israel's King he must, as Zechariah 9:9 had declared he would, present himself at Jerusalem.

But the reason why Christ's journey from earth to heaven must go via Jerusalem was not only historical: it was moral, spiritual, and redemptive. Jerusalem, the city favoured and privileged by God above all other cities had killed the prophets and stoned those who were sent to her by God (see 13:34). If Christ had come to expose and then to deal with human sin, then he must go to Jerusalem. There he would find the darkest form of rebellion against God that sin has ever produced: the rebellion not of open, sworn, avowed and honest enemies; but the rebellion of people who professed to be the most religiously enlightened and the most loyal to God of any people on earth. As he himself remarked, 'Nevertheless I must go on my way today and tomorrow and the day following, for it cannot be that a prophet perish out of Jerusalem.' (13:33 RV).

Moreover, at Jerusalem divine wisdom and love had determined to make Israel's murder of the Messiah the occasion of the atoning sufferings of Christ which should make redemption possible for Israel and the world; and for this very reason Jerusalem was the place from which it was ordained that the gospel should go out to the whole world: 'Thus it is written, that Christ should suffer, and rise again from the dead the third day; and that repentance and remission of sins should be preached in his name unto all nations, beginning from Jerusalem' (24:46 RV).

Then, as we have already noticed (p.165), just before Christ set out on his journey from earth to heaven, he invited all who would to follow him (see 9:23). He was to be the 'Pioneer of salvation' for all those many sons whom God proposed to bring to glory (Heb. 2:10). It is obvious, therefore, that here, too, the road along which disciples are invited to follow Christ must be understood in a double sense. For a few disciples contemporary with him, discipleship involved following Christ along a very literal road through Palestine to Jerusalem. But even progress along that literal road involved them daily in experiences which would call for, and produce, progress along the metaphorical road of discipleship. For all who have followed him since, however, following him does not necessarily involve travelling any particular literal road (except of course where duty involves literal travel of some kind) but is altogether a question of pursuing a road of moral and spiritual progress that leads to glory.

The journey, then, that Christ took from Galilee to heaven via Jerusalem was both literal and metaphorical, both spiritual and geographical; and that fact will necessarily have an important effect on the way in which Luke records the journey. To help us anticipate what these effects are likely to be, so that when we come across them they do not worry us, it will be helpful to construct a simple analogical model. The analogy will not, of course, be exact, but it will be exact enough for our practical purpose.

Suppose an American citizen rises from obscurity to become President of the United States, and eventually writes his autobiography. He entitles it *My journey from a log cabin to the White House*; and some visitor gives us a copy for Christmas.

What kind of journey shall we expect to find described in the book? A literal geographical journey from his birthplace to the White House in Washington? Or a metaphorical journey from poverty to wealth, from obscurity to fame, from political insignificance to being the most powerful political leader in the world? The answer is that we shall not expect the journey to be one or the other, but both. It would be a dull book indeed if it described only the geographical journey; on the other hand the metaphorical journey, though by far the more important and interesting, would be impossible without the geographical journey, and we shall therefore expect references to the geographical journey to keep appearing from time to time throughout the book.

Next – at the risk of casting doubt on our sanity – let us ask whether we may expect the words 'log cabin' and 'White House' in the book's title to refer to literal material dwelling-places whose geographical location could be pin-pointed on a map, or whether we are expected to understand them as symbols of humble obscurity in the one case, and dazzling political glory in the other. (We could ask the same kind of question about Luke's earlier record that Jesus was born 'in a manger' and 'in the city of David'). Again, of course, the answer is that our question poses a false alternative. The log cabin will turn out to be a very literal, geographically positioned building; and yet at the same time the words 'log cabin' will carry powerful emotional and metaphorical connotations. And the term 'White House', though a metonymn for 'presidency of the United States', will also refer to a very literal – and elegantly comfortable – house.

Now some commentators, though presumably recognizing that in theory our Lord's journey in Luke's narrative could be understood as both literal and metaphorical, have decided that in fact it is nothing but an artificial literary construct. They reason as follows. Having stated that our Lord set himself resolutely to go to Jerusalem, Luke represents him as leaving Galilee and proceeding through Samaria; but when Christ eventually approaches Jerusalem, he has him approaching it by Jericho, which he would not have done had he travelled by the direct route through Samaria into Judaea. Moreover they point out that after passages which indicate that our Lord has reached Samaria, come other passages that suggest that he is back in Galilee. They conclude that obviously Luke did not know the geography of Palestine very well, for if he had been familiar with it, he would have represented our Lord as proceeding directly from Galilee to Jerusalem, and he would not have later on let drop remarks which would imply that instead of resolutely proceeding to Jerusalem he was going in different directions all round the country. They feel, however, that the geographical inconsistencies do not matter, because the supposed geographical journey is not historical, but only an artificial literary device to create a thread along which Luke can string the large quantity of special material which he introduces into this part of his Gospel.

Our presidential autobiography can help us assess the validity of this kind of reasoning. Suppose the log cabin was situated a thousand miles due west of Washington. If the politician's journey to the White House were simply a geographical one we might expect the narrative to indicate that the route taken proceeded more or less directly due east. But we realize in advance that the journey is more than geographical: it is also the journey of a political career. We shall not be surprised to find then on reading the book that the one journey from the log cabin to the White House comprised hundreds of journeys in all directions all over the States and literally scores of journeys which our politician took as a congressman and then as a senator from his constituency to Washington – and back again! Yet in whatever geographical direction his journeyings might be taking him at any one moment we shall understand perfectly well that as far as he is concerned he is still taking the most direct route he knows to get to the White House. What kind of literary critics would people think us to be if we were to criticize the autobiography thus: the author of this book obviously does not know the geography of the USA very well. Having declared at the beginning that he was about to describe his journey from his log cabin in the mid-west eastwards to the White House he records that later on he made a speech in San Francisco which we all know is not on the way east from the log cabin to Washington but in the far west.

Our analogy may help us also with another difficulty that others have felt. Though there are in the second half of the Gospel a number of references to the geographical journey from Galilee to Jerusalem, these references are comparatively few when one considers that the journey narrative itself lasts for at least 400 verses. What is more, in the great majority of the items of narrative in this part of the Gospel there seems to be no explicit journey-motif present whatsoever. They are simply sermons and miracles which Christ preached and performed in the course of his journey to Jerusalem; but their meaning and message seem to have little to do with the fact that he was on his way to Jerusalem. This might suggest, therefore, that we ought not to make too much of this supposed journey-motif in the second half of the Gospel.

Before we accept this suggestion, however, let us look again at our presidential autobiography. We shall find that though the book contains, all told, quite a large number of references to geographical journeyings, these references tend to be fairly sparse and to come into the narrative irregularly. A tremendous lot will be made of a literal journey to New York, early in his career, and of a ticker-tape parade through its streets; and after that very little may be said about literal journeying until the chapter that deals with the first ever journey of an American Secretary of State to and through China. After that again very little of any consequence may be said for chapters on end about literal journeying. And that will not surprise us: literal journeys are after all only subsidiary to the main theme of the book, the one great metaphorical journey.

And then we shall notice another feature of the book. Large sections will go by without any explicit reference even to the metaphorical journey. For example, in one chapter our politician will describe at great length his diplomatic successes as the US Ambassador to Moscow. He will not stay to point out what relevance these successes had to his advancement along the road to the White House; not because they had no relevance, but because their relevance is self-evident.

As we apply this analogy to Luke's narrative of our Lord's journey, there is just one other thing we must remember. We must constantly recall our earlier observation that the goal of the road along which our Lord was journeying, and along which he invited his disciples to follow him, was not Jerusalem, but heaven. If we forget this and fall back into the mistake of thinking that the goal was Jerusalem, we shall naturally be puzzled that few of the stories, miracles, sermons and parables have anything to do with the journey to Jerusalem. But if we remember that the goal of the journey is 'being received up into glory', the exodus from this world to the one beyond, the leaving of time for eternity, we shall find that the material given us on the geographical journey is highly relevant to the metaphorical journey, and particularly to the progress of would-be disciples along that road. Many of the stories and parables, for instance, are concerned to warn us that some people will arrive at the end of the journey unprepared for heaven. Some, says 13:25, will arrive when the door is shut. Some, like the farmer in the parable of the rich fool (see 12:16–21), will arrive at eternity much sooner than they expected and unready. For some, like Lazarus, the end of the journey will mean the end of a life of pain and the beginning of eternal consolation; for others, like the rich man in that same story, the end of the journey will mean the end of any joy they ever knew and the beginning of eternal sorrow (see 16:19–31). The parable of the unjust steward (see 16:1–9) reminds us to be ready for the moment towards which we are travelling when like the steward we must be put out of our present temporary stewardship and enter the world of the eternal tabernacles.

Of course, it can be objected that if we are going to insist that the journey in the second half of Luke's Gospel is a journey from this world to the next, from time to eternity, then there is nothing in the whole of life, let alone in the second half of Luke's Gospel, that could not be said to be relevant both to the journey and to its goal. That is perfectly true; but then that is perhaps Luke's point. The whole of life is a journey. We are always on the move. There is no staying still. We can never say we have 'arrived'. But if we are uncertain of the goal, life's travelling, instead of being a deliberate journey towards a glad destination, can become an uncertain meandering or a purposeless going round in circles. And then, of course, Luke makes another point. While all men travel along some road or other, and all roads lead to eternity, not all roads lead to God's heaven. Which road is it then that can be trusted to lead us with certainty to God's heaven? Luke undertakes to show us. He will show first Christ himself travelling that road, passing through Jerusalem and the sufferings of the cross, and entering into glory; and then he will tell us how and on what grounds those who follow him may be certain of entering that same glory, and how they may rightly prepare themselves for what life will involve in that glorious world.

The path to glory

Preliminary survey

The movements

1 Its costs and sorrows   *(9:51 – 10:16)*
2 Its joys and triumphs   *(10:17–37)*

Stage 1

The path to glory

Preliminary survey

As is only to be expected the early paragraphs of the first stage of the Going make frequent references to the fact that Christ was now embarked on a journey. The first paragraph tells how he set himself resolutely to go to Jerusalem (see 9:51), sent messengers ahead to make necessary preparations (see 9:52) and when he was not received in one village because he was going to Jerusalem (see 9:53), went to another (see 9:56). The second paragraph begins by repeating the fact that 'they were journeying along the road' (9:57) and proceeds to record the lessons Christ taught three would-be disciples about what following him along that path would involve. The third paragraph likewise begins (see 10:1) by referring to the fact that Christ was travelling through the country, and tells how he sent a further seventy men on in front to every city and village which he would visit on the way.

Then there follow a further three paragraphs which make no mention of Christ's journey at all. At 10:17–20 the seventy return to Christ full of joy at their achievements and are both encouraged and corrected by Christ. At 10:21–24 Christ expresses his own joy and thanks to the Father for what is happening, and points out to the disciples their special blessedness. Finally, at 10:25–37 in answer to a lawyer's question Christ tells the parable of the good Samaritan. Only after this second group of three paragraphs does Luke resume the theme of Christ's journey with an explicit journey-notice 'Now as they went on their way he entered into a village' at 10:38.

It would be a reasonable working hypothesis, then, to suppose that the resumption of the journey-notices at 10:38 was meant to mark the beginning of a new stage in the journey narrative, and that the six paragraphs which we have just glanced at were intended to stand together as stage 1 of the Going. The hypothesis can easily be tested. Do these six paragraphs share any dominant theme or themes? Or do they show any other signs of being a coherent group?

We notice at once that the first (see 9:51–56) and last (see 10:25–37) paragraphs both involve Samaritans. This could, of course, be a superficial and insignificant feature; but indications are that it is not. First, both these stories are peculiar to Luke, and therefore his choice and placing of them must have been very deliberate. Next, these two stories are clearly variations on a common theme. In the first of them some Samaritans, moved by racial and religious hostility towards Jews, refuse Christ hospitality in their village. At that two apostles suggest calling down fire from heaven on them, and are rebuked by Christ for their unchristian attitude. In the second a Jew is viciously mugged and left half-dead by the roadside. Two fellow-Jews pass by and do nothing to help him; but a Samaritan, overcoming all religious and racial resentments, renders him first aid, transports him to a hotel and pays for him to stay until he has fully recovered. It is obvious that both stories are saying something important about what our reactions and attitudes should be towards people who are hostile to us on religious or racial grounds. And it is perhaps significant that while in the first story the Samaritans come out of the affair with little credit, since it was their initial action which provoked the Jewish apostles, in the second the Samaritan gets the credit for behaving far more nobly than the Jewish priest and Levite.

These two paragraphs, however, are not the only ones to deal with this theme. The third paragraph (see 10:1–16) tells of the sending out of the seventy. It is the longest (counting simply by verses) of the six, and it too is peculiar to Luke in the sense that no other evangelist records the sending out of these seventy, though the instructions given them are of course basically similar to the instructions given to the twelve on their earlier mission (cf. Mt. 10:9–13). What is significant for our present purpose is the fact that out of its sixteen verses this paragraph devotes three (see 10:10–12) to telling the seventy how to react to those who reject them and refuse them hospitality, three more (see 10:13–15) to a denunciation by Christ of Chorazin, Bethsaida and Capernaum for having rejected him and his message, and one final verse (see 10:16) to the enunciation of the general principle: 'whosoever listens to you, listens to me; and whoever rejects you, rejects me; and whoever rejects me, rejects him who sent me.' The rejection so heavily emphasized in these seven verses is not – or not simply – rejection of Jews by Samaritans, but more frequently of Jews by Jews; but it is, of course, rejection on religious grounds. And so we now have three paragraphs, all of them peculiar to Luke, and all of them carrying a common theme, stationed one at the beginning, one in the middle and one at the end of this series of six paragraphs. At the very least they act like a brace holding all six paragraphs together.

We look next, therefore, to see whether there is any recognizable flow or pattern of thought running through all six paragraphs, or whether the six are a mixture of likes and unlikes, of related and unrelated topics. Now we have already observed that while the first three paragraphs all explicitly mention Christ's journeying, the second three do not. There is nothing artificial about this arrangement. The first three paragraphs all deal with practical matters relating to the journey: (1) the sending out of a small advance party to make practical arrangements in some suitable village or town for the overnight stay of Christ, his apostles and all the other, perhaps quite numerous, disciples who followed him. Any village about to be descended upon by such a large crowd would need adequate warning so as to be prepared to put them up; (2) three would-be disciples are instructed on the demands which following Christ on his journey will make on them; and (3) seventy disciples are sent out in pairs in advance, to every town and village to be visited by Christ, not in order to make practical preparations for his coming, but to prepare the people spiritually for the tremendous choices that they will be faced with when Christ arrives and presents himself and his message. The reason why the next two paragraphs do not continue to talk of Christ's journey, is that at this point (see 10:17) the seventy return from theirs and proceed to give a joyful report of their achievements; and after commenting on their report Christ expresses in the next paragraph (see 10:21–24) his own joy at the events which the disciples are now witnessing. So what we have in these two paragraphs is not a record of the continuing journey, but reflections on the significance of the journey of Christ so far and of the journeys of the seventy. With that, one paragraph is left containing Christ's answer to a question posed at this time by a lawyer. At first sight both the question and the answer might seem to be merely incidental to the main flow of the narrative. Actually, as we have already seen, the answer continues what is in fact one of the dominant themes of this part of the Gospel, and that by itself could fully account for Luke's decision to select this parable and place it here. But there is also a further somewhat curious feature to be noticed about it: the story-line of the parable contains a tremendous lot about travelling, much more in fact than is strictly necessary to point the moral. The man who fell among thieves was, of course, on a journey and so likewise were the priest and Levite. Then came the Samaritan 'as he journeyed' (10:33) to where the man was and saved his life; and, as far as the lesson goes which the parable was required to teach, the story-line could have ended there. But it goes on: the Samaritan put the man on his own beast, transported him to an inn, and took care of him. Even so the story is not finished. In the morning when the Samaritan left, he paid the innkeeper sufficient to cover several days' further board and lodging for the Jew. Surely by now we have had enough detail to complete the picture of an extraordinarily kind, generous and caring Samaritan, who really loved his neighbour as himself. Perhaps we have, but the story is not yet finished: the Samaritan has some more travelling to do. As he leaves, he announces that he is coming back again, and promises on his return to reimburse the innkeeper for any additional expense he may have incurred.

Now the exegetes with their strict logic rightly insist that the parable of the good Samaritan was not intended as an allegory and must not be treated as one. On the other hand if Luke could be thought to have had some literary sense in addition to his concern for history and for strict exegesis, one would be tempted to a further comment: placed as it is in the opening stage of the Going with its necessarily heavy emphasis on Christ's journey and the journeys of the seventy, the parable of the good Samaritan with its similarly prominent theme of travelling, acts like a sub-plot would in a work of literature: it indirectly reinforces the work's major theme. And there might be even more to it than that; but for the moment we must turn to another preliminary observation.

We find ourselves with two sets of paragraphs with three paragraphs in each set. The first set opens with the famous remark:

'And when the time for his being received up was getting near . . .'
It refers to our Lord's ascension and it would be impossible to
exaggerate the importance and the significance of the elevation of
the man Christ Jesus to the right hand of God in heaven. But when
we look at the opening verses of the second set, we find Christ
announcing (10:18): 'I beheld Satan fall like lightning from heaven'.
Jesus ascending into heaven, and Satan falling from heaven – these
two events are so obviously complementary the one to the other
that it would scarcely be possible to comprehend fully the significance of the one without the other.

More of that later. The immediate question it raises is: if the ideas
of the opening paragraph of the second set so obviously complement the ideas of the opening paragraph of the first set, what about
the other paragraphs of the two sets? If they turn out to do the
same, we shall clearly have to take account of this fact in our
exposition. Here then is a table of contents for the two sets of
paragraphs, listing their main ideas side by side (see p. 192).

The movements

1. Its costs and sorrows   (9:51 – 10:16)

We must now consider the three paragraphs of the first movement
one by one. As we do so we should be aware that these paragraphs
form a natural progression, and to get a balanced view of the
matters which they present, we must hear their whole story
through to its end. In the first paragraph (see 9:51–56), for instance,
two apostles are rebuked for suggesting calling down fire from
heaven upon a Samaritan village that had refused Christ hospitality.
But in the third paragraph the seventy are told (see 10:11–12) that if
any city refuses to receive them, 'it shall be more tolerable in that
day for Sodom than for that city'. And we all know what happened
to Sodom: 'fire . . . came down from heaven and destroyed them
all' (see 17:29). Quite clearly, there are two sides to the question of
what should happen to those who reject Christ; but let us begin at
the beginning.

i. *Christ's path to his ascension into heaven (9:51–56).* We start now
the story of the journey destined to take the man Jesus of Nazareth
to the highest pinnacle of the universe, to be seated at the right hand

Stage 1 of the Going 9:51 – 10:37

1
Its costs and sorrows
9:51 – 10:16

2
Its joys and triumphs
10:17–37

1 Christ's path to his ascension into heaven 9:51–56

Disciples are incensed that the Samaritans should not allow Christ to stay in their village; they propose calling down fire from heaven on them. Christ corrects them. He is on his way to being welcomed in heaven 9:51.

1 Satan's fall like lightning from heaven 10:17–20

Disciples are overjoyed that the demons are subject to them in Christ's name. Christ foresees Satan's ejection from heaven. He corrects his disciples: they are to rejoice rather in their heavenly citizenship.

2 The demands and costs of following the Son of man 9:57–62

a The Son of man has nowhere on earth to lay his head.

b A would-be follower is told that his duty to preach the kingdom takes precedence over his supposed duty to bury his father.

c A disciple is warned against the temptation of 'looking back': no-one who, having put his hand to the plough, looks back is fit for the kingdom of God. (The Greek verb for 'look' is *blepō*).

2 The joy and blessedness of association with the Son of the Father 10:21–24

a The Son's Father is Lord of heaven and earth.

b The Son declares that all things have been committed to him by his Father, and that the mutual knowledge of Father and Son is known only by those to whom the Son wills to communicate it.

c The disciples' eyes are blessed for seeing what they see, since kings and prophets longed to see these things but did not see them. (The Greek verb for 'see' is *blepō*).

3 The journeyings of the seventy 10:1–16

a 'I send you out as lambs among wolves . . .'

b 'Heal the sick . . . and say . . . the kingdom of God has come near you . . .'

c 'The labourer is worthy of his hire.'

3 Travellers on the Jericho road 10:25–37

a 'A certain man . . . fell among robbers . . .'

b '. . . a Samaritan . . . came where he was . . . and bound up his wounds . . .'

c 'he gave the inn-keeper two silver coins and said "I will reimburse you for any extra expense on my return".'

of the power of God (see 22:69). The goal of the journey was inexpressibly glorious; but the road to that goal lay through indescribable sorrow: it must go through Jerusalem. Our Lord was under no illusion about what he must suffer there; but when the time drew near for his ascension, he resolutely set out for Jerusalem. In its early stages the journey lay through Samaria and Luke's story tells how when Christ's messengers went ahead to make arrangements for Christ to stay the night in a certain Samaritan village, the villagers would not receive him. We recall that when he came to earth, there was, by accident, no room for him and his parents in the inn (see 2:7); now as he began to go there was no room for him in the village. But this time it was no accident: the Samaritans could have put him up but refused.

Their reason was both sad and ironic. They rejected him because he was making for Jerusalem (see 9:53), and such was the religious animosity between Samaritans and Jews, that a Jew travelling to Jerusalem to take part in its religious festivals there was a *persona non grata* in Samaria. Little did they know that he was going to Jerusalem to be rejected by the religious authorities (see 9:22) and crucified. And still less did they realize that he was going to Jerusalem to die for their redemption. The bitterness of the religious hostility between Jews and Samaritans was not at his instigation nor did it have his approval. But that made no difference: to them he was a stereotype, a Jew going up to the religious festivals at Jerusalem, and without further enquiry they shut him out.

James and John were so enraged at this insult to their Master, that they proposed the immediate calling down of fire from heaven upon the Samaritan village. Now at 10:11–16 we shall be told what grave consequences must follow the knowing and deliberate rejection of Christ and his messengers. But there Christ is talking about rejection in the face of abundant and unmistakably clear evidence (see 10:13). Here the Samaritans were acting out of ignorant religious prejudice: they knew not what they did. Christ rebuked his apostles for even suggesting calling down judgment on their heads. Nor did he try to argue with the Samaritans; he quietly went to another village for the night, travelled on to Jerusalem and there died for them. Not long afterwards the Samaritans heard why he had died, and many of them – let's hope our villagers were among them – were converted to Christ (see Acts 8:5–25).

ii. The demands and costs of following the Son of man (9:57–62). James and John's experience shows that the disciple of Christ must be prepared to accept the world's hostility without retaliation or desire for revenge; the lesson taught to the first of the three would-be disciples of this paragraph shows that the disciple of Christ must be prepared to resist the allurements of its comforts. The Son of man, Christ pointed out, had not the comfort that even such lowly creatures as foxes and birds had: they had their own holes and nests, while he had no home of his own, no resting place to which he could retire, settle and be at ease. He must be always on the move, sleeping in other people's houses, or inns, without any base to which he could return. Following Christ on the road to Jerusalem would obviously involve a disciple in a similarly 'homeless' exist- ence. But the lesson surely has a deeper level of meaning. Those who start out to follow Christ on the road to glory, must be prepared to give up the idea of this world as their home; they become travellers, restlessly moving on, using life's lodging- houses on the way, but with no place to settle down this side of heaven.

The lesson taught to the second would-be disciple shows that a follower of Christ must be prepared not only to let go home- comforts: he must refuse the claim that home duties have priority. Called to follow Christ, this man agreed to do so but asked permis- sion first to go off and bury his father. It is perhaps unlikely that the man's father was already dead and that the man was asking for a two-hour delay in order to attend the funeral. It is more likely that the father was getting elderly and that the man with his Jewish sense of the religious duty of giving parents an honoured burial, was asking Christ for permission to delay following him until his father died (and, perhaps, also until he inherited his father's estate). Now it is a fact explicitly stated by Christ (see Mt. 15:3–9) that the care of elderly parents is a God-given duty which may not be put aside under any religious pretext whatsoever. If, therefore, anyone accepts Christ as Lord, Christ will direct him to fulfil this duty to his parents. But our man was making two mistakes. He asked permission to fulfil what he felt was a prior duty before becoming a follower of Christ. There can, of course, be no prior duty. If Jesus is God's Son, our first duty is towards him. A man who considers that he has a prior duty to fulfil before he is free to become a follower of Christ, has no concept of who Christ is. And secondly, the man was not asking permission to look after his elderly father, but to bury him. In asking to delay following Christ until he had buried his father, the man showed he had no concept of the urgency and importance of the task to which Christ was calling him. That task was to 'go and proclaim the kingdom of God' (see 9:60). People at large – his father included – desperately needed to hear that message: their eternal salvation depended on hearing it and on responding to its urgent call. It would be a very curious way of fulfilling his duty as a son to his father, to delay becoming a preacher of the gospel until his father was dead and buried. Moreover, Christ pointed out to the man that spiritually dead unbelievers could perform the task of burying his father when he died; but spiritually dead unbelievers could not preach the gospel to him or anybody else. 'Let the (spiritually) dead, bury the (physically) dead' said Christ (9:60). It is not an unkindness nor a failure in duty for a believer to let the spiritually dead do what they can well do to help themselves, so as to have more time himself to do for them what they cannot do for themselves. A surgeon does not waste his time cleaning his patient's boots.

The man's sense of duty towards his father, therefore, was false – false even to his father's deepest need. It was a sense of duty imposed not by the requirements of God's law or by the gospel, but by the social and religious conventions of the world. The claims of discipleship to Christ demanded that it be disregarded.

The lesson taught to the third would-be disciple shows that a follower of Christ must be prepared to break decisively the pull of family affection. A soldier called to fight to protect his nation and family must be prepared to leave his family and go off to the front. Our third disciple wanted to delay following Christ until he had gone home and said goodbye to his family. But saying goodbye according to the social customs of the time would have meant a succession of farewell dinner parties day after day, always putting off the time of departure until tomorrow (see, for instance, Jdg. 19:3–8), and making it ever more difficult to leave. 'No-one who puts his hand to the plough and looks back is fit for the kingdom of God', said Christ (9:62). It is a number one rule in ploughing that if you want to plough a straight furrow, you must keep your eyes riveted on the marker at the other end of the field. If you take your eyes off the marker and look behind you, the plough will go wandering all over the place. There is no denying that to put our hand to the plough of service in the kingdom of God is to face some sacrifice of the joys of family life, which may well increase as the plough advances. If when the going gets tough, we look back and hanker after the easier life we have left behind, we shall get our eyes off the goal we were supposed to be aiming at, our drive will falter, our efficiency will be impaired, our sense of direction will become confused and our ploughing may cease altogether.

iii. The journeyings of the seventy (10:1–16). If the first paragraph preached that a follower of Christ must be prepared to endure the world's hostility without retaliation, and the second made clear the costs of becoming a disciple and herald of the kingdom, the third describes what is involved in the actual work of being a herald. We cannot, of course, draw straight lines from the case of the seventy who served Christ before his crucifixion to our own who serve him after Pentecost. As we pointed out earlier (p.159) the instructions given on this occasion were later modified, and in some respects reversed (see 22:35 – 38). But we can try to see the significance of these instructions for the particular mission on which the seventy were sent, and then deduce certain general principles from them.

The situation was that Christ himself was about to visit a number of towns and villages on his way to Jerusalem and glory. Since he was the King, God's Messiah, Son of the Father, it meant that the kingdom of God was about to come near, very near indeed, to the people of these towns and villages. Theirs would then be the opportunity and responsibility of either receiving him and with him the kingdom of God, or rejecting both him and it. The consequences of Israel's rejection of him would be grave and far-reaching even in this world, as subsequent history showed; the consequences in the world to come would be immeasurable. Yet the time for consideration, choice and decision when he came and passed through their towns, would be brief enough. It was important, therefore, that they should be prepared for his visitation (see 19:44) and be presented with ample evidence on the basis of which to make up their minds. Hence the preparatory mission of the seventy: no man should be rushed into a decision without time to consider and understand the evidence.

Christ's first remark (see 10:2) revealed his sense of the great potential of the mission field, but of the dire shortage of workers. Nineteen centuries seem not to have changed the situation much.

Next he explained his tactics (see 10:3–12). He was under no illusion about the world's basic hostility to God, to his kingdom and to his Son. This world is a fallen world, his contemporaries were a perverse and crooked generation (see 9:41; 11:29), like a pack of wolves. Christ's tactics, however, were to send his disciples among them utterly defenceless, and dependent on their mercy. They were to carry no cash, spare clothes or provisions. The effect would be to force the townspeople to a decision as to what they should do with them. If the missionaries had enough money to support themselves, then letting them hire a room in a hotel would be a simple commercial transaction carrying no spiritual implication. But if the people were faced with penniless, destitute men claiming to be Messiah's own ambassadors, they would be forced to decide whether they would receive and entertain them as such, or reject them.

The missionaries were to make it clear that they were not on some merely social or casual visit: they were to greet no man on the way in oriental fashion; they were to make it evident that they had urgent business to do and must concentrate on it.

When they entered a house, they were to pronounce peace upon the house (see 10:5–6). That did not mean that if the occupants of the house were evil, they were to condone the evil by telling them that God is at peace with all men, however evil, and none will ever be lost. Far from it. Their pronouncement of peace was a declaration of their purpose: they had come to bring a message of peace and pardon. If there were people in the house open and prepared for salvation, they would enter into the good of the peace which the missionaries proclaimed. If the people of the house, having heard the message, were cynical and disbelieving, the offered peace would do them no good: it would return to the missionaries. Neither God nor his servants can pronounce peace on those who reject Christ.

And then the missionaries were to make clear that their evangelism was not a cover for any easy and enjoyable life. Whatever house received them, they were to stay there; even if the food and surroundings were poor, they were not to go around looking for some other house where they could get better food and more comfortable lodgings. They were not tourists on holiday, nor pseudo-evangelists sponging on the people (see 10:7).

Moreover, the differing cities they entered might well have

different food laws and customs. Never mind. Whatever city they went to, they were to eat whatever was put before them (see 10:8). They were not to raise difficulties and arguments about petty food laws, so obscuring the major issue of the gospel which they had come to present.

And then they were to make abundantly clear the issue at stake: healing the sick to authenticate their message they were to say that the kingdom of God had drawn near. They were to point out that Jesus was about to come: this would be the time of their visitation, their opportunity for salvation, their moment of decision (see 10:9).

If, on the other hand, the people of any town refused to receive them, they were not simply to leave. By the symbolic gesture of publicly wiping off the dust of the city that stuck to their shoes, they were to indicate the awful significance and implications of this rejection. They were to call on the people to see that they had had an opportunity of salvation: the kingdom of God had come near them. When judgment fell on them worse than that which fell on Sodom, they would never be able to say that they had never had an opportunity to be saved, that they never knew what they were doing in rejecting the Saviour (see 10:10–12).

At that point Christ seems to have been overwhelmed at the thought of cities like Chorazin, Bethsaida and Capernaum, which had witnessed his mighty works, and were still unrepentant and unsaved. Turning aside from addressing his disciples, he pronounced his woe of sadness upon them: 'And you Capernaum, shall you be exalted to heaven? You shall be brought down to hell.' (10:13–15). There are after all two destinations. To think of the stupendous opportunity and possibility that a man can accept the gospel and can follow Christ to the glory of heaven, is to be filled as Christ was at the beginning of his instructions (see 10:2) with a tremendous sense of the potential harvest to be reaped by the evangelists. But if heaven is a real possibility for man, so is hell. There are not two heavens, one for those who receive Christ, and one for those who reject him.

From addressing the cities, Christ reverted to instructing the seventy and pointed out the serious implications which rejection of them and their message carried: rejection of them was tantamount to rejection of him; and rejection of him was rejection of God (see 10:16). No man is fit to preach the gospel, no man has grasped what the gospel is, who does not see that for anyone to reject the

Saviour is unqualified disaster. But in all these instructions perhaps the thing that best prepared the seventy to be effective evangelists, was to stand and witness the profound distress of the Saviour's heart as he thought of the doom that awaited Chorazin, Bethsaida and Capernaum for their folly in refusing to repent.

2. Its joys and triumphs   10:17–37

Movement 1 has been grave and sombre, presenting with realism and due seriousness the costs and suffering involved in following Christ, the demands of discipleship and service, and the solemnity that inseparably accompanies the preaching of the gospel, when the possibility is present that those who hear may choose to reject it and so incur unspeakable loss. But there is another side to the story, which is bright with the exultant joy and wonder of being associated with the Son of the Father, of travelling after him the road to glory, and of witnessing the triumph of his work of redemption. Movement 2 puts this other side of the story, which we shall see if as we study its three paragraphs, we compare and contrast them with the three paragraphs of movement 1.

i. Satan's fall like lightning from heaven (10:17–20). The seventy returned from their mission exultantly joyful in a discovery they had made: 'Even the demons, Lord,' they said, 'are subject to us in your name' (10:17). Without their knowing it, theirs was the first expression of a theme which after Pentecost and the ascension was to rise to a mighty crescendo of joy and praise as the early Christians realized the significance of Christ's being 'received up' into heaven. 'He has gone into heaven' says Peter (1 Pet. 3:22), 'angels and authorities and powers being made subject to him.' God has . . . made him to sit at his right hand in heavenly places', says Paul (Eph. 1:20–22) 'far above all rule and authority and power and dominion and every name that is named not only in this age, but also in that which is to come; and God has put all things in subjection under his feet . . .'. Indeed Christ saw what was happening in this mission to Israel as the early successes in a war which would end in Satan's being cast out of heaven completely. 'I beheld Satan fall as lightning from heaven' he said (10:18). His vision was prophetic. The Christians after Pentecost were aware that they still had to fight against 'spiritual hosts of wickedness in the heavenly realms' (Eph. 6:12). But they had no doubt about the outcome (see

Rom. 16:20); and what excited them as it did the seventy was that here on earth they might exercise the triumphant authority of Christ's name. 'I have given you' said Christ (10:19) 'authority . . . over all the power of the Enemy, and nothing will by any means hurt you'. Again, the seventy were yet to learn that possessing this authority would not exempt them from suffering or even martyr-dom. It would mean, however, that nothing could hurt them by separating them from God's love; in all things they would be 'more than conquerors', and they certainly would never be hurt by the second death (see Rom. 8:37; Rev. 2:11).

It is understandable then that they were overjoyed. Yet without dampening their joy Christ gently corrected its focus: 'Neverthe-less', he said, 'do not rejoice in the fact that the demons submit to you, so much as in this that your names are written in heaven' (10:20). It is a wonderful thing to be allowed to perform effective service in the name of Christ here on earth; it is even more wonderful to be able while still here on earth to be sure of heaven. The Greek word for 'written' carries the connotation of 'being enrolled in the citizen-lists of a city'. It reminds a believer that if in the deepest sense he is 'homeless' on earth, he is already a citizen of heaven (see Phil 3:20). And it is surely significant that Christ did not wait till the end of the road before he allowed his disciples to know this glorious fact: according to Luke it was not long after they had started on the road home to glory (see 9:51) that he gave them this assurance. 'Rejoice above all in this', he said. Indeed, if a believer could not be certain of this, how could he rejoice at all? To believe in the reality of heaven, but to journey through life uncer-tain of ever arriving there, would be not joy but torture. It was the assurance of knowing that their names were already written in heaven that strengthened Paul in prison and nerved his fellow-workers in their labours for Christ in face of bitter persecution (see Phil. 1:29; 4:3).

We look back to the first paragraph of movement 1 (9:51–56). To be refused entry and hospitality in a Samaritan village rankled with the apostles at the time as an intolerable insult and privation. Perhaps now the discovery that they had full citizen rights in heaven helped them to see the matter in its true proportions.

ii. *The joys and blessedness of association with the Son of the Father (10:21–24).* At 9:58 our Lord pointed out to a would-be disciple that the Son of man had nowhere on earth to lay his head. That certainly shows us the staggering grace of his self-sacrifice. But there is another side to the matter: even as he was calling the man's attention to his homelessness on earth, he was enjoying the glorious fact to which he now (see 10:21) gives expression, that his Father was Lord of heaven and earth, owner of every square inch of earth and of heaven into the bargain. Christ felt no self-pity at his homelessness. Nor was there with him the slightest sense of disappointment or shame that after all his immeasurable sacrifice, so far his converts were not even the wise and intelligent of this world but only those who at best could be called intellectual infants. Quite the reverse. It filled him with joy that God in his sovereignty had hidden 'these things' from the intellectual and wise. Needless to say Christ was not giving vent either to exclusivism or to some kind of inverted elitism. He was observing that the knowledge of God and of his salvation is not one of those things that must yield up their secrets to a man if only he has sufficient intellectual power to analyse them. Atoms and molecules for instance and all things physical do belong to that lowly level. Granted they are very complicated, and granted that it takes intellectual powers bordering on genius to penetrate their secrets; but that is all it takes, precisely because physical things belong to such a lowly level. Move a little up the scale of things to the level of personhood, and then not all the giant intellects in the world could fully get to know a person simply by using their brains, if that person were unwilling to open up and let himself be known by communicating his thoughts and feelings. How much more so is it with God. The high mysteries of his person, his mind, his heart, his salvation are infinitely too exalted and wonderful to be penetrated and understood simply by submitting them to a sufficiently powerful intellectual analysis. By God's own choice and decree they remain hidden to the wise. And yet impenetrably mysterious though they are, the next thing that moved Christ to holy joy was his Father's ability and willingness to reveal them to intellectual infants. Again this was not exclusivism: anyone, if he has the sense to do it, can take the position of an infant before God's great mysteries. Nonetheless God's ability and willingness to reveal himself to the humblest of men is an exhilaratingly joyous thing to behold in action. Men of giant intellect often find it virtually impossible to communicate their profound philosophical insights to people of humble intellects. Not God. Take, for instance, the twelve apostles, humble men all of them, and the seventy. On Christ's own admission they were intellectual infants. Yet not only had they grasped profound things about God, and his Son and his salvation, but they had recently been out communicating these things successfully to many of their fellow-men.

Next Christ gave expression to the sense of infinite wealth that filled his heart (see 10:22). As Son of the Father he enjoyed unique knowledge of the intimate relationship that lies at the heart of the Godhead, and with that unique knowledge the unique privilege of communicating it to whomever he pleased. Here were unsearchable riches and incalculable wealth. Paul (see Eph. 3:8) became almost ecstatic at the thought of being allowed to share with Christ the privilege of opening up this wealth to the Gentiles. Who wouldn't? And yet there was one man, we remember, who with one eye on his duty to his father and one eye on the inheritance he was going to come into when his father died, asked to be excused preaching for Christ until his father was dead and buried (see 9:60). His sense of values looks a little odd in this context.

Finally (see 10:23) Christ congratulated his disciples on their extreme blessedness. With the Father's Son now on earth and already on the path that should lead him to the highest pinnacle of glory, they were seeing and hearing things that kings and prophets of centuries gone by longed in vain to see and hear. But now the long preparatory centuries were coming to an end. Now already the demons were subject to the disciples in Christ's name. Soon the power of the devil would be annulled. Soon the man Christ Jesus was to be received up in glory, far above all heavens; and one day they his redeemed would follow him to that glorious exaltation – their names were already written in heaven. And it was all beginning to happen in front of their very eyes. What a sight and what a prospect! To fix their eyes on these glorious things would help them as they 'followed the plough' (9:62) not to yield to the temptation to look longingly back to the attractions left behind.

iii. *Travellers on the Jericho road (10:25–37)*. The parable of the good Samaritan, the exegetes tell us, must not be interpreted as an allegory. And they are right, of course – although the temptation to read it as an allegory has proved practically irresistible to generations of Christians. The parable was constructed to give a very practical answer to a Jewish lawyer's very practical moral question, and to press upon him his duty of loving his neighbour as himself by giving him a practical example of what loving your neighbour as yourself means.

The lawyer had begun by asking what he had to do to inherit eternal life, and our Lord had referred him to the law which he knew so well and was able to quote so readily: 'You shall love the Lord your God with all your heart and with all your soul and with all your strength and with all your mind, and your neighbour as yourself'. But the lawyer wanted to justify himself. He did not want to appear to have asked a simple question to which he already knew the answer, as did everybody else. He had a problem with regard to the second of the two commandments: 'And who is my neighbour?' he asked. Now whether or not it was a genuine problem to him – Luke says his first question was designed to test the Lord (see 10:25) – the problem he posed is a real problem. Are we expected to treat every man jack in the whole of the world as our neighbour and love him as ourselves? And if that is impossible, where are we to draw the line? And are we to treat outrageous sinners and vicious tyrants and blaspheming heretics as our neighbours and love them, along with all others, as ourselves? Or may we with good common sense take the commandment as meaning by 'neighbour' the people in our family, or street, or synagogue, or at a stretch our fellow-nationals, but no more? Can we take it also that our political or national enemies, by being enemies, have ceased to be our neighbours?

The theoretical problem posed by the lawyer's question was not a frivolous, irresponsible question; but our Lord did not answer it at the theoretical level: he answered it by giving a practical example. And, as many commentators have observed, he did not directly answer the exact question which the lawyer asked, as is shown by his own final question to the lawyer (see 10:36). He did not ask 'Who was the neighbour whom these three were expected to love?', but 'Which of these three became neighbour, or, acted as neighbour, to the man who fell among the robbers?' From the practical point of view that was all the guidance that the lawyer, or anyone else, needed: whenever we come across somebody in our pathway in great need, we are to have compassion on them and help them as we would like them to help us if we were in need.

Our Lord, however, had chosen the characters in his parable with deliberate care. The man who fell among robbers was a Jew, the man who acted the neighbour to him was a Samaritan. When even the Jewish priest and Levite did not trouble to help their fellow Jew, it would be an astonishing thing for a Samaritan to help him. Such was the religious and racial animosity between Jews and Samaritans, that had the Jew been alive and well instead of half-dead, and the Samaritan had offered him so much as a glass of water, the Jew would have rejected it with venemous indignation. And yet the Samaritan was moved with a compassion that over-came all religious animosity, and treated the Jew with extra-ordinary generosity.

The moral is self-evident; yet it will be useful to compare the lesson taught here with the lesson taught at 10:10–12. The seventy were taught that if people rejected them and their message they were to wipe off the dust of their feet against them, and warn them in the most solemn terms that they were rendering themselves liable to the judgment of God. They were not to take the view that differences in religious belief at this level do not matter as long as we all love one another. They were to teach that rejection of Christ and of the gospel and of those who preached it will lead to eternal disaster. But now the parable of the good Samaritan puts the other side of the story. Suppose a Christian comes across his bitterest religious enemy, someone who has rejected him and his Christian gospel, and has even persecuted him – suppose he comes across this man in need, he must overcome all natural resentments, he must act the neighbour to his enemy, he must love the man as himself.

In the light of this it is difficult to understand how in past centuries professed Christians imagined they were advancing the cause of Christ by getting out their armies and fighting the Turks; and equally difficult to see how in our own day people can persuade themselves that it is right to defend the faith or promote the gospel by bullet and bomb.

This then was the practical moral lesson that the parable was meant to teach; and perhaps we ought now to leave the parable in case lingering over it we fall into the ways of allegory which we earlier rejected. Even so we may surely be allowed one simple practical question to finish with. It goes like this: if this is how Christ taught us to love our neighbour as ourselves, how well did he practise what he preached? We and all mankind were certainly fallen under the power of what Christ called 'serpents' and 'scorpions', and what is worse, under the power of the enemy himself (see 10:19). In that sorry plight we had no claim on the Father's pre-incarnate Son: we were not his neighbours nor he ours. But he chose by incarnation to come where we were; and in spite of the fact that human beings hounded him to a cross, he rescued us at his own expense, and has paid in advance the cost of completing our redemption and of perfecting us for unimaginable glory. What is more, when he comes again he will reimburse magnificently all who, like the seventy, the apostles and the disciples, have in any way helped him in his task.

On judging aright
life's necessities, priorities and proportions

Preliminary survey

The movements

1 Deciding life's paramount necessities (*10:38 – 11:28*)
2 Seeing God's Word in its true proportions (*11:29 – 12:12*)
3 Seeing possessions in their true perspective (*12:13–53*)
4 Assessing time and the times correctly (*12:54 – 13:21*)

Stage 2

On judging aright life's necessities, priorities and proportions

Preliminary survey

At 10:17, we recall, the seventy returned and reported to Christ what they had experienced on their travels throughout the country preparing people for his approach. That report is now over, and Luke resumes the record of Christ's journey with the notice that 'As they went on their way, he entered a certain village and a woman named Martha received him into her house' (10:38). After this there is no further journey notice until 13:22, which suggests that stage 2 is meant to extend from 10:38 to 13:21.

That gives us a long stage containing only two miracles and filled mostly with lengthy runs of teaching, conversation and argument. Apart from the village mentioned, but not named, at 10:38, no other village, town or city on Christ's route is referred to. Presumably, Luke's selection of material is meant to be a representative sample of the teaching Christ gave and of the discussion and controversy which his claims aroused in all the places which he visited. What in fact was happening is made clear very early on in the stage (see 11:20): through Christ's presence, his words and his supernatural works, the kingdom of God was being brought within the reach of the people in every village and town through which he journeyed; and they had to decide what they would do both with it and with him.

Nowhere in this stage does he claim in so many words to be the Messiah; but everywhere the magnitude and significance of his claims are unmistakable. At 11:31–32, for instance, he warns the crowds that his mission to them is more fateful than was Jonah's to the Ninevites and that their response to him will determine the verdict upon them at the judgment. Similarly at 12:1–4 he points out to his disciples that a person's confession or denial of him here on earth will determine whether he himself confesses or denies that person in heaven. In addition at 12:35–48 he tells his disciples that when he returns – and he must be referring to his second coming – he will call them to account for their service for him in his absence. The faithful servants will then be rewarded; but if any professing servant is shown by his record to have been unfaithful, false and in actual fact an unbeliever, it will have the gravest consequences.

Christ's claims, then, were momentous, and yet the time he had to spend in any one town or village presenting those claims and demonstrating the truth of them was at the best very brief: he was, after all, on a journey, passing through these towns and villages on his way from earth to glory. For the people there was so much to decide, so little time in which to decide it, with nothing less than the verdict of the final judgment hanging on their decision. True, indications were given that between his departure and his second coming there would be an interval of some length for reflection, repentance, faith and service. At 12:11–12, for instance, Christ talks of a time when his disciples will be brought before the courts and the Holy Spirit will use these occasions as an opportunity for witness to Christ. That, as we know, did not happen during his time on earth, but only after his resurrection and ascension. And the fact that he promises them that in their time of need the Holy Spirit (rather than he himself) will instruct them what to say, is further evidence that he is referring to the interval between his ascension and return. Again at 12:35–48, as we have seen, our Lord not only indicates that there will be an interval between his departure and his return during which his servants will have to act as stewards for their absent Lord, but he allows that the interval will be long enough for some servants to get the impression that the Lord is delaying his return (see 12:45). In spite of this, over and over again throughout this stage the urgency of the situation is emphasized. At 12:20 we are reminded that a man's life is only lent him, and could be asked back 'this very night'. At 11:49–52 Christ announces that the blood of all the prophets which has been shed from the foundation of the world will be required 'of this generation'; and at 13:6–9 he adds, in parabolic language, that this generation is living on borrowed time: the sentence has in fact already been delivered, and while stay of execution has been granted, the sentence will have to be carried out unless there is soon some genuine evidence of repentance on the nation's part. At 12:40,46 Christ's servants are warned that his second coming will take place when least expected; and at 12:57–59 a vivid metaphor warns not only Christ's contemporaries but all of us, that we are on a journey which will presently land us before the Judge of the Supreme Court unless in the fast diminishing interval between now and journey's end we take steps to settle our case out of court. In other words, in this stage the urgency of the human situation is shown to arise from various causes: sudden unexpected death from 'natural' causes (see 12:20), atrocities or disasters (see 13:1–5), or the intervention of God's providential judgment on an exceptionally wicked genera- tion (see 11:49–51), or the suddenness of the second coming of Christ (see 12:40,46), while over all hangs the poignant brevity of even the longest life compared with the duration of its eternal consequences (see 12:59).

Christ's claims, then, were immense and urgent; but stage 2 will also show us in some detail by what criteria his contemporaries judged him and his claims. Naturally enough, like people today, they judged him in the light of their preformed standards, their assumptions about what is most important in life, their concepts of fair play and justice, their ideas on religion, and their opinions, lay or professional, on what the Bible teaches. If Christ had fitted in more with their preconceptions on these matters, more people would doubtless have accepted his claims. As it was, this stage will show that he frequently had to point out that their assumptions, standards, values and concepts were maladjusted and mistaken, if not positively perverse and hypocritical. Consequently, when people discovered what Christ actually taught and stood for, their initial reaction was often astonishment (see 11:14,38) and some- times outrage and resentment (see 11:45, 53–54; 13:14).

At 10:38–42, for instance, a woman smarting at the unfairness with which she feels her sister is treating her, appeals to Christ to speak to her sister and demand fair play. Christ's reply is the very opposite to what she expects. At 12:13–15 a man, feeling he is being cheated out of his fair share of his father's estate by his brother, appeals to Christ to speak to his brother and insist on justice being done. Christ refuses to do any such thing and brands the man's appeal for justice as a form of covetousness. At 11:37 a

Pharisee invites our Lord to dinner and then is shocked by his complete disregard of religious observances which to the Pharisee are of the very essence of holiness. And when Christ proceeds to point out that his religious sense, moral judgment, motives, principles of biblical interpretation and application are all grievously unbalanced, ill-proportioned, false and hypocritical, he and his co-religionists are, not surprisingly, enraged (see 11:53–54).

In this stage, then, Christ calls for a radical reassessment of men's values, proportions, priorities and ambitions, and his call naturally meets with a varied response. The generation of Christ's contemporaries, says 11:29, was exceptionally evil; but on the other hand 13:17 records that the crowd was delighted at the glorious things which Jesus did. Martha, devoted disciple though she was, came near to questioning whether the Lord really cared for fair play (see 10:40); but, of course, she accepted the Lord's correction. Not so some others: they were prepared to denounce his healing of a dumb man as a work of the very devil (11:15–23).

With this we encounter what is one of the leading themes of this stage: no less than four paragraphs deal with various aspects of the intense hostility and division provoked by Christ's presentation of himself and his claims. At 11:14–28, as we have just seen, some people unable to deny that Christ's power is supernatural, but determined not to admit that it is of God, maintain that Christ is in league with the devil; and Christ takes their charge seriously enough to argue vigorously and extensively against it. At 11:53 – 12:12 the enraged scribes and Pharisees begin positively to hound Christ, and he has to warn his disciples that this persecution will grow to the point where they will be hauled before the courts, and maybe executed. At 12:49–53 Christ goes over to the offensive, so to speak, announcing that he has come to cast fire on the earth, not to bring peace, but to cause division; and he further indicates that the fire he has already set alight is nothing to the conflagration that will follow his death and resurrection. And at 13:10–30 there is a stand-up battle between Christ and a ruler of a synagogue, in which when the ruler criticizes Christ for delivering a woman from a spirit of weakness on the sabbath, Christ denounces him as a hypocrite in front of the whole congregation and exposes the ruler as standing perilously near Satan's side in the conflict. Obviously, Christ's journey through Palestine to glory was no mere joy-ride, nor even a ceremonial procession. It lay through enemy-infested territory, with many a citadel, out-post and ambush manned by the enemy's agents determined to resist to the very death the One who had come 'to destroy the works of the Devil' (1 Jn. 3:8), to invade his stronghold, to strip him of his armour and to set his captives free (see 11:21–22; 13:16).

If these, then, are some of the leading themes which re-occur throughout stage 2, the question arises whether we are meant to read the contents of this stage as a succession of independent and more or less unconnected narratives, or as one undivided whole, or as a series of movements of thought each concentrating for the most part on some aspect of the common themes. Here we can let ourselves be guided in the first instance by the four 'opposition' paragraphs, as we may call them, which we have just surveyed. First, we should notice that the fourth of these paragraphs is not only the last paragraph in the stage, but also forms a triumphal climax to the theme of opposition. When Christ refutes the synagogue-ruler's criticisms, we are told (13:17) 'all Christ's opponents were covered with confusion, and all the people were delighted at the glorious things which he was doing'. And this sense of triumph is further enforced by two parables depicting the progress of the kingdom of God: one involves a man who planted a mustard seed which grew to such proportions that the birds were able to lodge in its branches; and the other involves a woman who hid some leaven in three measures of meal until the whole was leavened (see 13:18–21). One can easily understand why Luke should have concluded the stage on this note of triumph.

Next, however, we should notice that the first 'opposition' para- graph (see 11:14–28) strikingly resembles this last 'opposition' paragraph both in contents and form. Both occasions involved a miracle, and both miracles involved the deliverance of someone from an evil spirit. In both incidents Christ was criticized and in both his triumphant rebuttal of the criticisms involved him in a discussion of Satan's power and tactics. Moreover just as the main discussion in the fourth paragraph is reinforced with two final stories, one about a man (Gk. *anthrōpos* – 'human being rather than 'male') and one about a woman, so in the first paragraph the main discussion (see 11:14–23) is followed first by a story of a man (Gk. *anthrōpos* again) from whom an evil spirit went out, but later came back with seven other worse spirits and, like the birds in the mustard tree, dwelled once more in the unfortunate man (see

11:24–26); and secondly by a story of a woman who wanted to praise Christ for his victory over his critics, but unfortunately did so indirectly by praising his mother and had herself to be corrected. It is at least obvious, then, that Luke intended us to notice the similarities – and the differences – between these two stories, and to reflect carefully on their significance. And if that is so, it would be a reasonable working hypothesis to suppose that the triumph of the first 'opposition' story was meant to serve as a minor climax in the course of the narrative, anticipating the major climax of the fourth 'opposition' story. Similarly with the other two 'opposition' stories. So let us draw up a table of contents for stage 2 on the basis of this hypothesis and see what it looks like. We cannot expect a stage, dominated by long runs of teaching with very little incident, to show the same clear-cut symmetry as other stages have done; but that matters little. The table of contents will at least enable us to take in the whole stage at a glance and to see what connections of thought, if any, there may be between the various parts of the stage (see pp. 214–215).

The movements

1. Deciding life's paramount necessities 10:38 – 11:28

i. A family dispute (10:38–42). The first story in movement 1 is brief and comes swiftly to its point: amid all life's duties and necessities there is one supreme necessity which must always be given priority, and which, if circumstances compel us to choose, must be chosen to the exclusion of all others. That supreme necessity is to sit at the Lord's feet and listen to his word (see 10:39, 42). It must be so. If there is a Creator at all, and that Creator is prepared to visit us and speak to us as in his incarnation he visited and spoke to Martha and Mary, then obviously it is our first duty as his creatures, as it ought to be our highest pleasure, to sit at his feet and listen to what he says.

But it is very easy to lose sight of the priority of this necessity and to let other necessities come crowding in and take first place. Nor does one have to be an atheist or a careless sinner to do so. Martha was no enemy of Christ. Far from it, she was one of his most devoted and spiritually perceptive disciples (see Jn. 11). When Christ came to her village, it was she who received him into her home, and it was love and devotion to the Lord that led her to go to an enormous amount of trouble (see 10:40–41) to entertain him as worthily as she possibly could. That meant, however, that what with the preparation of the guest-room, the buying of provisions, the cooking, baking and serving of the meals, and the washing of the dishes, she had very little time actually to sit and listen to the Lord talking. It was not of course that she did not enjoy his conversation: she would have enjoyed it as much as Mary; but she had very clear and very strong ideas on what things just had to be done when you were entertaining so important a guest as the Lord. If asked, she doubtless would have explained that true love is practical, and that work must be put before pleasure; and it was this that filled her with resentment when Mary left off working and went and sat at the Lord's feet and listened to his word. It meant that Mary was getting all the pleasure, and Martha was getting all the work, her own share and Mary's as well. To Martha's way of thinking, Mary was being selfish, unprincipled and unfair.

The trouble was that Christ was doing nothing about it; indeed, he seemed to Martha to be encouraging Mary in her wrong behaviour by letting her sit there and talking to her. That very fact, one might have thought, ought to have made Martha begin to suspect that her own ideas must be wrong somewhere; but instead of questioning her own list of necessities and priorities, she went up to Christ and suggested that he was being irresponsible in encouraging Mary to act so unfairly. Martha was wrong, of course, and it was a sad and ironic thing that her love and devotion to the Lord had led her through a wrong sense of necessities and priorities to a point where she questioned the fairness of the very One whom she felt obliged to serve so rigorously.

Gently but firmly Christ had to correct her. It was not that he underestimated the importance of service in general or of her service in particular. Later in this stage (see 12:35–38, 42–44) we shall hear him demand from his servants a readiness to serve at any time and faithfulness and fairness in that service; and what is more he will promise that when he returns he will reward his faithful servants by 'girding himself, making them sit at table, and serving them'. But when he visited Martha's house, he was on a journey (see 10:38). The time he had to spend with the two sisters was limited, and when he left, it would be a long while before he was back again. The question therefore was whether they would cut

Stage 2 of the Going 10:38 – 13:21

1 Deciding life's paramount necessities 10:38 – 11:28

1 A family dispute: a woman appeals to Christ to tell her sister to take her fair share of the work 10:38–42.

Christ's verdict
He refuses to take away from Mary the good part she has chosen. Martha is anxiously preparing many things, but has neglected the one necessary thing.

2 Lessons on prayer 11:1–13

a *Pattern prayer for the coming of God's kingdom*
'... Your kingdom come ... give us our daily bread ... forgive us our sins, for we ourselves forgive everyone who is in debt to us ...'.

2 Seeing God's Word in its true proportions 11:29–12:12

1 The people seek a sign but no sign is given except that of Jonah 11:29–36.

Questions of evidence
At the judgment the attitude of the Queen of the South and the Ninevites to the evidence available to them will be cited against 'this generation and secure its condemnation.

2 Woes on the Pharisees and lawyers 11:37–52

a *False proportions and aims in religious practice*
'... you clean the outside of cup and plate, but your inward part is full of extortion ... you tithe the mint and rue ... and pass over the judgment and love of God.'

3 Seeing possessions in their true perspective 12:13–53

1 A family dispute: a man appeals to Christ to tell his brother to divide the inheritance fairly 12:13–21.

Christ's response
He refuses to act as judge and divider, but tells of a rich fool who prepared large stocks for many years, forgetting that his life could be taken away that very night.

2 Blessings on true servants 12:22–48

a *False and true proportions and aims in respect of material things*
'... life is more than food, the body more than clothes ... you are more valuable than birds, more lasting than flowers ... do not seek food and drink ... seek God's kingdom ...'.

4 Assessing time and the times correctly 12:54–13:21

1 The people and signs: they can interpret weather-signs but not 'this time' 12:54–59.

Be your own judge!
It is better to judge your own case and to settle with your opponent out of court, rather than to come before the judge, lose your case and receive a long prison sentence.

2 Lessons on repentance 13:1–9

a *False interpretations of God's providential government*
'... do you suppose that these people were sinners and debtors above all others because they suffered these atrocities and accidents? No! ... unless you repent, you will all perish ...'.

b *The urgency of prayer*
Like the man who went to his friend at midnight seeking bread, we are to ask, seek, knock, because everyone who ... seeks, finds ... 'Your Father will give the Holy Spirit to those who ask him.'

3 **The opposition defeated:** Christ casts out a dumb demon and is accused of doing it by the power of Satan 11:14–28.

Christ answers his critics
Satan is not divided. Christ, the Stronger, has overcome the strong and set his victims free.

Warning example of a man to whom a demon returned with seven others and dwelled in him.

A woman congratulates Christ's mother, and is corrected. Blessed are those who hear God's word and do it.

b *Principles of accountability in teaching Scripture*
'... you load people down with burdens ... and you yourselves will not raise a finger to touch those burdens ... Your fathers killed the prophets ... you consent to what they did ... Therefore the blood of all the prophets shall be required of this generation ... You took away the key of knowledge ...'

3 **Overcoming the fear of the opposition:** Christ instructs his disciples how to behave when they are persecuted and brought before the courts 11:53–12:12.

... the Pharisees and the teachers of the law began to oppose him fiercely and to besiege him with questions waiting to catch him in something he might say ....

b *Principles of accountability in Christian stewardship*
'... if the servant begins to beat his fellow servants, to eat and be drunk, the lord ... shall come ... and cut him in two ... the servant who knew his lord's will and did not do it ... shall be beaten with many stripes ... the one who did not know ... shall be ... with few stripes. From the one to whom much is given much shall be required ....'

3 **Provoking the opposition:** Christ tells his disciples the true purpose of his coming 12:49–53.

'... I have come to cast fire on the earth ... not to bring peace but rather division ....'

b *The urgency of repentance*
For three years the owner has come seeking fruit from his fig tree and has found none. The tree has been given one more year to produce fruit: if it doesn't, it will be cut down.

3 **Triumph over the opposition:** Christ delivers a woman from a spirit of weakness and is criticized for healing on the sabbath 13:10–21.

Christ answers his critics
'Ought not this woman whom Satan has bound ... to be loosed from this chain on the sabbath?'

Parable of a man who sowed a seed which grew into a tree and the birds dwelled in the branches.

Parable of a woman who hid leaven in three measures of meal until it was all leavened.

down work to a minimum, content themselves with few and simple meals and so give the Lord the maximum amount of time to talk to them and enjoy their fellowship, or whether Martha would insist on putting on frequent and elaborate meals the preparation of which left her with very little time to sit and listen to the Lord. In those circumstances there is no doubt what Christ would have preferred – he would have preferred Martha's fellowship to her service – nor what he in fact regarded as more necessary for Martha. But Martha's idea of what had to be done, was different from Christ's, and as we can now see, it was false. She meant well, she loved the Lord, she thought she was serving him; but her sense of proportion with regard to what was necessary was in fact depriving the Lord of what he most wished for and depriving her of what was most necessary; and it had come about precisely because she had not first sat at his feet and listened to him long enough to find out what he regarded as the paramount necessity.

The story has its obvious lesson for us. We too are on a journey. Life at the best is short. We cannot do everything: there is not enough time. Like Mary, therefore, (see 10:42) we shall have to choose and choose very deliberately. Life's affairs will not automatically sort themselves into a true order of priorities. If we do not consciously insist on making 'sitting at the Lord's feet and listening to his word' our number one necessity, a thousand and one other things and duties, all claiming to be prior necessities, will tyrannize our time and energies and rob us of the 'good part' in life.

It is no accident, of course, that Martha and Mary's story stands first in this stage. Doubtless chronology decreed that it should stand first. But equally doubtless is the fact that logic (under the Holy Spirit's inspiration) played its part in Luke's selection and ordering of his material. This stage is going to be taken up largely with the need to get life's priorities and proportions right. How shall we ever do that, unless before we do anything else we first sit down at the Lord's feet and let him tell us what life's true priorities are?

ii. *Lessons on prayer (11:1–13)*. If life's first necessity is to let the Lord speak to us, its second necessity is surely that we should speak to the Lord. We must pray. Life's highest gifts do not come to us automatically, nor are life's most important goals attained unthinkingly. We are not mere cogs mindlessly revolving in some impersonal mechanistic universe. We are persons created by a personal God, made capable of holding converse with him. Next to the wonder of his being willing to talk to us, is the inexpressible honour of our being allowed to talk to him, and by asking him for gifts which he is pleased to give, to develop that personal relationship between ourselves and him which is the chief goal of our creation.

But what should we ask for? What are life's most important and necessary things? And among those things which should we put first as being supremely important and which second? Life is a journey, we are constantly moving forward, we feel we ought to be making some kind of progress. But towards what goal? What should be our chief ambition, what our highest aspiration?

Wisely, having listened to Christ himself praying, one of his disciples asked him to give them a pattern for praying, to tell them what to pray for and how to order their priorities in prayer.

In Luke's record of the prayer which Christ then taught them there are five requests. First come two requests relating to God's own interests: his name and kingdom; then three requests relating to our own: daily bread, forgiveness, and shielding from temptation. God's interests first, ours next. That obviously is the true priority for creatures at prayer.

God's interests first, then. And here, what God is, his character, his glory, these things stand first. We are to pray that his Name be hallowed, that is, set apart, regarded with awe as the most holy, valuable, glorious thing in all the universe. Life's values will never be measured properly or seen in their true light unless we see that God's Name is not only the chiefest value of them all but the source of all true value which any person or thing possesses. Let God's Name be devalued, and God himself dishonoured, then all that derives from him – which is everything – is correspondingly reduced in value and honour. Deny God altogether, and nothing ultimately will prove to have any value at all. And yet in this sorry world God's Name is not hallowed as it should be, not by the greatest saints, still less by us ordinary saints, not to speak of the profane and godless. We have lost the sense of God's holiness, and we live in a world where sacred things are progressively profaned and life becomes ever more cheap.

But it will not always be so. God has his purposes and plans to bring in his kingdom universally so that his will shall be done here on earth as it is in heaven, and his name be hallowed as it should, and all life's values shine with the lustre and brightness of the jewels of the new Jerusalem. That is God's purpose and it shall be accomplished. But we are not to regard its accomplishment fatalistically. We are actively to pray for it, to align our will with God's will, and to make the coming of his kingdom our chief desire, aim and ambition.

Often unfortunately we do not do so, for we have our own personal ambitions, plans, schemes and purposes in life, and if we are not careful constantly to pray as Christ taught us, they gradually come to fill our minds and horizons, leaving God's plans and purposes little time, space or consideration. Indeed it can happen that we pervert prayer itself by making its chief burden our personal and family interests instead of God's kingdom and purposes. And that is foolish even from the point of view of our own narrow self-interest. No purpose or ambition of our own can make ultimate sense or yield ultimate satisfaction if it is not subordinated to, and part of, the one great purpose behind the universe. It ought surely to be self-evident that it is far more important for our own good that God's kingdom come, than that our own shortsighted will and often misconceived ambitions be achieved. But even this is a dangerous consideration, if it leaves us thinking that our self-interest should be the prime concern in our praying. The first and chief point of the pattern for prayer which Christ has left us is that not our interests but God's must ever be given first place.

God's interests first, then; but after that it is right and good that we pray for our own. Of the three kinds of thing which Christ bids us ask for ourselves, one relates to our physical needs, two to our moral and spiritual needs. Again we notice the proportion. Our physical needs stand first: give us day by day the bread we need for existence (if that is the right translation, or perhaps, 'for the coming day'; see the commentaries). This is sane and practical. Physical existence with all its recurring needs is the necessary basis, in this world at any rate, for higher, spiritual experience. We are not to despise it, nor, on the other hand, to take it for granted. Indeed, the greatest enjoyment of our physical blessings is to be found in the consciousness that they come from God.

But to one prayer for our physical needs, we must add two for our moral and spiritual needs. Above all things physical we need forgiveness for the sins of our past, and deliverance from temptation lest we fall into sin in the future. And if we need forgiveness as much as we need our daily bread, so does our brother. If, therefore, we come asking God for this prime necessity for ourselves, God will insist that we show ourselves ready in our turn to forgive those who may be indebted to us.

This, then is the true ordering of priorities in the things which we should pray for. But there is another aspect of prayer that will reveal our sense of priorities and our estimate of what is really necessary, and that is, not what we pray for, but the motivation that leads us to pray for it and maintains us in our praying. This aspect Christ now deals with in 11:5–13.

In this connection let us notice first that the gift which the Father is ready to give and for which we should be praying is his Holy Spirit (see 11:13). For Christ's contemporaries this doubtless had a special significance. The prophets had declared that one day God would pour out his Spirit and effect a mighty regeneration of his people Israel (see Ezk. 36:26–27), and pour out his Spirit also on all mankind (see Joel 2:28–32; see also Acts 2:16). Generations of the godly in Israel would have prayed for the fulfilment of these promises; and now, though they did not know it, Christ's contemporaries stood on the very eve of Pentecost when the risen Lord having received from the Father the promise of the Holy Spirit, would pour out this Holy Spirit on those who believed (see Acts 2:33). How earnestly or otherwise some of Christ's contemporaries were praying for the Holy Spirit we shall see in a moment. For us who live the other side of Pentecost the situation is, of course, somewhat different. The Holy Spirit, who had not been given as long as Jesus was on earth and not ascended (see Jn. 7:39), has now been given. In that sense the believer on Christ no longer needs to pray to receive the Holy Spirit: he has received him (see 1 Cor. 12:13; Eph. 1:13). That does not mean, however, that there is no sense at all in which we who live after Pentecost need to pray for the Father's gift of the Holy Spirit. At Ephesians 1:16–19 Paul indicates that he unceasingly prays for those who have already been sealed with the Holy Spirit that God might give them a spirit of wisdom and revelation in the knowledge of him; and again at Ephesians 3:14–21 he declares that he prays God would give them to be strengthened with power through his Spirit in the inward man that Christ might dwell in their hearts.

By definition, therefore, asking for the Holy Spirit could not be

something which is done once for all. We must, says Christ (see
11:9) keep on asking, seeking, knocking.[1] That being so, two
things will decide whether or not we persist in prayer of this kind.
The first is our estimate of the necessity and urgency of the gift we
seek. We ought to be driven by a sense of its utter indispensability,
which will make us completely 'shameless' in asking for it (see
11:8).

At first sight shamelessness (Gk. *anaideia*, EVV 'importunity')
might seem to indicate a bad quality; and on some occasions, of
course, it does. But its meaning is not always or necessarily bad. It
simply describes a person who has no sense of shame, no compunction, in doing something or asking for something. If there are
reasons why the person ought to feel compunction or shame, then,
of course, shamelessness is a bad thing; but if a man's case is good,
then shamelessness in insisting on it, is not blameworthy, but
commendable. To illustrate the point Christ pictures a man who
has an unexpected guest arrive in the middle of the night, and finds
he has no food to offer his guest (see 11:5–8). Being an Oriental
with an oriental's sense of the importance of hospitality he has no
compunction whatever in going to a friend's house, midnight
though it is, and getting him out of bed to lend him the necessary
food to put before his guest. His friend might make some irritable
remarks about having to get up at that hour of the night; but he
would not find fault with the man's shamelessness. Sharing the
man's Oriental ideas on the duty of hospitality, he would recognize
his shamelessness as perfectly justifiable. In the West we do not
think the same way about the urgency of the need to feed visitors
who arrive in the middle of the night. An equivalent in our culture
would be the question whether or not you should call a doctor out
in the middle of the night to visit a sick person. We would feel
embarrassed if we called the doctor out for something that proved
to be only a minor upset. But if someone in the family suffered a
massive heart attack, we would have no compunction at all in
summoning the doctor whatever the hour of the night and whatever the weather.

This, then, is the analogy. It tells us that while all who ask for the
illumination and strengthening of their hearts by the Holy Spirit,

---

[1] The imperatives in the Greek are all present imperatives, indicating a repeated and not a once
for all action).

will most certainly receive the gifts they ask for, yet whether we ask and go on asking or not will depend on how indispensably necessary we regard the gift. If, for instance, today we ask for illumination by God's Spirit through his Word so that we may know God and his grace and his purposes more fully, and then tomorrow forget to ask, or to seek in his Word, or to knock on the door of heaven, and carry on forgetting for the next six months, it is obvious that we do not regard the gift we ask for as very important or necessary; and it is unlikely that we shall receive it.

On the other hand Christ guarantees that the one who diligently persists in asking, seeking, and knocking will most certainly be rewarded; and he backs up the guarantee by a second analogy (see 11:9–13). This time the analogy stresses not the shamelessness of those who ask, but the character of the Giver and the perfection of his Fatherhood. Human beings, Christ asserts (see 11:13), are evil, and yet in spite of it they know how to give good gifts to their children. No normal human father, being asked by his child for bread, would refuse it or deceive the child by offering it something superficially similar, but worthless or dangerous. If, therefore, very imperfect human fathers can be relied upon to give their children good gifts, how much more shall the Archetype and Perfection of fatherhood give the Holy Spirit to those who ask? (11:13). It was on this certainty, we notice, that Paul was in the habit of basing his requests: 'For this cause I bow my knees unto the Father, from whom every family in heaven or on earth is named, that he would grant you . . . that you may be strengthened with power through his Spirit in the inward man, that Christ may dwell in your heart through faith . . .' (see Eph. 3:14 –17).

iii. *The opposition defeated (11:14–28).* So far in movement 1 we have had two paragraphs. The first was about listening to the Lord speaking to us. The second was about our speaking to God. Now in the third paragraph we meet a man who was dumb. He could not speak to anybody.

All disabilities are sad, but there is something pathetic, almost uncanny about dumbness in a human being. The ability to speak and express oneself articulately, to communicate with others, is a characteristically human faculty, part of the distinctive glory of being man. Dumbness robs a human being of part of what it means to be human; it makes a prisoner of a human personality within his own mind and body.

Christ miraculously cast out the demon responsible for the man's dumbness. But if this miracle was like other miracles which Luke has recorded, it was more than a miracle: it was an enacted parable. Many people suffer from a dumbness that is worse than physical. As originally made man was intended to hold converse with God. Conscious of himself and of God, man could consciously respond to the Creator, and communicate in words with him who is the Word. But many men in actual fact never speak to God, never pray. They say that there is no Creator for them to talk to; or if there is, they are not interested in speaking with him; or they do not know how to, they cannot, pray. This is self-evidently the work of the enemy. If it is God's desire and design, and man's chief glory, that he should be the priest of creation and articulate creation's response to the Creator, that he should talk with God as a son with a father, then it is obvious why it should be of prime strategic importance to the enemy to cripple man's ability to speak with God, to lock up man's spirit within himself, and as far as God is concerned to turn this earth into (to borrow a phrase) a silent planet.

It was a glorious thing, therefore, that which the Saviour did when he cast out the demon responsible for the man's physical dumbness. Luke tells us that when the silence of years was broken and for the first time in life the man spoke, the crowd was amazed (see 11:14). As well they might be: they had grown so used to this man's being dumb, that they had never imagined he could be anything else. Even more glorious, however, is that great spiritual deliverance which Christ chose to illustrate by this miracle. To picture it we may perhaps be allowed to borrow some imagery from an analogy which he himself used in the argument that followed his miracle (see 11:21–22). 'When a strong man fully armed guards his own court, his goods are in peace'. That is, they remain undisturbed and secure, they give him no trouble or anxiety. There for you is the true state of prayerless, spiritually dumb mankind. Their peace, apparent contentment and spiritual silence is the peace of a prison. Chattels of the strong enemy, they ask God for nothing, not even for deliverance, because their prayerless tongues have been chained by a tyrant who has endless devices at his disposal for keeping them quiet and preventing any break-out or contact with the world above. Many of them have even been persuaded that there is no world above (*cf.* Eph. 2:1–3).

In that grim situation we may thank God that he did not wait for the prisoners to invite him in before he intervened. He took the initiative. Strong and fully armed as the enemy was, by means of the incarnation a stronger than he began to invade the prison, overpower the tyrant, and talk to the prisoners. His miraculous release of one prisoner from a demon of physical dumbness certainly astonished the rest of them; but the miracle was intended as more than an exhibition of supernatural power designed to demonstrate the existence of God and his kingdom. It was also meant as a sign to encourage men to break their silence, to set them free and get them talking to the Father. Since then, the Stronger than the strong by his death has invaded the deepest of the enemy's dungeons and broken his last stronghold. Multitudes have been set free (see Col. 2:13–18; Heb. 2:14–15). The risen and triumphant Lord has 'distributed Satan's spoils' (11:22).

We must rein in our fancy, and perhaps apologize to Luke, for we have taken what he records as a simple analogy and used it as though it were an allegory. For all that, we are not far from the imagery which other Christians used. When Paul says (Eph. 4:7–13) 'Christ has led captivity captive and has given gifts to men', the gifts he is thinking of are the once-time prisoners of Satan, whom the ascended Lord has set free and given to the church as apostles, evangelists and teachers.

Christ, then, delivered a man from the grip of a dumb demon. The power with which he did it was self-evidently supernatural: no-one questioned that. We might have supposed that it would likewise have been self-evident to everyone that this supernatural power was of God; but that would be to underestimate the enemy's hold on the minds of some people, and the sophistication of his opposition to Christ. Some in the crowd suggested that the power Christ employed was of the devil, and others thought that it could well be, and asked him to give them a sign from heaven to prove it wasn't (see 11:15–16). The suggestion was so foolish that we may well be surprised that Christ troubled to answer it. But the suggestion was not only foolish: it was ominous. Captives in Satan's prison they might be, but the kingdom of God had broken through to them (see 11:20). God's finger was touching them; God was speaking to them. What they had just witnessed was a direct, unambiguous, demonstration of the Holy Spirit. Now they must make life's ultimate judgment; and they were on the point of taking a decision which once deliberately made would be irreversible, and would make deliverance for ever impossible. Reject the Holy Spirit, call Ultimate Good evil, call Truth himself authenticated by Absolute Holiness, a lie, and God himself has no further evidence left, nothing further left to say, which could bring a man to repentance, faith and salvation. God himself is reduced to silence (see 1 Sa. 19:23–24; 28:6,15).

If then these men were determined to make this fatal choice, Christ was not prepared to let them make it without knowing exactly what they were doing. Certainly he would not allow them to suppose that it was reason, or true religion or morality that forced them to the choice. He pointed out that in order to reject the evidence of God's Holy Spirit working through him, they must defy common sense, reject common morality, and deny their own spiritual axioms and principles of behaviour into the bargain. Knowingly and deliberately they must call black that which in every other context and circumstance of life they would have called white. It is conceivable that for tactical reasons Satan would occasionally cast out a demon. To suggest that he would do it regularly as Christ did, and so divide and destroy his own kingdom was a manifest absurdity (see 11:17–18). Secondly, his opponents' sons also exorcised demons (see 11:19–20), and it was generally held that they did it by the power of God. Why, then, say differently about Jesus? For one very good reason which Christ proceeded to point out (11:20). Their sons did not claim to be about to introduce the kingdom of God. Christ did. If then it was divine power that had enabled him to cast out the demon, his claim stood vindicated. It was precisely their unwillingness to accept this claim and its implications for them personally that had led them to their absurd position of suggesting that Jesus was in league with the devil. Moreover – and here comes the analogy which we borrowed earlier – you cannot remove goods from a heavily-armed man who is guarding them unless you first overpower the man and disarm him. The very fact that Christ had delivered the dumb man from Satan's clutches was evidence enough that he was not on Satan's side: as the Stronger than Satan he had obviously overpowered him (see 11:21–22).

224

In the light of this Christ then gave two very strong warnings. First: 'he who is not with me is against me; and he who does not gather with me scatters' (11:23). Christ's critics were openly against him; and since Christ was engaged in fighting the enemy, it was apparent on whose side they stood. Many others in the crowd, however, may well have felt that while they were of course – like all decent-minded people are – against disability and demon-possession, and while they considered that Christ's critics were extremists, yet they need not themselves positively and actively take sides with Christ either. Christ warned these people that in the war which he was fighting such neutrality is in fact impossible.

Secondly, he warned the crowds that good as it is to cast a demon out of a man – and he had just admitted that his critics' sons did at times manage to do that – it is not enough (see 11:24–26). It leaves a man clean and refined, but empty; and the danger is that the demon will return with seven other worse demons and re-occupy the man, and he will have no power to resist them. So reformation without regeneration and the indwelling of the Holy Spirit is dangerously inadequate. Not for nothing did Christ earlier (see 11:9–13) urge his contemporaries, although the Judaism they belonged to had been purged of idolatry and thoroughly reformed by the exile, to seek ardently the gift of the Holy Spirit. And not for nothing was Peter inspired years later (see 2 Pet. 2:20–22) to describe so vividly the dangers of a moral clean up that is not accompanied by the new-birth and the receiving of the divine nature (see 1 Pet. 1:22–23; 2 Pet. 1:4).

Movement 1 is nearly over. It has dealt with many momentous things; but Luke still thinks it worthwhile to add one further detail (see 11:27–28). A woman in the crowd who had heard Christ answer his opponents so triumphantly, complimented Christ, perhaps also confessed his Messiahship, by remarking in oriental fashion how marvellous it must be to be his mother. So it was: Christ did not deny it. But wonderful as it was to be his mother, that in itself would not have saved anybody. It is spiritual relationship with Christ, not physical, that is vital. So, without contradicting her well-intentioned remark Christ pointed out where the superior blessedness lies: 'Blessed rather are those who hear the word of God and keep it'. At this our memory ought to be stirring. At the beginning of the movement we were told that the 'good part' in life is to sit at the Lord's feet and hear his word (see

10:39,42). That was true, of course; but not all the truth. After all it is not the hearing only, but the keeping of the word of God that counts.

2. Seeing God's Word in its true proportions (11:29 – 12:13)

i. *The people seek a sign (11:29–36).* At 11:16 in the course of movement 1 some in the crowd sought from Christ a sign from heaven. To this our Lord now refers at the beginning of movement 2, and in so doing he sets the theme which is going to dominate the movement: evidence. The claims of Christ faced his contemporaries with decisions which carried incalculably far-reaching consequences. It is understandable that they should ask him to give them indisputable evidence that his claims were true, if indeed they were.

It is therefore at first sight surprising to find him refusing their request. Had he not earlier assured his hearers that everyone who seeks shall be given what he seeks for? Why now refuse the miraculous sign which the people sought? The reason was not, of course, that there was anything wrong or unsatisfactory with the evidence of miraculous signs.[1] It was that there was something seriously wrong with the people: 'This generation is an evil generation: it seeks a sign and no sign shall be given it . . .' (11:29).

Now in one sense all men are evil (see 11:13); but Christ's generation was especially evil. Their very seeking of this additional sign was evil, a form, says Luke (see 11:16), of tempting Christ. Their seeking was not sincere. The proof they professed to be seeking was not logical or scientific proof that the power behind Christ's action was supernatural: everybody was agreed that it was supernatural. The proof they demanded was moral and spiritual proof that the miracle was of God and not of the devil. In theory this is a very important point, which incidentally our modern world is in danger of forgetting. Mere supernatural power is not by itself necessarily good; we need to ask about its moral and spiritual quality before we allow ourselves to be influenced by it.

But Christ had already done many miracles of which doubtless they had heard, and in addition, he had just healed a man of dumbness. The moral and spiritual quality of his acts of super-

---

[1] We should be careful not to misinterpret 1 Cor. 1:22–23 to the effect that there is something essentially unsatisfactory with our Lord's miracles as evidence. *Cf.* Jn. 20:30–31; Acts 2:22; 14:8–11; 19:11–12.

natural power was self-evident and consistent. To suggest that it was not clear, that there was a reasonable possibility that it was evil and that it needed some sign from heaven to prove it was not of the devil, was monstrously perverse. If the kinds of miracle Christ had already done did not prove it beyond all doubt, what kind of miracle would ever prove it? The fact is that the people who demanded another sign would not have been convinced by it or by any number of signs. Their seeking of a sign was not an indication of their willingness to believe if only adequate evidence were provided, but a rationalizing of their unwillingness to believe the perfectly adequate evidence they already had. And it was worse: it was a form of tempting Christ. Had he tried to give them another sign, he would, in their eyes at least, have been admitting that their doubts about the moral quality of his previous miracles were reasonable. Christ was not deceived by such a request for more evidence.

No further sign, then, was given except that of the prophet Jonah: 'for just as Jonah became a sign to the Ninevites so shall the Son of Man also be to this generation' (11:30). This raises the immediate question: in what sense did Jonah become a sign to the Ninevites? Matthew in his account (see 12:38–40) explicitly points out the parallel between Jonah's 'burial' in the whale and Christ's death, burial and resurrection. Luke does not explicitly draw attention to this parallel, and this has made some people think that Luke understood the parallel between Jonah and Christ to lie simply in the fact that they both were sent by God to issue a portentous clarion call to repentance to a people who were under the threat of God's imminent judgment. It may be that this interpretation is right; and if it is, it is apt and solemn enough. In dealing with people whose only response to evidence upon evidence is persistent prevarication, there comes a point where the only hope of bringing them to their senses and to repentance is a direct, unambiguous announcement of imminent divine judgment such as Jonah delivered so effectively to the Ninevites.

Two considerations, however, make it reasonable to think that Luke may have seen as much significance in the parallel as Matthew. First there is the meaning of the word 'sign' which forms the central point of similarity between Jonah's ministry and Christ's. In the context (see 11:16, 29, 30) 'sign' means 'miracle'. Jonah's mere appearance in Nineveh and his preaching were hardly by themselves a miracle. And if Christ's contemporaries were determined to reject the evidence of Christ's miraculous deeds, they were hardly likely to regard his preaching as a miracle either. It was the miraculous way in which Jonah arrived at Nineveh that gave force to his preaching and made him a sign to the Ninevites. It would similarly be Christ's death, burial and resurrection that made Christ God's ultimate sign to Israel (cf. Jn. 2:18–22).

Secondly, at 12:50, at the end of movement 3, Luke has Christ referring to his coming death, burial and resurrection as a 'baptism'. The other Synoptics record Christ's use of this figure on other occasions (see Mt. 20:22–23; Mk. 10:38–39); only Luke records it in this context. It is difficult to think that when he recorded the parallel between Jonah and Christ at 11:29–30, he saw no connection of thought at all between it and the 'baptism' which he was about to mention at 12:50.

If then we may think that by this parallel between himself and Jonah, Christ was referring to his death, burial and resurrection, it makes his pronouncement in 11:29 a message not only of judgment but of immeasurable mercy. Granted that it was pointless to give the people another sign, since what they needed was to be brought to repentance for their unwillingness to believe the miraculous signs they had already been given; yet God had evidence for them of a different kind, calculated precisely to lead them to repentance; evidence that he loved them in spite of their perversity. He would allow unbelief to crucify his Son. He would then raise him from the dead, and instead of deluging them with judgment forthwith, he would offer them pardon, reconciliation and escape from judgment in the name of, and through the sufferings of, the very One they had crucified. If they could not see that love like that was 'from heaven', they would never recognize heaven even if they saw it, and their hell would be self-chosen.

With this therefore Christ proceeds to tell his contemporaries how their case will be dealt with at the final judgment. Popular opinion has it that the judgment will concern itself with assessing how good or bad a person's works have been. And so, of course, it will, when it comes to passing its sentences (see Rev. 20:12). But just as no one will ever be saved on the ground of his works however good, so the verdict of final condemnation will turn not on the badness of a man's deeds, but on the fact that he did not believe (see Jn. 3:18) and that in consequence his name was never written in the book of life (see Rev. 20:15). That being so, the judgment will necessarily concern itself with assessing what opportunity a man had to believe, what evidence was available to him and what he did with that evidence. According to Christ, who after all will be the Judge on that occasion (see Jn. 5:22–24), witnesses will be called to show what other people did with the evidence available to them, and so to establish what the man in question could have done, had he wished, with the amount of evidence available to him.

In the case of Christ's contemporaries the witnesses called will be the Queen of the South and the Ninevites (see 11:31–32). The contrast between the Queen's attitude and that of Christ's contemporaries will convict the latter of culpable indifference to God's self-revelation. The only clue she had was a report of the remarkable wisdom of a distant king. Yet such was her keen desire for wisdom that she travelled the long distance to listen to Solomon. Compared with Christ's wisdom Solomon's was lowly indeed; but when Christ visited Israel many of his contemporaries made out that they could not see that he was particularly wise, some even condemned him without giving him a hearing (see Jn. 7:50–51). Their lack of interest in the wisdom of God incarnate and their spurning of him will be the ground of their condemnation at the judgment. It reminds us that though Christ no longer walks our earth, the report of him has reached us, and we are expected to follow it up actively and vigorously and to seek, ask, knock until we find him. Failure to be interested enough to seek the Lord is damning.

The contrast between the Ninevites and Christ's contemporaries will likewise convict the latter of moral obliquity. Jonah's moral teaching was simple indeed: just a warning that judgment was about to descend on them because of their sin. Gentiles though they were, with no law of Moses to instruct their consciences, they had no difficulty in seeing that they deserved God's judgment; and they repented *en masse*. Christ's Sermon on the Mount, for all its elevated morality, produced no mass repentance in Israel. They just could not see that they were in desperate need of repentance (see 3:7–9; 7:30–34). And Christ next explains why they could not.

For a man to be enlightened by some evidence or other, the evidence naturally has to be available to him. But that is not all. The light of the evidence must be allowed to enter the man through his faculty of perception. This faculty Christ calls the body's eye (see 11:34), and he compares its function to that of a lamp in a house. If the lamp is functioning properly and placed on a stand, the house is filled with light. If, however, someone were to hide the lamp in some secret place or cover it with a bushel, the house would remain dark. Similarly with a man's faculty of perception. If it is 'simple' (11:34), that is, open, honest, uncomplicated by ulterior motives and prejudices, it will admit the light of the evidence which God puts before it. But it is all too possible for his faculty of perception to be evil, to become clouded by evil desires and prejudices. In that case, no matter how clear the evidence is, its light will never illuminate his mind and personality, for the very faculty whose function it is to transmit the light now seriously distorts it, or else keeps it out altogether.

Christ warns us not to let this happen (see 11:35); and his warning implies that it is within each man's power not to let it happen. Even an unregenerate man, evil as he is, has enough moral sense to know how to give good gifts to his children (11:13) or to recognize in his quieter moments that he is allowing his ambition or greed or jealousy to distort his perception of some situation or other. So it is with the light of the evidence which Christ puts before him. It is useless, and dangerous, to protest that an unregenerate man cannot know when he is allowing his lust or his greed, his ambition or his fear, to distort his perception of the evidence. He can know it, says Christ, and what is more, he can do something about it, and will be held responsible to do something about it. If he wanted to, he could perceive Christ's wisdom as the Queen of the South perceived Solomon's and respond to it, as the Ninevites responded to Jonah's preaching. And if he does not, he will be condemned at the judgment for not doing what he could have done.

ii. *Woes on the Pharisees and lawyers (11:37–52).* We now leave the crowd and follow Christ into a Pharisee's house; but we may expect the topic that has so far been under discussion to be continued, for it was, says Luke (11:37), as Christ was speaking about the need to keep one's 'eye' from becoming 'evil' and from distorting or excluding the light, that this Pharisee invited him to dinner.

What we are about to witness is very sad. Here were religious people exceptionally devoted to the observance of the laws of the Old Testament. This, one might have thought, would have developed their moral sense and educated their conscience and so have prepared them to recognize the validity of Christ's moral teaching, the moral quality of his supernatural power, the rightness of his demand for repentance and the divine hallmark of the salvation which he proclaimed. Unfortunately, however, they had allowed their eyes to become evil, clouded with greed, vanity and heartless pride. As a consequence what light from the Old Testament had managed to get through to their minds had in the process of transmission been grotesquely distorted. Merely to observe their state will be a fearful warning to us. For let it be said at once that neither the Pharisees nor the experts in the law had deliberately set out to be perverse and wicked. The very reverse was their intention. But little by little they had allowed their sense of proportion and their moral judgment to become so distorted by religious pride and mere academic theology that perverse and wicked is what in fact they had become. And when Christ pointed it out, instead of repenting they became his most bitter enemies and relentless persecutors (see 11:53–54). Let us follow Christ's detailed analysis of their condition as Luke has recorded it.

First there was their preoccupation with religious symbols and rituals to the neglect of the moral realities and duties to which these symbols pointed. In the Old Testament God had backed up his demand for moral and spiritual cleanliness by giving Israel certain symbolic ritual washings to perform. The Pharisees made two mistakes over these symbolic rituals. In their zeal to keep the law they had extended these biblical regulations by a thousand and one rules that had no biblical warrant at all; and then they came to thinking that for anyone to disregard one of their additional rules was a serious breach of true holiness. When, therefore, Christ disregarded one of their man–made rules and ate his dinner without first performing a ritual ablution, they were genuinely shocked; their pseudo, man–made standards of holiness made Christ's true unsullied holiness look to them like sin (see 11:38) and prejudiced them against him.

Secondly, they had turned their observance of external rituals into a substitute for morality. Their scrupulous ritual cleansing of cups and plates from ceremonial defilement allowed them to feel they had attained to a high degree of holiness, when all the while they were doing little or nothing about the vastly more serious greed and wickedness which was filling their inner selves with real moral uncleanliness (see 11:39). The answer to greed is not to wash one's hands in water after coming in from the market, nor to cleanse the outside of the cup which one's extortionate profits have filled with good things. The answer is to give the ill-gotten gains away to the poor (see 11:41).[1] In this situation to concentrate on symbolic rituals is to risk turning them not into pointers to moral duty but into a substitute for it.

Christ's next charge was that in their keeping of God's laws the Pharisees had lost all sense of proportion between one duty and another: they tithed mint and rue and every herb, but neglected justice and the love of God (see 11:42). They took the letter of the law to fanatical extremes, but ignored and contravened its whole spirit and purpose. Now unlike the endless ablutions which the Pharisees had added to the law, tithing was commanded by the law itself. True, to extend tithing to the minutest herbs would suggest an over-scrupulous conscience; but if the Pharisees honestly felt that the law must logically be taken to this extreme, Christ would say nothing to offend their conscience. The law on tithing, he said (see 11:42), had to be kept. But when all was said and done, tithing was a minor duty compared with the immeasurably higher responsibility to love God and to act justly towards one's fellow men. Moreover tithing was instituted in Israel as a means of showing one's love for God by maintaining his temple servants, and then as a means of demonstrating the love of God to the stranger, the fatherless and the widow (Dt. 14:29). To tithe mint and rue, and at the same time to practise injustice towards the stranger, the fatherless and the widow and to show no love for God, made a complete mockery of the spirit of tithing and of its true purpose, and turned it into a heartless, mechanical, financial operation.

Next our Lord exposed the false motivation which invalidated much of the Pharisees' religious activity even when it was good in itself: they loved the chief seats in the synagogues and the salutations in the market-places (see 11:43). No man can do a religious act for the purpose of self-aggrandizement and simultaneously do it for the glory of God.

Moreover, the moment we admit self-aggrandizement into our

---

[1] This understands the Gk. of 11:41 as meaning: give away the contents, *i.e.* of the cup, as alms . . .'

motivation, we have distorted our moral judgment. Carried to an extreme, it can make faith in Christ impossible: 'How can you believe', said Christ on one occasion, 'you who receive glory from one another, and the glory which comes from the only God you do not seek?' (Jn. 5:44).

Finally, Christ pointed to the serious effect which these Pharisees' false holiness had on the people in general. Impressed by the Pharisees' outward show of strict devotion to religious rituals and regulations, the people were desensitized to the moral corruption which those same Pharisees indulged in in their private and business lives; and thinking that whatever such 'holy' men did was morally acceptable, they would follow their example of greed and wickedness with an untroubled conscience. The sad irony of the situation is vividly brought out by the metaphor which the Lord borrowed from their own ceremonial law in order to describe these Pharisees (see 11:44). According to the Old Testament (see Nu. 19:11–22) to touch a dead body or bone brought ceremonial defilement. In consequence graves were normally clearly marked, because, if they were not, a pilgrim, say, on his way to the temple could unknowingly walk over a grave, be defiled himself and spread defilement in the temple (see Nu. 19:13). Ironically the Pharisees' very concentration on the outward observance of ceremonial cleanliness coupled with their grievous neglect of true inner holiness, made them like unmarked graves, only worse: carriers of moral contagion among the unsuspecting public.

It goes without saying that not all Pharisees were like the ones whom our Lord denounced; and even his threefold expression 'Woe to you' (11:42–44) is more an exclamation of sorrow than a pronouncement of judgment. But it warns us that when it comes to the question of life's most important decisions, religion must be treated with great care: it is, and always has been, notorious for its tendency to get its proportions and priorities wrong.

Hearing Christ's denunciation of these Pharisees, the experts in the law remonstrated with Christ (see 11:45–52); for it was they who by their exegesis deduced from the Old Testament the elaborate rules and regulations which the Pharisees tried to keep. In denouncing the Pharisees, therefore, Christ was implying that the experts' exegesis of the Old Testament was invalid and perverse; and to imply that the system of exegesis current in the rabbinical schools was fundamentally wrong was such a radical thing to do, that the experts seem not to have been quite sure if Christ really intended to do it. Did he really understand the implications of his criticisms? 'Teacher', said one of them, 'when you say these things you insult us also'. But instead of apologizing, or modifying his remarks, Christ proceeded to denounce the theoreticians as directly as he had denounced the practitioners.

The first charge was that they bound burdens on the backs of ordinary people that were hard to be borne, and yet would not touch those burdens with one of their fingers (see 11:46). The heavy burdens were, of course, the ten thousand and one rules and regulations which they manufactured out of the biblical text by their (to them very clever and sophisticated, but to us often very strange) rabbinic analysis and exegesis. So complicated were these rules and regulations that one would have needed to be a highly qualified lawyer oneself to know whether one was breaking the law or not; and a serious attempt to keep the rules turned moral and religious duty into an intolerable burden (*cf.* Mt. 11:28–30). The second part of Christ's charge, however, has been variously interpreted. Some have thought that Christ meant that having bound burdens on others, the theoreticians made no attempt to practise what they preached, but rather used their skill in casuistry to invent endless loopholes and escape clauses to avoid carrying those same burdens themselves. Certainly this was in part true of the Jewish theoreticians; it is in fact a temptation to all religious theoreticians to feel sometimes that their superiority in biblical study and knowledge somehow exempts them from the necessity of actually carrying out the rules which they impose on other people. But the Jewish theoreticians did carry out many of the regulations which they invented, and prided themselves on it. It would seem more likely therefore that our Lord was referring to their heartless, compassionless legalism which delighted in laying down the law, but had little interest in helping the common people whom they despised (see Jn. 7:49), or in relieving them of their burdens. Examples of that attitude are ready to hand in the context. We have already met (see 11:15) those who claimed that Christ's deliverance of a man from dumbness was a work of the devil. At 13:10–16 we shall meet another of the same kind: their compassionless legalism will insist that people must not be healed on the sabbath; they must be left in their misery.

The second charge against the experts in the law was that their hearts were no different from those of their ancestors who had murdered the prophets. 'You build the tombs of the prophets, but it was your fathers who killed them' (11:47). In building these tombs Christ alleges (see 11:48) they were not only witnessing to the fact that it was their fathers who had killed the prophets, they were thereby showing that they consented to the deeds of their fathers.

At first sight that may seem a hard or even unfair charge. Was not their building of the prophets' tombs a sign of repentance, an attempt to make up for what their fathers had done? Christ will not have it so. The way to honour a dead prophet and to derive spiritual benefit from him is to carry out his message. If Hosea said in God's name 'I will have mercy and not sacrifice' (6:6), the way to honour Hosea is not to build him an elaborate tomb and venerate his shrine, but, as Christ exhorted the legalists (see Mt. 9:13), to obey his words and show mercy and compassion. But these theoreticians were the very men who along with the Pharisees were about to persecute Christ for criticizing their legalism and moral inconsistency, with the same murderous hatred as their fathers had shown to the prophets who had rebuked them in their day (see 11:53–54). For such men to venerate the relics of the dead prophets was nothing but superstition.

To this second charge therefore Christ added a still more solemn pronouncement (see 11:49–51). His contemporaries were the most favoured of all the generations in Israel's history: on them would come the divine wrath and vengeance that had been building up all through the centuries. This pronouncement raises a very important principle of God's providential judgment. If God is going to intervene in judgment in the course of history, and not wait until the final judgment outside the course of history; and if he is not going to visit each generation with judgment immediately it sins, then the question arises how it is right that one particular generation should have to suffer the visitation of God's accumulated vengeance and not another. [1]

That question Christ now answers (see 11:49–51). His own generation was busy building the tombs of the prophets whom their ancestors had killed. Lest anyone should be deceived into thinking that this was a sign of repentance, the divine wisdom had

---

[1] The Flood and the exile are examples in Old Testament history of this kind of judgment.

determined to send to this generation prophets and apostles the like of which no previous generation had ever been privileged to hear: John the Baptist, greatest of all the prophets; then the Messiah himself; then the Christian apostles. Their message would be a more marvellous, more glorious statement of the gospel than any previous generation had ever heard. And in rejecting these prophets and apostles and this gospel this generation would show that they consented with their ancestors who killed the earlier prophets, and thus shared their guilt; and were more guilty than their ancestors because of their rejection of the greater prophets and apostles. Rightly and justly then the vengeance would fall on this generation for the murders of all the prophets from the beginning of the world.

This solemn principle of judgment operated in AD 70 and again in 135 when God allowed the Romans to destroy Jerusalem and its temple, to decimate its citizens, to deport droves of them as captives and to turn Jerusalem into a Gentile city (21:20–24; 1 Thes. 2:14–16). It will operate in even greater measure on apostate Christendom and Judaism at the end of this age.

Christ's final denunciation of the experts was perhaps the most damning of all. 'Woe unto you, lawyers! for you took away the key of knowledge; you did not enter in yourselves, and those who were entering in you hindered' (11:52). Ater all, it was the lawyers' task to expound Scripture so that ordinary people might the more easily understand it, repent, believe, be saved and enter into the spiritual riches of God's word. Yet so divorced from its original purpose had their exegesis become that not only did it leave them ignorant of the true riches of Scripture themselves, but it made it ten thousand times more difficult for the ordinary man to understand God's Word than it was before they started. Such exegesis stands self-condemned.

This denunciation of the Pharisees and of the lawyers is one of the most solemn passages in the whole of Scripture. It is not without its lessons for us. If by its citation of Mary and of the unnamed woman movement 1 has encouraged us to hear the word of God and keep it; if in its early part movement 2 has encouraged us by the example of the Queen of the South to seek the wisdom of God; then certainly the rest of movement 2 is a fearful warning on how not to hear the Word of God and on how not to treat the wisdom of God. God's Word is given us for our salvation: it is possible to misuse and pervert it to one's own destruction (see 2 Pet. 3:16).

iii. Overcoming fear of the opposition (11:53 – 12:12). At the end of the dinner party the atmosphere in the Pharisee's dining room must have been very tense. When he left the house 'the scribes and the Pharisees began to press him fiercely and to provoke him to speak of many things, lying in wait for him, to catch him in something he might say' (11:53–54). To describe their attitude adequately Luke has to use the vocabulary of the hunt. They were pursuing Christ as men pursue a wild animal, pressing him here, worrying him there, pushing and provoking him to say something indiscreet which they could pick on as a ground of accusation, or use to trap him. Meanwhile (see 12:1) the crowds gathered in such numbers that they were trampling on one another. For the disciples it must have been very frightening, just the situation in which they might be tempted to tell themselves that faith is a personal and private matter, and that there was no need to advertize their loyalty to Christ too publicly. So Christ began to teach them first that they must confess him publicly, however frightening it might be to have to do so, and secondly how to cope with their fear and overcome it.

He began (see 12:1–3) by warning them against hypocritically trying to hide what they really believe; and the ground of his warning was that in the end it is in fact impossible to hide it anyway: 'There is nothing covered up, that shall not be revealed, and hid that shall not be known. Therefore whatever you have said in the darkness shall be heard in the light; and what you have spoken in the ear in the inner rooms shall be proclaimed upon the housetops.'

The word for 'hid' in the Greek of verse 2 is *krypton*, and it takes us back to 11:33 where Christ remarked that 'no one, when he has lit a lamp, puts it *eis kryptēn* (*i.e.* in some hidden place) . . . but on the stand so that those who enter in may see the light.' There our Lord was warning against the danger of allowing our eye to become so be-clouded that the light of God's truth cannot get into our darkened hearts. Here in 12:1–3 he warns us against the opposite danger of refusing to allow the light of God which has penetrated our hearts to get out and be known publicly.

But how can anyone overcome the fear that tempts him to keep his faith dark? We can never totally eliminate fear (true, healthy fear, that is, not the neurotic kind): we were never meant to. Fear is a protective mechanism which the Creator himself has put within us. Christ therefore does not simply tell us not to fear, but rather to make sure we fear the things that ought to be feared the most; and fearing them will deliver us from lesser fears. It is an undeniably frightening thing to be threatened by men who have power to kill the body; but when they have done that, they can do no more. It would therefore be very short-sighted to let fear of man's persecution lead us to deny God, for God has infinitely more that he can do: 'But I will warn you whom you shall fear. Fear him who after he has killed has power to cast into hell; yes, I say to you, Fear him' (12:5). And this bigger fear will deliver us from the smaller fear.

But fear of God's power is only one element in our cure: the other is faith in God's sense of comparative values (see 12:6–7). The odd sparrow that is thrown in for nothing if you buy four others, is present to God's awareness. Even the hairs on our head are numbered. Whether we live or die, therefore, God is at every moment aware of what is happening to us. If that is so, the only other thing we need to know is how much he values us. You are of much more value than many sparrows, says Christ; and his cross tells us how much more.

Next there follows (see 12:8–9) an exhortation to get our priorities and proportions right in another area. We should be inhuman if we did not find it a very hurtful thing to be rejected by our fellow man. But to confess Christ will at times involve such repudiation. We must therefore remember that there are two courts to be considered here. There is the court of human society and the opinion of men. There is the court of heaven and the august company of the angels. We must decide which court's recognition is more worth having. To deny Christ before men on earth is to be denied before the angels of God in heaven; whereas to confess him before men is to be confessed by him before the angels of God (see 12:8–9).

Finally, in 12:10–12 Christ bids us consider the comparative seriousness of different sins. A word spoken against the Son of man can be forgiven, but blasphemy against the Holy Spirit cannot be forgiven; and the relevance of the remark here is shown by the final verses, 12:11–12. Believers in Christ, so Christ now warned his disciples, might expect eventually to be dragged before the courts.

That would be a frightening experience for many of them but Christ comforted them and steadied their nerves by two considerations. First they need not worry what to say when the time came to make their defence: the Holy Spirit would teach them what to say. Secondly, the Holy Spirit would use the Christians' witness in order to present before all in the court his supernatural, divine and final witness to the person of Christ. On trial would be not so much the Christians as the court. Let any judge, any prosecutor, any witness, consciously and knowingly and deliberately blaspheme the witness of the Holy Spirit through the believers, then in their folly they would commit the unpardonable and eternal sin; while still living they would pass beyond the point of no return. The possible consequences for the witnesses, the judge and the jury being potentially so grave, it might induce in the believer on trial more compassion for his persecutors than pity for himself (see Acts 7:60).

3. Seeing possessions in their true perspective (12:13–53)

1. A family dispute (12:13–21). The first story in movement 3, like the first story in movement 1, is about a family dispute. The similarities between the two stories are obvious; what is more to our point at the moment is to notice the differences. The story in movement 1 was concerned with the sensible division of time between work on the one hand and listening to the Lord's word on the other. The story in movement 3 is concerned with rightly sharing out material possessions. So the theme is set: movement 3 will be largely dominated by the question of material possessions, and the need to see them in their true perspective and to adopt the right attitude towards them.

'Teacher, speak to my brother that he divide the inheritance with me', said the man out of the crowd; and we cannot tell whether the man had a just case against his brother or not, since Christ refused to act as judge or arbitrator. Perhaps he did have a good case; but Christ did not consider it to be his office to adjudicate in the business disputes of men who were not his disciples (see 12:14). One day, of course, he will act as a 'judge and divider' over all men; but that time had not yet come when he was on earth. It still has not come. Moreover, he made his refusal to act in this case the occasion of issuing a warning against covetousness; and the connection of thought seems clear. When it comes to material possessions Christ does not hold that getting our legal rights is necessarily the best thing for us to do. It is possible (though not necessary) that in going for our legal rights in the matter of possessions we could be (sometimes, though not always) motivated by covetousness. In which case, getting our legal rights would be a victory for our covetousness. Christ will never help us to achieve such a 'victory'. 'Watch out' he said, 'and beware of all (that is, every kind of and every instance of) covetousness' (12:15). Covetousness, apparently, comes in many guises, and more situations display instances of it than we may be aware.

Now the Greek word for covetousness, *pleonexia*, is interesting: it means 'having, or wanting to have, more (more, that is, than one's fair share)'. But the reason Christ gives (see 12:15) why we should beware of such covetousness is even more interesting. The older versions, such as the AV, and many of the modern ones, render the Greek of this verse 'a man's life does not consist in the abundance of the things which he possesses'. But the English word 'abound', like the Latin word from which it comes, can mean one of two somewhat different things. It originally meant 'to overflow' and therefore 'to be more than enough', 'to be in excess', 'to have in excess'. From that meaning it has come to be used very often to signify not 'to be in excess', but simply 'to be plentiful'. So likewise the related noun 'abundance' is normally used nowadays to mean 'plentifulness'. Now in our Lord's saying at 12:15 the Greek word could likewise have either of these two meanings; but the parable which our Lord then uses to illustrate his saying shows quite clearly that the word is intended in the sense of 'excess', 'being more than enough'.[1]

Translated literally the Greek says: 'Not in his having more than enough of them does a man's life consist from the things which he possesses.' Our Lord is not saying, then, that a reasonable supply of goods in this life is either wrong or unnecessary: he is saying that necessary to life as enough goods are, a man's life does not consist in what he has over and above what is necessary to meet his needs.

The rich farmer in the parable had a problem. His farms produced such bumper crops that he had not only enough to meet his immediate needs but enough for many years to come (see 12:17,

---

[1] On the other three occasions where the verb occurs in this Gospel, the idea of excess is clearly present as the RV recognizes: 'the fragments which *remained over*' (9:17); 'food enough and to spare' (15:17); '*of their superfluity*' (21:4).

19). His problem, therefore, was to know what to do with the excess. He decided to store it. But that led to another problem: Where? He had not the room to store it in (12:17). He solved this second problem by deciding to pull down his existing barns and to build greater, to store the excess in them, and then to retire and enjoy life for many years to come.

And God called him senseless for deciding to store his excess in that way. In the first place he had forgotten that his physical life was only lent to him. It could be asked back any time. Indeed it was to be asked back that very night. And with his physical life taken away, it would become immediately apparent that he had made two grievous mistakes in deciding to store his excess goods on earth. Firstly, he would never enjoy them, and they would fall into other hands (see 12:20). Secondly, having planned to use the excess to lay up treasure for himself and not to invest it in God's eternal interests, he would not be rich towards God.

From this we gather the first major lesson of this movement. Material goods are given to us not merely in order to maintain our lives in this world, but so that we may use them in order to become rich towards God; so that investing them in God's interests, we may turn temporary, material, earthly goods into eternal riches. Not to invest them in this way is to deprive oneself of the only riches which are ultimately worth having.

ii. *Blessings on true servants (12:22–48)*. The parable of the foolish farmer was addressed to the crowds; but it has a voice for disciples as well. So now Christ enlarges on the topic of being 'rich towards God' for the benefit of his disciples. Here the first lesson is concerned with the pull that treasure exerts on our hearts: 'where your treasure is, there will your hearts be also' (12:34). Store up your treasure on earth, and it will inevitably pull your heart in the direction of earth. Store it in heaven, and it will pull your heart, and with it your goals, ambitions and longings, towards heaven. Heaven is scarcely a reality to a man who is not prepared to invest hard cash in it and in its interests; but by that same token it becomes more of a reality to the man who is.

To invest in heaven in this fashion, we shall need to be freed from anxiety (see 12:22) and fear (see 12:32). If we are anxious that we shall not have enough food and clothes, we shall, if we are not careful, allow our quest for food and clothes to become the major

241

pre-occupation of our lives to the neglect, or even to the complete exclusion, of far more important things. It is vital therefore that we see food and clothes in their true perspective. Both are necessary to keep life going. But the main purpose of life is not simply to feed ourselves so that we can stay alive. Nor are we given our bodies simply so that we can spend our time and energies clothing them (see 12:22–23). Body and life are given us so that we may seek God's kingdom, his rule, his will. 'Seek', says Christ, 'his kingdom' (12:31), thus recalling and reinforcing his exhortation in 11:2 that our prime request in prayer should be for the coming of God's kingdom. That is what life is primarily about: to seek the rule of God and its development in our own lives here and now; to seek the extension of that rule in the lives of others; to look for and pray and work for the coming of the kingdom of God worldwide at the return of Christ. And Christ guarantees that if we refuse to live like worldly people who make food and clothes their prime objective in life, and if instead we make the kingdom of God our foremost aim, God our Father, who knows we need food and clothes, will see to it that we get them (see 12:30–31).

Consider the ravens, says Christ. They do not sow nor reap, nor store up food. One might have thought, therefore, that in this very competitive world they would not survive. But they do. God feeds them (see 12:24).

Several comments are in order here. Christ is not saying that birds do not have to work to get their food. Birds have to work very hard at it. Secondly, Christ is not saying that because ravens do not sow or reap or store up food for the winter, we should not either. God feeds them in spite of the fact that he has not given them the ability to do these things. To the squirrel God has given the instinct to store food (not, of course, for the next twenty years like the foolish farmer!); it is God's way of feeding the squirrel, and if the squirrel does not use this ability, it will not be fed miraculously. We have incomparably greater God-given abilities than either ravens or squirrels. That is God's normal way of feeding us. Thirdly, Christ is not so unrealistic as not to have noticed that birds fall prey to old age, disease, enemies, famine: Matthew 10:29 quotes him as saying that not one sparrow *falls* without your Father knowing. Nor does he imply that no beliver will ever die of hunger or cold. What Christ is saying is that as long as it is necessary for God to leave us in this world to learn and practise the principles of the kingdom, and to work for its extension and to pray for its coming, so long does God undertake that we shall have the food and clothes necessary for the course. When in God's wisdom, the time for the course runs out, we cannot by worrying add the smallest amount to our life-span anyway: and with that gone, we shall not need food and clothes any more. Why, therefore, worry about them, the smaller things, when worrying about the largest thing of all is no use? (see 12:25).

Let us take one practical example to show the bearing of all this on daily life. To engage in bribery and corruption is obviously against the principles of the kingdom. A Christian business man, threatened with dismissal from his firm if he does not consent to practise bribery, will have to accept dismissal and face many sacrifices in order to be true to the kingdom. But God guarantees him enough goods and clothes to make obeying the rule of God in this world practical. Suppose, on the other hand, he is afraid to trust God, and engages in bribery in order to keep his job and get food and clothes for himself and his family. He will, by Christ's standards, have lost the very purpose of life which made the food and clothes necessary in the first place.

We are then of much more value than the birds (see 12:24). In 12:6–7 Christ used almost these same words in order to strengthen his disciples to face persecution. Now in 12:24 Christ uses them again to strengthen his disciples to resist temptation in the workaday business world. In some countries Christians face persecution, in other countries they do not. It may be that the temptations of the workaday business life are sometimes more difficult to resist than is outright persecution.

Christ has talked about food (see 12:24): now he talks about clothes (see 12:27–28). In this connection not birds, but flowers are used as an object lesson, since it is not our greater value that is now in question, but our greater permanence. The flowers last but a very brief time; and yet God takes great pains in adorning them. They are so shortlived that we might think it was not worthwhile spending much effort on them. But God does. And will God not make provision for our clothing and adornment (no mere utilitarian drabness with either Solomon or the lilies) when we must last so much longer?

12:22–31 then have dealt with the question of getting food and clothes; now 12:32–34 deal with the question of what we should do with life's goods once we have got them: 'Sell your possessions and give alms' (12:33). To see the command in its true proportion we must pay attention to its context. Christ is not insisting that no Christian should own anything. Martha was not sinning in having a house (see also Acts 5:3–4) in which Christ himself was glad to stay. Nor is Christ saying that it is wrong for a Christian to have treasure. Quite the reverse. He should aim to have as much endurable treasure as he can. That means, however, transferring as much as he can to the heavens, where it is safe from loss, devaluation, robbery or decay. And that in turn means giving as much as he can now to the poor (of whatever kind).

Here the great obstacle to obeying Christ is fear (see 12:32). Our little possessions seem to us so important and valuable that we are afraid of the loss involved in giving them away. To counteract this Christ puts our possessions in their right perspective: 'Fear not, little flock, your Father has been pleased to give you the kingdom'. Notice the past tense. He has been pleased to, he has decided to. Indeed, the inheritance has now been confirmed and guaranteed by irrevocable covenant (see Gal. 3:15–29). Heirs to an eternal kingdom, why should we be afraid to give away a few temporary possessions? Indeed how are we not afraid to keep hold of too many of them and so fail to turn them into eternal treasure (see 12:33). Pray God we do not fall into the mistake of the Pharisee of 11:39–41: externally and ritually religious, but in practice mean and grasping.

And now in 12:35–48 Christ turns to another consideration that will put material possessions into their proper perspective for a disciple: the second coming of the Lord. The lesson is twofold. First (see 12:35–40), we must not allow our attitude to material goods to render us unprepared for the Lord's coming. Second, (see 12:41–48), when he comes, all his servants will be accountable to him for what they have done with their material possessions and with all other gifts and trusts committed to them.

First then we do not know the time of Christ's second coming; but whenever it may be, he expects to find us ready to serve him. His expectation is reasonable. To borrow the language of his parables and similes, if we expect God to be ready to answer us when we knock on his door (see 11:9), it is only right that we should be ready and prepared for whatever Christ wants us to do when he comes and knocks on our door (see 12:36). One danger with material goods is that we get so pre-occupied with them that we forget the Lord, have little time for spiritual fellowship with him now or for his service. In that case, if he were suddenly to come, how do we suppose that we should instantaneously be found prepared to be granted that degree of intimate and personal fellow-ship which he promises to his faithful servants (see 12:37)? More-over daily life with its practical business of work, food and clothes, is meant, as we have just seen, as a training ground where we learn to put into practice the rules of God's kingdom. If like worldly men (see 12:30) we have used life simply to lay up treasures for ourselves on earth; if like the Pharisees of 11:48 we have made little attempt to put the love and justice of God into practice in daily living; how could we suppose that when the Lord comes we shall suddenly find ourselves ready actively to reign with him (see 2 Tim. 2:12) and to practise and enforce love and justice as responsible executives in his kingdom?

The second lesson is brought home to us by the analogy of a steward in a large household who has been entrusted with his lord's goods to use them in his lord's absence for the good of his fellow-servants. To understand and apply the analogy correctly, we ought first to ask the question which the first lesson prompted in Peter's mind: 'Lord, are you addressing this parable to us (that is, to your truly converted, believing disciples) or to everyone else (including unregenerate, non-Christian people) as well?' (12:41). The answer that the rest of the New Testament would give to this question would surely be that while true disciples of Christ are stewards of special spiritual gifts (see 1 Cor. 4:1–5; Tit. 1:7; 1 Pet. 4:10–11), when it comes to material goods and natural gifts no man is an absolute owner of these things: all men are merely stewards. We brought nothing into this world and, like the foolish farmer (see 12:20), when we go we shall take nothing out. Goods and natural gifts are temporarily entrusted to men by God, so that they can use them for the good of their fellow-men.

The true believer in Christ will demonstrate that he is such by being a faithful steward; and when Christ returns, he will be rewarded for his faithfulness in the things of this life, by being put in charge of unimaginably larger responsibilities (see 12:42–44). If, however, a man acts as an unfaithful steward and is false to his trust, uses his material goods and natural gifts to indulge himself, cheats his fellow-men, oppresses the poor, or persecutes the true servants of God like the Pharisees and lawyers of 11:47–51, then his unfaithfulness as a steward shows him to be an unbeliever. When Christ returns he will pronounce the man an unbeliever and deal with him accordingly (see 12:45–46).[1] There are, it is true, degrees of faithfulness and unfaithfulness, and the best of believers would freely admit that he is an unprofitable servant (see 17:10). But at 12:45–46 our Lord is describing an extreme and clear case. Let a man profess what he will: if he constantly and consistently behaves in an unchristian way, he is not a true believer (see Eph 5:5; 1 Jn. 3:10), and the second coming of Christ will expose him for what he is. Let us therefore make sure that at the coming of the Lord we qualify both for the blessing (see 12:37–38) and for the reward (see 12:44) of the genuine servant of Christ.

Mention of the punishment which shall be meted out to the unbeliever at the second coming leads our Lord finally to state two principles on which his judgment will proceed. First, the more knowledge of the Lord's will there was, the more severe shall be the punishment of the man who failed to do it (see 12:47–48). Secondly, the more a man has been entrusted with, the greater will be his responsibility (see 12:48).

iii. *Provoking the opposition (12:49–53)*. At the beginning of the present movement we found Christ refusing to be 'a judge and divider' over men (12:14) during his time on earth. At 12:41–48 he has been pointing out that at his second coming he will most certainly act as judge and divider over all men. Now in this final section of the movement he indicates that there is a sense in which he is already in this present age the supreme divider of men: contrary to popular opinion he has not come to bring peace on the earth, but fire and division (see 12:49, 51).

This statement, like all others, must be read in its context. It is not meant to contradict in advance the later statement of the New Testament: 'and he came and preached peace to you who were far off, and peace to those who were near' (Eph. 2:17). But men are sinful and under the power of Satan. To enter into peace with God, they must be roused out of their complacency, repent, believe and

---

[1]The Gk. word *apistos* can mean either 'unfaithful' or 'unbeliever'. Its opposite, *pistos*, in the analogy of 12:42, is rightly translated 'faithful' rather than 'believing'. But in 12:46, where the application of the analogy is to the fore, *apistos* is surely intended to have the meaning 'unbeliever' as it does everywhere else in the NT.

be saved. Even to attempt to alert men to their true condition will provoke both human and Satanic opposition as we have already seen at 11:15 and at 11:53–54, and as we shall see again at 13:14–17. And since all will not repent, nor desire to be saved, division must come, and so must its temporal and eternal consequences. Christ was not playing at the redemption of mankind; preaching for him was not a game. He had not come to tell people that it did not matter what they believed, that good or evil were all one, both now and eternally, whether they believed the gospel or not, whether they accepted the Saviour or rejected him. He had come to bring, and to force, division. Decision must be made: for Christ or against him (see 11:23), for God or the devil (see 11:15–20), for salvation or perdition, for heaven or hell. And if decision brought division even within the family, then it must be (see 12:52–53).

For the past two years or more he had been preaching to his generation and sooner or later the time must come for forcing the division. In one sense our Lord was impatient for that time to come: 'I have come to bring fire on the earth, and how I wish it were already kindled!' (12:49 NIV). And yet the consequences of Israel's decision would be so serious that in God's great mercy and to Christ's infinite cost Israel would not be forced to a final decision about Jesus until they had been presented with the full evidence of his baptism: his sufferings, death, burial and resurrection (see 12:50). Certainly one part of the purpose of his coming was 'to cleanse his threshing-floor' (see 3:17); but in his divine compassion he would not 'burn up the chaff with unquenchable fire' until by his own suffering of the wrath of God he had made it possible for all who would to be rescued from that fire.

4. Assessing time and the times correctly (12:54 – 13:21)

i. The people and signs (12:54–59). The theme of the judgment which has been so prominent in the earlier movements of this stage continues unabated into this final movement. Here its inherent solemnity is given an added urgency by considerations of time, of the shortness of the interval that separates the present moment from imminent temporal and eternal judgments, and of the length of the sentences that the High Court will impose. The lessons taught in this final movement will naturally be those which our Lord taught his contemporaries in their special historical situation; but the principles underlying these lessons are relevant still.

The first lesson was that judgment was imminent; and Christ rebuked the people's hypocrisy in pretending that they could not see it was so. They could interpret nature's physical signs of approaching storm or scorching heat. How could they not read the signs of the moral and spiritual storm that was blowing up around them (see 12:54–56)?

Surely, to start with, they could sense the growing animosity against him of some of the leading scribes, Pharisees and Sadducees. In a nation that had a long record of persecuting its prophets, what did that animosity portend? The charges that they had already brought against him were no trifles: some had already gone so far as to accuse him of being in league with Satan (see 11:15). The charge was absurd; but it showed their determination to deny that he was of God. Soon that must mean a religious trial with its foregone conclusion: a verdict of blasphemy and a sentence of death. Why could the people not see it?

And when the authorities eventually got their way and had him executed, what would that mean? As surely as a south wind would be followed by scorching heat, so surely would the judicial murder of the Lord's Anointed (see 4:18) be followed by the wrath of God upon Israel. Both morality and history must warn the people that it was inevitable. Israel's rejection and persecution of their prophets in centuries gone by had eventually been followed by God's judgment in the form of the exile. Christ was greater than Solomon and Jonah and all the prophets. He was in fact the Coming One of whom the prophets had spoken (see 4:17–21). The Pharisees and lawyers were already vigorously opposing his claim. If they carried their opposition to the point of executing him, the case would pass out of their hands into the hands of the divine court; and the sentence which that court would impose on Israel would be long and severe indeed (see 12:57–58). Israel needed to do some very serious and very quick thinking; to see how empty their case against him was and how strong God's case was against their sins; and to come to terms with Jesus before it was too late.

We, of course, know what happened. Israel officially persisted in their opposition and within a comparatively few months condemned Jesus to death. He neither resisted nor retaliated but 'committed himself to the One who judges righteously' (1 Pet. 2:23). The Judge declared in favour of Jesus by raising him from the dead and sending forth the Holy Spirit in his name (see Jn. 16:8–11; Acts

2:36). Israel was then given space to repent; but when the nation as a nation refused to repent, 'wrath came upon them to the uttermost' (1 Thes. 2:16). Israel was scattered among the Gentiles and Jerusalem was given over to the Gentiles to be trodden down until the times of the Gentiles should be fulfilled (see 21:24). It would take Israel a long time to pay the last farthing.[1]

Israel's national experience of God's temporal judgments, however, is only part of the story. There still remains the case between every individual Jew and Christ, and the possibility of that case one day entering the supreme and final court and receiving an eternal sentence. Immediately we begin to think in these terms, we must surely realize that not only Jews but we Gentiles as well are in the same position. Life is a journey soon to be over; and after death comes the judgment (see Heb. 9:27). We all should do well to settle matters between ourselves and Christ before we reach the end of the road, so that our case never comes into that court.

Christ is not any man's legal opponent (the meaning of the Gk. word, *antidikos*, which lies behind the AV and RV translation 'adversary' in 12:58). Adversary in this sense is what the devil is said to be (see 1 Pet. 5:8). Nor will Christ accuse anyone, Jew or Gentile, before the Father (see Jn. 5:45) as the devil constantly does (see Rev. 12:10). On the other hand Christ does witness to us that there is a case against us: our deeds are evil (see Jn. 7:7); and he urges on us his salvation. If we dispute these things with him, or ignore him, and our case comes before the final judgment, he warns us that the verdict cannot be anything other than guilty, and the sentence anything other than eternal (see Jn. 3:18–19,36). He urges us therefore to judge our own case ourselves and to get it settled here in this life so that it never comes into the court of the final judgment.

Elsewhere in the New Testament he tells us simply and straightforwardly how this can be done: 'The one who hears my word and believes on him who sent me, has eternal life, and does not come into judgment, but has passed over from death into life' (Jn. 5:24). The Greek of this statement is decisively clear. It does not simply assert that the believer will not be condemned, though that of course is true. It asserts that his case will not even come into court,

---

[1]It goes without saying that the fact that God used Gentiles to execute his temporal judgments on Israel, no more justifies their barbaric cruelties against Israel than in times past it justified Assyria's atrocities against Israel. The Gentiles shall yet be punished for their anti-semitism. See Is. 10:5–15.

since it has already been settled, and the believer has already passed over from death into life (*cf.* Rom. 8:1).

Now many people make no attempt to settle matters like this with Christ, because they do not realize it is possible to do so. Somehow or other they have got it into their minds that it is impossible to anticipate the verdict of the final judgment. They need to let Christ who will be the judge at that judgment (see Jn. 5:22) assure them that it is possible.

Others see no urgent need to settle matters with Christ. They have not as yet discovered that their case is hopelessly bad, and that God has already declared it to be so (see Rom. 2:1; 3:19–23). They drift on through life towards the final judgment under the comforting, but completely false, illusion that though they are not perfect, they are not bad enough to be damned. If they persist in such unrealism, damned is precisely what they will be. They urgently need to be shown what the real state of their case is. It is to them and people like them that Christ's next lessons are addressed.

ii. Lessons on repentance (13:1–9). The first lesson here is on how we should interpret atrocities, such as Pilate committed on some Galileans (see 13:1–2), and accidents, such as befell certain men in Siloam (see 13:4). Believing as they did in God's providential government Christ's contemporaries, like many before and since, were apparently inclined to think that the victims of these atrocities and disasters must have been guilty of extraordinary sins which up to this point might have been kept secret, but which were now exposed by the special sufferings which God had allowed to come upon them as a punishment for those sins. Christ said their interpretation was wrong.

The modern humanist, noticing that atrocities and disasters often happen to good people while thoroughgoing rogues escape, conclude that the unfairness of it all proves their contention that there is no God. Their interpretation is wrong too.

Some atrocities and disasters may be allowed by God to fall on certain people or nations as a temporal punishment for their particularly heinous sins. But not all atrocities and disasters are to be viewed as God's visitation of the victims' special sins. To deduce the right lesson from these happenings we must start off on a different tack altogether. We are all sinners. If we compare ourselves with other people, we shall notice real, and sometimes large, differences. They are differences in degree only, however. They do nothing to ameliorate the fact that we all come grievously short of God's requirements. We are all guilty and without excuse. We all stand under God's displeasure. Our lives are all forfeit (see Rom. 1:18–20; 2:1; 3:19). The wonder is not that some people are allowed to suffer atrocities and accidents, but that anyone is spared. Certain it is, and Christ solemnly affirms it twice (see 13:3,5), that unless we repent, we shall all perish, not necessarily in some earthly accident or atrocity, but under the wrath of Almighty God eternally. Moreover the fact that we have not already perished is not because we are in any way better than people who have been swept into eternity by some atrocity or accident. It is due to an altogether different cause, as the second lesson in this section will now make clear.

This second lesson (see 13:6–9) is in the form of a parable – which tells of a fig tree whose owner came for three years in succession seeking fruit from it. Finding none he ordered it to be cut down. But the gardener pleaded for a stay of execution for one further year to give him one more chance to do what he could to induce the tree to bear fruit. If after that it still failed to bear fruit, the owner should then have it cut down. He could not be expected to wait more than one year more.

It may be uncertain how many details in this parable are meant to have allegorical significance; but three major lessons stand out clearly. Firstly, Christ was telling his contemporaries that if they did not produce fruit to God's satisfaction they could not be spared indefinitely. Nor, of course, can any other man in that condition.

Secondly, we may notice the difference between what Christ said here and what John the Baptist said in his day (see 3:9). Using the same figurative language the Baptist warned the people that the axe had already been laid at the root of the tree. It was waiting only for the order from the Owner, and the gardener would pick it up and cut down all unsatisfactory trees. But by the time Christ spoke the present parable, the Owner had already issued that order. He had waited three years (the time of Christ's earthly ministry?) for evidence of repentance, and finding no such fruit he had given orders for the fig tree to be cut down. And the tree would already have been cut down, if the gardener had not interceded with the Owner and gained for the tree a temporary reprieve, so that he could make one last effort to prevail upon the tree to produce the required fruit. Christ's contemporaries, then, were living on borrowed time. So are we (see 2 Pet. 3:9–12). We deceive ourselves if we think that the verdict of the final judgment against the unrepentant and unbelieving is as yet uncertain. The verdict has already gone out (see Rom 3:19). We must repent or we perish.

Thirdly, Christ's contemporaries did not owe their reprieve any more than we owe ours, to their own goodness or merit, and certainly not to their moral superiority over other people whom they chose to think were exceptionally bad sinners. They owed it, if we may so understand the parable, to the intercessions of Christ. True, at 12:49–53 we saw him divinely impatient to cast fire on the earth and to bring matters to their final issue. Here we see the other side of his character: that same Jesus in his divine compassion pleading for a stay of execution of the sentence that men might have an extended opportunity to repent and be saved.

iii. Triumph over the opposition (13:10–21). We now enter the last section of movement 4. Like the first two sections it too is concerned with the question of the shortness of time. But while the first two sections gravely warned us that men have very little time in which to repent and be saved, this last section joyfully puts the other side of the case: however long anyone may have been in bondage to Satan, he or she can be saved instantaneously. As far as God is concerned no one needs to wait so much as five minutes. This lesson, however, Christ had to teach in the teeth of opposition from a ruler of a synagogue, who held that respect for God's law would require a certain woman's salvation to wait until the sabbath day was over. We need to consider, therefore, the nature of the woman's condition, the nature of the miracle which Christ performed on her, and the true significance of the sabbath.

We earlier saw (p.222) that the incident of the dumb man and his healing at 11:14–26 was not only a miracle but also a parable. It is so likewise, and very naturally, with the miraculous healing of the woman in our present story. Whatever name is given to her physical condition, it had certainly robbed her of a significant part of her human dignity: she was permanently bent over and unable to straighten herself up. From one point of view it was simply a physical condition. On the other hand, man's upright stance is more than a mere anatomical fact. Like the faculty of speech of which the demon had robbed the man in 11:14–26, it is a something distinctively human, an appropriate physical expression of man's moral, spiritual and official dignity as God's viceroy, created in the image of God to have dominion over all other creatures (see Gn. 1:26–27). By that same token the bent back is the typical physical posture of the burden-bearer and the slave under the yoke, and so becomes a natural and vivid metaphor for the effects of oppression and slavery. Moreover the woman's physical condition was not due simply to physical causes. Christ declared it to be a bondage induced by Satan, whose malevolence has always sought from the very beginning to rob man of his dominion and dignity and degrade him into a slave. Few men and women have bent backs physically: but morally and spiritually all men and women find themselves sooner or later bent and bowed by weaknesses of one kind or another from which they have not the strength to free themselves.

One day, however, so the story tells us, the woman shuffled her way to the synagogue to hear the Word of God, for it was the sabbath. What word would the Bible have for her and her condition? Left to itself, uncomplicated by Pharisaic traditions of interpretation, the Bible would have spoken clearly enough. This perhaps: 'The seventh day is a sabbath unto the Lord your God: you shall not do any work . . . you shall remember that you were a slave in the land of Egypt and the Lord your God brought you out from there by a mighty hand and by a stretched out arm' (Dt. 5:14–15). Or even this: 'I am the Lord your God who brought you out of the land of Egypt so that you should not be their slaves; and I have broken the bars of your yoke and enabled you to walk upright and erect.' (Lv. 26:13). The ruler of the synagogue, however, was a Pharisee, and he would have told her that if ever God would be willing to set her free to stand up straight, it certainly would not be today: this was the sabbath, and it would not be glorifying to God for her to be set free from bondage on the sabbath. But before he had the chance to say anything, mighty arms stretched out and laid their hands on her, and another voice said, 'Woman, you are released from your weakness'; and immediately she stood erect and glorified God (13:12–13).

The ruler of the synagogue was indignant and tried to lecture the people on the wrong of coming to be healed on the sabbath; but Christ exposed his hypocrisy and silenced him. He and his ilk were quite happy to release their oxen and asses from their stalls and lead them to watering on the sabbath, on the grounds that it was a necessary act of mercy. Yet here was no mere animal but a human being; and not only a human being but a daughter of Abraham (see 13:16), the friend of God, called like Abraham to walk before God (see Gn. 17:1); and for eighteen years Satan had bent and bound her double, so that she could no longer hold her head high, lift up her eyes to heaven or look her fellow-men in the face, but only shuffle along in the most abject bondage. was there mercy for animals, but not for her? Must legalistic religion be allowed, instead of releasing her, to bind on her already broken back burdens impossible to carry (see 11:46)? Christ would have none of it, but demanded that the releasing of a human being from the bondage of Satan was a necessity that must not be delayed: indeed the release was fittingly performed on the sabbath.

At this the ruler of the synagogue and his co-religionists were covered with confusion, and the whole congregation was delighted at the glorious things which Christ was doing (see 13:17). Christ had triumphed. True, the release and restoration of one unknown woman in an unnamed synagogue in Palestine was in one way a very small triumph. But from the tiny seed of that victory would grow a tree greater and more majestic by far than Nebuchadnezzar's (see Dn. 4:10–22). Its ramifications would one day spread to the bounds of the universe, until creation herself would be delivered from the bondage of corruption into the glorious liberty of the sons of God, and all in heaven and earth would find security, satisfaction and delight in the magnificence of his dominion. His work on earth was obscure: few in the world had yet heard of him. But like leaven hidden in meal it would spread until there would be no place in heaven, earth or hell but would feel the force of his triumphant authority (see 13:18–21).

Meanwhile the risen Christ has continued his fight against all perversions of God's gospel that would hold men in bondage, or try to recapture them after they have been set free. Hear him protest through the mouth of Peter: 'Why then do you tempt God by trying to put a yoke on the neck of the disciples which neither our fathers nor we were able to bear?' (Acts 15:10). Read what he writes by Paul's pen: 'For freedom did Christ set us free: stand fast, then, and do not be entangled again in a yoke of bondage' (Gal. 5:1). May he make us his fellow-workers to 'open people's eyes so that they may turn from darkness to light and from the power of

Satan unto God' (Acts 26:18), until man released from his
dumbness and woman from her weakness reign in life to the glory
of the Creator through Jesus Christ our Lord (see Rom. 5:17).

The destination that awaits us

Preliminary survey

The movements

1 The glorious company of the saints (*13:22 – 14:6*)
2 The satisfactions of the Messianic banquet (*14:7 – 15:2*)
3 The joys of redemption (*15:3 – 16:18*)
4 The comforts of heaven (*16:19 – 17:10*)

Stage 3

The destination that awaits us

Preliminary survey

Stage 3 lies between the two journey markers at 13:22 and 17:10. The very first paragraph (see 13:22–30) sets its dominant theme. Describing the coming kingdom Christ says 'People shall come from east and west and north and south, and will take their places at the feast[1] in the kingdom of God' (13:29 NIV). At 14:15–24 this metaphor is extended into a parable in which Christ likens the coming kingdom to a great supper. Now both these passages have counterparts in Matthew (see 7:21–23, 8:11–12; 22:1–14); but at 15:11–32 Luke records the parable of the prodigal son which no other evangelist records. In this parable the joy at the home-coming of the prodigal expresses itself in a banquet with music and dancing (see 15:23–25) and corresponds to the joy which earlier verses (see 15:7,10) say breaks out among the angels in heaven over repentant sinners. Then again at 16:19–31 Luke has another major story which no other evangelist records. It tells of a rich man whose everyday meals were glittering banquets (see 16:19) but who in the life to come suffered unquenchable thirst (see 16:24); but it also tells of Lazarus the beggar who in this life longed for a few crumbs to still his hunger, but who in the world beyond rested in Abraham's bosom and was comforted (see 16:21,23,25).

Now the contemplation of these coming delights is itself delightful; but for that very reason this stage is also marked by unutterable

[1] AV 'sit down' represents Gk. *anaklinomai* which means 'to recline at table'. At banquets in NT times the guests did not sit but reclined round the table.

sadness. Prominent in all the four leading paragraphs which we have just mentioned are people who for one reason or another miss these delights. Two groups, we shall find, miss them unintentionally, though each of them for different reasons; and their eventual frustration is terrible. The other two groups miss them on purpose, though each of them again for different reasons; their deliberate rejection of salvation is appalling.

It is, of course, only natural that as Christ's journey brought him ever nearer to his own destination of glory, he should remind people ever more frequently of the two possible destinations that await them at the end of their journey through life: inside the Father's house with its banquet of joy and satisfaction, and outside the Father's house with its eternal frustrations and pains. And since it is possible for people to miss the Father's house, it is understandable that he should spend a great deal of time analyzing for us the various reasons why some people's journey through life will end so disastrously. His aim is obviously to warn us not to adopt their foolish and fatal attitudes.

Now from one point of view the thought-flow in this stage runs on in one unbroken stream, the last paragraph of one movement serving also to introduce the theme of the next movement. If, however, we make out a table of contents giving pride of place to the four paragraphs that carry the dominant theme, it will help us to see more easily how the individual parts of the stage relate to each other and to the whole (see pp.260–261).

The movements

1. The glorious company of the saints   (13:22 – 14:6)

i. *The pleas of the lost refused (13:22–30).* The first movement comes immediately to the urgent and exceedingly practical question which is going to dominate the whole stage: the question of salvation and of entry at last into the coming kingdom of God. 'Lord', someone asked 'are those who are going to be saved few in number?'

The Lord did not answer his question directly, but in the end he answered it very plainly: when the door into the kingdom is eventually shut – and we should notice the solemn fact that one day it will be shut – there will be many shut out. Not only so: many will be shut out who thought they were going to get in. They will discover, when it is too late, that their expectation was groundless and false: they have missed salvation, all unexpectedly and unintentionally.

Our Lord notices two things about these people: first their surprise at being shut out and then their disappointment and frustration. Their surprise is shown by the fact that when they knock for admittance and the Master of the house replies from behind the closed door that he does not know them or where they come from, they protest that surely he must know them, since in times past they ate and drank in his presence and he taught in their streets (see 13:25–26). From this we gather what Matthew makes explicit (see 7:21–23) that the Master of the house is none other than Christ himself, and that these people are referring to the fact that when he was on earth they were fellow-guests, or even hosts, at dinner-parties which he attended: they knew him socially. And what is more they had been present on occasions when he preached: they knew his views and had taken some interest in his sermons. This they obviously felt was enough to gain them entry into the kingdom of God. They are astounded when they discover it is not enough.

Then what is necessary for entry? The Master makes it clear: for anyone to enter Christ must know him or her personally (see Jn. 10:14–15, 27–29) through a mutual direct relationship. The people standing outside the closed door have obviously never had any such personal dealings with Christ. They are still what they always were: 'workers of iniquity'. While they were on earth they never radically repented of their sinfulness, never sought and obtained from Christ forgiveness and the gift of eternal life. They never became one of 'his own' (Jn. 13:1); they were never born of God through personally receiving Christ as Saviour and Lord (see Jn. 1:12–13). And having never so received him, they must now depart from him.

If their surprise is terrible, their frustrations are bitter indeed (see 13:28–29). In the figurative language which Christ uses, they are pictured as standing outside the closed door but able to see through some chink or window in the door into the great banqueting hall of the kingdom of God; and they can actually see the guests arriving and taking their places at the banquet. The guests come from every period of history: there is Abraham, Isaac and Jacob and all the

1 The glorious company of the saints
13:22 – 14:6

1 *The pleas of the lost refused* 13:22–30

a There shall be weeping . . . When you shall see Abraham . . . and all the prophets in the kingdom of God and you yourselves cast out

b . . . the door is shut . . .

c You . . . stand outside . . . and knock, saying, Lord, open to us; and he shall say, I do not know you . . . depart from me.

2 *Christ's attitude to certain rejection* 13:31–35

a It is impossible that a prophet perish out of Jerusalem.

b Go tell that fox . . .

c . . . how many times I would have gathered your children . . . and you would not . . .

3 *Man's needs and God's due* 14:1–6

When he went into the house . . . to eat a meal . . . they watched him. Right opposite him was a man with dropsy . . . And . . . he said, Which one of you would have an ass or an ox fall into a well, and would not pull it out *at once* on the sabbath day?

2 The satisfactions of the Messianic banquet
14:7 – 15:2

1 *The Lord's invitation declined* 14:7–24

Three parables
1 To guests: the honour of being exalted.
2 To hosts: the eternal reward of true hospitality.
3 The Messianic banquet. . . . they all began to make excuse . . . Then the master of the house was angry . . .

2 *The cost of discipleship* 14:25–35

a Who of you . . . does not first sit down and count the cost . . .

b Any one of you who does not renounce everything which belongs to him cannot be my disciple.

3 *The Pharisees criticize Christ* 15:1–2

The complaint is that he is too lax: The Pharisees and the teachers of the law muttered angrily among themselves: 'This man welcomes sinners and eats with them.'

3 The joys of redemption
15:3 – 16:18

1 *The father's entreaty rejected* 15:3–32

Three parables
1 The joy of finding a lost sheep.
2 The joy of finding a lost piece of silver.
3 The welcome-home banquet.
... the elder brother ... was angry and would not go in; and his father ... entreated him ...

2 *The calculations of stewardship* 16:1–13

a How much do you owe ... ? 100 measures ... ? Sit down quickly and write 50.

b If you have not been faithful with what belongs to someone else, who will give you what belongs to you?

3 *The Pharisees scoff at Christ* 16:14–18

The complaint is that he is too strict: The Pharisees who were lovers of money ... scoffed at him. And he said ... It is easier for heaven and earth to pass away than for the tiniest part of the law to become null and void.

4 The comforts of heaven 16:19 – 17:10

1 *The pleas of the lost refused* 16:19–31

a And in Hades ... being in torment he sees Abraham afar off and Lazarus in his bosom.

b ... a great gulf is fixed.

c And he said, Father Abraham, send Lazarus ... to me ... to my brothers. Abraham refuses both requests.

2 *Disciples' attitude to inevitable occasioning of stumbling* 17:1–4

a It is impossible but that occasions of stumbling should come ...

b If your brother sins rebuke him.

c And if he sins against you seven times a day and seven times turn again ... you shall forgive him.

3 *The Lord's due and his servants' needs* 17:5–10

But which one of you, having a servant ploughing ... will say to him when he comes in from the field, Come *at once* and sit down to a meal, and not Prepare my supper first ... and then have your own?

prophets. They come, not merely from the Jews who had national links with these great patriarchs, but from every nation and every quarter of the globe. What a vast assemblage of faith, what an accumulated wealth of experience. What table-talk there will be at that eternal banquet, with all of every nation knowing and understanding and enriching each other because each one in the course of life's journey came to know the Master of the house.

To have been so near to Christ on earth without receiving him and without coming to know him personally, and therefore to be shut out for ever from the glorious company of the saints, while others from distant times and cultures have found the way in (see 13:30) – who shall measure the disappointment and frustration of it? There shall there be weeping and gnashing of teeth (see 13:28). It ought to be for us a matter of supreme concern to make sure that we shall be among those who enter the narrow door (see 13:24).

ii. *Christ's attitude to certain rejection (13:31–35)*. The first paragraph has told us what, when we first hear it, must sound strange if not shocking: the time will come when Christ himself shall bar people from eternal bliss in spite of their entreaties to be let in. But the first paragraph must not be read without the second, which puts the other side of the story.

We are now told therefore how the Pharisees relayed to Christ Herod's intention of killing him if he stayed within Herod's borders. Herod's dim understanding of what Jesus stood for (see 9:3–9) probably made him fear that Jesus would lead some messianic uprising, and he wanted no disturbance in his territory. Herod was not interested in the heavenly banquet and the glorious company of the saints: he had already murdered John the Baptist at one of his own banquets (see Mt. 14:3–11). He was interested only in political power and self-indulgence. Christ despised his values, his petty-minded cunning and his threats, and sent him a sharply worded rebuke (see 13:32). Christ was following a divinely foreordained course through this world, expressing God's love to men through innumerable acts of mercy and salvation. Herod's threats would not lead him to speed up or cut short his ministry. Nor could Herod's death threats frighten him either: he was willing and ready and indeed intending, to die. Only it would not be given to some petty politician like Herod to kill him in the interests of some minor political skulduggery. When Christ died, he would die in such a place and at the hands of such people as would give his death the utmost significance. And when we have grasped that significance, it will explain why he must eventually reject the pleas of the lost.

Jerusalem had a centuries-long reputation for killing the prophets whom God sent to her (see 13:34). The Saviour knew that before he came into the world. He came nonetheless. Jerusalem stood in danger of the wrath of God for her rejection of God's prophets. Christ offered himself therefore as her Saviour, and urgently called her citizens, like a hen calls her chicks, to find shelter and salvation under his redeeming protection. When he first called, they refused, as he knew they would; but the fact that he knew they would, did not deter him from calling, or lessen the sincerity of his call, or his willingness to save. He called again many, many times (see 13:34); but they would not be saved. If one day he has to refuse their pleas, it will be only because they first refused his over and over again.

But there is more to it. When they set their will to reject him, he respected their will, and accepted their rejection. Jerusalem was Messiah's own capital city; and in Jerusalem was the very house of God. Christ did not raise an army, nor use his miraculous powers to drive out his enemies from Jerusalem and throw Israel's rebellious priesthood out of his Father's house. Instead he let them throw him out of both the temple and the city; and what had been his Father's and his, he left in their hands: 'your house', he said, 'is left to you' (13:35). It is an awesome thing to contemplate: if men use the free-will God has given them to reject the Saviour, neither God nor Christ will overrule that free-will or remove it. That does not mean, of course, that puny man has the power to defeat the will of the Almighty: it was always God's will that man's will should be genuinely free, and man be able to say no to God, if he chose. But when they arrive unrepentant at that house of which he is the indisputable Master, he will not be obliged to let them in there too.

Above all let us notice in what way Christ accepted Jerusalem's rejection. When the last of his many pleas met with their determined rejection, he could, as we imagine, have abandoned his final journey to Jerusalem, and have consigned his nation to the hopeless and endless suffering of the consequences of their fatal decision. He did the opposite. He continued on his foreordained path to Jerusalem, determined to die at their hands. One day, however long it took, that death would be the means of bringing Israel to repentance (see Is. 53:3–5), and the means of their cleansing (see Ze.

12:10–13:1), so that when at his second coming they look on him
whom they pierced they might be able to say through their tears of
repentance, 'Blessed is the One who comes in the name of the Lord'
(13:35).

iii. *Man's need and God's due (14:1–6).* 'Lord, open to us' say those
who stand outside the door knocking for admittance, 'we ate and
drank in your presence' (13:25–26). In case we should imagine that
their plea is evidence of genuine repentance, Luke now relates an
incident which shows us what 'eating and drinking in the presence
of Christ' meant for the likes of these people when he and they
were on earth. One of the rulers of the Pharisees invited Christ into
his house for a meal. 'And there right in front of him' says Luke
dramatically (14:2) 'was a man suffering from dropsy'. Christ could
not have failed to notice him.

The question is how he came to be there and so prominent. As
the commentators all point out, he apparently was not a guest:
when Christ healed him he sent him away. It seems he had been
deliberately planted there by the Pharisees who then watched (see
14:1) to see what Christ would do. They held that to heal on the
sabbath was to break the law. They knew what he believed and
taught; but they had set up the situation to see if he would dare to
defy them to their faces, heal the man and so brand himself as a
law-breaker. He asked them if it was right to heal on the sabbath.
There was stony silence (see 14:3–4). So he healed the man and then
asked another question. Again stony silence. They had no answer
with which to justify their position (see 14:5–6). But that did not
mean that they were prepared to repent or even to rethink their
ideas. They held that Christ was wrong, and the whole incident
had been arranged to demonstrate how wrong he was. They
hoped, of course, to be admitted one day to the Messianic banquet;
they did not believe that Jesus would be the Master of the house.

The mere fact of disagreeing with him was in itself serious; but
serious also was the matter over which they disagreed. It concerned
nothing less than the attitude of God towards man's need and man's
salvation. Their position was that the honour due to God and to his
law meant that no work might be done on the sabbath. On that
everyone was agreed, for that was what Scripture said. They
added, however, that healing a man on the sabbath was work, and
therefore God's honour and obedience to his law demanded that the

man's need however great must not be attended to on the sabbath. It must wait.

Such severity appeals to some minds as being evidence of great holiness, self-denial and devotion to God. Christ showed that it was hypocritical and false. In the first place, Christ pointed out that if their son or ox[1] fell into a well on the sabbath, any one of them would run and pull him out at once. Leave the boy or animal so much as a few minutes and he might drown. Yet here was a man whose body was morbidly filling up with water; soon, none of them knew how soon, it would prove fatal. Why make him wait to be rescued when they would not make even their animals wait?

The answer had nothing to do with God's honour, but everything to do with their pride and self-interest. They held that by keeping God's law they gained merit; and upon their merit depended acceptance with God and eventual entrance into his kingdom. So they added regulations to the law of sabbath, which made it not just a day of rest and delight in God, but a rigorous test of ability to keep endless, strict regulations. Their motive was that the more and the stricter were the rules they kept, the more merit they piled up for themselves. Their interpretation allowed them to pull their ox out of a well on the sabbath, because if their animal drowned, they lost money. But they enforced their rule against a man's being healed on the sabbath: if he died, they lost nothing. It was not God's honour, nor man's good, but their own self-interest and pride of attainment that concerned them.

According to Christ – and this is what angered the Pharisees – their merit was useless. Their bloated sense of religious attainment was a spiritually pathological state more dangerous than the physical dropsy which threatened the patient's life. In the first place, acceptance with God and entrance into his kingdom do not, cannot, and never will depend upon a man's merit. Moreover God never authorized nor approved of their addition of these strict rules to his sabbath law; and therefore their keeping of them brought them no merit in his eyes. Worse still, their rules amounted to a slander on the character of God. His honour and due never demand that man's salvation must wait. If man is in desperate need and danger, God will always give that need priority: Calvary has subsequently shown us to what extreme he is prepared to go in doing so.

---

[1]Some manuscripts read 'ass or ox'

The Pharisees, however, were not prepared to give up their imagined merit. According to them Jesus was wrong, and his concept of God and of salvation was wrong as well. When eventually they arrive at the door of the kingdom, they will hardly gain entrance simply by pointing out that after all they did invite Jesus to dinner and attend some of his theological lectures, even though they disagreed with him. Christ is not the democratically elected chairman of a religious club to which everyone, whatever his views, whether he agrees with the chairman or not, has right of entry. He is the Son of the Father and Master of the house. The banquet is his expression of what God is like. To reject his teaching is to reject the banquet.

2. The satisfactions of the Messianic banquet (14:7 – 15:2)

i. The Lord's invitation declined (14:7–24). At 14:1–6 Christ was at dinner in the house of a Pharisee. The three parables which Luke now records were told while Christ was at table with fellow-guests in someone's house. We need not stay to decide whether it was the same Pharisee's house and the same occasion or not: we can afford to leave that decision to the exegetes. For our purposes it is sufficient to notice that the thought flow follows on from movement 1 without a break.

The first two parables deal with the question of what the attitude of guests and hosts should be to earthly entertainment; the third deals with the question of people's attitude to the Messianic banquet. The two questions are not unrelated: false attitudes to earthly entertainment can help to pervert people's thinking about the heavenly banquet.

First, then, Christ commented on the fact that for some people the chief satisfaction of a wedding feast is the opportunity it gives them to advertize their own imagined merit and distinction. They cannot humbly enjoy the feast and the company as a gracious gift given to them quite independently of their own importance, and allow the host, if he chooses, to confer unexpected distinction on them; they must sit themselves down in the chief seats so that everyone can see how distinguished they are, or else they do not really enjoy the feast at all.

Secondly, Christ commented on the tendency of some hosts not to invite poor guests who could not possibly pay them back for their hospitality. Their dinner-parties were rather a calculated quid pro quo. Their guests would thank their host as if the dinner were free, but they knew in their hearts that they were expected to repay him. It considerably altered the significance of the host's lavish dishes, and his guests' enjoyment of them.

Christ's criticisms of these less than ideal attitudes prompted one of his fellow-guests to remark 'Blessed is the man who shall eat at the banquet in the kingdom of God' (14:15). The sentiment was true enough: no-one is invited to that feast on the basis of his merit and distinction and no guest therefore will spoil the occasion by parading his own supposed worthiness. Nor is any guest expected to pay the Host for the feast by good behaviour, self-denial or religious observance; nor will it ever be possible for any guest to repay the Host. The feast is a genuinely free gift, provided by the unadulterated generosity of the Host. The remark led Christ, however, to speak further of the Messianic banquet but this time with certain differences from his description in 13:25–30.

First he called attention to the lavish provision: it is to be a great supper with many guests and with all the dishes well prepared (see 14:16–17). Doubtless the satisfactions to be enjoyed in eternity will be of a higher order than mere physical satisfaction; but even in this world a banquet is much more than a means of satisfying physical hunger. The metaphor of feasting, as distinct from merely eating a meal, assures us that no true potential appetite, desire, or longing given us by God will prove to have been a deception, but all will be granted their richest and most sublime fulfilment.

Secondly, his description of the guests who eventually enjoy the feast does not mention, as 13:28 did, the illustrious saints, Abraham, Isaac, Jacob and all the prophets, but the poor, the crippled, the blind, the lame (see 14:21). These are people whose experience in this world has seemed to mock them by giving them some concept of what life could be like if it were truly fulfilled, and then frustrating their potentials, cheating their appetites and leaving deep longings unsatisfied. Many are the people to whom life has done this kind of thing, if not physically, then emotionally and spiritually. Salvation will more than compensate them with unstinted satisfaction.

Thirdly, just as at 13:25–30 there were some who missed the feast, so there are here, but with this difference: those missed it unintentionally, pleading to be let in, but shut out; these miss it intentionally, invited to come, summoned at the appointed hour to take their seats, but deliberately declining the invitation. They make polite excuses but the excuses are transparently thin. They could come if they wished: they have no wish to come. The supper apparently, is not good enough for them.

The parable reminds us that there are multitudes who reject salvation for this very reason. They enjoy the Creator's gifts: the Creator himself they regard as a bore. They reject salvation deliberately. Life on earth they admit is not all it could be, but it satisfies them; eternal life, they know without even tasting it, would not please them. They will have their choice: they will never taste of the banquet (see 14:24).

ii. The cost of discipleship (14:25–35). The heavenly banquet is free. It fulfils all Christ's conditions for true hospitality: it has not to be paid for or merited; the Host can never be repaid. But because it is free that does not mean it is cheap. Quite the reverse. This paragraph is about to tell us that salvation is so valuable that if receiving it as a gift involved us in the loss of everything else, we should be foolish indeed not to accept the loss. Thousands have been and still are confronted with this choice right at the outset of their Christian lives. They see, as clearly as Saul of Tarsus saw, that salvation is a free gift. Equally clearly they see that confession of faith in Christ will cost them career, friends, family, perhaps life itself; and they have to decide between Christ and salvation on the one side and all else on the other. All disciples of Christ must be prepared for that choice at any time. They must be ready to 'hate', that is, to give second place to, and if need be to let go, all else (see 14:26).

Secondly, Christ insists that no-one can be a disciple of his without carrying his own cross and following him (see 14:27). He must be prepared to accept the same hostility from the world as Christ suffered. But more. A man carrying his own cross along the street of some ancient city was normally a condemned criminal or a defeated rebel sentenced to death, deprived of all rights and possessions, and on his way to execution. Everyone who claims forgiveness because Christ died as his substitute, thereby confesses himself as a sinner who has forfeited all his rights and everything except what the grace of Christ gives him.

There is no denying, then, that discipleship is costly, both at the beginning and all the way along the road. Christ does not hide the fact. The disciple faces a tremendous project. As with any other major project of building or conquest, the costs of carrying it through to completion should be carefully calculated and faced in advance (see 14:28–33). A guide might offer to take a party of inexperienced travellers on a highly dangerous journey. He might guarantee that he would bring them safely through. He might offer to do it for nothing and refuse any reward. But he also might very reasonably lay it down as a condition that for the duration of the journey everyone in the party should hand over themselves and all their possessions and provisions to his control and yield unquestioning obedience to his authority. Christ guarantees that he will bring every true disciple through life's journey to the heavenly banquet. On the way he will teach them the behaviour that will be expected of them at the banquet. The banquet itself is free; and Christ requires no payment for his services. But he lays it down as an indispensable condition that every disciple must renounce all rights to his property (see 14:33). That does not mean that he must give everything away to other people. As far as other people are concerned (and that includes the church), his right of private property remains (see Acts 5:4). 'All that a man has' includes not just money and goods, time and energy, talent and body and soul, but wife and children as well. Obviously, a disciple is not called upon to give his wife and children away to other people. But them and all else he must surrender to Christ, and be prepared unquestioningly to accept Christ's authority over everything. Salt is good; but salt that has lost its saltiness is useless. Is it worth calling it salt? A traveller who is not prepared to stir out of his armchair in his study, is not a traveller. A disciple who is not prepared to follow the Master or do what he says, is no disciple (see 14:34–35).

iii. The Pharisees criticize Christ (15:1–2). At 14:1–6 the Pharisees planted a sick man at a dinner-party to which they invited Christ in order to force a show-down: either he submitted to their rabbinic regulations for the sabbath and left the sick man sick, or else he healed the sick man on the sabbath and showed himself to be sinfully irreligious, in their eyes, by disregarding the ceremonial law.

Now they criticize him again, this time on grounds of moral laxity: Christ welcomed tax-collectors and loose-living people, and was prepared to take a meal with them. This, according to the Pharisees, was to condone these people's immorality. The criticism was grossly unfair. It overlooked Christ's unambiguous teaching against immorality, which was in fact far stricter than that of the Pharisees themselves (see 16:18; Mt. 5:27–32); and it also overlooked both the purpose for which the tax-collectors and sinners sought his company and his motive in taking a meal with them. They were coming in order to hear him preach (see 15:1) and they knew exactly what moral standards he stood for. But like the prodigal unsatisfied with his husks (see 15:16–17), and wistfully searching for something more satisfying, they were taking their first tentative steps back home to the Father. Of course Christ welcomed them, and not only to his formal public preaching. He had for them an invitation to a banquet which could satisfy their truest longings with wholesome and magnificent pleasures, instead of the husks with which they had tried to gratify their perverted cravings. How and where better could he explain the invitation to them and show them that it was genuine, and how to accept it, than by taking a meal with them and talking with them over the table? The Pharisees derived great personal satisfaction out of successfully keeping their own religious rules; but they had little interest in the joy of retrieving for God those who had broken God's laws. And that was serious, for as movement 3 is about to tell us, one of the chief delights which the Master of the house invites us to share with him at his banquet is his joy as the Redeemer of men.

3. The joys of redemption (15:3 – 16:18)

1. The father's entreaty rejected (15:3–32). Like the first paragraph of movement 2, our present paragraph consists of three parables, the third one of which depicts a banquet. Luke presumably wants us to see the similarities between these two paragraphs, but more particularly the differences. Like the people of 14:16–20 who refused the invitation to the great supper, so the elder brother of 15:25–32 refused to go in and take part in the welcome-home banquet for his brother; only unlike the people of 14:16–20 he objected to going in not because the banquet was not good enough, but because in his estimation it was too good. Too good, that is, for his waster of a brother. The father came out and pleaded with him to go in, but he was angry and refused (see 15:28). He objected most srongly to the whole idea. If his brother could go off, live a dissolute life, bring disgrace on the family, waste all his money and opportunities, and then come home, make some kind of a profession of repentance and immediately be received, made a fuss of, treated as if nothing had happened, indeed treated better than he had ever been in his life before, then that put a premium on sin and evil living. It made a mockery of all the long years of hard work that he himself had put in on the farm serving his father like a slave. If that was his father's idea of forgiveness, of 'saving the lost', he wanted nothing to do with it.

The parable, we are explicitly told (see 15:1-3), was aimed at the Pharisees. They had been objecting to Christ's receiving tax-gatherers and notorious characters, and it is not difficult to see how the parable was meant to apply to them. Perhaps the first point to be made is the one which the two short introductory parables prepare us to notice in the third major parable: there is a tremendous joy to be experienced in the finding of the lost. In everyday affairs everybody recognizes it. The Pharisees themselves (see 15:4,8) would experience a spontaneous joy at finding a lost sheep, or a lost piece of silver, and their friends would recognize the natural validity of that joy if they were called upon to share it. The joy is in fact the analogue in humble earthly experience of the joy which angels at their far higher levels experience at the conversion of a sinner. The father in the third parable therefore understandably protested to his complaining elder son that it was perfectly right and reasonable of him (the father) to put on a banquet with music and gladness to celebrate the finding of his lost son, and perfectly reasonable and right of him to expect the elder son to join in (see 15:32). But the elder brother would not go in to the banquet; to him his father was being soft, indulgent and grossly unfair. The merriment was immoral.

The parable, then, told the Pharisees that they were out of sympathy with the Father and with the angels, and that they were in danger of excluding themselves deliberately from one of the chief joys of the heavenly banquet. The parable did more: it analysed for the Pharisees why they felt no joy in the redemption of tax-gatherers and sinners. The older brother's grievance was that he had worked like a slave for his father for many years, never transgressing any of his father's orders, and he had never got anything out of it to rejoice over with his friends, not even so much as a kid. Yet his brother, who had done no work, but instead had wasted his father's resources in disgraceful debauchery, had only to come home to be given the calf which the family kept fatted up ready for some special celebration. That was to reward sin and selfishness, and to penalize honest endeavour to behave as one should.

The Pharisees felt the same about Christ's gospel of forgiveness and salvation by grace. They had honestly toiled hard to keep God's commandments. Like the elder brother they were proud of their record; but it had never brought them any joy, and sense of acceptance with God, or any assurance of salvation. How could it? Salvation and acceptance with God can never be enjoyed on those terms (Rom. 4:4–7; Eph. 2:4–10). Yet here were some of these tax-gatherers and sinners who had broken practically every commandment and lived disgracefully, and now through simple repentance and faith they were enjoying the welcome of Christ, and sensed the very kiss of God's acceptance in their hearts; it was for them as though the great banquet had already begun. It made the Pharisees angry; and, of course, they had to brand it as bogus.

The parable conveys yet another answer to the Pharisees' criticism. Astonished at his elder son's sense of grievance the father pointed out that in welcoming home the prodigal, he had not penalized the elder son in any way or robbed him of what was his. 'All that I have', he said, 'is yours'. But that did not pacify him. 'All these years I have slaved for you', he said; and he had a slave's mentality. He had no feeling of being the heir to all the father had, simply because through no merit of his he was the son of his father. Like a slave he thought only of earning everything for himself by his own hard work. Generosity to a bankrupt but repentant prodigal was to him not an expression of his undeserved wealth as the heir of all the father had, but the squandering of hard-won earnings which he could not afford to give away. He would not join in the joy of a banquet provided at such expense.

So, and for similar reasons, many still intentionally shut themselves out of the possibility of sharing with God the joys of redemption both now and hereafter.

ii. *The calculations of stewardship (16:1–13)*. The parable of the prodigal son introduced a young man who wasted his resources in dissolute living (see 15:13). The parable of this second paragraph presents a steward who wasted his master's goods, or so it was said (see 16:1). The first of the two parables teaches us that if we sinfully waste our lives and then, even at the eleventh hour, come back to

God in true repentance and faith, the fact that we have wasted our lives will make no difference at all to the pardon we shall receive or to our acceptance with the Father. The second parable puts the other side of the story: if we waste our lives, it will in another sense make an eternal difference.

The steward's methods may not have been altogether just: we are not meant to copy them. But we are to copy his foresight. Realizing that he would soon have to leave his post and that he would not have control of his master's goods much longer, he used his temporary stewardship of those goods to make friends for himself, so that when he had to leave his job, they would receive him into their homes.

We are in a similar position. Nothing we have in this life belongs to us. We brought nothing into this world and we shall take nothing out of it (see 1 Tim. 6:7). We are simply stewards. One day we must go and leave it all. While we have in our control, therefore, what our Lord here calls 'the mammon of unrighteousness' (so called because, in this disordered world, it is unfairly distributed?), we are to use it, not indeed in order to gain salvation, for nothing can buy that: it is a gift; but in order to make friends. Not fickle friends of the sort that the prodigal son is said to have made; but friends who will welcome us in the eternal world, and remain our friends eternally. 'Make to yourselves friends by means of the mammon of unrighteousness, that when it shall fail, they may receive you into the eternal tabernacles' (16:9).

We need to bring a little practical realism into our anticipation of what heaven will be like. In some respects it may not necessarily be all that different from what life is like now. We should consider that while all believers will be equally welcome in heaven and all be loved equally, not all will have equally as many friends. If when accounts are rendered and it becomes known in heaven that it was your sacrificial giving that provided the copies of the Gospel of John which led a whole tribe out of paganism to faith in Christ, will not that whole tribe show towards you an eternal gratitude which they will not show towards me who spent my spare cash on some luxury for my own enjoyment? Moreover when it is a question of our relationship with Christ as Saviour, then of course it is a one-way process in which he does all the saving. But when it comes to our relationship with him as Friend, the relationship is a two-way process: 'you are my friends', he says (Jn. 15:14) 'if you do the things which I command you'. If our side of this friendship has been lacking here, will it make no difference at all there?

In the verses following the parable Christ proceeds to list some of the eternal differences which unfaithful stewardship will make (see 16:10–13). Compared with the real and eternal riches, the mammon of unrighteousness is a very small matter (see 16:10–11). But our employment of it gives enough opportunity to demonstrate whether we have been faithful or unjust. If then we have not been faithful, says Christ, in the unrighteous mammon, who will commit to our trust the true riches? Moreover, nothing that we have in this temporary world is our own. It is only lent to us on trust for the time being. In that eternal world it will be different. There awaits us there an eternal inheritance covenanted to us in and through Christ (see Gal. 3:15–29). But owning it is one thing; being put in active, practical administration of it is quite another. If therefore in this life we have not been faithful in what belongs to Another, who will put us in active administration of our own things in the age to come (see 16:12)? And finally, in our use of mammon here in this life an extremely important matter is at stake. We can use mammon in the course and in the cause of serving God; or we can serve it as an end in itself. If we do the latter, it means, as God sees it, that we are despising him and giving him second place (see 16:13). No one can suppose that a life thus spent in despising God will make no difference when we reach eternity.

iii. The Pharisees scoff at Christ (16:14–18). At 15:1–2 the Pharisees criticized Christ for being too lax. Now at 16:14, having heard his teaching on the right use of money, they sneer at it as being too strict. They were, says Luke, lovers of money; and that accounts for their sneering. They had to be told that the standards which they had set themselves and which they prided themselves on keeping were immeasurably too low for God's acceptance. And not in money-matters only. Christ did indeed eat with prostitutes and tax-collectors in his desire to get them converted; but his teaching on sexual morality, marriage and divorce insisted on a divine ideal that some of the critics of his gospel, content with mere legality, were not prepared to rise to, nor even to contemplate (see 16:18).

Still today mere religion will often discourage a man from accepting salvation by faith, on the grounds that it is bound to lead to careless living; and in its place it will urge him to do the best he can to keep God's law. Then when 'doing his best to keep God's law' has not produced anything like holiness of life, mere religion will comfort him with the thought that God is after all very reasonable: only a fanatic would suppose that he meant us to keep his law all that strictly. But mere religion of that kind is bogus: no heaven worth the name could possibly be built upon it. Indeed, the man who comforts himself with such lax views of God's law is in mortal danger, as the next paragraph will point out.

4. The comforts of heaven (16:19–17:10)

1. The pleas of the lost refused (16:19–31). The Pharisees who sneered at Christ's teaching on the right attitude to money, are not said to have been rich, but rather lovers of money (see 16:14); and that is a different thing. The dangers inherent in the love of money are now solemnly brought out by our Lord's story of a rich man who dressed in the most expensive materials and whose everyday meals were glittering banquets; but when he died, he found himself in hell.

Like the people of 13:25–30 the rich man missed heaven unintentionally. He no more expected to find himself on the wrong side of the fixed gulf (see 16:26) than they expected to find themselves on the wrong side of the shut door. He pleaded for alleviation of his torment, as they pleaded for the door to be opened; but his pleas were refused as theirs were. Why was it, then, that he missed salvation?

Here we shall need to proceed carefully, for it would be easy to jump to the conclusion that he missed salvation because he was not generous enough with his money and had no compassion on the poor. Such a conclusion would be true, but only half of the truth; and like so many half-truths it could be dangerously misleading. It could lead some to imagine that if, doing the opposite to the rich man, they compassionately give a hefty contribution to the world's poor and hungry, they will by that means secure themselves right of entry into God's heaven. It is not so, of course. Scripture explicitly asserts that salvation is not by works, but by faith (see Eph. 2:8–9; Tit. 3:5).

On the other hand, while salvation is not gained by love and good works, it invariably leads to love and good works. A profession of faith that does not show its reality by good works is not genuine (see Jas. 2:14–24).

So it was with the rich man: he had never really believed what he professed to believe. He was not an atheist. We must not even suppose that he was a Sadducee who believed that there was no afterlife. Like the Pharisees to whom Christ was telling his story, he would probably have claimed to believe that Scripture was the Word of God and that after death there was a judgment. His mistake was that never for one moment had he ever got round to taking it seriously. We can see that from his behaviour. The second greatest commandment in the Old Testament ran, 'You shall love your neighbour as yourself'. At his very door, so near that he nearly tripped over him every time he went out, there had lain a beggar infested with sores and starving. Some of the bits and pieces that fell from his table may have reached the beggar; but he himself personally made no attempt to show the man any love or compassion. He did not think it mattered whether he obeyed God's law or not – at least he did not think it mattered enough for God to send him to hell for not obeying it. Only the narrowminded and fundamentalist took the Bible as strictly and literally as that. The very idea that God would ever send him or any of his cultured, sophisticated, very pleasant and polished friends to hell was to him preposterous. None of his set believed that. He certainly didn't. And the unbelief that lay behind his inaction eventually became explicit in his final conversation with Abraham (see 16:27–31). When he pleaded for Lazarus to be sent to warn his brothers, Abraham replied that there was no need, since his brothers had the Bible and could read what it said. At that the rich man protested that it was no good supposing that his brothers would take what the Bible said seriously enough to repent, unless they were sent some spectacular apparition. The rich man was sure of it: he himself had not really believed what Scripture said, and that was why he was now in hell.

Abraham persisted in his refusal to send Lazarus to warn his brothers, and it is instructive to notice why. It was not that Abraham, or God either, was determined to give people no more than the minimum of evidence. If seeing and hearing an apparition would have brought the brothers to repentance, every room they sat in, every street they walked down, would have been alive with apparitions. But apparitions would not have helped them. They did not need to be convinced that the afterlife is real, or that after death there comes the judgment, or that there is a hell. They needed to be convinced that their neglect of God's law was serious enough to land them personally in hell. And that was a moral issue, and ultimately a question of God's moral character. The highest possible evidence in the matter therefore was the plain statement of his Word directed to the brothers' moral conscience and judgment. And so it is with us. If our moral judgment is so irresponsible that it can make light of the Bible's warnings of our guilt before God (see Jn. 3:18; Rom. 1:18,20; 2:1 – 3:20), no amount of seeing of apparitions would convince us that we personally were in danger of perdition unless we repented.

Now the story of the rich man and Lazarus is not said to be a parable, and it is obviously not one.[1] But the language it uses to describe their ultimate condition is obviously figurative. It will be instructive to compare the figures used here with those which our Lord used at 13:22–30. There the lost were represented as being able to see Abraham and the other guests arriving for the banquet, as pleading themselves to be allowed in, but as being kept out by a shut door. There is, of course, no thought of the door being shut to stop the guests coming out. In our present passage the rich man is similarly represented as being able to see Abraham and Lazarus, but this time they are said to be far off (see 16:23). Between them there is not a closed door, but a gulf, which moreover not only prevents the rich man from crossing over to Lazarus but also prevents Lazarus from crossing over to the rich man (see 16:26).

On earth there was no gulf between the rich man and Lazarus: the beggar lay at his garden gate. Nor was it difficult for the rich man to see Lazarus' need: his disease was hideously evident. How clear was the lesson which God had set the rich man, and how easy and near the opportunity to love his neighbour as himself. Any time he wished he could have brought him into his house, treated his sickness and invited him to a meal. Lazarus so treated would have been the means not only of bringing a new joy and satisfaction into his life, but of developing his moral character. But the rich man put an impassable gulf of compassionless selfishness between himself and the sick beggar.

Now in the eternal world a great gulf of another kind separates

---

[1] A parable is based on actual things and activities in this world, *e.g.* wheat, tares, sheep, oil-lamps, *etc.*, which are then used as parables of higher realities. But heaven and hell to which Lazarus and the rich man went respectively, are not parables of higher realities: they are themselves the ultimate realities.

them for ever. The rich man cannot pass over to Lazarus to do him any good: Lazarus does not need it anyway. Nor can Lazarus pass over to the rich man to relieve his condition or improve his state. The rich man has had to leave behind all his wealth and sumptuous dishes: but he has brought his character with him. Such as it is, it is fixed for ever. Even his concern for his brothers has lost eternally any opportunity of helping them in the things that he now sees matter most. And it torments him.

Let our last thoughts be of Lazarus. After life's sufferings he is comforted (see 16:25). He is pictured 'in Abraham's bosom'. On earth he was obviously a true son of Abraham, the father of the men of faith. Certainly it must have taken a very strong faith indeed to endure the role that he was called upon to fill in life without abandoning belief in God completely. The problem of suffering is a great mystery. But this much is clear: the suffering of some provides opportunities, whether taken or not, for the development of qualities in others that would scarce have been developed apart from that suffering. The believing medical missionary who shows the reality of his faith by devoted services to lepers, develops a character of sterling and eternal worth, and will surely be rewarded by God in the life to come. But all this has been occasioned by the fact that there were lepers for him to serve; and it is a much more difficult role to be a leper than it is to be a much applauded medical missionary. What then of the lepers? We may not think that the mere fact of their suffering entitles them to heaven any more than the rich man's riches automatically consigned him to hell. But if the lepers are true sons of Abraham, their faith, refined by their sufferings, 'will result in praise, glory and honour when Jesus Christ is revealed' (1 Pet. 1:7). And God will comfort them for all the suffering which became the means in his hand of perfecting the character of others. Some people, it is true, sneer at the doctrine that the Lazaruses of this world will be comforted in the next. They say it encourages the better off to think that it does not matter too much if they neglect them. They seem to forget what Christ said happened to the rich man who neglected Lazarus.

ii. Disciples' attitude to inevitable occasions of stumbling (17:1–4). If true, genuine and active faith is as eternally important as we have just seen it is, no sin against a fellow-man can possibly be more serious than to do something by act or word to stumble him in his faith, or to break that faith, in God, in the deity of Christ, in the authority of his Word, in the value of his redemption or the reality of his salvation. In this imperfect world, Christ says, it is impossible but that such stumbling-blocks will occur; but the consequences for the people responsible for their occurrence will be so grave, that it would have been better for them, before they injured someone's faith, to have been flung into the sea with a millstone round the neck where they would be safely out of the way and unable to influence anybody.

A true disciple, therefore, has two special duties in this connection. He must rebuke his brother when he sins (see 17:3). Some people seem to enjoy doing it; and if they do, they are obviously not doing it in the manner in which it should be done. Most of us find it unpleasant and in cowardly fashion err by not doing it at all. But if our silence encourages a man to think that his sin does not matter, where might he not end up? In this as in all things Christ is our example. He rebuked 'that fox Herod', for example, even though in doing so he was humanly speaking endangering his own life (see 13:31–33).

Secondly the true disciple must forgive his repentant brother, even if he sins and then repents seven times a day (see 17:4). God himself never refuses forgiveness to genuine repentants. But what a tragedy it would be, if a man who professed to know Christ were to refuse to forgive his fellow man when he repented, and his fellow man got the impression that repentance is useless, and therefore ceased to repent thereafter of his sins towards men or towards God either. So if seven times a day seems an impossible number of times to have to forgive a sinning brother, let the disciple remember Christ. He called on Jerusalem to accept his protection. How many times they rebuffed him. And how many times, in spite of it, he renewed his offer of mercy (see 13:34).

iii. The Lord's due and his servants' needs (17:5–10). Faced with such demanding duties as those outlined in the second paragraph the apostles asked Christ to increase their faith.

They received the stimulating reply that even faith as small as a mustard seed would uproot a tree and plant it in the sea. To faith so strong few duties would prove difficult. But powerful faith such as that might possibly create in us wrong attitudes: the very success it achieved might make us spiritually overbearing and arrogant. And so Christ proceeds to teach us what our attitude toward God must ever be as his servants.

'Which one of you', asks Christ, 'having a servant ploughing or keeping sheep, will say to him when he comes in from the field, 'Come at once and sit down to eat'', and will not rather say to him, "Get my dinner ready, and dress yourself and wait on me until I have eaten and drunken, and after that you shall eat and drink"?' (17:7–10). The form of his analogy and the crucial stress on the words 'at once' may profitably recall for comparison the passage at 14:1–6 and the lesson it taught us (p.265). If God will always put man's salvation before the ceremonies and celebrations of his own praise, we who have been saved must always put God's service before our own interests. We certainly must never get it into our heads that we have served God so superbly well that now we have a right to put our own needs and satisfactions before his requirements. And never can we put God in our debt by serving him. If after we have served him well, as we think, he appears not to thank us or to be grateful (see 17:9), why should we expect him to? When we have done everything he asks of us, it is what we were only duty-bound to do anyway. At the great banquet the Master himself will serve us (see 12:37). Does not that inspire us to grasp every opportunity of serving him first?

Preparing to reign with Christ

Preliminary survey

The movements

1 On the coming of the kingdom (*17:11 – 18:14*)
2 On entry into the kingdom (*18:15 – 19:28*)

Stage 4

Preparing to reign with Christ

Preliminary survey

Stage 4 lies between the journey-marker at 17:11 and another at 19:28. Much of its material is peculiar to Luke either in substance or position.

At 17:22–37 a long paragraph deals with the coming of the Son of man. Apparently much of this material was repeated during Holy Week (see Mt. 24:26–28, 37–41); Luke alone tells us that Christ first gave it on his way up to Jerusalem.

The parable of the widow and the unjust judge at 18:1–8 is peculiar to Luke. It makes explicit reference to the coming of the Son of man (see 18:8).

The theme of the parable of the pounds at 19:11–27 is the reward of Christ's servants at his second coming. Only Luke records the fact that our Lord told this parable during his ascent to Jerusalem.[1]

The coming of Christ, then, and his reign over the earth are the themes which will dominate this stage. By this time our Lord was far advanced on his journey, and it was natural that the nearer he got to the capital city, the more frequently questions would be raised as to when the kingdom of God might be likely to appear. Some imagined that it was about to appear at any moment (see 19:11) and it must have been awesomely exciting for them to think that they were accompanying the Son of David on the last few steps towards his enthronement and universal dominion.

---

[1]Matthew's counterpart is the very different parable of the workers in the vineyard (20:1–16), spoken during the ascent and likewise dealing with the question of reward.

What lessons, then, according to Luke, did Christ think appropriate and necessary for people at this stage in the journey? Obviously he had to correct their perspective on time. Twice he spelt out that the events which lay immediately before them were his rejection, crucifixion, burial and resurrection (see 17:25; 18: 31–34). Then he told the parable of the widow and the unjust judge (see 18:1–8) to forewarn them that their faith might well be tested by an apparent delay in God's vindication of his people and in the coming of the Son of man (18:1,8) even though by God's reckoning these events would come soon.[1] And the parable of the pounds, we are explicitly informed (see 19:11), was told in order to counteract the popular idea that the kingdom of God was imminent, and to teach his disciples that they would have an interval of responsible service between his ascension and return.

Granted these corrections and explanations, however, the main aim of our Lord's teaching at this stage was to concentrate his disciples' attention on the coming kingdom. Suffering there would be at Jerusalem. But he was on the way 'to a distant country to receive a kingdom and to return' (19:12); and if his disciples could not accompany him all the way to the distant country at this time, they would need to know what to expect when he returned and how to prepare themselves for it.

We may notice first of all, then, not only what prominence, but also what balance Luke gives to his coverage of our Lord's teaching on the coming of the Son of man. The long paragraph at 17:22–37 deals with that coming as a time of catastrophic judgment comparable to the Flood and to the destruction of Sodom. The long passages at 18:18–30 and 19:11–27 look at other aspects: they consider not only the coming of the kingdom, but entry into it, and they talk of the coming of Christ mostly, though not exclusively, as the time when Christ shall reward his servants (note particularly 18:28–30).

Next we should notice the devices by which Luke weaves his major and minor themes together so that the stage as a whole shall present a coherent message. First among these is a simple feature of his vocabulary. Through the stage he constantly plays on the twin ideas of 'appearing' and 'seeing' at both the physical and the meta-

---

[1]For a long and helpful discussion of the translation of 18:7 see Marshall 674–77. The renderings given in RSV and NIV are doubtful in themselves and spoil the thought-flow of the passage.

phorical levels. At the second coming, we are told, the Son of man will be 'like the lightning' which suddenly bursts forth and is simultaneously and inescapably visible everywhere (see 17:24). The Son of man will be 'revealed' (17:30). The kingdom of God will 'appear' (19:11). In the meantime Christ's disciples will desire to 'see' one of the days of the Son of man and shall not 'see' it (17:22). They are moreover warned against being deceived into going looking for the Messiah here or there (see 17:23). The idea is, then, that the Son of man and his kingdom will for an indeterminate period be hidden, veiled, invisible; and then suddenly the veil will be removed and the King and his kingdom will come in visible form.

But – and here is Luke's point – the Son of man who will be revealed at that time and universally recognized, will prove to be none other than the One who earlier visited our earth and travelled the road from Galilee to Jerusalem. Comparatively few saw who he was then. But some did; and their perception saved them. One leper out of ten saw not only that he had been physically healed (see 17:15), but saw its significance and so returned to Christ, from whom he received the additional gift of spiritual salvation (see 17:19). Similarly, the blind man near Jericho perceived that the One whom the crowds saw as Jesus of Nazareth was in fact the Messianic Son of David; and his perception brought him not only physical sight but salvation and a completely different way of life (see 18:35–43). Again, Zacchaeus, the chief tax-collector, conceived a desire 'to see who Jesus was'; and what he saw led to a thorough-going conversion: 'salvation came to his house' (19:1–10).

On the other hand a rich ruler, in spite of the flattering way in which he addressed Christ (see 18:18–19), did not really perceive who Christ was. As a result he rejected Christ's word and so threw away his opportunity of entering the kingdom of God when it eventually comes (see 18:23–24). Likewise in the parable of the pounds, one servant out of the ten throws away all possibility of active participation with the Lord in the government of his coming kingdom; and he does it as a result of his perverted view of what the Lord is really like (see 19:21).

Another device which Luke uses to weave his various themes together in this stage is to allow, as he has often done before, one of the prominent features of a later story to recall a prominent feature of an earlier one. A single example will suffice. The lesson taught by the parable of the widow and the unjust judge is the need for persistence in prayer in spite of discouragements (see 18:1), and it assures those who 'cry out to God day and night' (18:7) that their crying will be heard and eventually rewarded. The Greek word Luke uses for 'cry out' is *boaō*. Some twenty-five verses later he begins to tell another story (see 18:35–43). It is about a beggar who 'cried out, Jesus, Son of David, have mercy on me' (18:38). The Greek word Luke uses for 'cry out' is again *boaō*. The crowd tried to silence him, but he persisted until he got what he cried for (see 18:39–42). The echo between the parable and the story is unmistakable; what the point of it is we shall have to consider later on.

Yet another device which Luke has again adopted quite frequently in this stage, is to place side by side two paragraphs which deal with a common theme from opposite but complementary points of view. But this and other features can most easily be seen if we now as usual make ourselves a table of contents (see pp. 286–287).

The movements

1. On the coming of the kingdom (17:11 – 18:14)

i. The return of the leper (17:11–19). The first thing to notice about this story is the crucial part played by geographical and spatial details in the development of the narrative. Luke is not content to tell us that this incident took place in a village somewhere on the journey to Jerusalem, as he did for instance at 10:38. He specifies that it happened as our Lord was travelling along the border between Samaria and Galilee. Now the Galileans were Israelites, but the Samaritans, as our Lord later points out, were aliens (see 17:18). Mention of the border area between the two gives the story its first hint of separation, distance, alienation. 17:12 gives us the second: there ten men with leprosy met him. They 'stood at a distance' and had to shout to make their voices carry across the intervening space. The law did not allow lepers to come near healthy people. We notice next that Christ did not go to them, touch and heal them as he had done with other lepers (see 5:12–13). He kept his distance and simply told them to go and show themselves to the priests. Only as they went were they cleansed. But by now, of course, the distance between them and Christ was increasing.

1   On the coming of the kingdom 17:11 – 18:14

(A) *1*   *The return of the leper* 17:11–19

Ten lepers are cleansed; only one returns to give thanks, but that leads to his receiving salvation as well as healing.

(B) *2 (i)*   *The coming of the kingdom is not visible* 17:20–21

It is a question of heart-attitude to the kingdom which is already among you.

(ii) *The coming of the Son of man will be visible* 17:22–37

A warning based on the rejection of Christ's claims and illustrated by the days of Noah and Lot that preoccupation with material goods and wordly activities will leave people unprepared for the coming of the Son of man.

(C) *3 (i)*   *The widow and the unjust judge* 18:1–8

A parable about persistence in prayer: a widow in spite of being discouraged by an unjust judge keeps on pleading until he avenges her.

(ii) *The Pharisee and the tax-collector* 18:9–14

A parable of two men at prayer: a Pharisee boasting of his good works and criticizing a tax-collector is not justified; the tax-collector who simply appeals to God for mercy is.

2   On entry into the kingdom 18:15–19:28

(B′) *1 (i) The blessing of the infants* 18:15–17

Entry into the kingdom is determined by heart-attitude: anyone who does not receive it as a little child will never enter it.

   (ii) The rich ruler 19:18–34

A warning based on the example of a ruler that the possession of riches makes it difficult for men to enter the kingdom. Sacrifice for the kingdom will be rewarded, but is to be viewed in light of Christ's rejection and suffering.

(C′) *2 (i) A blind beggar* 18:35–43

He cries out, 'Jesus . . . have mercy on me'. The crowd tries to silence him, but he persists until Jesus gives him what he asks for, saying, 'Your faith has saved you'.

   (ii) A rich tax-collector 19:1–10

He desires to see Jesus. The crowd criticizes Jesus for going to stay with a 'sinner'; but the tax-collector gives half his goods to the poor and makes restitution for wrong. Jesus replies: 'Today salvation has come to this house'.

(A′) *3   The return of the Lord* 19:11–38

Ten servants are each given a pound to trade with until their lord returns. At his return he rewards the faithful. One servant has not used his pound and abuses his lord. The pound is taken from him and given to the servant who already has ten pounds.

Presently one of the lepers realized that he was cleansed. He was of course grateful to God; but it is the way in which he expressed his gratitude to God that is crucial to the lesson which this story has to teach. He could, we might think, have been grateful to God while carrying straight on to the priests without ever coming back to Christ. But no! What Christ expected him and all the others to do was to 'return, that is to return to Christ, in order to give glory to God' (17:18). Nor was it that Christ merely wanted them to thank him personally as well as thanking God, though the returning leper did that; this phrase at 17:18 implies that in order to give true glory to God in this affair they had to return to Christ.

One leper did return, and it is delightful to see how as he did so all distance and alienation of every kind between himself and Christ, between himself and God, was removed. The need for social separation was gone, of course. He no longer had to stand at a distance: he came and fell at the Lord's feet. He was a Samaritan, Jesus was a Jew; the national and religious barrier meant nothing now. True, leprosy had long since brought him together with nine Jewish lepers in a common separation from both Jews and Samaritans; but cleansing had brought him to recognize the divine power of Jesus the Jew and to accept its implications. But most important of all, as grateful recognition of God's power in Christ brought him back to the Person through whom that power had been expressed, that Person was able to grant him salvation (see 17:19): not just physical healing such as the other nine received, but forgiveness and reconciliation and eternal life, and the removal of all alienation and distance between himself and God caused by his sin and moral uncleanness.

What then of the nine? The story does not tell us what happened to them. We may not suppose that they went to the priests like a bunch of atheists grudgingly submitting to religious ceremonies which they did not believe in. For all we know they may have gone to the priests like good orthodox Jews singing grateful praise to God. That was not good enough for Christ. Vague general gratitude to God was no adequate response to what had happened. The miraculous power of God had manifested itself to them through Christ. In Christ, to borrow an earlier phrase (see 11:20), the very kingdom of God had come upon them. They were expected to respond by returning to Christ in order to give their praise to God (see 17:18).

Ingratitude for the general gifts of the Creator is bad enough (see Rom. 1:21); and many have been the people who in dire trouble have called on God for special deliverance and being granted it, have ungratefully gone further from God than they were before. But our story is dealing with something even more sad and serious. The healing of the lepers was not an ordinary common gift of the Creator to his creatures, nor simply some special gift of providence. It was a miraculous sign intended to point them to Christ so that through faith in Christ they might receive salvation and eternal life. It had that effect with the alien Samaritan: the sign after all was not difficult to see nor the direction in which it pointed. But the Jews in the party were like the crowds at the feeding of the five thousand. Those crowds saw the miracle, but they were not interested to see what it was a sign of, nor to seek the One to whom it pointed, except in the hope of getting more bread and fish (see Jn. 6:26). So with the nine lepers. Salvation and eternal life and the kingdom of God had come within their reach; but not even gratitude could interest them in anything more than their physical healing. In their leprosy they had at least come near Christ; when he gave them physical healing, they walked out of his life, as far as we know, for ever. All God's gifts are meant to lead us to the Person who is his Supreme Gift to men. It is strange behaviour to take them and ignore him.

iia. The coming of the kingdom is not visible (17:20–21). There follow now two distinct paragraphs, one addressed to the Pharisees, the other to the disciples. Both deal with the coming of the kingdom, but each from a different point of view.

In this first paragraph, when the Pharisees ask 'When will the kingdom of God come?' our Lord replies 'The kingdom of God does not come with observation', that is, you could watch very carefully for its coming and you would never see it come. 'Neither', he adds, 'shall they say, See here! or there!'; and the reason for that is that it does not come in any externally visible way, and therefore it is no good looking to see it come.

Now in saying this our Lord was obviously not intending to deny in advance what he was about to tell his disciples about the universal visibility of the coming of the kingdom in its future outward form (see 17:24). What he was telling the Pharisees was that there was another and prior sense in which the coming of the kingdom must be thought of. In that sense the kingdom of God was already among them (see 17:21).[1] They were at that very moment looking at the King himself, though they did not realize it. Their inability to see who he was, moreover, was not due to any lack of signs. He had done many. But the signs were only pointers; actually recognizing Jesus to be God's Messiah was, and remains, a matter of inner revelation and spiritual sight (see 10:21). Similarly, entering the kingdom in its spiritual phase was an essentially inner process of repentance, faith and a spiritual rebirth brought about by the Spirit whose activity was as invisible as the wind (see Jn. 3:3–8). It still is.

What the Pharisees urgently needed to do, then, was to concentrate a little less on the future external form of the kingdom and a little more on its present spiritual phase; to recognize the King and to enter the kingdom. Failing that, they would be unprepared for the coming of the kingdom in its future form even if they saw it come.

iib. The coming of the Son of man will be visible (17:22–37). On the other hand it would be equally wrong to fall into the opposite mistake from the Pharisees and so to concentrate on the present spiritual phase of the kingdom as to forget or even deny the fact that one day the kingdom will come outwardly in power and great glory. Far from being invisible that coming will be instantaneously and universally visible (see 17:24).

In regard to this coming our Lord proceeded to issue two warnings. First, his disciples would naturally come to long for his appearing; but that very longing could lead them into wishfully thinking he had come when he had not. He therefore pointed out once more the folly of those who would say 'See, there,' or 'See, here' (17:23); only this time the folly lay differently from before. There (see 17:21) it was foolish to say 'See, here', when what was supposedly being pointed at was by definition invisible. Here (see 17:23) the folly lies in suggesting that something needs to be pointed out when in fact it is impossible for anyone not to see it. The disciples, therefore, were to be wary of all claims that the Messiah had been actually sighted somewhere or other, or that the

---

[1] It is a mistake to translate our Lord's phrase 'the kingdom of God is *within* you'. See Marshall, 655.

kingdom had already come. When the Son of man appeared, no one would need to tell anybody.

The second warning was (see 17:25–30) that before his glorious appearing he must 'first be rejected by this generation'. When his disciples eventually saw him suffer, this prediction would steady their faith (*cf.* 24:6–8). But in its context in the discourse it serves another purpose as well. It explains why in spite of generations of Christian preaching, the second coming will take the world by surprise. The term 'rejected by this generation' points specifically to the fact that his generation would examine his claims to be Messiah and repudiate them. As long, therefore, as Israel or the nations for that matter held that view, they would deny the very possibility of his return. Hence their surprise and unpreparedness when it takes place.

Two analogies are used to drive the lesson home. During 'the days of Noah' men disbelieved his preaching (see Pet. 2:5); the day of the flood surprised and destroyed them. During 'the days of Lot' the Sodomites mocked at his testimony; the day Lot left, to their consternation the judgment of God actually fell and destroyed them.

In the same way, after a long period of warning largely disregarded by the world, there shall come a day when the Son of man shall suddenly and unexpectedly be revealed (see 17:30; 1 Thes. 5:3). It will be a day of apocalyptic judgment (see 2 Thes. 1:7–9; 2:8–12).

Now Noah's contemporaries and the Sodomites of Lot's day were particularly evil (see Gn. 6:11–13; 19:1–11); but it was not their indulgence in lurid sins which left them so unprepared for God's judgment when it came. According to Christ it was their total preoccupation with life's normal activities, all of them quite proper in their way, to the total exclusion of any concern for God's warnings and gospel (see 17:27–28). Indeed, with Sodom already burning behind her under the wrath of Almighty God, Lot's wife still looked longingly back to the goods and activities she had so reluctantly left behind; and in doing so she perished (see 17:32). Human nature changes little. Some people are so taken up with material things, that Christ thinks it necessary to warn them that on the very day in which he will be revealed to execute the wrath of God on evil centres and conglomerations of human iniquity, they will be tempted to go back into the house or city to get their favourite possessions because they cannot imagine life without them. For the sake of things they will lose life itself (see 17:31–33).

Now when the flood came upon a godless world it 'took them all away', (Gk *airō*), says Matthew 24:39; 'it destroyed them', says Luke 17:27. It thus removed the mass of corruption which was filling the earth (Gn. 6:13). The believing righteous, safe in the ark, were left untouched. So shall it be again when the Son of man comes: evil people shall be removed. In that night two shall be in one bed, the one shall be taken (Gk. *paralambanō*), the other shall be left. There shall be two women grinding together, one shall be taken, the other left (*cf.* Mt. 13:41–43). The disciples ask where this discriminating judgment will take place. It seems that the Lord's warning not to return to the city or to their houses had led them to think that the judgment would be focused on a particular place or places. The Lord replied somewhat enigmatically: 'Where the body is, there the vultures will assemble.' (17:37). Scavenging vultures are a repulsive sight, but they do a very necessary job. They are nature's way of removing masses of putrefaction from the face of the earth. The judgment is no pleasant topic; but one day to stop evil corrupting the earth beyond redemption, Christ will come and 'destroy those who destroy the earth' (Rev. 11:18).

iiia. The widow and the unjust judge (18:1–8). For the ungodly, then, the coming of the Son of man will be an event of unrelieved disaster; but the paragraph which now follows looks at that coming from a completely different point of view. For God's elect the assurance of that coming is a veritable gospel, for then all the wrongs which they have suffered will be put right. All down the ages God's elect have from time to time suffered injustices and persecutions, and the sufferings which they will be called upon to endure at the end of the age before the appearance of Christ will be of unparalleled severity (see Mt. 24:21–22). It is only natural that they should cry to God, not for revenge on their enemies, but for God to intervene and put a stop to all the evils perpetrated on them by unprincipled individuals and governments. After all, is God not interested in justice and in seeing justice done?

True, some have considered this cry for injustice as a somewhat sub-Christian attitude, appropriate perhaps for Jews of the pre-Christian era, but hardly in character for Christians. Christians should follow the example of Jesus who prayed forgiveness for those who crucified him. But Scripture tells us also that Jesus 'committed himself to him who judges righteously' (1 Pet. 2:23); and the very exhortation to the Christian not to avenge himself is based on God's personal assurance 'Vengeance belongs to me; I will repay, says the Lord' (Rom. 12:19).

The problem then is not that Christians should cry to God to be avenged but that when they cry he remains silent and appears to do nothing until in the end God's elect are tempted to think that it is no use appealing to God. Either he does not hear them, or else he does not really care. Yet, Christ insists, it is imperative that God's elect should persist in praying and not give up (see 18:1); for to cease praying would be to call in question the very character of God. The judge in the parable was wicked and unprincipled enough, caring for neither God nor man. But even he eventually gave in to the widow's persistent pleading. And shall we give up appealing to God and so make him out to be more unfeeling, more unjust than the unjust judge himself? To give up praying would be calamitous: it would imply that God, if there is one, is so indifferent to justice that we can have no reasonable hope for a coming reign of justice on earth nor of any heaven above worth going to.

One day God will avenge his elect. Christ stakes his truthfulness on it (18:8). God will intervene: the Son of man will come. Justice will be done. But will he find us still believing in God's justice (18:8)? If meanwhile we have stopped praying, how shall we then satisfactorily explain to him why we doubted his character?

iiib. The Pharisee and the tax-collector (18:9–14). The thought of Christ coming to execute the judgment of God on all evil and unrighteous men leads on naturally to the question raised in this next parable: who are the unrighteous, and who are the just? Here we need to be very careful. It is all too easy for people, particularly if they have suffered some injustice or other – and even if they haven't – to regard themselves as the innocent and good, and to take it for granted that it is other people who are wicked. We need therefore to watch the stance we take before God in our prayers; for if our persistence in prayer shows what we think of God's character, our prayers also reveal, sometimes without our realizing it, what we think of ourselves. And that could be disastrously wrong.

The Pharisee in the parable was a very religious man, and doubtless he and his friends had often been unjustly treated by tax-collectors. This led him therefore to take his stand before God on the ground of his own good deeds and to point out to God how much better he was than the loose-living men around him and, of course, than the tax-collector over the way. This was misguided indeed. By men's relative standards of justice he might perhaps have been better than the tax-collector; but he was forgetting that judged by God's absolute standards of justice he in common with all men, religious and irreligious, cheated as well as cheaters, persecuted as well as persecutors, stood under God's condemnation as a sinner who fell short of his glory. Taking his stand on his own merits, the Pharisee went home from the temple, unaccepted, unjustified and still under God's displeasure.

The tax-gatherer took a different stance: he stood at a distance (see 18:13), like the lepers of 17:12, owning the gulf that his sins had put between himself and God, and making no attempt to bridge it by any talk of what good deeds he had to his credit. Feeling himself unworthy even to look up to God's heaven, he confessed the absolute justice of God's condemnation of his sin, and in his utter spiritual bankruptcy simply cast himself on the mercy of God. On those grounds God accepted him. Nor did he have to wait until the second coming to know it: he went home from the temple justified (see 18:14). All distance between himself and God was gone forever. He could await the coming of the Lord in confidence and peace.

2. On entry into the kingdom of God (18:15 – 19:28)

If movement 1 has dealt largely with the coming of the King and with his future kingdom, movement 2 will deal with the question of entry into that kingdom. Here again, as in 17:20–37, we shall need to think both of the present spiritual phase of Christ's kingdom and of its future outward manifestation, for if we wish to enter the latter, we must make sure we enter the former. So first there come two stories dealing explicitly with the conditions for entry into the kingdom.

ia. The blessing of the infants (18:15–17). At 17:20–21 the Pharisees, intent on looking for the glory and power of the coming kingdom, failed to recognize the King himself standing in front of them. Apparently he was not grand enough for them. Now the disciples make the opposite mistake. Some mothers bring their babies for Christ's blessing, and the disciples rebuke them. Obviously they thought that babies were not important or grand enough for Christ to spend time and effort on them; and our Lord had to correct them; 'of such' he said 'is the kingdom of heaven'. A little child takes its food, its parents' love and protection, because they are given, without beginning to think of whether it deserves them, or whether it is important enough to merit such attention. So must we all receive God's kingdom and enter into it (see 18:17).

Most Christians, to be sure, would have no difficulty in adopting the child's attitude themselves in this context; it is when, like the apostles, we start engaging in 'Christian work' that we are liable to fall into the temptation of thinking that it is more important to attract 'leaders' and 'magnates' to Christ rather than the Mrs Mopps of this world. According to James (see 2:1–13) that is to break the whole law. The fact is that when it comes to entry into the kingdom of God none is more important than another.

ib. *The rich ruler (18:18–34).* On the other hand, this next paragraph will teach us that the King and his kingdom are important beyond all else, and if we do not believe them to be all-important, scarcely shall we enter into the kingdom. The rich ruler is the classic example of the principle. Being rich he had presumably enjoyed life in this age and he thought he would like to have eternal life in the age to come as well. He had always been able to pay for what he had in this life, and he was quite prepared to pay, so he thought, for eternal life in the kingdom: 'what must I do', he asked, 'to inherit eternal life?' (18:18). In actual fact he had woefully underestimated both the King himself and the kingdom.

He approached Christ with a polite 'Good teacher', but Christ pulled him up sharp. Did he really understand and mean what he said? No one was good except God alone.

It was no theological quibble. If Jesus was in fact God incarnate and the ruler had come to see that was so, then of course the ruler would be prepared to do whatever he said without question. It would be nonsense to ask for admittance into the kingdom and yet from the very outset to refuse to do what the King himself said. But the ruler was not prepared to do what Jesus told him. His 'Good teacher' turned out to be mere polite talk.

He had come, we recall, asking what he had to do to inherit eternal life. Christ told him how he could have not only eternal life but treasure in heaven (see 18:22). But when he discovered that he would have to choose between treasure in heaven and his consider-able earthly possessions he decided that the latter were after all the more valuable of the two. That is the difficulty with those who are in any way rich. Not only can pre-occupation with possessions leave them unprepared for the judgments that will accompany the coming of the kingdom (see 17:26–33), but their present posses-sions make the kingdom of God appear very much less than the one supremely valuable thing. It becomes at best a thing which they would gladly have in addition to their riches if they could con-veniently do so, but not something to be chosen if need be to the exclusion of all else. And as long as they think of the kingdom like that it is doubtful if they will ever enter it.

Now when Peter saw the rich man caught in the snare of riches, he felt moved to point out to Christ that he and his fellow apostles had left everything in order to follow Christ (see 18:28). His remark seems to have carried the unfortunate suggestion that their sacrifice was, compared with the rich young man's attitude, wonderfully meritorious. Christ corrected it immediately by making one observation (see 18:29–30) and later by making another (see 18:31–34). First he pointed out that every disciple is abundantly compensated for any loss he may incur for the sake of the kingdom of God. Not only does he get eternal life in the age to come, but here and now in this world he receives many more friends, homes and 'family' than ever he has to leave behind. Sacrifice for Christ is not really loss: it is an investment that provides both dividend and capital growth.

Secondly, sometime later – how much later Luke does not tell us – Christ took the apostles aside and told them more (*cf.* 17:25) of the detail of the sufferings that awaited him at the end of the road and how after those sufferings would come the resurrection. Had they immediately understood what he was saying, perhaps Peter would have been embarrassed at having recently reminded Christ of what he and his fellow apostles had given up for Christ's sake. But they did not understand; and Luke uses three clauses (18:34) to stress that fact and its explanation: 'this saying was hidden from them'. One day, of course, their eyes would be opened.

iia. A blind beggar (18:35–43). The next two stories will strike echoes in our minds. First they will recall our Lord's warning against riches: 'how hard it is for those who have riches to enter the kingdom of God' (18:25), and his audience's reply: 'Who then can be saved?' (18:26). Our two stories give the answer. One is about a poor beggar (see 18:35–43), the other about a rich tax-collector (see 19:1–10). The poor man was saved (18:42); yes, but so was the rich man (19:9–10), proving the truth of our Lord's earlier comment: 'things that are impossible with men are possible with God' (18:27). The rich man, of course, needed to be saved. His way of making a living was to some large extent fraudulent; salvation would need, among other things, to save him from that way of making a living. But in case we should think that the poor man was automatically better than the rich, Luke points out that the poor man also needed to be saved. His begging was equally degrading; he too needed to be saved from his unsatisfactory way of making a living.

The key to the poor man's salvation will revive other echoes in our minds. How the eyes of his heart had been enlightened (see Eph. 1:18) we are not told; but long before he received his physical sight he had seen in Jesus far more than other people discerned. They saw in Jesus simply the man from Nazareth (18:37). He saw in him the Royal Messianic Son of David (see 18:37–38) with all the resources of the kingdom of God at his command. Vigorously he appealed to him for the gift of sight and the King gave him his request. He never begged again; his prayer had gained him true independence. Even today someone who suffers from some dis-ability which makes him totally dependent on others in one sense, can find in prayer a means of conferring on others far greater benefits than they confer on him.

When the beggar first appealed to the Lord, however, the crowd tried to silence him (see 18:39). His persistence in crying out until he got what he wanted cannot but recall the widow who, in spite of endless discouragements, persisted in her pleading with the unjust judge until she too got what she wanted (see 18:1–8). Their tactics were the same: but it will be instructive to consider the difference in what they received. The widow managed to get the judge at last to give her justice against her adversary; and our Lord used the par-able, we remember, to direct our faith to the time when the Son of man shall come (see 18:8) in all his divine power and majesty to execute God's justice and put right earth's wrongs. That vision of the coming Christ is true, and will sustain us in times when we are called upon to bear injustice.

But it was a very different vision that filled the eyes of the blind man when his persistence was rewarded: not, of course, the Son of man appearing in the glory of his Father and of the holy angels; but not even a figure in royal clothes, with a noble entourage, on his way to his throne. Simply a dust-stained traveller on his way to Jerusalem, and, as we have just been reminded (see 18:31–33), on his way to being mocked, insulted, spit on, scourged and killed. Yet the blind man's new sight was not playing tricks with him: this *was* the Son of David, this was what he was like, this was what being the King must mean for him. The blind man followed him on his road (18:43), grateful to God that the Son of David had ever come his way. When he eventually saw what happened to the King at Jerusalem, perhaps he realized that if the King had not come near enough for men to spit on him, he might not have come near enough to hear a blind man's cry. Be that as it may, the King's character will never change. The King who served and suffered for men on earth, will serve them still in glory (see 12:37; 22:27). Hence the delight of being in his kingdom.

Meanwhile in the sure knowledge that one day our prayers will be heard and the Son of man will come and put all our wrongs right, we too are still called, says Peter (see 1 Pet. 2:18–24), to follow the King on his road to innocent suffering in the cause of men's salvation. 'The road to entry into the kingdom', says Paul (Acts 14:22), 'lies through many tribulations'. Indeed if our eyes have been opened to see and understand what was hidden from the apostles (18:34) that the King's sufferings are his chiefest glory; if we have seen the King who was rich become poor for the sake of us poverty-stricken beggars that we through his poverty might become rich; then we shall willingly hasten to suffer with him now, that we may share his glory then (Rom. 8:17).

iib. A rich tax-collector (19:1–10). Rich Zacchaeus was also saved, and it was a sight of the Lord Jesus that in its way saved him too. He was a short man (19:3), perhaps with a short man's inner urge to prove himself and gain recognition. If so his wealth had brought him no sense of acceptance either with God or men. The synagogue disapproved of him and the people shunned him: they despised him and his misgotten wealth; and he would have discovered the hard way that money cannot compensate for lack of acceptance. He was lost. How then could a man who was lost find his way into the kingdom? He couldn't, of course; but he could be found and brought in, if someone was prepared to come and seek for him and bring salvation to his very house (19:9–10).

And now Luke is telling us, with even more frequency than usual, that Christ was on a journey (18:31,35; 19:1,4,5,7,9,10). He had been on the journey a long time, but as he passed through Jericho certain things came swiftly together. Zacchaeus conceived a desire – who shall say where from? – to see who Jesus was and climbed up a tree to get a fuller view; and Jesus with the precision of an eternal purpose made for the tree, stopped, looked up into Zacchaeus' downward peering face, and told him to come down because he had to stay at his house. In that moment Zacchaeus not only saw who Jesus was, he discovered his own long-lost identity. He was a man loved by God with an eternal love, and longed for so much that God had sent his Son on purpose to find him and to rescue him from his lostness by coming personally to his home and bringing the sense of acceptance with God into his very heart.

Zacchaeus presently discovered something else. Acceptance with God had given him what he had sought in vain for years from wealth. The compulsive drive to make money had gone. Indeed, he felt he no longer needed half his wealth and he gave it away. In addition, the thought of entertaining Christ to a meal paid for by money which he had got by fraud, now seemed repulsive and impossible. He confessed his sinful practice and promised to make full restitution and to compensate his victims. It was a programme of social concern more generous by far than the Pharisee himself had announced as he stood in the temple (18:11–12). It was not the criticisms of the crowd that made him do it (19:7); their criticisms had never produced any such result before. And certainly Christ had not made it a condition of his acceptance of him. But through being accepted Zacchaeus had recovered his true identity: a true son of Abraham (19:9) that very rich ancestor of his, who was first justified by his faith (Gn. 15:6) and then lived to justify his profession of faith by his works (Gn. 22; Jas. 2:21–23).

With this we perceive once more the care with which Luke has selected and arranged his material. The tax-collector of the parable at 18:9–14 was justified by God's grace even though he had no good works to boast of like the Pharisee had. Zacchaeus was accepted and justified on the same ground. But his salvation led to a completely changed attitude to his social responsibilities. And it was important that it should: for if Zacchaeus was going to reign with

Christ in Christ's coming administration, he needed to learn and practise the Christian attitude to wealth in this present age. To profess conversion and then to carry on behaving like the rich ruler is a contradiction in terms.

iii. *The return of the Lord (19:11–27)*. All through this second movement we have been thinking of what it means and takes to enter the kingdom of God. For the most part we have been thinking of entry into its present spiritual phase by personal faith in the Saviour. Now we must in this final paragraph think what it will mean to enter the kingdom in its future outward form at the coming of our Lord Jesus Christ.

It will mean for all true believers eternal life (see 18:30). It will mean more. Much of this parable is a self-evident allegory of the ascension of Christ and of his return with the kingdoms of this world finally and fully committed to his authority (see Rev. 11: 15–18). Even if we avoid the mistake of confusing the allegory with the thing allegorized, the parable still clearly teaches that when the Lord returns to reign, his people shall reign with him (see 2 Tim. 2:12; Rev. 3:26–27).

What then will reigning mean? It will mean sharing the glory of the reigning house (see Rom. 8:17; Heb. 2:5–10). For some, for most perhaps, it will mean active participation in the government (see Mt. 19:28; 25:31; 1 Cor. 6:2–3). But here the parable teaches us a number of exceedingly important principles.

First, the amount of practical responsibility that will actually be given to each individual believer in the coming kingdom will in part depend on that believer's faithful use and development of the resources committed to his or her trust by the Lord during his absence. In this connection we might well remember the apostle Peter's observation (see 2 Pet. 1:10–11): it is one thing to enter into the eternal kingdom, and all believers will do that. It is another thing to be given an abundant entrance into that kingdom. That will be for those who in the power of their faith have availed themselves of God's resources and added to their character the necessary graces and qualities (see 2 Pet. 1:3–8).

Second, the Lord has entrusted some of his resources to every one of his servants: the number ten in the parable is presumably a representative number.

Thirdly, at his return, he will call all his servants to account for what they have done with their trust. The faithful will be rewarded; and the reward will be in terms of further responsibility and added trust and increased work, as well as the enjoyment of joining with Messiah in his unimaginably vast new enterprises. But what of the unfaithful?

There is one such in our parable and he presents us with a problem. His counterpart in the parable of the talents (see Mt. 25:24–30) is thrown into the outer darkness amid the weeping and gnashing of teeth. He seems evidently to represent a false servant exposed at last as an unbeliever. But ours is a different parable; and in our parable the unfaithful servant is treated differently. He has his pound taken away; but he is not said to be thrown out into the outer darkness, and he seems to be distinguished from 'these my enemies' who are brought before the King and slain (19:27).

What is it, then, that still makes it difficult to think that the unfaithful servant in our parable represents a true believer? It is his whole concept of the King. Asked to account for his failure to work for his lord, he replies that it is his lord's fault for being a person who always expected to get something for nothing, to get something out where he had put nothing in (see 19:21). Fear of him, fear of doing wrong, he adds, has paralysed him.

Our question, then, resolves itself into this: could anyone who truly believes that Christ gave his life for him, ever turn round and tell the Lord that in asking him to work for him, the Lord was asking for something for nothing? People can be ungrateful, witness the nine lepers. But would a believer ever be so ungrateful? And would any one who believes that Christ's death has secured him forgiveness for all his sins, ever tell Christ that he was afraid to work for him in case he made a mistake?

Perhaps our question is too theoretical or too literary. Perhaps we had better ask ourselves what we imagine our own behaviour is even now telling the Lord about ourselves and about what we think of him, if we likewise are not faithfully engaged on the business he has entrusted to our care.

Believer or unbeliever, the unfaithful servant had his pound taken away. Failure to work for the Lord will not cost a believer his salvation; but it will certainly cost him his reward (see 1 Cor. 3:15).

Let us end, however, on a happier note. The leper who was grateful to the Lord for what he had done for him and returned to give him thanks, found that his gratitude led on to something higher: in addition to his healing he received the gift of salvation. So the servant in our parable who worked faithfully for the lord found his faithfulness had a snowball effect. The one pound gained ten; the ten pounds brought him authority over ten cities (see 19:16–17); and over and above all that he was given the unfaithful servant's pound as well. Given his way with pounds, this additional pound would soon turn itself into an additional city. It is a law of the kingdom, apparently, that to the one who already has, more shall be given (see 19:26).

The King enters into his glory

Preliminary survey

The movements: first suite

1 Jerusalem and the first coming of the King (*19:29–48*)
2 The King and the question of religious authority (*20:1–19*)
3 The King and the question of political authority (*20:20 – 21:4*)
4 Jerusalem and the second coming of the King (*21:5–38*)

The movements: second suite

5 The King eats in Jerusalem: symbols of his suffering (*22:1 – 22:38*)
6 The King arrested and tried by the religious authorities (*22:39–71*)
7 The King sentenced and crucified by the political authorities (*23:1 – 56a*)
8 The King eats in Jerusalem: evidence of his resurrection (*23:56b – 24:53*)

Stage 5

The King enters into his glory

Preliminary survey

We have reached the final stage of the Going. It is the longest of all the stages, fittingly so for it forms the climax of the great journey which began at 9:51 and has been proceeding ever since. Its leading theme is self-evident, so that all we need to do in our preliminary survey is to investigate the way in which Luke has arranged his selection of material. That arrangement will give the events of this last stage the frame and focus in which Luke intends us to see them.

When the journey began at 9:51 we were carefully told that while the goal of the journey was to be nothing less than Christ's being received up into heaven, the last stage on the road would be Jerusalem. It had to be. As Son of the Most High to whom the Lord God had promised to give the throne of his father David (see 1:32), our Lord was heir to all the promises made by God to David, and Jerusalem was his capital. When therefore he finally presented his claim formally and officially to the nation, it would have to be done at Jerusalem. In fact, throughout the whole of this climactic visit Luke will constantly describe Christ's movements in relation to the city. We shall see him approach the city and weep over it (see 19:29–44). It will be pointed out that each night to obviate premature arrest he was obliged to leave the city and take to the dark shadows of the Mount of Olives (see 19:47–48; 21:37–38). We shall hear him predict the city's destruction and its centuries-long subjugation (see 21:20–24). Luke will tell us with some poignancy of the secret arrangements which the King had to make in order to be able to eat the Passover in his own capital city (see 22:7–15). We shall see him at last led out of the city to crucifixion; and on his way warning the 'daughters of Jerusalem' (see 23:26–31). And after his resurrection we shall find him rallying his dispirited disciples to Jerusalem (see 24:13,33), instructing them to wait in the city for empowering by the Holy Spirit, and directing them to make Jerusalem the starting point for their mission to the nations of the world (see 24:46–49).

There is much more involved in all this of course than mere topography; but in this stage the higher levels of meaning and significance are built on topographical foundations. The stage itself begins (see 19:28–46) as Christ reaches Bethphage and Bethany, and from Bethany in the company of his disciples descends the Mount of Olives and enters Jerusalem city. It ends (see 24:33, 50–51) as he leads his disciples out of Jerusalem city back up the Mount of Olives until they are over against Bethany, and there leaves them.

In the course of the stage Christ makes two very carefully prepared entries into the city, and Luke calls our attention to the fact by the similarity of his descriptions. At 19:29–35 he tells us that Christ sent two of his disciples into the nearby village to borrow an ass, with careful instructions what to say to its owners (see 19:31–34). And going, the two disciples 'found even as he had said to them' (19:32). They then took the ass to Christ who rode it into the city. In the days that followed he daily made many minor entries and exits, but, of course, only the initial entry was made in ceremonial style on the ass. The days were filled with teaching and discussion; and then Luke brings this part of the stage to an end with the general summary remark: 'And every day he was teaching in the temple . . . and all the people came . . . to him in the temple . . .' (21:37–38).

Then comes the second carefully prepared entry (see 22:7–13). Christ once more sent two disciples into the city, this time to borrow a room, with careful instructions what to say to its owner. And going, the two disciples 'found as he had said to them' (22:13). Momentous events followed that entry; but when at last they are all over Luke brings this second part of the stage to an end likewise with a general summary remark: 'And they . . . returned to Jerusalem . . . and were continually in the temple' (24:53).

These two major entries, then, are obviously similar in their basic pattern, but their differences are striking, and we must try to see their significance. By the time our Lord enters Jerusalem at the beginning of this stage we have been well prepared and know what to expect: he will be rejected and crucified (see 9:22, 31; 17:25; 18:31–33). At the same time we have been left in no doubt that he is God's Messiah (see 9:20, 35) and the royal Son of David (see 18:38–39); and, therefore, it has also been explained, sometimes explicitly and sometimes in parabolic language, how the matter of his suffering will fit into the programme for bringing the Son of David into his kingdom. After his crucifixion he will rise from the dead (see 9:22; 18:33), and ascend into heaven (see 19:11) and eventually come again to reign (see 9:26; 17:22–37; 19:15). The question arises, therefore, as to how exactly the sufferings relate to the reigning. Is it that the sufferings are simply a temporary obstacle between his claiming to be King and the actual establishment of his kingdom? Or, perhaps, a divinely foreseen interlude that will allow the King's servants to travel the world and spend the centuries preparing the nations for the King's coming reign? Or are his sufferings something more than an obstacle or more even than a useful interlude?

It is as if to answer these questions that Luke draws our attention to the highly significant fact that when at last our Lord came officially to his capital city as Zion's King, he made not one but two carefully arranged entries into the city. At the first entry he arranged things so as to gain for himself maximum publicity; at the second with equal care he arranged things to secure maximum secrecy. On the first occasion he borrowed an ass from its owners, and on the second an upper room from the master of a house. On both occasions these immediate arrangements were made to facilitate the fulfilment of age-long plans. When on the first occasion Christ borrowed an ass he did so in order to fulfil the prophecy given centuries earlier through Zechariah (see 9:9) that one day Jerusalem's King Messiah would come riding into the city on an ass. When on the second occasion he borrowed an upper room in Jerusalem it was in order that there he might eat the very last passover before the prophetic promise inherent in the symbols of that historic institution should be fulfilled by his own suffering at Calvary (see 22:16). On the first occasion, he claimed the role of Zion's King; on the second the role of Israel's true passover-lamb. The second role was no improvisation thought up to take advantage of Israel's unexpected rejection of her King.

In Israel's history the institution of Passover preceded that of Kingship by centuries; the promises inherent in its celebration had prior claim to fulfilment. But what perhaps is most significant of all is that on the first occasion when his claim to kingship was publicly rejected, he prophesied that he himself would be 'thrown out of the vineyard' and murdered, and that in his absence the city would be overrun by the Gentiles until the time of his second coming (see 21:20–36). When, however, he entered the city secretly on the second occasion, he proceeded there and then to set up his kingdom by instituting the new covenant by whose laws his subjects would from now on be ruled. He did it first in the upper room by means of symbols (see 22:20), and shortly afterwards at Calvary in actual suffering and blood.

Christ's sufferings then were no mere temporary obstacle, nor merely a fortunate interlude; they were the very basis on which his kingdom was set up. But Luke's careful emphasis on the fact that there were two entries one public and one private reinforces the lesson that we have already met with in the Gospel, namely that there are two senses in which we must think of the establishment of the kingdom. At his first entry Christ publicly presented himself as King and both he and his kingdom were publicly rejected. In that public open sense the kingdom will not be established until the second coming. At the second entry the kingdom was set up, as it were, secretly. Its covenant was concerned with the writing of God's laws in the human heart (see 22:20; Je. 31:33–34). The world at large eventually saw his sufferings, blood and death, but they had no idea that by that very blood he was ratifying the covenant and so establishing his kingdom. The significance of his death and the institution of the covenant were announced and explained in the secrecy of the upper room, as was appropriate for a kingdom which until he comes again must exist solely in spiritual form.

We shall find then that Luke has arranged the movements of this final stage in two groups, headed by the two entries of the King into his capital city. Once more a table of contents will help us to grasp the major themes of the movements and the thought-flow between them.

Stage 5 of the Going 19:29–24:53

1 Jerusalem and the first coming of the King 19:29–48	2 The King and the question of religious authority 20:1–19	3 The King and the question of political authority 20:20–21:4	4 Jerusalem and the second coming of the King 21:5–21:38
1 The coming of the King 19:29–40	**1 The King questioned 20:1–8**	**1 The King questioned 20:20–26**	**1 The coming of false messiahs 21:5–19**
a 'Blessed is the King who comes in the name of the Lord.'	*a* 'By what authority do you do these things? Who gave you this authority?'	*a* They watched him … that they might … deliver him up … to the authority of the governor.	*a* 'Many shall come in my name …'
b … the Pharisees … said, 'Rebuke your disciples' …; he said … 'if these keep silent, the stones will cry out'.	*b* 'The baptism of John, was it from heaven or from men?'	*b* 'Is it lawful … to give tribute to Caesar or not? … Render to Caesar's and to God the things that are God's.'	*b* 'I will give you a mouth … which all your adversaries shall not be able to withstand …'
2 Destruction of Jerusalem 19:41–44	**2 Murder and vindication of Messiah 20:9–18**	**2 Resurrection and enthronement of Messiah 20:27–44**	**2 Destruction and redemption of Jerusalem 21:20–33**
a '… your enemies shall … compass you round … and … dash you to the ground and your children within you.	'… I will send my beloved son … They … killed him … "The stone which the builders rejected, the same was made the head of the corner" … if it falls on anyone, it will scatter him as dust.'	'… neither can they die any more, for they … are sons of God being sons of the resurrection … How say they that the Christ is David's son? … "Sit at My right hand until I make thine enemies thy footstool".'	*a* '… Jerusalem compassed with armies … Woe unto those who are with child … they shall fall by the edge of the sword …'

b '... but now they are hid from your eyes ... because you did not know the time of your visitation ...'

3 Christ enters the temple 19:45–48

'... My house shall be a house of prayer: but you have made it a den of robbers.' And he was teaching daily in the temple. But the chief priests ... sought to destroy him, and they could not find what they might do, for the people all hung upon him listening.

3 Reaction in the temple 20:19

'... And the scribes and the chief priests sought to lay hands on him in that very hour, and they feared the people, for they perceived that he had spoken this parable against them.

3 Assessment of temple offerings 20:45 – 21:4

'... Beware of the scribes ... who devour widows' houses, and for a pretence make long prayers ...': A widow gives her whole living to the temple treasury.

b '... then shall they see the Son of Man coming ... when you see these things ...know that the kingdom of God is nigh ....'

3 Final admonition in the temple 21:34–38

'... Take heed to yourselves lest your hearts be weighed down with dissipation ...': And every day he was teaching in the temple ... and all the people came ... to hear him.

Stage 5 of the Going 19:29 – 24:53 cont'd

5 The King eats in Jerusalem: symbols of his death 22:1–38	6 The King arrested and tried by the religious authorities 22:39–71	7 The King tried, sentenced and crucified by the political authorities 23:1–56a	8 The King eats in Jerusalem: evidence of his resurrection 23:56b–24:53
1 Necessary preparations 22:1–13	*1 Arrest: priests and the authority of darkness* 22:39–53	*1 Civil trial: Pilate and the authority (v.7) of Herod* 23:1–25	*1 Unnecessary preparations* 23:56b–24:12
'Go and prepare for us the passover . . . Where do you wish us to prepare . . .' And they . . . found as he had said to them, and they prepared the passover.	'Father, if thou be willing remove this cup from me: nevertheless not my will but thine be done . . .' And being in an agony he prayed more earnestly . . .	And Pilate spoke, willing to release Jesus . . . but they were instant with loud voices . . . and their voices prevailed. . . . Pilate gave sentence that what they asked for should be done. . . . Jesus he delivered to their will.	They came . . . bringing the spices which they had prepared, and they found the stone rolled away . . . and they found not the body of the Lord Jesus . . . 'Remember how he spoke to you . . .'
2 Eating with his disciples 22:14–38	*2 Christ is led away to the High Priest's house* 22:54–65	*2 The leading away and crucifixion* 23:26–49	*2 Eating with his disciples* 24:13–43
a 'With desire I have desired to eat this passover . . . before I suffer, for . . . I will not eat it until it be fulfilled (22:15–16). . . . The Son of Man goes as it has been determined (22:22) . . . And I appoint	*a* And a maid . . . said, 'This man also was with him'. But he denied, saying, . . . 'I do not know him . . . . And Peter remembered the word of the Lord . . .	*a* And he said, 'Jesus, remember me' . . . and he said. . . . 'Today shall you be with me in paradise.'	*a* 'O . . . slow of heart to believe after all that the prophets have spoken. Ought not the Christ to suffer these things and to enter into his glory . . .' he interpreted in all the

unto you a kingdom ... that you may eat ... at my table in my kingdom' (22:24–30) ...

b And he took bread, and brake it and gave it to them saying, 'This is my body ... this do in remembrance of me ...' (22:19)

3 Provision for mission 22:35–38

'When I sent you forth without purse ... did you lack anything ... But now he who has a purse let him take it ... let him sell his cloak and buy a sword, for ... this which is written must be fulfilled in me ...'

---

b And the men ... mocked Jesus and beat him ... saying, 'Prophesy, who is it that struck you?'

3 The decision of the council 22:66–71

The assembly of the elders ... led him away into their council ... He said ... 'the Son of Man shall be seated at the right hand of the power of God ...' And they said, 'What further need have we of witness'.

---

b And the rulers also scoffed ... and the soldiers mocked ... and one of the malefactors ... railed on him.

3 The decision of a councillor 23:50–56a

And ... a man named Joseph, who was a councillor ... he had not consented to their counsel and deed ... who was looking for the kingdom of God ... went to Pilate ... asked for the body ... and laid him in a tomb ....

Writings the things concerning himself (24:25–27) ... 'Have you here anything to eat?' ... and he took it and ate before them (24:41–43).

b And he took the bread ... and broke it and gave to them ... and he was known to them in the breaking of the bread (24:30,35).

3 Briefing for mission 24:44–53

'All things which are written ... concerning me must be fulfilled ... And behold I send forth the promise of my Father upon you: but wait ... until you are clothed with power from on high.'

The movements: first suite

1. Jerusalem and the first coming of the King   (19:29–48)

i. The coming of the King (19:29–40). When at the end of the long journey Christ eventually came to Jerusalem, he put beyond all doubt the capacity in which he came. Zechariah had prophesied (see 9:9) that Zion's King should come to her 'just and having salvation, lowly and riding upon an ass, even upon a colt the foal of an ass'. When, therefore, Christ reached Bethphage and Bethany, he sent for an ass and in full view of Jerusalem rode it solemnly in royal procession thronged by his disciples down the slope of the Mount of Olives over the last few furlongs of his approach to the city.

Even before the procession started he had asserted the rights of his lordship. Two of Christ's disciples were sent into the nearby village, where, so Christ told them, they would find a colt tethered. They were to untether it and bring it to him. And then Christ added: 'If any one ask you, Why are you untethering it? You shall say as follows: The Lord has need of it' (19:31). The two disciples went off and, says Luke, they 'found even as he had said unto them' (19:32). Clearly this was no chance operation: Christ had the whole thing under his control perhaps by prior arrangement. At this point, then, all Luke need have said to complete the story was that the disciples did and said exactly as they had been told. Instead he chooses to repeat the detail: 'And as they were untethering the colt, its owners said to them, Why are you untethering the colt? And they said, The Lord has need of it' (19:32–34). Twice over, therefore, we hear the question raised: What right has Christ to take somebody's ass?, and twice over the reply is given: 'The Lord has need of it'. His needs are paramount.

If, however, his riding into the city on an ass still left it uncertain that he was claiming to be Zion's King, his disciples put the matter beyond doubt. In an expression of personal homage 'they threw their garments on the colt and set Jesus on them.' As he moved forward, 'they spread their garments in the way' for him to ride over. Then as the procession came over the brow of the Mount of Olives and began the descent towards the city, they burst into spontaneous, joyful thanksgiving to God for all the miracles which they had seen Christ perform, and openly acclaimed Jesus as Messiah: 'Blessed is the King who comes in the name of the Lord: peace in heaven and glory in the highest' (19:35–38).

Among the bystanders were some Pharisees. They suggested to Christ that he could not really approve of the exaggerated claims which his disciples were making and they invited him to restrain their excessive zeal. Far from doing so, Christ affirmed in the strongest possible language that the claim the disciples were making was true and could not be silenced. If the disciples did not make it, the very stones of the city would cry out in recognition of her King and shame the silence of her inhabitants. In the preceding months Jesus had forbidden his disciples to publicize the fact that he was Messiah (see 9:21); but now the time had arrived for him to present himself formally to the nation: with unambiguous clarity and maximum publicity he announced himself as Zion's long promised Messiah and King.

ii. *The coming destruction of Jerusalem (19:41–44).* But for all that there was no ambiguity or uncertainty about the King's approach to his capital, the King was under no illusion that the city would either recognize or receive him. There follow now therefore two paragraphs, in the first of which he laments the consequences that must follow on Jerusalem's failure to receive him, while in the second he diagnoses its cause. For the consequences he had tears; for the cause nothing but divine indignation.

There was no self-pity or injured pride in his weeping over Jerusalem, nor any threat of revenge. To him the city was a mother whose instinctive concern was for the protection of her children; and he had come not merely as her King, but as One 'having salvation' (Ze. 9:9). Certainly she had need of him. Long experience had shown that her walls and bulwarks by themselves without the protection of God's presence were insufficient to keep her enemies at bay (see Ps. 48; Is. 26). If now she rejected her God-sent King and Saviour, her walls would become the prison in which her ruthless enemies would confine and then slaughter her and her children. Ruination was inevitable.

Our Lord did not even blame Jerusalem. As a mother she would do what she felt was best for her children. But she was blind: 'the things which belong to peace were hidden from her eyes' (19:42), and 'she did not recognize the time of her visitation' (19:44). Blindness may not be blameworthy, but it would not mitigate the

313

tragic consequences of her rejection of her Saviour-King. The anticipation of those consequences moved him to tears; subsequent history has shown that his tears were not groundless.

iii. Christ enters the temple (19:45–48). On entering the city Christ went directly to the temple, as Malachi (see 3:1) had said he would. It was not merely that as the Father's Son he would wish before all else to pay his respects to his Father's house. It was that as Zion's King who was about to be rejected by Zion he would go immediately to the source of the trouble and expose the cause that blinded Zion to the rightful claims of her owner-King: robbers had infested the very temple of God. The outward evidence of that robbery was the blatant commercialization of the temple services; bad in itself it was but the sympton of a deeper malaise.

Somebody, of course, had to sell the required sheep and birds to would-be worshippers; but these sales should have been left to secular trade, unassociated with the sacred precincts and activites of the temple. For the temple authorities not only to allow this trading to go on in the temple courts, but to profit unduly from the sales themselves was not only inappropriate, it was scandalous. Instead of being priestly intermediaries to help men find worship and be blessed by God, they had become middlemen, turning their priesthood into a commerical monopoly in order to make financial profit out of men's quest for God.

Thus they robbed men, for it is difficult to experience the grace of God and the free gift of his salvation through the services of men bent on making money out of one's spiritual need. They also robbed God, treating his Word and sacraments as though they were the stock-in-trade of their business, and treating God's people not as God's possession, to be developed for God's enjoyment, but as a market to which they as the professionals had exclusive rights.

In high indignation Christ drove out those who sold, and began to teach the people daily in the temple-courts. It was the beginning of a fight to the death. On the one side were the temple authorities determined to maintain their status, power and income. On the other side was the Messiah, 'come in the name of the Lord' to secure the divine rights. At stake were the faith, love, obedience and devotion of the people; and from now on this struggle for the hearts of the people will be one of Luke's main concerns (see 20:1,6,19,26,45; 21:38; 22:2,6; 23:2–5,14,35; 24:19–20). The temple authorities would have liked to destroy their 'rival' forthwith; but his immense popularity with the people made any immediate attempt at arrest and execution impossible and tactically unwise. To upset the people would have put at risk the very thing for which the battle was to be fought (see 19:47–48). Subtler and more sophisticated tactics would have to be used.

2. The King and the question of religious authority (20:1–19)

i. *The King questioned (20:1–8)*. The expected attack soon came. One day as Christ was 'teaching the people in the temple and preaching the gospel', the religious authorities descended on him and in front of the people demanded to know what authority he had to do these things, and who gave him the authority (see 20:1–2).

Uppermost in their mind was not his teaching so much as his, to them, highly irregular and shocking conduct in driving out the merchants from the temple ('by what authority is it that you *do* these things?'); and the form of their question – 'who gave you this authority?' – shows that what they were thinking of was official authority. According to their way of thinking Jesus had no official authority, and they doubtless thought that if they could force him to admit it in front of the people, it would, if not discredit him, at least justify them before the people in arresting him.

They made the mistake that all religious 'establishments' are prone to make. The first question that ought to be asked of any teacher or preacher is whether his message is true, not whether he has a licence to preach. Similarly the first and major question to be asked about Christ's cleansing of the temple was whether it was morally and spiritually valid and whether the Scripture he appealed to (see 19:46; Is. 56:7) justified his action; whether he had an official permit from the dean and chapter to act in this fashion was altogether a secondary matter. Actually, as Messiah he had all the official authority he required without applying to the chief-priests and temple-captain for their permission. But the ultimate question was, as it must always be, one of moral and spiritual, and not of official, authority. Perhaps, of course, they sensed that to raise the question of the moral and spiritual authority of Christ's cleansing of the temple in front of the people would be embarrassing and dangerous: the people might find it difficult to see that it was morally and spiritually right for the temple authorities to make so much money out of their sacrifices. At any rate what they challenged was his official authority.

Christ did not answer them directly; instead he asked them a carefully phrased question about John the Baptist (see 20:3–4). Now John had not conferred any authority on Jesus; but he had claimed to be the forerunner foretold by Isaiah (40:3–4), and he had declared Jesus to be the Messiah. Christ, then, could have asked the priests quite simply 'Do you not remember that John said I was the Messiah?' But that would merely have raised the further question 'But how do we know that John was a true prophet and had the authority to say these things?' What Christ asked therefore was: 'The *baptism* of John, was it from heaven, or from men?'; and the question, put thus, immediately focused attention on the moral and spiritual authority of John's ministry. John had proclaimed on the authority of Isaiah that for the nation to be prepared to recognize and receive Messiah would require radical and thoroughgoing repentance on the part of every member of the nation; and John had demanded that repentance be signified by baptism. It was in fact the tremendous moral and spiritual power of John's preaching of this baptism of repentance that had convinced the people that John was a God-sent prophet.

Now many of the Pharisees, Sadducees, priests and theologians had refused to be baptized by John (see 7:30; Mt. 3:7); presumably they had privately decided that they did not need this baptism of repentance. But to be asked publicly in front of the people whether or not John's baptism was of God was highly embarrassing. To deny the moral and spiritual authority of John's preaching would have destroyed the people's respect for them completely. To say that while the people in general needed his call to repentance, they themselves did not, would not work either: religious leaders cannot altogether hide their moral failings from the people. But to admit that John's baptism was of God and obligatory on everyone would have been to own in front of the people that they were in rebellion against God by refusing to be baptized and to accept the Messiah to whom John had testified. So they tried to take refuge in uncertainty: 'we do not know', they said 'what authority John's baptism had.'

Now if it had been true that they did not have enough moral and spiritual discernment to decide about such an important matter,

they would not have been fit to be the religious guides of the
people. Their ignorance, however, was a pretence, and by it they
negated the sacred responsibility of their priestly office. If they
really believed that John was not of God, they had a duty to tell the
people so; and if the people stoned them they had a duty to suffer it
in the cause of truth and faithfulness. Deliberately to blur the truth
and fudge the issues in order to keep their hold on the people was to
descend to the level of mere religious politicians, more concerned
with position and power than with truth.

ii. The murder and vindication of Messiah (20:9–18). The religious
authorities, then, had tried to discredit Christ in front of the people
by questioning his authority for what he was doing. Christ exposed
their dishonesty and refused to answer their enquiry. Instead, he
turned to the people (see 20:9) and in front of their leaders told
them a story designed to state exactly what his authority was and
how it would be vindicated, and at the same time to warn the
people that their leaders were about to perpetrate the gravest possible abuse of their religious office.

The story took a well-known Old Testament metaphor (see *e.g.*
Is. 5) and turned it into a parable in which the people were represented as a vineyard, God as the Owner of the vineyard and the
religious leaders as contract-workers responsible to cultivate the
vineyard for the Owner's satisfaction. On this basis Christ levelled
a double charge at Israel's religious establishment. First, in the past
they had frequently thwarted the wishes and satisfaction of the
Owner; and secondly in the present they were about to commit
that crowning abuse of office to which religious establishments are
prone, to take over the vineyard as if they were its owners in open
rebellion against the Owner.

In the past when God had sent his servants the prophets to call
for repentance, reform and true worship from the people, the
religious leaders had often resisted their reforms, suppressed, persecuted and sometimes destroyed the prophets, and so had cut off
from God the response he sought from his people, the very satisfaction which it was their office as the religious establishment to
promote.

In the present they were about to do even worse. In the language
of the parable Christ claimed that the Owner had now sent his
'beloved son' (20:13), and it is beyond all doubt that he was refer-

317

ring to himself and indicating with the utmost clarity 'what authority he had to do these things and who gave him this authority' (20:2). The Son had come for the same purpose as the prophets, but as the Owner's Son he stood in a completely different relationship to the vineyard from either the prophets or the religious leaders. They were simply servants; he was the heir, joint-owner with the Father, with rights not only to the fruits, but to the vineyard itself. In other words, the people were his property; he personally had a claim to their faith, love, obedience and service, and it was the duty of their religious leaders to guide the people to place their faith in the Son and yield him their obedience. Instead of that Christ announced that they were going to put him, the Owner's Son, to death, not because they thought his claims were false, but because in their heart of hearts they knew that he really was the Owner's Son, and they were determined not to surrender the control of the people to him but to keep it in their own hands. It had taken the coming of the Owner's Son to expose the fact that they had turned their office from being a humble service to God and to his people into a usurpation of God's rights over his people, in the same way, we may add, as all kinds of extra-scriptural organizations subsequently usurped the rights of Christ over his churches, suppressed his Word and persecuted his evangelists.

Next the parable predicted the consequences of their usurpation of the Owner's rights. The Owner, Christ said, would respond to his Son's murder by destroying the contract-workers and giving the vineyard to others. God's spiritual interests in the earth and the care of people who believed in and served the true God of Israel would pass out of the hands of Judaism's priesthood and eventually to a large extent out of Israel's hands altogether.

When the crowd heard this they were shocked (see 20:16). A cynic might have said that the severity of Jesus' charge against the religious authorities was really caused by the fact that he wanted to do the very thing he accused the priests of, to control the people of God. The answer to such a charge lies in the way Jesus said his claims and his diagnosis would be vindicated. In the first place his parable informed the people that the religious authorities would succeed in putting him to death; and he made no attempt to rally the people to his defence. He was content to let the Owner of the vineyard vindicate him after his death.

Secondly, he pointed to the fact that both his diagnosis of the situation and the vindication of his claim were predicted by Scripture. Psalm 118 was by common consent regarded as messianic, which is why the Pharisees objected so strongly when Christ's disciples applied its phraseology to him as he rode into Jerusalem claiming to be Zion's King (see 19:38=Ps. 118:26). But that Psalm in a context about the house of the Lord and the sacrifices of the altar referred in its figurative way to 'the builders'. Who could they be but Israel's priests and religious leaders? It also indicated that these leaders would reject the stone which God would subsequently instal as the keystone of his people's worship. Who could that keystone be but the Messiah? Precisely because he knew himself to be that Messiah, Jesus would make no attempt to resist the priests, to rally the people and take over the vineyard by their support. He could afford to let God vindicate his claim and set him as the keystone in the key position among his people.

Finally, however, he warned both the people and the religious leaders of what the consequences must be if they persisted in rejecting him. He was after all the Owner's Son and heir to the vineyard (to the universe in fact, see Heb. 1:2). He would one day be made the keystone in the eternal spiritual temple of God's universal praise. To repudiate that Stone and try to build one's life on some other foundation would be to court brokenness and ruin, while active opposition would eventually be crushed and removed (see 20:18).

As we read these solemn words we must not forget that at 19:41–44 he wept when he thought how Jerusalem's blind rejection of his salvation would expose her to destruction at the hands of her enemies. But his compassion for the blind and ignorant must not lead us to forget what he must do to those who knowingly and deliberately usurp the rights of God, and especially to those who cloak their usurpation under the cover of religious office. There is no vineyard anywhere in the universe where creatures may usurp the authority of the owner and of his son and then continue for ever to enjoy the grapes.

iii. Reaction in the temple (20:19). At 19:47–48 Luke reported that the religious authorities would have liked to destroy Christ but were unable to do so because of the people. Now at 20:19 things have got worse, and Luke tells us that the authorities wanted to arrest him at once '*and* they feared the people'. That is, fear of the people was no longer a reason why they could not arrest Christ, but a reason why they felt they must arrest and destroy him as soon as possible. That was because, as Luke explains, 'they (presumably the people as well as the authorities) realized that he had spoken this parable against them (that is, against the religious authorities)'. The people were beginning to get their eyes opened to the way the religious leaders had been, and still were, abusing their authority. In Christ, moreover, they had now discovered someone who was not afraid to stand up against the religious establishment and denounce them to their face. There was no telling what the people might do if things went on like this. In their fear of the people the authorities decided they must proceed against Christ at once.

3. The King and the question of political authority (20:20 – 21:4)

i. *The King questioned (20:20–26)*. In movement 2 Luke showed us what Christ's claim to be King meant in relation to the established religious authorities in Judaism, and why those authorities repudiated his claim. Now he will devote the most of movement 3 to showing us what Christ's claim to be King meant in relation to the political powers of the day. Luke does that by relating what the Jewish authorities did when they found they could not break Christ's popularity with the people by undermining his religious and spiritual authority: they decided to trap and destroy him at the political level.

The compulsory payment of taxes to the Romans understandably rankled with many Jews. For some the resentment sprang from simple economic considerations, with others from nationalistic feelings. The religious right wing in Judaism went further: they held that to pay tribute to the Romans was an offence against God, a misdirection of revenues that rightly should be given to their divine Ruler, the Almighty. Moreover the major prophets had plainly declared that when the Messiah came God would grant Israel complete deliverance from Gentile domination. In consequence any messianic figure who was prepared to teach the people that it was a religious duty to refuse to pay tribute to the Romans would get an immediate and large following among the masses. Among the nation's religious leaders there was naturally more caution. The high-ranking priests in particular, who held office virtually by grace and favour of the Romans, looked with alarm and disfavour on any messianic movement (see Jn. 11:47–50) which might upset the Romans and thus eventually threaten, or even destroy (as eventually happened), their temple, priestly power and income. So they waited for a suitable occasion when there should be large crowds listening, and then using a judicious amount of flattery and appealing to his sense of justice and righteousness (see 20:20–21) they asked him about paying tribute to the Romans. Was it right to pay it, or to refuse to pay it? The question was designed to catch him on the horns of a dilemma. If he said it was right to pay the tribute, he would immediately alienate the masses and as a religious leader that would be the end of him. If on the other hand he said that it was right to refuse to pay tribute, they could report him to the Roman governor who would have him executed for political subversion. That too would be the end of him. Christ's answer is proverbial. Calling for a denarius he got his questioners to recognize that the image and susperscription on the coin were Caesar's, and he then laid down the principle 'Render to Caesar the things that are Caesar's and to God the things that are God's' (20:25).

We notice at once that the principle enunciated by Christ turns on the question of 'ownership', and this inevitably recalls the diagnosis of the religious situation which Christ has just given in the parable of the vineyard. The whole point of that parable was that Israel's religious leaders, priests and theologians were usurping the rights of God the Owner and of his Son and Heir over the love, loyalty and obedience of the people. In eloquent contrast here Christ does not say that in demanding tribute from Israel Caesar is usurping the ownership rights of God. Nor does he say that now that the Messiah and heir to the throne has come, Caesar must give up his right to tribute, or his power over Israel. Quite the reverse. He asserts that Caesar is acting within his legitimate rights of ownership: render to Caesar the things that are Caesar's. It was a confusion of categories to suppose that faith in the truth and justice of God (see 20:21) meant taking political steps to overthrow the government of Tiberius Caesar, cruel and corrupt though that government was. And, as we shall later be told in detail, it was a misreading of the prophetic timetable and misunderstanding of Messiah's methods and strategies to suppose that faith in Jesus as Messiah must lead his followers to attempt to restore Israel's ancient ideal of a theocratic state by mounting political programmes of civil disobedience or outright warfare against the Gentile imperialists.

What then was Christ's timetable for the setting up of his kingdom? And what were to be his methods? And what was the nature of his kingdom? To these questions the subsequent paragraphs and movements turn.

ii. Resurrection and the enthronement of Messiah (20:27–44). It so happened that around this time some of the Sadducees – and most of the leading priests who had been disputing with Christ were Sadducees – engaged Christ in public debate on the topic of resurrection. Unlike the Pharisees the Sadduccees did not believe in resurrection (see Acts 23:8) and they tried to show that in the light of the sane, practical commands of holy Scripture the whole idea of resurrection made nonsense. For argument's sake they supposed the case of a woman whose first husband died without producing a son and heir. The law (see Dt. 25:5–10) required the deceased's brother to marry his widow and produce a son who should be counted as the deceased's son and heir. This therefore was done. But the second husband also died without producing a son, and so did all the others, seven in all, who attempted to fulfil their obligations under the law. 'Then', said the Sadducees, advancing what they thought was an irrefutable objection to the idea of a resurrection, 'in the resurrection whose wife shall she be, for the seven had her to wife?'

Now we have no means of telling whether the Sadducees had perceived that in the parable of the vineyard and in the citation of Psalm 118 Christ was implying that after his execution by the authorities he would rise again, and were therefore wanting to scotch the idea before it took hold of the popular imagination (see Mt. 27:62–66), or whether they were simply anxious to win a debate with this Galilaean prophet on a major doctrine of their theological school. But of this we may be certain: the synoptic evangelists will have seen the crucial importance and relevance of this question to Jesus' claim to be the Messiah and Saviour of the world. If there is no such thing as resurrection, Jesus is neither Messiah nor Saviour and there is little or nothing in Christianity (see 1 Cor. 15:12–19). All three Synoptics therefore record at length both the question and Christ's answer to it.

According to Christ (see 20:34–40) the Sadducees' objection was based on two false presuppositions. The first was that conditions in the world to which resurrection admits a man are simply a continuation of this life, and that therefore the marriage relationships which people have contracted here will continue there. That, of course, is not so. In the resurrection the redeemed will be like the angels in two respects: they will never die, and they will not marry.

The second mistaken presupposition lay at the other extreme. It implied that the relationship formed between God and men in this life was only temporary. But that is not so. God being eternal, the relationships he forms are eternal. Centuries after Abraham, Isaac and Jacob lived, God was announcing himself to Moses, so Christ pointed out, as the God of Abraham and the God of Isaac and the God of Jacob (see 20:37). The eternal cannot be characterized by something that no longer exists. Resurrection then is not a fantasy dreamed up by the wishful thinking of less than rigorous theologians; resurrection is a necessary outcome of the character and nature of God.

Christ, however, was not content to leave the matter there, but went over to the offensive and in his turn cited a passage from the Old Testament. In Psalm 110:1, Christ observed, David called Messiah his Lord. What sense could that possibly make if (1) Messiah was not already existent in David's day, and (2) if by the time Messiah was born, David had completely ceased to exist? How could David call a non-existent Messiah his Lord? How could Messiah be Lord of a non-existent David? Moreover no oriental father, let alone an oriental monarch, would ever call one of his own sons Lord. Joseph's brothers might eventually call him Lord, Jacob never did! But David called Messiah his Lord: how could he therefore be simply his son?

The rest of the New Testament supplies the answer to these questions: Messiah was not simply the son of David. He was and is both the Root and Offspring of David (see Rev. 22:16). He could have said with reference to David what he said with reference to Abraham: 'Before Abraham was I am' (Jn. 8:58). It was, therefore, impossible for him to be executed and then to cease to exist. He was the Owner's beloved Son in the fullest possible sense of the term. His death would inevitably be followed by his resurrection.

If we go further and ask what the programmme was to be for the setting up of his kingdom, the rest of Psalm 110:1 will tell us. The command from God to the Messiah, 'Sit at my right hand' would be pointless if in fact Messiah had always uninterruptedly been sitting there. The command implies a time when Messiah came forth from the Father (see Jn. 16:28), and was not sitting at the right hand of God; and it equally implies his subsequent resurrection, ascension and session at the right hand of God. The verse then indicates that there will be an interval between his ascension and the time when his enemies are put as a footstool beneath his feet (see Heb. 10:13). How and when that operation is to be staged will be the function of movement 4 to tell us.

iii. Assessment of temple offerings (20:45–21:4). At 19:45–46 Christ denounced the priests for turning the temple into a den of robbers. Now he denounces a similar abuse on the part of the scribes who were the experts in the interpretation of holy Scripture (see 20:46–47). His charge against them was that they used the authority which their expert knowledge of Scripture gave them to demand from a not altogether willing public excessive adulation for themselves; and secondly that their professional prayers were often mere camouflage over their unscrupulous and hard-hearted extortion of money, not only from the well-to-do, but from defenceless widows. It is to be noticed (see 21:1–4) that these grave abuses of Israel's religious system did not blind Christ's eyes to the genuine piety, indeed the spectacular devotion of many private individuals such as the widow to whose sacrifice of two mites he gave eternal commendation and universal fame. At the same time it is evident from his denunciations that the Judaism of his day was gravely distorted by corruptions such as in later centuries have proved so great a scandal in Christendom (see 1 Tim. 6:5). These very corruptions, unrepented of, would one day destroy the temple.

We should therefore notice the relevance of Christ's critique of Israel's temple-worship to the political question with which this movement 3 began. In Jeremiah's day there were many who thought that no matter how corrupt their religious, social and commercial behaviour was, God would never allow the great Gentile empire of the day to overrun and destroy the temple in Jerusalem. Jeremiah, therefore, was directed by God to stand in the gate of the Lord's house and to warn all who came in to worship that that was precisely what God would allow the Gentiles to do (see Je. 7). The temple would afford them no protection. In Christ's day the religious leaders, and particularly the aristocratic high-priestly class, professed to be afraid that if they allowed Jesus to continue to propagate his messianic claims, it might lead to a popular political rising, and the Romans would retaliate by destroying both Jerusalem city and the temple (see Jn. 11:47–53). Actually, as movement 3 has shown, Christ's messianic claims posed no threat either to the Roman Caesar or to the Jewish temple. What was beginning to make the destruction of the temple inevitable was first the corruption of Israel's worship at the hands of the religious leaders and secondly the treatment which they were plotting to hand out to the Messiah. They would in fact succeed in getting the Romans to execute Jesus; a generation later those same Romans would ruthlessly destroy their temple.

4. Jerusalem and the second coming of the King (21:5–38)

Movement 1 made it clear from the very beginning that when Christ came officially to Jerusalem riding ceremonially on the ass as Zion's long-prophesied King, he was under no illusions as to what was going to happen. Jerusalem, he knew, would reject both him and his salvation (see 19:41–44). Immediately on entering the city he had gone to the chief trouble-centre, the temple and its perversion of the worship of God (19:45–46); and since then movements 2 and 3 have enlarged on the determination of Israel's religious leaders to destroy him. In those circumstances there could be no thought of Christ's proving himself to be Zion's Saviour by delivering Jerusalem from Gentile domination. All the major prophets had declared that God himself had deprived Israel of her political independence and theocratic constitution because of her sins. Christ was certainly not going to wave a magic wand and deliver Israel from Gentile domination in spite of the fact that she still had not repented and was at this moment intending to murder the Owner of the vineyard's Son. Daniel in the ninth chapter of his prophecy had recorded the solemn lesson that God's promises to restore Jerusalem would never be completely fulfilled as long as Israel remained obdurate in her sin and in her rejection of her Messiah; and in movement 3 we have heard Zion's King himself tell Israel to continue paying taxes to the Gentiles since Gentile domination was to continue indefinitely.

Now we come to movement 4, and we shall hear more solemn things still. Israel will not only continue under the Gentile yoke, but after Messiah's murder the temple, the headquarters so to speak of Israel's rebellion against her Messiah and her God, will be swept away and Jerusalem city overrun by the Gentiles.

But all is not gloom. Daniel in his seventh chapter had prophesied of the time when Israel should finally be set free from Gentile imperial domination, and he had associated that deliverance with the coming of the Son of man in the clouds of heaven (see Dn. 7:13). Here in movement 4 our Lord will affirm Daniel's prophecy: Jerusalem's redemption shall eventually take place at the coming of the Son of man in a cloud with power and great glory (see 21:27–28).

i. The coming of false messiahs (21:5–19). Granted the solemn fact of the temple's impending destruction and the glorious prospect of Jerusalem's future redemption at the second coming of Christ, the main question to which the detail of movement 4 addresses itself, is the order of events that shall lead to these two momentous happenings.

The disciples were warned in the first place against the many false messiahs that would come preaching the imminence of the end (see 21:8) on the basis of quite fallacious evidence. To save them from such deceptions Christ informed his disciples that the signs of the imminence of that end would be nothing less than a combination of wars, earthquakes, famines, plagues, along with terrifying cosmic disturbances (see 21:11).

In the second place the disciples were to know not only that the destruction of Jerusalem would take place long before the second advent and before the end (see 21:24–27) but also that there would have to be a period of time after Christ's departure even before Jerusalem and the temple were destroyed (see 21:12–19). The reason for that was that before the destruction took place, the nation would be given an opportunity to repent together with new and altogether exceptional evidence designed to lead it to repentance. That evidence would take the form of the supernaturally inspired witness of the early Christians at all levels of society, and the maintenance and growth of that witness by divine power in spite of severe and often unnatural persecution. Israel should thus have such powerful evidence that they had been mistaken in crucifying Jesus and such compelling offers of forgiveness and reconciliation, that they would have no excuse for continued opposition, nor ground for complaint when God eventually allowed both their city and temple to be destroyed.

ii. The destruction and redemption of Jerusalem (21:20–33). We know
from the Acts of the apostles that some thousands of individual
Jews took advantage of the period given them for repentance; but
officially the nation persisted in its rejection of Jesus. Christ, of
course, foresaw it would, and so did the prophet Daniel. In his
famous chapter on Jerusalem city Daniel had forecast that: '. . . the
Anointed One will be cut off and will have nothing. The people of
the ruler who will come will destroy the city and the sanctuary.
The end will come like a flood. War will continue until the end, and
desolations have been decreed' (9:26 NIV).

So now Christ indicated that the time given for Jerusalem to
repent would come to its end, and in its place there would come her
desolation (see 21:20) and 'the days of vengeance, that all things
which are written may be fulfilled' (21:22). When the disciples saw
the Gentile armies approaching, they were to abandon the city.
They were not to hope for some miracle of divine deliverance. The
time for the execution of God's wrath had come: they were not to
try to resist it (see 21:20–22). In his compassion he lamented again,
as he had done earlier (see 19:41–44), the terrible human suffering
that would be inflicted on the city, and particularly on the women
and children, as the city's inhabitants were either slaughtered or else
taken into captivity and exile (see 21:23–24). But with the precision
of divine righteousness he pointed out the chief form which the
divine wrath upon Jerusalem would take: '. . . they shall be led
captive into all the Gentiles, and Jerusalem shall be trodden down
by the Gentiles until the times of the Gentiles be fulfilled' (21:24).
One cannot escape the solemn repetition. Jerusalem had once represented all that was distinctive from the Gentile way of life and from
its system of values. But now her official religion had become
corrupt, as Gentile in spirit as any pagan religion. Jerusalem's
religious leaders were about to take their Messiah and force the
Gentiles against their will (see 23:1–25) to execute him. It was
appropriate therefore that her streets should suffer what her values
had already suffered. God was going to allow Jerusalem not so
much to be destroyed as to be overrun and trodden down by the
Gentiles. Jerusalem, the holy city, would become a Gentile city,
run by Gentiles according to Gentile values.

The temple would of course be destroyed, its age-long testimony
to God obliterated (see 21:5–6). But when its chief priests took the
Father's well-beloved Son and killed him God was not prepared to

327

allow their temple to continue indefinitely as an alternative witness to the true God. A religion which officially denies that Jesus is the Son of God 'has not the Father' says John (see 1 Jn. 2:23).

Here we should perhaps make the obvious, naïve point that the destruction of Jerusalem was not something which God gave to the Christians to do: he gave the task to pagan Gentiles, as in earlier centuries he had given it to the Assyrians (see Is. 10:5–15). The anti-semitism of mediaeval and modern so-called Christian countries has been nothing but diabolical and satanic in its origin.

But next we should notice that divine mercy had limited the divine wrath on Jerusalem even before it began: Jerusalem, said Christ, was to be trodden down by the Gentiles but only 'until the times of the Gentiles be fulfilled' (21:24). The times of the Gentiles would be marked by centuries of opportunity for the Gentiles to hear of the Saviour and of the gospel which Judaism had officially rejected; and, as we now know, millions would respond. But in themselves the pagan nations would prove to be no better, or less sinful, than Israel; their opportunity to receive the gospel would not last for ever either, nor their ascendancy over Jerusalem. Moreover, as Paul later had to remind his Gentile fellow-Christians, apostasy would eventually rob Christendom of its role as the leading witness to God in the earth as surely as it had robbed Judaism of it; and Israel being at last converted would be restored to her place of witness for God (see Rom. 11:13–32). One day, then, Jerusalem's desolations shall be over. The Son of man shall come in power and great glory (see 21:27) amid premonitory cosmic disturbance; redemption shall be completed (see 21:28); the kingdom of God shall come (see 21:31). The long waiting will be past.

At 19:29,37,41 Luke carefully recorded the increasing nearness of our Lord's approach at his first official ceremonial 'Coming' to Jerusalem. Here at 21:28,30–31 he records likewise the signs which Christ gave of the nearness of the approach of his second coming. As surely as men standing in Jerusalem once saw him slowly descending the Mount of Olives and then ascending the opposite hill into the city, so surely shall the world one day see the Son of man descending the heavens. Not then shall he come as the meek and lowly: he shall come with power and great glory. Not then shall he come riding on an ass: he shall come in a cloud, the emblematic carriage of Deity. Not then shall he have to borrow a donkey: then his advance preparations shall be the roaring of the sea and the shaking of the powers of the heavens.[1]

iii. Final admonition in the temple (21:34–38). It is a fact much noted by commentators that the setting of our Lord's prophetic discourse is different in Luke from what it is in Mark and Matthew. Mark (see 13:1–2) and Matthew (see 24:1–2) both relate that as Jesus was going out of the temple his disciples called his attention to the mighty stones of which the temple was built. Luke does not tell us that Jesus went out of the temple. At 21:5 Christ is still inside the temple, and what the people call his attention to is not only the stones of the temple but the votive offerings which of course would be hanging inside the temple. At the end of the discourse, moreover, Luke places two summary verses (see 21:37–38) which seem to indicate that the teaching he has recorded from 20:1 – 21:36 was all of it given during our Lord's daily teaching sessions in the temple. It is altogether likely that Christ began his prophetic discourse inside the temple in the hearing of the general public, and that when he went out and sat on the Mount of Olives his disciples came to him privately, as Matthew and Mark say, and in answer to their request for further elucidation Christ went over much of the same ground but with appropriate additions and differences of emphasis. It is the kind of thing that still happens with lecturers and students during conferences nowadays.

Be that as it may, one cannot escape the emphasis that Luke has

---

[1]Our Lord's affirmation that 'this generation shall not pass away until all these things happen' (21:32) has led to much debate on the meaning of the term 'generation'. For a full discussion of the problem see Marshall, 779–81. The event has shown that 'generation' was not intended in its temporal sense. Of the other possible interpretations perhaps the best is to take the whole phrase as a strong asseveration that all these things shall be accomplished, in the same spirit as the next verse (21:33): *i.e.* this nation would perish first before these things should fail to find fulfilment. Another way would be to follow the Jewish usage in which certain generations were thought and spoken of as peculiarly wicked, notably the generation of the Flood, whom God had to destroy, and the generation in the wilderness, who apostatized from God and were condemned never to enter the Promised Land. Of all the perverse generations ever to have lived that surely was the most perverse that rejected its King Messiah and delivered him over to the Gentiles to be put to death. Christ himself called it an evil generation (11:24), and affirmed that from it should be required the blood of all the Old Testament martyrs (11:50–51). In saying, then, that this generation should not pass away until his second advent, our Lord may have been indicating that the nation that rejected him would continue officially to reject him until his second coming. There would be no qualitative change.

On the other hand he could have been using the term 'generation' in its other (Greek) meaning i.e. 'race' or 'nation', and so meaning that in spite of all the scattering of Israel for their rejection of their Messiah, the race itself should not perish before the destined redemption and reconciliation should take place at the second coming.

placed on the temple throughout these chapters. Every movement
so far has ended with a description of some perversion or other in
the temple (see 19:45–48; 20:19; 20:45 – 21:4); and now movement
4 ends fittingly enough with a warning against another perversion.
The movement began (see 21:5), as we have noticed, with people
calling our Lord's attention to the votive offerings in the temple. It
is understandable that such beautiful things, expressive of great
religious devotion, should excite people's admiration. But it is all
too possible for such admiration to be nothing more than an
aesthetic appreciation which because it produces feelings of awe
and delight is mistaken for true spirituality, when all the while it
leaves a person's self-indulgence and worldliness unchanged and
the person morally and spiritually unprepared for the coming of
Christ (see 21:34–36). Rather than that the glories of the temple
should lull unregenerate hearts into complacent unpreparedness for
Christ's coming, it were better for it to be swept away.

The movements: second suite

5. The King eats in Jerusalem: symbols of his suffering (22:1 – 22:38)

i. Preparations for the feast. (22:1–13). The first suite of movements
has taken our minds from the official coming of the King to
Jerusalem through the story of his rejection, the prophecy of his
death and vindication and on in thought to the destruction of the
temple, the overrunnning of Jerusalem and finally to the glorious
second coming of the Lord.

Now as the second suite opens Luke brings our thoughts back to
the situation as it was in Jerusalem just before the Passover at the
end of Holy Week. The religious authorities naturally had their
preparations to make for the celebration of the national feast.
Pressing even more urgently on their minds, however, was the
necessity of isolating Jesus from the crowds so that they could
destroy him. Presently Judas gave them the opportunity they were
looking for, and they went ahead with their preparations for the
kill.

And now we are to behold the most spectacular demonstration
of the way God governs a rebellious universe. Human rebellion,
initially induced in Eden's garden by Satan, is at this stage in

history by Satan's continued inspiration (see 22:3) determined that Jesus shall die. And Jesus for his part in order to counter that rebellion and to establish God's kingdom here on earth in the very teeth of that rebellion is determined – to die! To that end he once more makes preparations to enter Jerusalem, and sends two disciples, not this time to borrow an ass on which to ride in ceremonial procession as Zion's King, but to borrow a room in which to eat the Passover. The Passover of course had to be eaten at night; but, humanly speaking, it was dangerous for Christ to be in the city at night without the protection of the crowds around him, which is why all through the past week as soon as evening came and the crowds dispersed our Lord had left the city and disappeared into the dark shadows of the Mount of Olives to avoid premature arrest (see 19:47–48; 21:37–38). His entry into the city at night and the place where he would eat the Passover had to be kept secret. The two disciples were therefore given certain pre-arranged signals that would eventually bring them to an unnamed man who was prepared to lend Christ a room in his house in which to celebrate the Passover in Jerusalem. It was the King's own capital city; but the authorities had a price on his head and Jerusalem was now the earthly headquarters of rebellion against the King.

ii. *Eating with his disciples (22:14–38).* So 'when the hour was come, he sat down and the twelve apostles with him' (22:14). We notice the precision of the timing. Messiah was about to suffer (see 22:15); but it was neither an accident nor unforeseen. The Son of man was about to go (see 22:22); but the going had been fore-ordained before the foundation of the world (see 1 Pet 1:20). In the course of history therefore when Israel had needed deliverance from Egypt God had ordained that the deliverance should be effected by the blood of a literal Passover lamb. Thereafter the annual celebration of Passover served two functions. It was a memorial of Israel's original deliverance which was of course a genuine historical event of immense significance in its own right. At the same time it was designed as a prototype and promise of that immensely more significant deliverance that God would eventually effect through the sacrifice and blood of his Son.

And now in the course of God's government (see 22:16) the time had come to redeem the promise. The final preparations had all been carefully made and the King came with a strong desire to eat the last Passover before Passover's promise should be fulfilled. The anticipation of his suffering had long weighed heavily upon him (see 12:50), and the prospect that now it would soon be over doubtless contributed something to that desire. But in addition, the eating of that Passover on the eve of his death would allow him to imprint on the minds of his apostles and on the minds of all his followers ever afterwards, that his death was no disaster, nor simply the sad achievement of human envy, Satanic power-lust and religious perversion. Rather it was the divinely foreordained sacrifice for the deliverance of men from their bondage to those very lusts and perversions and for their reconciliation with God. So effective indeed would that sacrifice be that however long it took before the kingdom of God should finally come (see 22:18), he should never again need to drink of the fruit of the vine either as a common meal or as a Passover symbol: the great redemptive sacrifice would be complete, his work on earth would be finished.

Moreover, in addition to celebrating the Passover in Jerusalem, Christ also instituted a completely new ordinance, the Lord's Supper (see 1 Cor. 11:20). It was to serve his disciples until he came again as a set of vivid symbols to remind them of his body and blood given for them and for their deliverance; it was to serve also as a sign of the new covenant that he was about to inaugurate in his blood (see 22:19–20).

The terms of the new covenant, published by God through Jeremiah (see 31:33–34), had long since made its nature and purpose clear. Like the old covenant which it replaced it was to be an instrument of government: 'I will put my laws into their minds and on their heart also will I write them: and I will be to them a God, and they shall be to me a people: and . . . all shall know me, from the least to the greatest of them. For I will be merciful to their iniquities, and their sins will I remember no more.' In handing his disciples the cup of the new covenant in his blood Christ was doing nothing less than announcing the inauguration of his kingdom into which those who accepted redemption through his blood, would be admitted, and there by the regeneration, teaching and power of the Holy Spirit would be trained in obedience to their Lord and King. The establishment of this spiritual phase of his kingdom moreover would not need to wait until his second coming: it could begin as soon as the blood of the covenant sacrifice sealed the covenant.

Christ had no sooner announced the establishment of his king-dom, however, than he called attention to a great irony. Satan had infiltrated his agent Judas into the very upper room and he now sat with his hand on the table (see 22:21) to mark Christ's every movement, to plan Christ's arrest, to facilitate Christ's crucifixion and death; and the very table on which the traitor's hand lay carried symbols which being now decoded by the King proved to be announcing that it had been God's eternal purpose all the way along that the King should die and by that death break Satan's power and inaugurate his own kingdom. Judas' sin was inexcusable; but his traitorous hand would but serve the plan of God for the destruction of the power of his diabolical master.

The King went further. In addition to announcing the establish-ment of his laws in the hearts of his disciples he disclosed his plans for training them to share in his government both here and here-after. They were to be schooled to renounce the Gentile concept of government as domination over others, and to follow the ideal which he had set before them, that of the Servant-King (see 22:24–27). Their schooling done and their loyalty to the King tested by the sharing of his suffering, they were to be rewarded in the age to come with the delight of close personal fellowship with him in his glory and with active participation with him in the government (see 22:28–30). Meanwhile the disciples were not to be shielded from Satan's attacks, and they would suffer temporary, partial defeats; but the vital lifeline of their personal faith in the Saviour would be maintained by the intercessions of their King-Priest as in the case of Peter; and the lessons learned in defeats would be turned to the further strengthening of the group (see 22:31–34). The King would not only defeat his Enemy: he would use Satan's opposition for the perfecting of his own disciples.

iii. Provisions for mission (22:35–38). If the nation's rejection of the King meant that he had to announce the inauguration of the king-dom in the secrecy of the upper room, it did not mean that the vigorous missions of the past years must now cease. Far from it. Instead of being confined to Israel, Christian missions would now be extended to cover the world (see 24:47). But the fact that the King himself was about to be outlawed and executed by the nation, meant that his missionaries could no longer expect the nation to meet the costs of their maintenance as on previous occasions (see

9:1–6; 10:1–16); they would have to pay their own expenses and fight their own way with no financial help from the nation or the unconverted.

Misunderstanding his metaphorical reference to the need for a sword, the disciples found two swords and offered them to him. He brushed them aside without further explanation: the next few hours would show them quite clearly that he was not talking of literal swords, or advocating violence, either in the propagation, or in the defence, of the faith (see 22:49–51). But the new situation, and the new relationship which it would necessitate between Christian missions and the world were, he pointed out, no unforeseen, temporary difficulty. This too was a fulfilment of what Scripture had long since indicated should happen (see 22:37). The fact that at the cross 'Christ was reckoned with the transgressors' is the very basis of the gospel of forgiveness and peace; but that same cross has of necessity set up a relationship between the King and his followers on the one hand and the world on the other which likewise is a fundamental part of the gospel of the Crucified. The relationship cannot be compromised without compromising the gospel (see 1 Cor. 1:1 – 2:5; Gal. 6:14).

With this Christ completed the announcement of his programme and strategies for the establishment of his kingdom. But symbols, programmes and prophecies are no use if they are not put into action and fulfilled. 'What is written must be fulfilled in me', said Christ, '. . . for that which concerns me has an end' (22:37). And when he had said that, the King went out to set up his kingdom.

6. The King arrested and tried by the religious authorities (22:39–71)

i. Arrest: priests and the authority of darkness (22:39–53). When the King came out from the upper room, he went, so we are told (see 22:34), 'as his custom was' to 'the place' (22:40) on the Mount of Olives where every day throughout the past week he had gone when he left the temple at nightfall, the place which Judas knew well and to which he would soon come with the arresting party. There was no thought of running away. If the kingdom of God was going to be set up, then the battle with the powers of darkness must be fought and the sooner it was joined the better.

'Pray', said Christ to his disciples, 'that you enter not into temptation'. Hell itself would now unite all its forces and combine with human evil to prevent, if possible, the will of God from being done. And this would be their temptation: to avoid facing the battle, to give in, to run away, to fail to do the will of God.

So then, as if to make clear where at this crucial, fateful hour in the history of the universe the battle-centre lay, he withdrew from his disciples about a stone's cast (see 22:41). The battle and its outcome would depend on him alone. If he failed all would for ever be lost: if he triumphed, he secured irreversible victory.

And he kneeled down. What a sight! What a victory! The King kneeling on the Mount of Olives! Only a few days ago he had come riding down this same Mount of Olives in royal procession rightly acclaimed as the King (see 19:35–38). But he had found Jerusalem his capital city in the hands of rebels, the temple infested with robbers. How could such opposition be overcome? How could such rebels be saved from the condemnation of God and the penalty of their rebellion, and restored to obedience and the worship of God? Riding on the royal mount through the streets of the city would hardly do it. Pomp and ceremony never yet turned a rebel into a saint. If ever Jerusalem, Israel and the world were to be brought back to God's obedience, it must all start here: Messiah must himself establish the will of God on earth by obeying it himself.

So the King kneeled down. He would obey on his own behalf as always, but on behalf of Israel as well, on behalf of all the human race. 'For as through the one man's disobedience the many were made sinners, even so through the obedience of the one should the many be made righteous' (Rom. 5:19). There was in his prayer of obedience no pretence that the cup was sweet. Obedience in an unfallen world may, for all we know, be nothing but ecstatic pleasure. But when obedience was confronted in our world with the purpose of God for the redemption of fallen men, the cup could not be other than immeasurably bitter. In all sincerity Christ pleaded that the cup might be removed without his having to drink it. Here was no cheap unthought-out enthusiasm or superficial devotion like Peter's (see 22:33) professing a readiness to suffer and die that was the product of irresponsible unrealism. For any one to welcome the prospect of being made sin by God would be either fatuous ignorance or Promethean defiance of the All-holy. For Holiness Incarnate to welcome the prospect would be unthinkable. Sincerely he prayed for the cup to pass – if it would be God's will.

335

But if not, then even if every emotion in his heart, every fibre and cell in his flesh rose up against the prospect, and his body sweat blood in its agony, he would positively pray 'Not my will but thine be done'.

When he returned to his disciples, he found them sleeping for sorrow and he gently chided them. Yet their very failure will help us to see an important distinction. Under the weight of evil circumstances and sorrow they had given in to nature's weakness and the comfort of sleep. That of course did not make the evil go away, it made them only oblivious of it and unprepared for its onslaught. Christ gave in to nothing: he positively asserted the will of God in the face of all evil. His prayer as he knelt on earth, 'Thy will be done', was the cry of the Conqueror: for 'he who does the will of God abides for ever' (1 Jn. 2:17).

With that the arresting party arrived, and the sudden shock of seeing through Judas's sickening pretence and of realizing what was going to happen provoked an instantaneous reaction from the other disciples: 'Lord shall we use our swords on them?' One of them indeed did not wait for permission, but drew his sword and with poor aim but stout intention cut off the right ear of one of the high-priest's servants. This reaction was natural, the all too natural reaction of mere human nature, unprepared by prayer, ungoverned by the will and wisdom of God, and utterly inappropriate and inadequate to the nature of the conflict that was now upon them. What they were up against was not mere flesh and blood but principalities and powers, the world-rulers of this darkness (see 22:53) whose power lies in twisting all that is genuinely human and true into a diabolical but specious lie. That is not a power from which a man can be delivered by physical weapons. Christ restrained his followers and healed the man's ear. One man at least should hear loud and clear, in spite of all the confusion in the garden that night, exactly what Christ really stood for, as Christ now exposed the deceit of the chief priests, captains of the temple and elders who were conducting the operation. There they stood professed ministers of God, guardians of his temple, upholders of his sanctity and truth, making out they were on an expedition against some political activist. The whole thing was a deliberate pretence; and we can now see how beautifully Peter would have unthinkingly played into their hands, if he had been allowed to continue with his armed resistance. Then they could have told the

336

public that they had caught Jesus at dead of night at the head of an armed band, engaged on some subversive guerrilla action, and that when challenged, he and his followers had attacked the authorities with weapons. How Satan would have laughed to see the Saviour of the world represented as a guerrilla fighter who thought that the problem of evil could be solved by political subversion and armed conflict.

The fact is that publicly in broad daylight they had been unable to find any basis for a political charge against him and they were obliged therefore to concoct one and try to pin it on him under cover of darkness. Their very tactics and the timing of their arrest proclaimed the source of their power: 'This is your hour', said Christ 'and the authority of darkness' (22:53).

ii. Christ is led away to the High Priest's house (22:54–65). By this time most of the disciples had run off and abandoned Christ. Peter, to his eternal credit be it said, had at least followed him; but all of a sudden he now found himself ranged on the wrong side in the battle. He had not intended it: but he had not perceived the nature of the battle nor the weapons and the resources with which it is ultimately won. The battle is between the Truth and the lie, the Truth being ultimately a Person. It is settled not by physical force – how could it be? – but by spiritual strength (see 2 Cor. 10:4). What is required of a man is to stand with the Truth. Whatever the consequences, he has triumphed if he has remained standing with the Truth; he has lost, if success has meant deserting the Truth.

In the courtyard of the High Priest's house the servants lit a fire and sat around it. Peter sat among them. Presently in the semi-darkness the fire blazed up, the light shone on Peter's face, and his face gave him away (see 22:56). They made him talk, and his Galilaean accent gave him away (see 22:59). 'In truth' the last servant said, confidently asserting what he knew to be true (22:59); and it gave Peter his last opportunity to win his battle and stand with the Truth. But he denied the Truth, taking refuge, as it felt at the time, in the shelter of pretended ignorance: 'I do not know him', 'I am not one of them'. 'Man, I do not know what you are talking about' (22:57–58,60). Just then, when he had denied the Truth for the third time and seemed to have cut off all connection between himself and Christ, somewhere out in the darkness of the night a cock crowed, and the Lord turned and looked on Peter.

'And Peter remembered the word of the Lord, how that he said unto him, Before the cock crow this day, you shall deny me thrice' (22:61).

Peter got up and in great distress fled out into the cover of the night. But now the darkness would never swallow him up completely: the link between Christ and him had been maintained, and Peter's faith in the truth of the word of Christ was actually at this moment stronger than ever. He had proved Christ's word to be true. And if Christ had been right about the denial, right too even about the detail of the cock crowing, he would be right in regard to the rest of his prophecy (see 22:31–32): Peter would turn again and strengthen his brethren. The memory of that assured statement saved Peter from ruinous despair. The intercessions of the King-Priest had secured for Peter that his faith did not fail (see 22:32). They will do the same for every believer on every battlefield of life.

But now for the remainder of the night Jesus stood alone. His guards were cruel and coarse men who cared little about truth. To them religion was always good for a joke, particularly prophets who tried to scare you with warnings about a God who is supposed to be able to see everything you do, and will one day punish sinners. So they blindfolded Jesus. 'There now', they said, enjoying their new-found freedom to punch him without his being able to see who did it, 'prophesy now and tell us which of us it was who punched you'. It was crude thinking; but how were they to know that in Peter's denial a prophecy had just been fulfilled under their very eyes?

iii. *The decision of the council (22:66–71).* As soon as daylight came (see 22:66) the religious authorities held what was ostensibly an investigative council. 'If you are the Messiah', they said to Jesus, 'tell us'. In actual fact they were not interested in trying to find out the truth. They were not prepared either to believe what he said, or even to discuss the matter with him. It was pointless trying to explain things in detail, or to offer any defence. They were determined to find grounds for condemning him to death. Forseeing their verdict Christ therefore stated his identity in terms of his resurrection and ascension. 'From henceforth shall the Son of Man be seated at the right hand of the power of God' (22:69).

They understood him to be claiming virtual equality with God, both in position and power, and they were delighted with the statement because to them it was the height of blasphemy and gave them ample grounds for having him executed. They just checked, however, to make sure that he was claiming to be the Son of God in the fullest possible sense of the term; and finding that he was, they concluded their investigation. Now they could get him executed. Ironically their execution of him would be but the first step in the process of translating their prisoner to his seat at the right hand of the power of God.

7. The King tried, sentenced and crucified by the political authorities (23:1–56a)

i. The civil trial: Pilate and the authority of Herod (23:1–25). The religious authorities saw clearly that a charge of blasphemy would scarcely secure the verdict they wanted from the civil courts, so when they brought Christ before Pilate they charged him instead with subversion in the cause of political messianism (see 23:2). It was a lie, of course, so obviously a lie that Luke does not trouble to point out the fact. Pilate examined the accused and soon concluded that the charge was baseless. Learning, however, that the prisoner belonged to Herod's authority Pilate referred him to Herod. The very suggestion that Jesus was a contender for political kingship struck Herod as so ludicrous that he and his men made a mock of the whole business, dressed Jesus up in mock-royal garb, and eventually after much merriment sent him back to Pilate. There was nothing in the charge. Pilate reconvened the court and announced the verdict of the double enquiry; but then he found that the priests were not prepared to bow to his authority, nor Herod's either. They insisted that Jesus be executed and that a certain Barabbas be released.

The situation was beginning to become crazy. Here were priests demanding the execution of Jesus on the ground that he was attempting to overthrow the political authorities. Yet these very priests would not themselves bow to the political authorities; and what is more, they were calling for the release of a known political activist who in a recent civil disturbance in the city had committed murder. Pilate decided the time had come to assert his own will. 'Willing (Gk: *thelōn*) to release Jesus', he again addressed his accusers (see 23:20). But they shouted, 'Crucify him.' Pilate made a third attempt to have his will done; but again they shouted him down and he gave in (see 23:22–23).

339

At this crucial moment in the narrative we cannot help noticing the insistent repetitions in Luke's language: 'But they insisted *with loud voices asking* that he might be crucified. And *their voices* prevailed. And Pilate gave sentence that *what they asked for* should be done. And he released one who for insurrection and murder had been cast into prison, *whom they asked for*; but Jesus he delivered up *to their will*' (Gk. *thelēma*). It is only a few verses since we were listening to the prayers of another petitioner before another authority: 'If thou be willing, remove this cup from me; nevertheless not my will, but thine be done' (22:42). That was the King at prayer, and one day as a result of that prayer he would sit at the right hand of the power of God and have the government of the universe entrusted to him. How different the priests and the people. Standing before the properly constituted political authority (see Rom. 13:1–7) whose sacred God-given task it was to protect the innocent and condemn the guilty, these priests insisted on overriding the will of the political authority and on having their own will done. Their own will was that the innocent be condemned and a murderous insurrectionist be released. But whatever becomes of people who insist on their own will like that?

ii. The leading away and crucifixion (23:26–49). If Jesus Christ is indeed the Son of God, his crucifixion here on our planet obviously raises profound questions about God's moral government of the universe. And if, as we have been told (see 22:20), Christ by his death was going to establish the new covenant as the basis of his government, it is hardly surprising to find that Luke's narrative of Christ's death draws our attention to some of the basic principles on which divine government operates.

The first matter to be noticed is how God gets his will done in a rebellious world. As Christ was led away to execution (see 23:26) the Roman army press-ganged a passer-by and made him carry Jesus' cross. The man had no choice: the army wanted it done and they compelled the man to do it. And that was that. How different has God's method been. It was the divine will and foreordination that the Son of God should die as a ransom for sinners (see 22:22). The High Priest and the chief priests, Judas, Satan and the people have all had a part in bringing God's Son to his death. None of them has been forced by God to do it. All have their own reasons and their action is altogether voluntary. Yet in the end they do what God's power and will has decided beforehand should happen (see Acts 4:28).

The second matter is the law of inevitable consequences. Among the crowds who followed Jesus to his place of execution was a large number of women who bewailed and lamented him. It was, it seems, a psychological reaction to the sight of 'such a nice young man' being so rudely taken out to such a hideously cruel death. It had nothing to do with moral conscience or repentance. In a month's time they would have forgotten it. Christ wanted no such pity. He told them rather to weep for themselves and their children since before them lay such suffering as would reverse all nature's normal desires and values: childlessness would come to seem the happiest thing, and death to be preferable to life (see 23:29–30).

This is terrible; but it proceeds from the law of act and inevitable consequence, of sowing and reaping. The people of Jerusalem, led by their priests, elders and rulers, had just called on Pilate to condemn an innocent man to death and to release a murderous political activist in his place. When Pilate, in the name of just government, tried to refuse such an outrageous demand, they shouted and raved and insisted on having their own way against all justice and governmental restraint. They got what they called for. Alas they did. As a direct, if distant, consequence of calling for this injustice they would one day call again, this time for the mountains to fall on them to save them from the consequences of what they insisted on calling for the first time.

'For if they do these things in the green tree, what shall be done in the dry?', said Christ (23:31). If citizens, living in a reasonably civilized society under a fairly stable and reasonably just government, can overrule the government and insist on the execution of an innocent man, not to mention the fact that he was God's Son and their Messiah; if priests in a nationally recognized religion which stands for divine law, morality and ethical behaviour, can use lies to pressurize the civil power to commit judicial murder; what kind of behaviour will prevail in a society that has lost all respect for justice, law, morality, religion and God? It may take a long while to turn a green tree into a dried-up trunk, a paradise into a desert. But bleed the moral life-sap of a nation, and the result, however long-delayed, is inevitable.

These then would be the consequences of the nation's murder of Messiah. But sin brings more than consequences: it brings divine retribution. The Owner of the vineyard, so Christ warned (see 20:15–16), would not stand idly by after the contract workers had taken his beloved Son, thrown him out of the vineyard and killed him. The Owner would 'come and destroy these workers'. Yet solemn as is the fact of divine retribution, it allows the possibility of divine forgiveness, and the narrative now shows us on what conditions forgiveness is granted and how it affects the question of the consequences of sin.

First come the soldiers who without realizing the significance of what they were doing crucified Christ along with two malefactors as if he were just another malefactor, and drove the nails through his quivering flesh. We should notice the grounds on which Christ prayed forgiveness for them: 'Father, forgive them *for they know not what they do*' (23:34). This prayer, uttered in the moment of fearful pain, on behalf of those who were causing the pain, has rightly moved the hearts of millions and become the ideal which has taught countless sufferers not to yield to blind retaliation, but to seek the good of even their enemies (see Mt. 5:43–48). It detracts nothing, however, from the glory of Christ's prayer to point out that it was prayed on behalf of the soldiers who in all truthfulness did not know what they were doing. False sentiment must not lead us to extend the scope of his prayer beyond his intention. To pray forgiveness for a man who knows quite well what he is doing and has no intention of either stopping or repenting would be immoral: it would amount to condoning, if not conniving at, his sin. Christ certainly did not do that.

Next comes the principle on which Christ makes it possible for people to be saved from the wrath and retribution of God. We hear it first, distorted as a jibe, on the lips of the rulers mocking his inability to save himself: 'He saved others; let him save himself, if this is the Christ of God, his chosen' (23:35). They were thinking in physical terms. They admitted that at this level he had brought deliverance from disease to many in the nation. But now here he was physically nailed to a cross and apparently unable to free himself. How could he be the God-sent Messiah, God's chosen? If he could not prevent his enemies from crucifying him, or miraculously come down from the cross and deliver the nation from their political enemies, what use would he be as a Messiah?

At this the Roman soldiers joined in. They knew nothing of the terms 'Messiah of God, his chosen' and the meaning these terms would have for Jews who knew their Old Testament. But according to their own simple concepts a king who could not save himself was altogether a non-starter in the struggle for political power. If Jesus was all that the Jews could put forward to contest the rule of Judaea with Caesar, the whole claim to kingship was ludicrous. In contempt they nailed over his cross an inscription: 'The King of the Jews this'. It was laughable; and until Christ comes again in power and great glory, all attempts to represent Christ and true Christianity as a political kingdom in competition with other political kingdoms will in the end incur similar contempt in the eyes of the Gentile powers.

But we know what neither the rulers nor the soldiers could know. When Christ entered the city at 19:29–48 he certainly entered claiming to be King; but when he entered the city at 22:7–38, he came to fulfil the Passover and effect that deliverance of which Passover was a prototype. Now the first Passover was of course a deliverance from the political oppression of Pharaoh; but even that literal, political deliverance necessitated two stages for its achievement. In the second stage Israel were delivered from the power of Egypt as God destroyed the Egyptian army in the Red Sea. But in the first stage, which was clearly the far more important of the two, Israel had to be delivered, not from the power of Pharaoh, but from the wrath of God. The night of the first Passover was a night of the execution of God's judgments (see 12:12–13); and Exodus makes it very clear that when God rose up to execute judgment on Egypt, Israel was just as liable to the wrath of God as the Egyptians were. The distinction between oppressor and oppressed counted for little. All were sinners. Israel's firstborn would therefore have perished as certainly as the Egyptians' firstborn, had God not provided the blood of the Passover Lamb as a protection against the destroying angel (Ex. 12:21–23).

It was, then, as the true Passover Lamb that Christ had deliberately come to Calvary to deliver sinful and guilty mankind by his blood from the wrath of God. Without that deliverance, all other deliverances would ultimately be in vain. To mock Christ, as the rulers and the soldiers did, was sublimely misconceived: they might as well have mocked a literal Passover lamb because, while it saved others, it could not save itself.

Granted then that Christ's death makes divine forgiveness possible, on what conditions does anyone receive that forgiveness?

And granted that forgiveness releases a man from divine retribution which is the eternal penalty of sin, what effect does that forgiveness have, if any, on the consequences of sin? Answers to these questions are now given in the narrative of the two malefactors.

The first malefactor was suffering the consequence of his misdeeds in the form of temporal punishment inflicted by the government of the day. For all his pain there was with him apparently no fear of God, no confession of guilt before God, no expression of repentance, no request even for divine forgiveness. He was prepared to believe that Jesus was the Messiah if he would do a miracle and release him from the temporal punishment that was the consequence of his crimes. When Jesus made no attempt to do that he cursed him and his religion as a cheat. But to save people simply from the temporal consequences of their sins without first bringing them to repentance and reconciliation with God, would be no true salvation at all. It would but encourage people to repeat their sins under the impression that any ugly or inconvenient consequences could and would be miraculously removed by a fairy godmother. No paradise could be built on such an irresponsible attitude to sin.

It was different with the second malefactor. Reflection on the fact that Christ was innocent and yet was suffering along with the guilty convinced his conscience that there must be in the world to come a judgment in which the injustices of this world are put right. That in turn awoke in his heart a healthy fear of God, which led him to repentance and a frank acknowledgement of his sinfulness. Even the temporal punishment inflicted by the state, he owned, was well deserved and he made no request for a miracle to be done to let him off the consequences of his sins (see 23:40–41). Again reflection on the fact that Christ was suffering innocently led him to believe that he was indeed Messiah the King; and that if he was Messiah and there was a God who cared about justice, then all he had heard about resurrection must be true: Messiah would be raised from the dead and 'come in his kingdom'. Perhaps it was hearing Christ's prayer to his Father to forgive the soldiers who crucified him; perhaps it was an instinct born of the Holy Spirit; but whatever it was that caused it, there arose in his heart the faith to realize that while there was no question of his being released from the temporal consequences of his crimes, there was every possibility of his being delivered from the wrath of God and from the eternal penalty of sin. With that there also came a change deep within his heart. He no longer wanted to be a rebel; he wanted nothing more than to be allowed to become a subject of the King in his eternal kingdom, if the King would have him. 'Jesus', he said, 'remember me when you come into your kingdom' (23:42).

The King's reply granted not only immediate forgiveness but also spelled out for the dying malefactor, and for all who repent and believe, what forgiveness involves: immediate and complete acceptance with God; the assurance that upon death he would be received directly into the presence of the King, without any interval he would be 'with Christ'; and admission to paradise where there shall be no more pain, crying, sin or curse (22:43). 'Today' said Christ, 'you shall be with me in paradise.' A rebel had been converted: is not that the true work of a king?

Finally Luke shows us that the government of God arranged that there should be vindication for Christ even in his suffering and death. His resurrection, of course, would provide further and greater vindication; but at his death there were two divine interventions, one in the realm of nature and one in the realm of religion (see 23:44–45).

The darkness that came cannot be explained as an eclipse, but its effect on those who had witnessed the spectacle of the crucifixion (see 23:48) and now witnessed this eerie disturbance in nature must have been profound. Let the normal processes of nature be unaccountably disturbed, and men's sense of insecurity will make them conscious, if ever they are going to be, of their own littleness, and of the awesomeness of God, and it will induce in them a consciousness of guilt and an honesty at least with themselves over moral issues.

Now the centurion in charge of the execution squad was merely doing his duty, and may at first have taken little interest in the issue at stake between the Jewish leaders and Jesus, beyond being aware that it involved certain religious questions. The darkness obviously deepened his interest and set this crucifixion for him in a profounder context. Luke does not tell us of Christ's cry of dereliction; he records simply the confidence and peace with which Christ went to meet God, as a son going to his Father (see 23:46). It was this that finally decided things for the centurion. 'Surely this was a righteous man' he said; right not only in his dispute with the Jewish religious leaders, but right in relation with God. A man who could die like that in those circumstances and conditions must be right. The effect on the crowd was the natural corollary of this: the innocent sufferings of Christ, the manner of his death amid the unnatural disturbance of nature brought them by contrast to consciousness of, and self-condemnation of, their own sinful state: they went away beating their breasts (see 23:48).

Few people standing round the cross would have been aware that the veil in the temple had been torn in two; but when it did become known, that not only had it happened, but that it had happened when Jesus died, the phenomenon took on profound symbolic meaning. Without the veil to hide the presence of God, no Jewish priest would have dared to enter the holy place of the temple. The tearing of the veil made the Jewish system of worship temporarily unworkable. Later as people came to see that they could have forgiveness through the death and sacrifice of Christ, and immediate acceptance with God and spiritual access into his presence (see Heb. 10:19–22), their very enjoyment of those spiritual realities made them feel that Judaism's symbolic sacrifices and temple were now obsolete. By that same token it made them feel that the cross of Christ and what he has achieved by it are the chief of all his glories.

iii. The decision of a councillor (23:50–56a). The next step in the vindication of our Lord was his burial in a separate tomb by himself. Had his body been flung into a mass grave along with other bodies, it would subsequently have been impossible to point to the empty tomb as clear evidence of the resurrection. As it was, Luke carefully indicates how and where the body was laid (see 23:53) and further emphasizes that the women who had followed Jesus from Galilee saw both the tomb and exactly how the body was laid in it (see 23:55). When upon their return they found the tomb empty, it would not be because they had mistakenly come to the wrong tomb or because they had not originally known exactly how or where within the tomb the body was laid.

For the moment, however, interest centres on the way God achieved this necessary part of his Son's vindication. He achieved it through the effect of the death of Christ on the moral conscience of one of the Jewish councillors, Joseph of Arimathaea.

He, Luke tells us (see 23:50–51), was 'a good man and a righteous' and had dissented from the counsel and deed of the council, obviously on the grounds that he regarded the council's act as totally unjust. But the council was a national body, their act a public act; and Joseph was a member of the council. He came to see therefore that it was not enough to dissent privately: if he wished to free himself from implication in the judicial murder of Christ, he must publicly dissociate himself from the council's act.

But Joseph was, so Luke explains (see 23:51), more than 'a good man and a righteous': he was also 'looking for the kingdom of God', that is, he was a man who on the ground of the Old Testament expected the coming of the Messiah to inaugurate the kingdom of God. Now many a man might wish to maintain that Jesus had been unjustly executed, as indeed many do today, without wishing to go further and assert that Jesus was that Messiah. Moreover at the council Jesus had claimed an utterly unique relationship with God, to be the 'Son of God', destined to share the throne of God. If this was not true it was blasphemy and, according to Jewish law, worthy of death and Joseph ought to have agreed with the sentence.

If on the other hand Jesus was the Messiah, it was not enough simply to protest that his execution was unjust. Joseph realized that both logic and loyalty demanded that he confess his faith in the truth of Jesus' claim and publicly associate himself with Jesus now in this moment of his profound humiliation, if he wanted to be owned by Christ at his exaltation, whenever and however that exaltation should be brought about. So he went to Pilate, and he buried Jesus, and doubtless very soon the council knew all about it, and saw not only the moral, but the theological and religious implication of Joseph's act.

The so-called dying thief was taken to paradise within a few moments of confessing faith in Christ, and so was not called to demonstrate the sincerity of his faith. We who like Joseph are left to live in a world where God's Son was crucified, might well ask ourselves what we have done and are doing to make it clear publicly where we stand in relation to the claims of Christ.

8. The King eats in Jerusalem: evidence of his resurrection (23:56b – 24:53)

All four evangelists, as is natural, record the triumphant fact that on the third day Jesus our Lord rose from the dead. The special feature of Luke's record is without doubt his story of the journey to Emmaus. Apart from a brief possible reference to this journey in Mark 16:12–13 there is nothing like it in any of the other gospels.

The story occupies the centre of Luke's resurrection narrative and plays a key role in the development of its thought. It lies between the perplexity, disbelief and puzzled surprise of the apostolic band at 24:4, 11–12 and the final dispersal of all disbelief by our Lord's appearance to the apostolic band at 24:36ff (see especially 24:41). It starts with two disciples in deep disillusionment; their unbelief in the resurrection was, we may suppose, typical of the rest. It then shows the Lord analysing the causes of their unbelief, banishing it and replacing it with joyous and unshakable faith. Finally it records that it was as they were recounting their experience to the apostolic band that the Lord suddenly appeared among them, demonstrated the nature of his resurrection body and briefed them for their world-wide mission (see 24:44–49).

It is not of course accidental that the story which Luke has chosen to fill the centre of his resurrection narrative is the story of a journey; but Luke is anxious that we should notice that the journey was not simply to Emmaus. It was from Jerusalem to Emmaus and back again to Jerusalem. As the two disciples leave Jerusalem he tells us that the distance to Emmaus was about seven miles (see 24:13); and at the end of the story he tells us that no sooner had the Lord disappeared than they got up at once and returned to Jerusalem in spite of the distance and the fact that it was now night (see 24:29,33). In the immediate and in the greater context of the Gospel both their leaving Jerusalem and their return are highly significant.

At the very outset of his narrative of our Lord's journey from earth to heaven Luke told us that Christ 'resolutely determined to go to Jerusalem' (9:51); and after that he kept reminding us that Christ and his followers were on their way to Jerusalem (see 13:22; 17:11; 18:31; 19:11). Christ's arrival there showed us why it was so important that he should come to the city: he came to Jerusalem as Zion's King, and to publicize the fact he had the great crowd of his disciples escort him into Jerusalem with royal honours and acclamation.

Now two disciples were leaving Jerusalem and going back home for reasons which carried the most serious implications. They had virtually decided that the crucifixion of Jesus by the authorities had proved that he was not the King after all (see 24:19–21) and they were in danger of abandoning not only Jerusalem but all the hopes they originally expressed by escorting Christ into the city. Christ could obviously not allow that retrograde journey to end in

Emmaus; he must bring them back to Jerusalem. As Zion's King he had not done with Jerusalem yet. True, the religious authorities 'had thrown him out of the vineyard and killed him' (20:14–15); but there was another side to that story. His death at Jerusalem had been his own deliberate strategy for the establishment of the new covenant and the setting up of his kingdom. Now that his Passover sacrifice had been completed, he had his 'exodus' to accomplish (see 9:31).[1] He was not going to retreat from Jerusalem as a thwarted and defeated King and complete his journey to heaven from some other point in Palestine. His exodus should be accomplished, as previously announced to Moses and Elijah, at Jerusalem. He had come to Jerusalem as King; he would leave from Jerusalem as triumphant Lord. It was at Jerusalem therefore that he would appear to the eleven and brief them for their world-wide mission (see 24:36–39). Jerusalem, he would direct, must be the starting point for the spread of the gospel (see 24:47). It would be to Jerusalem that the Holy Spirit would come to empower them for their mission and they were to wait in the city until he came (see 24:49). It would be from Jerusalem that Christ himself would finally lead them out to witness his ascension (see 24:50); and it would be to Jerusalem that they returned (see 24:52) and to its temple in which they constantly assembled in joyful praise from the ascension to Pentecost.

First, however, he had to rally his dispirited disciples and convince them that he was risen; and it will be the function of the first two paragraphs of the movement to explain why that was necessary and why it was at first so difficult.

i. Unnecessary preparations (23:56b – 24:12). When the women came to the tomb of Jesus on the first day of the week, they were carrying spices with which to embalm the Lord's body. Obviously they were not expecting him to rise from the dead; and therefore when they found first the stone rolled away and then no body in the tomb they were perplexed. Presently two angels appeared and pointed out the cause of their perplexity: they had not remembered what Christ had plainly told them while he was in Galilee – and these women came from Galilee (see 23:55) – about his impending death and resurrection (see 24:5–8).

---

[1] AV, RV 'decease', NIV 'departure'=Gk. *exodos*.

We should notice how Luke's careful phraseology presses this fact on our attention. When at Christ's instructions two disciples had gone to borrow an ass 'they found just as he had said' (19:32). When at his word two disciples had gone to borrow an upper room 'they found as he had said and there they made their preparations for the Passover' (22:13). If the apostles and disciples had listened to the Lord's words in Galilee, the women would not have prepared any spices or brought them to the tomb; and if they still had come to the tomb they would not have been surprised to find it even as he said – empty.

When the eleven were reminded of our Lord's Galilean prediction of his death and resurrection by the women's report, it still apparently made no difference. They simply refused to believe that the women had seen any angels or that the angels had announced that the Galilean prediction had been fulfilled (see 24:11). Peter did go to the tomb and find it, as the women had said, empty except for the grave-clothes (see 24:12). That surprised and puzzled him; but it still did not make him think that Christ's prophecy of his resurrection had come true.

Why the apostles found it so difficult to believe the Lord's words about his resurrection, will be explained in the next story. For the moment we should grasp the significance of the facts which this first paragraph is relating. Luke will presently tell us that the gospel which the apostles were commissioned to take to the world was the offer of forgiveness to the repentant on the basis of Christ's death and resurrection (see 24:46–47). In this first paragraph he is emphasizing the fact that this gospel originated with Christ. It is not true to say, as some have said, that the message which Jesus preached was the simple lesson of God's love for man and man's love for God and his neighbour, and that it was his apostles who subsequently invented the gospel which claims that Christ died for our sins and rose again the third day (see 1 Cor. 15:3–4). Jesus could have preached love to God and man without going anywhere near Jerusalem. But it was an essential prerequisite for the gospel that he was about to launch on the world that he should go up to Jerusalem, be crucified there and rise again; and that being so, the purpose of the journey, so Luke solemnly affirms, was stated by Christ in Galilee before the journey began. The disciples did not invent it: for some time, in fact, they neither understood it nor believed it. It originated with Christ.

ii. Eating with his disciples (24:13–43). It was kind of the Lord, having journeyed from Galilee and entered Jerusalem as King, to travel back with two of his disciples down the road of their disillusionment and listen to all their reasons why they now doubted whether after all Jesus was King. Before they left they had heard the women's report of the empty tomb and the message of the angels, and they were able to tell the Stranger that some of the apostolic band had checked Jesus' tomb and found it empty, adding with tremendous unconscious irony as they looked the Stranger straight in the face: 'But they did not see him' (see 24:24). They even pointed out to the Stranger that this was the third day since Jesus had been crucified (see 24:21), and still the idea that the resurrection had taken place seemed not to register with them as a serious possibility. Why not?

First there was the fact that for ordinary members of the public, the priests and religious authorities still carried enormous influence. Their decisive dismissal of the evidence on which the disciples had built their hopes and their execution of Jesus were obviously a severe blow to the disciples' faith that Jesus was the Messiah (see 24:19–20).

More important still was the fact that death and resurrection formed no part of their concept of Messiah's office and programme, which is why they had not really taken in what Jesus had said about his coming death. They were hoping for a Messiah who would break the imperialist domination of the Romans by force of arms. A Messiah who managed to allow himself to be caught by the Jewish authorities, handed over to the Romans and crucified before he had even begun to organize any guerrilla operations, popular uprising or open warfare – what use was he? If the Old Testament prophesied a liberator who should not die, but be triumphant, Jesus was already disqualified: he had died. After that, it was almost irrelevant to talk of resurrection.

The first thing the risen Lord had to do, therefore, in order to establish for Cleopas and his companion the fact of his resurrection was to demonstrate that according to the Old Testament the Messiah had to die; and secondly that the kind of redemption which Messiah was to effect could only be effected by his dying. Their expectations of a triumphant Messiah were not wrong, of course, but they were built on a very selective reading of the Old Testament. They had fastened on to those passages which talked of victory over Israel's enemies and the restoration of Israel's land, king and independence. The passages that talked of Messiah's sufferings and death had not made sense to them – even supposing they had read them; and they had passed them over: they formed no part of their expectations of the Messiah. They had believed what the prophets had spoken: they had not believed *all* that the prophets had spoken (see 24:25).

And so the Stranger had to demonstrate at length and in detail that the programme laid down for the Messiah was that he must 'suffer these things and enter into his glory' (24:26–27): that is to say, his sufferings were to be the actual means by which he should enter into his glory. His death would not be an obstacle in the way of his redeeming Israel, but the very method by which that redemption should be accomplished. In the upper room (see 22: 14–20) Christ had referred to the typology of the Passover and to Jeremiah's prophecy of the new covenant. Now he took our two disciples through all the types and prophecies of the Old Testament (see 24:27) which spoke of redemption in terms of forgiveness of sins and reconciliation with God through Messiah's sacrificial death.

Throughout the conversation so far, however, the disciples had been kept from recognizing who the Stranger was. What the Stranger had established was simply that Jesus' death was no obstacle to his being Messiah: rather it made Jesus' claim to be the Messiah more compelling and the report of his resurrection more credible. But if Jesus was alive again, where was he? And how could anyone recognize him and be sure it was he, if they saw him.

This latter question is perhaps of even greater interest to us than it was to the two disciples. If it was widely recognized that according to the Old Testament Messiah had to die and then rise again, what was to prevent some religious opportunist after Jesus' death from dressing himself up like Jesus and deceiving the early Christians into thinking that he was Jesus come back from the dead? How in fact, we ask, did the Stranger convince the two disciples that he was Jesus?

Certainly not by simply saying, 'I am Jesus'. Any impostor could have said that. He did it by an action that no impostor would have thought of, and in a way that was so characteristic of Jesus and so eloquent of the very heart of what he had secretly told his disciples about himself that no impostor could have known about it, let alone have done it.

Seated at table, he took the bread in his hands, said the blessing, broke it, and gave it to them. That inevitably called their attention to his hands, and maybe, as it did so, they would have seen the nail marks in his wrists. But it was not the nail marks which they afterwards cited to the apostles as the means by which they had known him, but rather the action of breaking the bread itself: 'they related . . . how he was known to them in the breaking of the bread'.

On two exceedingly significant occasions the Lord had broken bread in his hands and distributed it to his disciples. The first occasion was at the feeding of the five thousand (see 9:16). The disciples who were close enough to see what was happening would never have forgotten the astounding sight as the bread multiplied itself in those hands. What is more, the miracle had been subsequently used by the Lord as a parable of the giving of his flesh and blood for the life of the world (see Jn. 6:32–59). Now the Stranger, who had just completed a long survey of the Old Testament showing that the divine plan was for Messiah to give his body for his people's sins, took the bread into his hands, blessed, broke and distributed it to them. At once they knew him: it was an inimitable gesture of self-revelation.

The second occasion had been in the upper room at the celebration of the last Passover and the institution of the Lord's Supper. Cleopas was not present on that occasion; for all we know he may not have been present at the feeding of the five thousand either. He would certainly have heard of both. The mysterious talk on both occasions of Christ's giving of his body and blood had obviously not made sense to the apostles let alone to Cleopas, not even after he died, until just now the Stranger had demonstrated that the Old Testament was full of prophecies, ceremonies, types and prototypes of Messiah's destined sacrificial self-giving. Now as the Stranger once more broke the bread and gave it to them, it all came together and made sense. 'Their eyes were opened and they knew him.'

Still today, though at a deeper level, we recognize the authentic Saviour of the world by that same gesture: none other in the world of human history offered up his body for our personal redemption.

That same night the two disciples returned to Jerusalem. The last time they had gone up to Jerusalem they had been hoping that Jesus would prove to be King and redeem Israel (see 24:21). This time it was different. Now they knew he was King. Now they had become aware of a redemption infinitely bigger than the limited political deliverance they had originally been hoping for. And now their faith and hopes were based on a foundation that neither opposition nor even death itself could overthrow.

In Jerusalem they found the eleven and others gathered together and reporting that the Lord had indeed risen and appeared to Simon. Then he appeared again, and this time they were temporarily terrified. On the road to Emmaus he had come alongside them naturally as any fellow-traveller might have done; but on this occasion he suddenly appeared in the midst of them. Instinctively they thought that this must be a spirit and not the man, Jesus of Nazareth, whom they had known; and they felt that terror which human beings sense in the presence of bodiless or disembodied spirits.

To calm their fears he demonstrated, insofar as they could grasp it, what 'resurrection' means. He first asserted his essential identity with the Jesus they had known: 'it is I myself', he said (24:39). Moreover the identity was not merely at the level of the human spirit, but at the physical level of the body. 'See my hands and my feet', he said. John tells us they still carried the marks of the nails (see Jn. 20:27); but what Luke records is that Christ invited his disciples to use their sense of touch to establish that in resurrection he still possessed a body of flesh and bone. They still found it too good to be true; so he asked for something to eat, and ate the fish they gave him, in order to demonstrate further that while in one sense even as he stood in their midst he was no longer with them (see 24:44), but was already in another world, subject to different physical laws from theirs, yet he was the same Jesus as he was when he was with them.

He had eaten with them before he suffered (see 22:15–16) the literal Passover lamb which bespoke his death. He ate now (see 24:43) a literal fish to demonstrate the physical reality of his resurrection. When, therefore, we hear the King promise (see 22:30) that we shall eat and drink with him at his table in his kingdom, we might be unwise to suppose that 'eating' is absolutely nothing more than a metaphor for spiritual fellowship. Doubtless eating there will be a very different thing from eating here. But different as that world may be from this, it is not completely different: it now holds the real, glorified, but still human, body of Jesus Christ our Lord.

iii. Briefing for mission (24:44–53). At 22:35–38 at the end of the Passover meal Christ had briefed his apostles for their world mission. Now at the end of this meal he briefs them again. On the former occasion he had concentrated largely on the question of the source of supply of the money and other material things necessary for their missionary work. On this occasion he concentrated on the spiritual aspects of their mission. First the basis and content of the gospel they were to preach. Their message was not a philosophy built by logic on the basis of general axioms. It was a gospel based on certain historical events prophesied in the Old Testament and fulfilled in history by Jesus, namely the sufferings, death, burial and resurrection of the Messiah; and the fact that his life, death, burial and resurrection fulfilled those biblical predictions was itself to be part of the gospel (see 24:44–46).

Secondly, their gospel was to offer to all who would repent forgiveness in the name of Jesus: not in general terms in the name of God's general kindness and love but specifically in the name of the historical person Jesus who suffered died and rose again (see 24:47).

Thirdly, this gospel of forgiveness was to be preached world-wide to all mankind without discrimination of any kind. At the same time the preaching of this gospel was to start from Jerusalem (see 24:47). The gospel was not to spring up simultaneously in several different parts of the world as though it were based on some general or universal self-evident truth that might simultaneously occur to different people in different times and in different places. The preaching was to start from Jerusalem because the forgiveness it offered was based and should for ever remain based on what took place when God's incarnate Son suffered, died and rose again just outside the city of Jerusalem. And the proclamation of this unique salvific event was to be made in the first instance by men who could act as witnesses to its historical truth (see 24:48).

Fourthly, there was the question of the empowering of the mission (see 24:49). Important as the historical basis of the proclamation was, the kingdom of the King was not to be advanced by a simple recitation of the historical events. The messengers were to be empowered in their witness by the Holy Spirit sent upon them by the ascended Saviour; and conversion to Christ would be effected in the hearers by his supernatural work of regeneration.

Such then was the briefing which Christ gave to his apostles and disciples after his resurrection in Jerusalem.

And now the last stage of the King's journey on earth is complete, and he must proceed to the goal that was always in view from the time the journey began: the King 'having suffered these things will now enter into his glory'. Today he must go alone, and leave his servants to do his service, preach his gospel and spread his kingdom here on earth; one day he will return and introduce them too into his glory. With this Luke comes to describe that indescribably august event, the ascension of the King:

'And he led them out until they were over against Bethany: and he lifted up his hands and blessed them': no dumb priest he, like Zecharias silent before a bewildered people (see 1:22), but true High Priest, who at his ascension drew from his people such a response of praise to God as shall never die away.

'And it came to pass, while he blessed them, he parted from them, and was carried up into heaven. And they worshipped him, and returned to Jerusalem with great joy, and were continually in the temple, blessing God'.

For the moment there is nothing more to be said. Let us join them, and all the great multitude of the redeemed, in their joy and worship of the King.

Appendices

1. On the validity of applying Aristotle's canons of literary criticism to Luke's work.

The objection mentioned on p.15(fn. 3) would certainly be valid if we were proposing to apply the whole of Aristotle's critical theory *tout court* to Luke's work. Needless to say, we are not proposing any such thing, but merely suggesting that some of Aristotle's observations on the importance of the careful selection, proportioning and arrangement of material, and on the desirability that a work should have a certain coherence, a beginning, a middle and an end, in other words a rational thought-flow, are applicable to all serious works, whether of literature or of history, in whatever period they are written. We are not for one moment implying that Luke has moulded his source material with the same kind of freedom as that with which the Greek playwrights reshaped the myths from which they made their tragedies. Judged by Aristotle's own distinction that the historian tells of things that actually happened, whereas the poet tells of things of a kind that could or would happen[1], Luke is unhesitatingly to be classed as a historian. On the other hand Aristotle himself points out[2] that whereas generally speaking poetry is concerned with universal truths and history with the particular facts of what someone or other actually did, yet some of the things that have actually happened in history have been instances of universal truths. Now once more this observation cannot be applied without modification to Luke's work; but it may serve to remind us of an important feature of the Gospel narratives. The evangelists' stories of, say, Christ's miracles are in the first place records of things that actually happened; but instinctively believers all down the centuries have read them as being in addition parables and paradigms conveying truth of universal applicability. This understanding of Christ's

[1] *Poetics* ch.9.
[2] *Ibid.*

miracles is explicit in the Fourth Gospel in for example its treatment of the feeding of the five thousand (see ch.6) and the giving of
sight to the blind man (see especially 9:39–41). It would be difficult
to think therefore that when Luke recorded, say, the giving of sight
to the blind man at Jericho (see 18:35–43) he saw nothing more in it
than a particular fact of history. Once admit, then, that Luke will
have seen in such miracles truths and lessons of universal
applicability, and one is automatically led on to ask whether in
selecting and arranging the records of these miracles Luke intended
the lessons he saw in them to stand in isolation as self-contained
units, or whether he meant those lessons to chime in with the
matters being discussed in the contexts in which he places them.
We are back with the question of thought-flow.

2. On the question whether the use of literary sym-
metry in a historical work is consistent with strict historicity.

If it were the duty of a historian to record everything which the
subjects of his history did and said on every day of their lives, then
doubtless he could not be true to history if he tried to present the
facts in symmetrical patterns: life's happenings are too multifarious
and unrelated for that. Nobody, however, imagines that a historian
or biographer either could or ought to attempt to record everything. He must make a selection, and since selection necessarily
involves interpretation, the basic questions to be asked of any
historian or biographer are whether the facts he relates are true and
his interpretations correct. We should observe, therefore, that the
use of symmetrical structure by an ancient historian or biographer
is simply his way of achieving interpretation which a modern
historian would achieve by different methods. As a method symmetrical structure is not in itself necessarily false to historicity any
more than the modern historian's method.

Take an imaginary case of a man who was a famous general and
then became a politician and eventually president of his country.
An ancient biographer wanting to be fair to the man and to represent his many-sided and versatile personality might well select for
record two of his campaigns and two mutinies which he quelled,
and arrange them either in close proximity or with intervening

material so that they formed a symmetrical structure: one campaign won through the use of lightning strikes, and a succession of massive pitched battles; one mutiny quelled by the use of draconian severity; another mutiny quelled by the use of judicious clemency; another campaign won by deliberate avoidance of pitched battles and the adoption of delaying tactics and intrigue. And the ancient biographer might well leave his selection and symmetrical structure to convey his interpretation without adding much or any comment of his own. The modern biographer in his turn might well wish to give the same interpretation of the general's personality, and he might well illustrate it from the same two battles and the same two mutinies. But he would do it differently. He would probably place the battles and mutinies together in a chapter devoted to the study of his subject as a general; and all the way through he would add his own explicit comments and observations on the general's versatility to bring out and back up his interpretations. The modern reader might feel more comfortable with the modern biographer because he explicitly pointed out that he was adding his interpretion to the historical facts; but it is difficult to see why the ancient biographer's use of symmetrical structure without explicit comment should have necessarily involved him in being false to the historical facts.

Again another historian, ancient or modern, interested in the same man but primarily as a politician might select just one of the campaigns, neglecting the other three stories, and place it in an altogether different sequence of social, economic and political happenings designed to show how his success as a general helped to sweep him to political power. No one would imagine that his selection of only one battle and his placing of it in a different sequence of events was necessarily a distortion of the historical facts.

Now the question whether Luke's selection of material, or his departure from strict chronological order, or his use of symmetrical structure does in fact involve him in a misinterpretation of his sources or a distortion of the historical facts, is a question that can be settled only by a detailed investigation of every individual case, since to prove that in ninety-nine instances it does not, need not prove the same for the hundredth instance. Such an investigation is obviously beyond the scope of this work. What we do wish to claim here, however, is that Luke's construction of symmetries is not by itself necessarily inconsistent with strict historicity.

3. On the questions raised by different and mutually exclusive analyses of the literary structures of biblical narratives.

Many literary structures have been proposed for Luke by different scholars.[1] The suggestions of these scholars are naturally supported by detailed literary analysis and argument, and it would obviously be impossible to offer a fair critique of the work of even one of them in the minute space available to the present writer here. What he proposes to do therefore is simply to state briefly his own attitude to literary structures and what he expects of them and then to give one small example of the kind of question he would wish to ask about any suggested structure.

The primary concern of the present work has been to detect meaning and thought-flow rather than to establish symmetrical structures. Even that more limited concern can, it is freely admitted, involve a great deal of subjective interpretation, witness the suggestions of the ancient Jewish 'juxtaposition-exegetes' and their attempts to trace the thought-flow between one paragraph and another in the Torah (see Babylonian Talmud, Berakoth, 216 and for an example, the comments in the Midrash Rabbah on Nu. 20:14–29). The present writer, therefore, would look to literary structure to control his exposition in two ways. First, if the author has placed two stories one opposite the other in a symmetrical structure, it forces the expositor to consider the similarities and differences between the two stories and so to consider features in the stories that he otherwise might miss or pass by as insignificant. Secondly, any suggested exposition of a story can be tested by asking whether it makes sense within the structure in which the author has placed it.

On the other hand while the present writer would look to literary structure to facilitate and to control exposition, he would not regard it as a strait-jacket. In the body of this work for instance he has indicated that symmetrical structure demands that the two stories of the woman in Simon's house and the woman subject to bleeding should be interpreted each in the light of the other. To miss their similarities and contrasts would be to miss something that Luke intended us to think about. But that said, the present writer would

---

[1] A very useful account of them is to be found in Charles H. Talbert, *Literary patterns, theological themes and the genre of Luke-Acts* (Scholars Press, 1974) and in Kenneth E. Bailey, *Poet and Peasant, a literary-cultural approach to the parables in Luke* (Eerdmans, 1976.)

certainly not wish to claim that it was illegitimate to take, for example, the story of the woman in Simon's house and to compare and contrast, say, her use of ointment on the Lord with the ill-advised intention of the women in 24:1–9 to honour the Lord's dead body with spices. It may well be that it was not in Luke's mind that his readers should compare these two stories, but since his work is a record of historical events it is open to his readers to compare and contrast any two or more of his stories as they please.

Moreover the present writer does not claim that the structures which he has proposed are the only ones that can rightly be detected in Luke. An intricate artistic design will often present one symmetry when viewed from one angle or starting point, and a different symmetry from another. The present writer has himself pointed out that depending on what theme or themes one is following through Matthew's Gospel, for instance, one can make out a strong case for the existence of two or three major patterns running through the book.[1]

Now here is a part of a symmetrical structure proposed by Professor C. H. Talbert[2] for part of Luke's Gospel.

4:31–41 Jesus is in conflict with demons. One cries: 'What have you to do with us, Jesus of Nazareth? Have you come to destroy us? I know who you are, the Holy One of God.'

1. *8:26–39* Jesus is, in conflict with demons. They say: 'What have you to do with me, Jesus, Son of the Most high God? I beseech you not to torment me.'

5:1–11 Jesus is in a boat with Simon. A nature miracle takes place.

2. *8:22–25* Jesus is in a boat with his disciples. A nature miracle takes place.

5:17–26 While Jesus is in the company of some Pharisees there arises the question of Jesus' forgiving sins. Jesus tells the man: 'Man, your sins are forgiven you.'

3. *7:36–50* While Jesus eats with a Pharisee the question of forgiveness of sins arises. Jesus tells the woman: 'Your sins are forgiven.'

5:27 – 6:5 Jesus and his disciples are shown eating and drinking in contrast to John's disciples who fast often.

4. *7:31–35* John came neither eating nor drinking. The Son of man came eating and drinking.

6:12–16 The twelve are chosen. This immediately precedes Jesus' teaching within the hearing of the crowds.

5. *8:1–3* Jesus is with the twelve. This immediately precedes Jesus' teaching the crowds.

6:17–49 Jesus teaches the multitudes. The conclusion concerns 'hearing' Jesus' teaching and 'doing' it.

6. *8:4–8, 16–21* Jesus teaches the multitudes. The conclusion concerns 'hearing' Jesus' teaching and 'doing' it.

[1]See 'Structure littéraire de Matthieu, XIII, 35 à XVIII, 5', *Revue Biblique*, 85, 1978, pp.236–38.
[2]*Op. cit.*, p.40.

Let it be said again quite clearly that we are not offering here a full-scale critique of Professor Talbert's work supported as it is by very detailed and scholarly analysis. We are simply citing this small part of his work to provide an example of the kind of questions the present writer would wish to put to many of the literary structures proposed by various scholars.

First, can we really think that the original composition was meant to be symmetrical, if to obtain the symmetry the order of Luke's narrative has to be rearranged drastically as in the right-hand column? Secondly, can a proposed structure really be thought to be symmetrical if it has to omit passages like the healing of the leper (see 5:12–16) and the healing of the man with a withered hand (see 6:6–11) as well as others? But more important than these two queries would be the two questions: what is the point of the symmetry as a whole? And how does the structure help us to see the significance of its individual components?

Take for instance the proposed correspondence between 5:1–11 and 8:22–25. Granted that both passages record a nature miracle, how does the lesson which is taught by the second miracle help us to understand more fully the lesson taught by the first miracle? The detail of the first story is very full and concerns Peter's obedience to the Lord's command, his conviction of hitherto unrealized sin and his commissioning for his apostolic ministry. How does the detail of the second story cast further light on or further emphasis on the detail of the first story?

Finally, how does the existence of this proposed structure help us to see how the story at 5:1–11 is related to its immediate context? 5:1–11, as we have recalled, comes to its climax with Peter's confession of sin. In that respect it has more in common with the two stories 5:17–26 and 7:36–50 than it has with the story at 8:22–25. But how does the structure help us to see the connection of thought that made Luke place the story of the leper (see 5:12–16) immediately after 5:1–11?

In other words the present writer would regard literary structure as simply a practical (and very subordinate) device aimed at helping the reader to grasp more fully the detailed meaning and thought-flow of the narrative. As soon as it has fulfilled that function it is best forgotten; and if it does not fulfil that function, it is of little use.